THE INDIAN TRIBES
OF NORTH AMERICA

THE INDIAN TRIBES
OF NORTH AMERICA

WITH BIOGRAPHICAL SKETCHES AND
ANECDOTES OF THE PRINCIPAL CHIEFS

THOMAS L. McKENNEY

and

JAMES HALL

EDITED BY

FREDERICK WEBB HODGE

and

DAVID I. BUSHNELL, Jr.

Volume II

ROWMAN AND LITTLEFIELD

TOTOWA, NEW JERSEY

THIS EDITION FIRST PUBLISHED IN THE UNITED STATES 1972
by Rowman and Littlefield, Totowa, New Jersey

ISBN 0 87471 119 3

THIS REPRINT TAKEN FROM THE
1934 EDITION

by John Grant, Edinburgh

This edition published by
kind permission of the copyright holder,
John Grant,
31 George IV Bridge, Edinburgh

Reprinted in Great Britain by
Scolar Press Limited, Menston, Yorkshire

THE INDIAN TRIBES
OF NORTH AMERICA

HUNTING THE BUFFALO

THE INDIAN TRIBES
OF NORTH AMERICA

WITH BIOGRAPHICAL SKETCHES AND
ANECDOTES OF THE PRINCIPAL CHIEFS

THOMAS L. McKENNEY
AND
JAMES HALL

A NEW EDITION, EDITED BY
FREDERICK WEBB HODGE
AND
DAVID I. BUSHNELL, JR.

Illustrated with 123 *full-page Plates in Colour (chiefly from the Indian
Gallery, formerly in the War Department at Washington), Photogravure
Portraits, and two Maps*

VOLUME II

EDINBURGH: JOHN GRANT
31 GEORGE IV. BRIDGE
1934

CONTENTS

CONTENTS

BUFFALO HUNT

THE frontispiece prefixed to this volume exhibits a lively representation of the noblest sport practised upon this continent—the hunting of the buffalo. These animals were formerly spread over the whole of the great western valley, and formed the most important article of food, not only for the natives, but the early white settlers of that fertile region. They retired as the country became settled by civilised men, and are now found only on the great prairies of the Far West, whose immense extent, with the scarcity of timber and water, renders them uninhabitable by human beings. Here these animals are seen congregated in numbers which seem almost incredible. As the eye roves over a verdant surface, nearly as boundless as that of the ocean, the herds are beheld grazing over the whole of the wide space, in countless multitude.[1]

The buffalo, though large and unwieldy, is not easily approached by the hunter. Extremely vigilant, and gifted with an exquisite sense of smelling, they readily discover the scent of a human being, and fly before him with precipitation. The Indians overcome this wariness by a variety of devices. Sometimes, having killed the prairie wolf, of which the buffalo has no fear, an Indian wraps himself in the skin, keeping the head in its proper position, and drags himself slowly towards the grazing herd, taking care to advance from the leeward, so that the watchful

A

animal shall not scent his approach upon the tainted breeze. When the object is first seen, the buffaloes raise their heads, and eye it suspiciously, but the appearance of the wolf's head, with which they are familiar, reassures them—nor are they undeceived until their wily foe darts his arrow into one of the fattest of the herd, with an aim so true that it is sure to pierce a vital part. Pitfalls and inclosures are also sometimes contrived. But, although these devices are practised, the number thus taken is inconsiderable; and the only mode of taking this noble prey, which is commonly practised, is that of meeting him openly in the field. For this purpose most of the tribes who reside in the vicinity of the great plains resort to them, after having planted their corn in the spring, and spend the whole summer and autumn in the chase. As the buffaloes often change their pastures, and the laws which direct their migrations are but imperfectly known, the wanderings of the natives in search of them are often long and wearisome; hundreds of miles are sometimes traversed, by a way-worn and starving band, before they are gladdened by the sight of their favourite game. Sometimes they are mocked by discovering the footprints of a retreating herd, which they pursue for days with unavailing toil; not infrequently a hostile clan crosses their track, and they are obliged to diverge from their intended course; and sometimes, having reached a suitable hunting-ground, they find it preoccupied by those with whom they cannot safely mingle nor prudently contend.

At last the young men, who scout in advance of the main body, espy the black, slow moving mass wading in the rich pasture, and preparations are made for a grand hunt. An encampment is made at a spot affording fuel and water; the women erect lodges, and all is joy and bustle. But the hunting is not commenced without due solemnity. [It is not a mere sport in which they are about to engage, but a national business, that is to supply the summer's sustenance and the winter's store, as well as to afford a harvest of valuable articles for traffic.] Horses and harness are inspected; weapons are put in order; the medicine men practise incantations; offerings are made to the Great Spirit; the solemnities of the dance are gone through; and the more superstitious of the warriors often impose upon themselves the austerities of fasting, wounding the body, and incessant prayer, during the night, or even a longer period, preceding the hunt. Duly prepared at length, they mount for the chase, well furnished with arms, but divested of all superfluous clothing and furniture—and approach the herd cautiously from the leeward, keeping some copse, or swell of the land, between themselves and the game, until they get near enough to charge, when the whole band rush at full speed upon the herd. The affrighted buffaloes fly at the first appearance of their enemies. The hunters pursue; each selects his prey, choosing with ready skill the finest and fattest of those near him. The horse being the fleeter animal, soon overtakes the buffalo. The hunter drops the bridle rein, fixes his arrow, and guiding his well-trained horse with his heel, and by the motion of his own body, watches his opportunity to let fly the weapon with fatal aim. This he does not do until his steed is abreast of the buffalo, and the vital part, immediately behind the shoulder, fairly presented; for it is considered disgraceful to discharge an arrow without effect. Usually, therefore, the wound is fatal, and instances have been known when the missile has been sent with such force as to pass through the body of this sturdy quadruped. If, however, the first arrow is but partially successful, the hunter draws another, the horse continuing to run by the side of the buffalo. But the chase now becomes more dangerous, for the wounded buffalo not infrequently turns upon his assailant, and dashing his horns furiously into the flank of the horse, prostrates him, mortally wounded, on the plain, and pursuing his advantage, tramples on horse and rider, unless the latter escapes by mere agility. When, however, the hunter discovers that the first or second arrow has taken effect, he reins up his steed, pauses a moment until he sees the huge beast reel and tumble, and then dashes away into the chase to select and slay another victim. Thus an expert and well-mounted hunter will kill several buffaloes in one day —especially if the band be numerous, and so divided as to have reserve parties to meet and drive back the retreating herd.

When the slaughter ceases, the hunters retrace their steps to gather the spoil, and the women rush to the field to cut up and carry away the game. Each hunter now claims his own, and the mode of ascertaining their respective shares is simple. The arrows of each hunter bear a distinctive mark, and each carries an equal number. The carcass, therefore, belongs to him by whose arrow it is found to be transfixed; and these being carefully withdrawn, every hunter is obliged to produce his original number, or to account for the loss of such as are missing, in default of which he suffers the discredit of having missed the object, or permitted a wounded buffalo to escape with a weapon in his flesh.

The animating scene which we have endeavoured to describe, will be better understood by an inspection of the beautiful drawing of Rhinedesbacker,[2] a young Swiss artist of uncommon talent, who, lured by his love of the picturesque, wandered far to the West, and spent several years upon our frontier, employing his pencil on subjects connected with the Indian modes of life. His was the

fate of genius. His labours were unknown and unrequited.
Few who saw the exquisite touches of his pencil knew
their merit. They knew them to be graphic, but valued
slightly the mimic presentations of familiar realities. They
might wonder at the skill which placed on canvas the
war dance, or the buffalo hunt, but they could not prize
as they deserved, the copies of exciting scenes which they
had familiarly witnessed. Since his death these beautiful
pictures have attracted attention, and some of them have
passed into the possession of those by whom they are
properly appreciated. In that which graces this number
there are slight defects, which we notice only because
we are jealous of the fidelity of our work. The prominent
figure in the foreground is a little too much encumbered
with drapery. The costume is correct in itself, but
misplaced; and there is a slight inaccuracy in the mode
in which the arrow is grasped by the right hand. All
else is true to nature. The landscape and the animals
are faithfully depicted; and the wild scene which is daily
acted upon our prairies is placed vividly before the
eye.

The chase over, a scene not less animated but widely
different is presented. The slaughtered animals are cut
up, and the most valuable parts carried to the camp.
A busy scene ensues. The delicious humps are roasted
and the warriors feast to satiety. The laborious women
prepare the skins for use and for market, and the meat
for preservation. The latter is cut in thin slices and dried
in the sun or over a slow fire, and is then packed in
small compact bales, suitable to be carried. If, however,
more is taken than can be conveniently transported, the
surplus is buried in holes, which our hunters call *caches*—
from the French word which signifies "to hide." A *cache*
is a hole dug in a dry spot, and carefully lined with bark,

grass, or skins, in which the Indians deposit jerked meat, or any other valuables which they cannot conveniently carry away. They are carefully covered over, and the leaves and rubbish that naturally cover the ground replaced, so that the deposit is completely concealed. Property thus left is reclaimed at leisure, and sometimes furnishes timely relief to a famished war party, or an unsuccessful band of hunters. The skins of the buffaloes are very ingeniously dressed by the Indian women, either with or without the hair. This is done by partially drying the hide, then rubbing it laboriously from day to day, with the brains of the animal, until the juices and fleshy parts are entirely absorbed, and the fibre only left, which remains soft, white, and flexible. The lodges of the Indians and their clothing are made of these dressed skins; and immense quantities are annually sold to the traders.

NOTES

1. The extinction of the buffalo as a wild animal has been so recent that it seems hardly necessary to refer to it. For valuable information on the subject, consult Allen in *Memoirs of the Geological Survey of Kentucky*, Vol. I., pt. 2, 1876 ; Hornaday in *Report of the U.S. National Museum for* 1887, Washington, 1889.

2. See Vol. I., note 2, p. 4, this work. A collection of eighteen water-colour sketches by Rindisbacher, now belonging to the United States Military Academy, at West Point, New York, includes the original of the frontispiece of this volume. But nothing is known of the history of the sketches, neither when nor how they were acquired by the Academy. One of the paintings, representing a mounted warrior, was crudely reproduced as a wood engraving, and appears in *Burton's Gentleman's Magazine*, Philadelphia, April, 1840, p. 181, as an illustration in the fictitious *Journal of Julius Rodman*, by Edgar Allen Poe. This, together with the fact that two of the sketches were reproduced as illustrations in McKenney and Hall's work, makes it appear highly probable that at one time the entire collection was in Philadelphia.

Rindisbacher also appears to have made duplicates of his sketches, for among those at West Point is one that may have served as the original of the frontispiece of Vol. I.

Only four additional sketches by this artist are known; they now belong to D. I. Bushnell, jr. Two of these are represented by replicas, or by the originals, in the West Point collection; the others are different from any in that collection.

HALPATTER-MICCO, OR BILLY BOWLEGS

(A SEMINOLE CHIEF)

In the sketches of other Seminole chiefs, and in the general Indian history, some account of this singular tribe of our aborigines has been given. Halpatter-Micco's history possesses peculiar interest, because he was among the very last few leaders of the fugitive race who were associated with the stirring scenes which transferred the remnant of it to the lands west of the Mississippi.[1]

His father, Secoffer, was an ally of the English, and cherished bitter hostility towards the Spaniards, taking the field against them in the troubles that followed the recession of Florida to their sovereignty.[2] When dying, at the age of seventy, he called to his side his two sons, Payne[3] and Bowlegs, and solemnly charged them to carry out his unfinished plans; and, at any cost, complete the sacrifice of one hundred Spaniards, of which number he had killed eighty-six. This bloody offering, he affirmed, the Great Spirit had required at his hand to open for him the gate of Paradise.[4] We need scarcely add, that such requests were sacredly regarded by the Indians in their uncivilised state. Their fidelity to their vows and treaties was in sad and singular contrast with the faithless dealing of their white invaders.

In 1821, Florida came into the possession of the United States, having within its limits four thousand

8

HALPATTER-MICCO, *or* " BILLY BOWLEGS "
A Seminole Chief

Seminoles, including the women and children, and eight hundred slaves. The log-cabins, environed by cultivated clearings, or grouped together in villages, dotted the country from St Augustine to Appalachicola River, and attracted the covetous eye of emigrants flocking into the territory. The Seminoles' plea of right to the lands by possession had little weight so long as the Government did not recognise the claim.

Two years later, the Indians were pressed into a relinquishment of lands by treaty, and restriction within certain original boundaries.[5] Slaves ran away from white masters, and the Seminoles refused to send them back; property was stolen, and reprisals made; and the occasions of quarrel readily embraced by the settlers, until a sanguinary conflict seemed ready to open its horrors upon the mixed population. Then came the celebrated "Treaty of Payne's Landing," made on the 9th of May, 1832, which Mr Gadsden, commissioned by Secretary Cass, after much difficulty, induced a part of the Seminole chiefs to sign.[6] A delegation was to visit the lands west of the Mississippi, and if the report was favourable, the Florida possessions were to be ceded to the whites, and the removal of the Indians was to follow. In this treaty, the name of Halpatter-Micco[7] makes its first appearance in public affairs. A youthful sub-chief of Arpiucki, or "Sam Jones," he seems to have been bribed or flattered into giving his sign, while Micanopy's who was the real head of the nation, and that of other well-known chiefs, were wanting on a document which, in the result, sealed the doom of the Seminoles. Indeed, the delegation repudiated the treaty, and Asseola,[8] a sagacious, crafty, and daring Indian, determined to out-general the framers of the instrument. In private life, he nevertheless ruled the councils of the aged Micanopy, and laid a deep plot of resistance to the Government. A negotiation, and a feigned treaty of removal,[9] were used as means of delay, to give time for preparation to make war. It was resolved that if a Seminole sold his property to go west, he should be slain. Months passed by, and as autumn ripened the fields, Charley Amathla,[10] a prominent chief, was waylaid and killed, because he had commenced the sale of his cattle, and the money in his possession forbidden by Asseola to be touched, he declaring that "it was the blood of the red man." December 28th, 1835, occurred the murder of General Thompson and Lieutenant Smith, as they walked on a sunny afternoon out of the fort, by Indians in ambush, within sight of the fortress.[11] A larger force was sent to meet Major Dade, who was advancing from Fort Brooke.[12] On the same day that Asseola's band dispatched General Thompson, this body of savages, numbering one hundred and eighty, fired from behind forest-trees, without a sound of warning—the leaden hail bringing down half of the men at the first fire. Only four privates, out of the eight officers and one hundred and two troops in the ranks, escaped. This was the opening of the Florida war, whose havoc and death cost the nation not less than $40,000,000 and three thousand brave soldiers.

Asseola, who had himself broken treaty, was treacherously betrayed, and sent to Fort Moultrie[13] to die of a broken heart. Coacochu, or *Wild Cat*,[14] surrendered, and successively bands were scattered, and the remnant of the tribe was driven toward the dark, impassable everglades. In July, 1839, Halpatter-Micco made himself conspicuous by a bold and daring exploit to retrieve the falling fortunes of his people. Under an arrangement by Commander Macomb with "Sam Jones," a leading chief, assigning certain limits beyond which the Indians should not pass, and within which protection should be excluded, Colonel Harney[15] was sent to establish a trading-post. He encamped with thirty men on an open, desolate plain, near the Caloosahatchee River, and held unsuspecting intercourse daily with the Seminoles. As the dawn of the 22nd of July fell on the white tents, Halpatter-Micco, at the head of two hundred warriors, rushed upon the sleeping inmates. The surprise was so complete, no resistance was offered. Twenty-four were killed[16]; the rest fled, Harney himself barely escaping by swimming from the river-bank to a fishing-smack anchored in the stream. From this successful raid dates the sudden and growing greatness of the leader, who was soon elevated to the position of principal chief, in place of "Sam Jones," deposed because of his advanced age and infirmities. The sovereignty was now a narrow one, including not more than two hundred and fifty souls, of whom eighty were warriors. Halpatter-Micco saw that the stake was lost, and treaty alone left for his people. He found this was possible, for the United States Government was weary of the terrible struggle, and appeared at headquarters to avail himself of the only hope. The result was, the allotment of a small territory, as a planting and hunting-ground, and the announcement, August 14, 1842, that the Florida war was closed.

The peace thus secured continued more than half a score of years, when, in 1856, rumours were abroad that a reopening of the conflict was at hand. Skirmishes followed, and affairs were unsettled for two years. Halpatter-Micco, by money, "fire-water," and "parley," was induced to join his brethren in Arkansas. In the spring of 1858 he left his native Florida with thirty-three warriors, eighty women and children, and embarked for New Orleans. "Sam Jones," almost a century old, with thirty-eight warriors, refused at any price to leave; the women following the departing chief, "King Billy," with shouts of derision, because he had sold his people to the pale faces. He was accompanied by his lieutenant, "Long Jack," a brother-in-law; Ko-Kush-adjo, his inspector-general, a fine-looking Indian; and Ben Bruno, his interpreter and adviser, an intelligent negro.

At New Orleans he was the "lion" of the day. He illustrated the humiliating fact, that contact with the whites has been destructive to the sobriety of the Indian, and generally demoralising;—an account to be adjusted at the last assize, before an impartial Judge. The libations were freely offered and accepted, until the Seminole chief was a reeling inebriate in the streets of the Crescent City.

He reached his lands in Arkansas,[17] and, without any notable events in his history, a few years later, died, about fifty years of age.

In personal appearance he was called good-looking. His forehead was broad and high, and under it flashed a sharp black eye, indicating the shrewdness and sly cunning characteristic of the man. His height was above medium, and his person stout, though not corpulent.

His immediate family comprised two wives, one of them comparatively young; six children, of whom five were daughters; and fifty slaves. He had, when he left Florida, a fortune of one hundred thousand dollars. The costume he wore was national and picturesque. On his breast were two medals, bearing the likenesses of Presidents Van Buren and Fillmore.

The name "Bowlegs" was simply a family cognomen, having no reference to any physical peculiarity.[18] We believe there is no evidence that he renounced his native heathenism and embraced the Gospel of Christ;—a sad but not a singular fact, with the lessons of his intercourse with the supplanters of his race.[19]

NOTES

1. See also OPOTHLE-YOHOLO, note 14, p. 34. All the tribe was not transferred to Indian Territory. In February, 1842, General Worth recommended that a body of Seminole, estimated at 301, including 112 warriors, be permitted to remain in Florida, south of Peace River, and his recommendation was approved. The number now in Florida is about 350. The strictly correct form of "Halpatter-Micco" is *Halpŭda Mikko*, and signifies that the chief (*mikko*) belongs to the Alligator (*Halpŭda*) clan, according to Dr Frank G. Speck.

2. This, of course, refers to the retrocession to Spain, in 1783, by Great Britain, of the territory known as East and West Florida, including a part of the present Alabama and Mississippi, that had been ceded to Great Britain twenty years before. West Florida was sold to France in 1795, and after the purchase of Louisiana in 1803, the United States claimed the territory to the Perdido as part of the purchase; but the claim was not pressed at the time. In 1810, however, the Spanish Government being overthrown, the United States took possession of all but Mobile, which was occupied during the War of 1812. Spain virtually having lost control of East Florida by reason of the state of affairs at home, it became a refuge for fugitive slaves, as it was already the rendezvous of Indians, notably the Seminole, who raided into Georgia. President Madison was authorised by Congress in 1811 to take temporary possession, but nothing was done. In 1818 General Jackson invaded the territory for the purpose of punishing the Spaniards, who had been withholding the fugitive negroes and giving aid to the Seminole in their depredations, capturing St Mark's and Pensacola and hanging two British adventurers, Arbuthnot and Ambrister, who had been furnishing the Indians supplies. By the treaty of February 22, 1819, Spain ceded East Florida to the United States, the latter assuming claims of American citizens against Spain amounting to $5,000,000. The treaty was ratified by the Senate in 1821.

3. This individual, better known as "King Payne," was, like his brother, only a minor chief, his reputation having been gained principally by his hostile attitude toward the white settlements on the Georgia frontier, especially in 1812. On September 26th of that year, an encounter between 117 men under Col. Daniel Newman, of the

Georgia volunteers, and King Payne and Bowlegs (whose correct name
was probably *Bolek*), at the head of 150 warriors, resulted in the capture
of Payne and the wounding of Bowlegs, but by desperate fighting on
the part of the Seminole they recovered their leader.

4. Following the plan to preserve *the* statements of the authors,
however incorrect some of them may be, we permit this sentence to
stand, although the concept that it is designed to convey was totally
foreign to such uncivilised Indians as were the Seminole at that time.
It is sufficient to say that the law of retaliation in the case of the killing
of a member of a tribe was quite common among the Indians.

5. This was the treaty with "the Florida tribes of Indians," concluded at camp Moultrie, Florida, September 18, 1823, and ratified
January 2, 1824. The commissioners on the part of the United States
were William P. Duvall, James Gadsden, and Bernard Segui. The
reserve first set apart for the use of these Indians contained so little
tillable land that Gadsden recommended an additional tract, which
was granted by the President, July 29, 1824. In 1826 another tract
was set aside for their use, but the whole was ceded to the United
States by treaty of Payne's Landing, May 9, 1832, as is subsequently
mentioned.

6. James Gadsden (1788-1858) was a friend of President Jackson,
under whom he had fought in the Florida campaign of 1818 which led to
the arrest of Arbuthnot and Ambrister (see note 2 above). In June, 1853,
he was appointed Minister to Mexico by President Pierce, and in this
capacity negotiated with that Government, in the same year, the
purchase of what is now southern Arizona and New Mexico, a transaction,
as well as the tract itself, still known as the "Gadsden Purchase."

7. Billy Bowlegs' name is not apparent in connection with this
treaty. Possibly he is identical with Hola-at-a-Micco. Jones was the
sixth of the fifteen signers.

8. That is, Osceola. See p. 360, this volume.

9. The treaty concluded at Fort Gibson, March 28, 1833, the first
Seminole signer of which is "John Hicks, representing Sam Jones."

10. Under the form "Charley Emartla" his name is signed to the
treaty of Payne's Landing, above mentioned. The name Emathla,
strictly *Imá'la* (or *Imá-hla*), signifies "leader." This Indian having
refused to join his tribesmen in their opposition to the enforced
removal of the Seminole, was murdered by Osceola and a small party
on November 26, 1835.

11. General Wiley Thompson, Indian agent for the Seminole, and
Lieutenant Constantine Smith. The Indians were under the immediate
command of Osceola. The fort alluded to was Fort King, situated
near the present Ocala, Florida.

12. Major Francis L. Dade. Fort Brooke was at the present Tampa, 130 miles south-west of Fort King. The massacre occurred in the palmetto country, which afforded a perfect ambush for the Indians, in the present Sumter county, Florida, near the Withlacoochee River. Dade's command numbered 139 men, equipped with a six-pounder fieldpiece and a wagon with ten days' provisions. Lewis, the negro slave of a Spaniard, was enlisted as a guide, but proved the traitor by informing the Indians of the intended march, with the disastrous result noted.

13. Near Charleston, South Carolina, Osceola's death occurred, January 30, 1838. His grave is marked by a monument immediately outside of the principal gate of the fort.

14. Coacochu, or Coacochee, was the son of the so-called King Philip. These two Seminole attacked Fort Mellon, on Lake Monroe, February 8, 1837, but were repulsed after a stubborn fight lasting three hours. Wild Cat and Osceola surrendered at the same time. The former was confined in a dungeon at Fort Marion, but effected a remarkable escape, and continued his depredation as a leading chief after Osceola's death. He was recaptured by Colonel W. J. Worth on the Kissimee, in February, 1841, Coacochee being arrayed in gorgeous attire which he had stolen from a band of strolling actors near St Augustine. He was permitted to visit his people for the purpose of effecting their surrender, but time and again returned with the complaint that he could do nothing with his band, and demanding whisky. The patience of the officers finally becoming exhausted, he was seized in June, and was on the way to Indian Territory when he was recalled and placed in irons on a vessel in Tampa Bay. With separation from his people staring him in the face, he agreed now to bring about peace by sending a deputation to the members of his warring band, and in October, with 210 of his people, he departed for their new home in the West. Coacochee was always a friend of the negroes among the Seminole, and in 1850 went to Mexico with 300 blacks in order to prevent the Creeks from enslaving them. Returning after two years, he escaped with a number of slaves belonging to the Creeks, and it is said was afterward heard of as living with the Comanche in the Far West.

15. Colonel (later General) William Selby Harney, who fought in the Black Hawk War of 1833, and later became distinguished as an Indian fighter. See his Life by L. U. Reavis (St Louis, 1887).

16. Figures vary as to the mortality, but what is probably a more trustworthy account gives the number killed as 18 out of a force of 30. One of the leaders with Billy Bowlegs in this attack was Checkika, a chief of the "Spanish Indians," who was killed by a detachment under Harney during an excursion into the wilderness south of Peace River.

17. That is, between the north and south forks of the Canadian River, Indian Territory, near Oklahoma.

18. See note 3, above.

19. The portrait of Bill Bowlegs was probably painted by King in the winter of 1825-6, when a Seminole delegation visited Washington. The portrait, however, is not listed as among those in the National collection. There is no copy in the Peabody Museum collection, and from the fact that the portrait does not appear in the earliest editions of McKenney and Hall (see Introduction, Vol. I., p. lix.), it may perhaps be assumed that it was painted at a later date. See Rhees' *Catalogue*, Nos. 36, 63, 68, 107, 111, 118, for other Seminole who visited Washington at this time.

OPOTHLE-YOHOLO
A Creek Chief

OPOTHLE-YOHOLO

(A CREEK CHIEF)

THE last home of the Creek Indians, on the eastern side of the Mississippi, was in Georgia and Alabama, from which, in conformity with the provisions of a treaty with the United States, made in 1832,[1] they emigrated in 1836-7. They were divided into what were called the Upper and Lower towns, the former of which were situated upon the banks and among the tributaries of the Tallapoosa and Coosa Rivers. Over these towns the *Big Warrior*[2] was chief, under whom Opothle-Yoholo[3] held the rank of principal councillor, or speaker of the councils, over which he presided with great dignity. His influence was so great that the questions submitted to the council were generally decided according to his will, for the Indians, considering him as the organ of their chief, supposed he only spoke as he was directed. The great council house of the Upper towns was at Tuckabatchee, where the Big Warrior resided, and near which was the residence of Opothle-Yoholo.

We have, in the biography of McIntosh,[4] pointed out the singularly embarrassing circumstances in which the Creeks were placed at this time. The United States, by a compact made with Georgia, when the limits of that State comprehended the territory which afterwards was formed into the State of Alabama, became bound to remove all the Indians within the boundaries of Georgia, whenever it could be done peaceably.[5] To comply with this engagement, and to fulfil a benevolent policy, having for its object the civilisation of the Indians and the securing to them a permanent home, the United States set apart a fertile and extensive tract of wilderness, beyond the Mississippi, upon which they proposed to settle the several remnants of tribes that still lingered within the states, and were becoming demoralised and destroyed by contact with a race with whom they could not amalgamate. Unhappily some of the tribes were not willing to emigrate, and among them the Creeks. The pledge of the Government to remove them, although qualified by the condition, "when it could be peaceably effected," was yet to be at some time redeemed; and while the Creeks were on the one hand averse to the removal, the more intelligent among them saw, upon the other, that the existence of such a compact doomed them to an exile which, although it might be delayed, could not be avoided. Year after year the Government, to redeem its promise to Georgia, sent commissioners to purchase from the Creeks their lands, who as often returned unsuccessful, or succeeded only in part, while the inhabitants of Georgia and Alabama discovered a disposition to resort to more urgent measures, and frequent collisions between the white people and the Indians were the unhappy consequence. The Creeks themselves became divided: McIntosh, the head chief of the Lower towns, advocating the removal, and the Big Warrior, who ruled the Upper towns, opposing that measure. The Little Prince, an aged chief who ruled the whole nation, was willing to leave the question to those whom it immediately concerned.

In 1824, Messrs Campbell and Meriwether were sent by the Government to effect this long-desired purchase, and held an ineffectual treaty at a place called the Broken Arrow,[6] where they found a few of the chiefs willing to yield to their views, but others so decidedly opposed that, forgetting the grave and decorous courtesy which usually prevails in their solemn councils, they would give no other answer than a sullen but emphatic "No." The deputy of the Big Warrior said that he would not take a houseful of money for his interest in the land, and that this was his final answer. Failing in their object, the commissioners called another council, to meet at Indian Springs, in February, 1825.

Previous to this period little is known of the character of Opothle-Yoholo, except that he was considered in early life a youth of promise. The first public service in which he distinguished himself, was at the council at Indian Springs, to which he was sent to counteract the influence of McIntosh, and to remonstrate with him against selling any part of the Creek country. It is said that he executed this mission with great fidelity; he pursued his object with unyielding firmness, and his remonstrances were marked with energy and eloquence.

The substance of his address to the commissioners was as follows:—"We met you at the Broken Arrow, and then told you we had no land to sell. I heard then of no claim against our nation, nor have I heard of any since. We have met you here upon a very short notice, and I do not think the chiefs present have any authority to treat. General McIntosh knows that we are bound by our laws, and that what is not done in public council is not binding. Can the council be public if all the chiefs have not had notice, and many of them are absent? I am, therefore, under the necessity of repeating what I told you at the Broken Arrow, that we have no lands to sell. No part of our lands can be sold except in full council, and by consent of the whole nation. This is not a full council; there are but few here from the Upper towns, and of the chiefs of the Lower towns many are absent. From what you told us yesterday, I am inclined to think it would be best for us to remove; but we must have time to think of it, and to consult our people. Should the chiefs now here undertake to sell our country, it would cause dissension and ill-blood among ourselves, for there are many who do not know that we have been invited here for that purpose, and many who would not consent to it, if they were here. I have received a message from my head chief, the Big Warrior, directing me to listen to what the commissioners have to say—to meet and part with them in peace—but not to sell any land. I am also instructed to invite you to meet us at the Broken Arrow three months hence, when a treaty may be finally made. I gave you but one speech at the Broken Arrow, and I give you but one here. To-morrow I return home. I have delivered the message of my head chief, and have no more to say. I shall listen to whatever you may think proper to communicate, but shall make no further answer."

This speech was delivered with the calmness and dignity becoming the occasion; respectful to the commissioners, yet decisive in tone and language, it was the refusal of a little band of untutored men, confident of right, to the demand of a powerful nation. All that was fiery and alarming was reserved for McIntosh, who was supposed to have already promised to accede to the proposed transfer. Turning to that ill-fated chief, with an eye full of meaning, he extended his arm towards him, and in the low bitter tone of prophetic menace, he added, "*I have told you your fate if you sign that paper. I once more say, beware!*" On the following morning he left Indian

Springs, and returned to Tuckabatchee. McIntosh persisted in his determination to sell the country, signed the treaty, and, as we have narrated in another place, paid the penalty with his life.

Arrangements were soon after made to send a deputation of chiefs to Washington, to protest in the name of the Creek nation against the execution of the treaty of Indian Springs, and to conclude one which should be more acceptable. Opothle-Yoholo was placed at the head of this deputation, and proceeded with his colleagues to the seat of Government. In all the negotiations connected with that exciting occasion he conducted himself with great dignity and firmness, and displayed talents of a superior order. He was cool, cautious, and sagacious; and with a tact which would have done credit to a more refined diplomatist, refused to enter into any negotiation until the offensive treaty of Indian Springs should be annulled. The executive being satisfied that the treaty had not been made with the consent of the nation nor in accordance with its laws, but in opposition to the one, and in defiance of the other, disapproved of it, and another was made at Washington in January, 1826,[7] the first article of which declares the treaty of Indian Springs to be *null and void*. By the same compact the Creeks surrendered all their lands lying within the chartered limits of Georgia, except a small strip on the Chattahoochee, which formed afterwards the subject of much dispute. The intention of the parties, as declared and understood at the time, was to convey the whole of the Creek country, but in undertaking to lay down boundaries, from an office map, wrong lines were assumed, and the Creeks left in possession of a tract which they were afterwards induced, by the advice of indiscreet friends, to insist upon retaining. It was in reference to this tract that a correspondence took place between the Executives of the Federal Government and Georgia, characterised, on one side at least, by much warmth.

As the great object of the purchase of the Creek country was to remove that tribe from the vicinity of a people with whom they lived in constant contention, and from the limits of a state which insisted on their departure, as of right, the retention of a portion, however small, and whether effected by accident or artifice, defeated alike the wishes of Georgia and the intentions of the United States. Several ineffectual attempts were made to settle the question by a further purchase that should include the whole of the disputed territory; the Federal Government adhering to its usual conciliating policy, and preferring to buy again what had been already purchased, rather than practise the slightest injustice, while Georgia, stimulated by the discontent of her citizens, and offended by what she conceived an artful evasion on the part of the Creeks, vehemently urged a speedy decision. All these efforts having failed, a special commission was issued in 1827, to Colonel McKenney, directing him after discharging certain duties upon the Upper Lakes, to cross over to the Mississippi, descend that river, and hold councils with the Chickasaws, Choctaws, Cherokees, and Creeks—and, if possible, to bring this unhappy controversy to a close by purchasing the disputed tract.[8]

Fully appreciating the character of Opothle-Yoholo, the first object of Colonel McKenney, on his arrival in the Creek country, was to conciliate that chief, on whose decision he foresaw the result would depend. A messenger was accordingly despatched to Opothle-Yoholo, to announce his arrival and solicit an interview at Fort Mitchell.[9] That politic leader, understanding well the purpose of this visit of the Commissioner for Indian Affairs, declined the pro-

posed meeting under the plea of indisposition. This was
considered a subterfuge to gain time until the attendance
of two educated Cherokees, who were the secret advisers
of Opothle-Yoholo, could be procured; and another
messenger was despatched to inform him that if he was
not well enough to ride on horseback, a suitable convey-
ance should be provided, and that the business to be
discussed was of great interest to him and his people. In
short, he was told emphatically that he must come. The
next day he made his appearance, and entered with
apparent frankness upon the subject of Colonel McKenney's
mission. In the interview of that gentleman and Colonel
Crowell, the agent, with this chief, he discovered a tact
which the more enlightened might imitate with advantage.
He spoke of his readiness to do whatever might be most
acceptable to his Great Father; and admitted that the
land in question was not worth much to his people while
it was a bone of contention between them and Georgia.
In evidence of the unhappy state of things which existed,
and that he deplored, he stated, that when his people
crossed the Chattahoochee, to look after their cattle or
hogs that roamed in the woods, they were shot by white
men, against whom he could have no redress. He had,
therefore, every desire to comply with the wishes of the
President, but insisted that he could not sell the land
except in open council, and by consent of the nation. He
would most cheerfully do anything to promote peace, but
he was only an individual, unauthorised to act for the
nation, and unable to control its decision—and, finally, he
expressed his belief that the Creeks would not be willing
to sell the land.

He was told in reply that it was not intended to make
the purchase except in conformity with their laws—that
he was sent for because he was known to be the friend of

his people, and of their welfare—and that, by advising
them in open council, where it was proposed to meet them,
he could do much towards satisfying their minds of the
justice and propriety of settling this controversy in the
mode proposed by the Government. It would be *just*,
because the intention of the parties to the treaty at
Washington had been to embrace all the land of the
Creeks within the limits of Georgia, and this strip was
excluded because the maps were incorrect upon which the
lines were traced. It would be *proper*, because the safety
of the Indians and the quiet of the borders could in no
other way be insured. In a word, he was told that the
Creeks were required to carry into effect the treaty according to its true intent, and that the Government proposed
again to purchase that which was already theirs by solemn
compact. The Creeks were not asked to make a new sale,
but to ratify and execute a contract which had been previously made. Still their Great Father was willing to
remunerate them for their expected compliance with his
wishes—he knew they were poor, and would again pay
them for the land.

The reply of the wary chief showed, as his previous
conversation had indicated, that his object was to gain
time. It was smooth, plausible, and evasive. At last it
was agreed to hold a council at Tuckabatchee,[10] and runners
were sent out to invite the chiefs of the towns to be present.
At the appointed time from twelve to fifteen hundred Indians
had assembled, and after some delay Opothle-Yoholo, as the
chief person present, was called upon to open the council.
He still hesitated, and, upon various pretences, consumed
three days, when it was understood that the two educated
Cherokees had arrived. These persons having learned the
white man's art of talking upon paper, were much esteemed
by the chief, who probably expected through them to be

able to protect himself from any artifice that might be practised in the phraseology of the treaty that should be proposed, while they used their advantage, on this and other occasions, to thwart the designs of the Government, and keep alive the existing agitation.

No other apology for delay remaining, certain ceremonies, preparatory to the council, were performed with a solemnity and careful attention which showed that they were considered of great importance. These were not only singular, but, as we believe, peculiar to the Creek nation; and they form one of the many curious examples exhibited in savage life, in which the human intellect is seen to act, on an occasion demanding the exertion of its highest powers, with an absurdity which intentional levity could scarcely surpass. In the centre of the square of the village, four long logs were placed, in the form of a cross, with their ends directed towards the four cardinal points, and a fire kindled at the intersection. The Indians were seated around in groups. A decoction had been previously prepared, called the *black drink*, which is made by boiling the leaves of a small bush, greatly esteemed and carefully preserved by them, which they call *arsee*.[11] The black and nauseous liquid, thus produced, was poured into large gourds, each holding three quarts, or a gallon, and being handed round by persons appointed for the purpose, was drank in such liberal quantities as to fill the stomach. The disgusting draught acted as an emetic, and was drank and thrown up until the evidences of the hideous ceremony covered the square. Having thus purified themselves for business, a messenger was sent to inform the commissioner that the council was ready.

But little hope was entertained that this council would lead to a successful result; for it was ascertained that during the previous night the proposition of the commissioner had been debated, and a negative reply decided upon. It was believed that the two half-breed Cherokees had prevailed upon Opothle-Yoholo to refuse to make the transfer of the disputed territory until a government could be organised, like that which had been established by the Cherokees, after which the sale was to be made, and the money put into the Creek treasury—one of the half-breeds being the prospective minister of finance. Unpromising as the prospect appeared, the commissioner determined to leave no effort untried to effect an object essential to the peace of the frontier and to the preservation of amicable relations between the Federal Government and Georgia. When, therefore, in reply to the proposition he was instructed to make, he received the decided negative of Opothle-Yoholo, in which the council unanimously concurred, he availed himself of the information he had received of the secret intrigue of the Cherokees, and boldly disclosed the plan to the assembled Creeks. For the first time perhaps in his life Opothle-Yoholo became alarmed. He knew the jealous and vindictive temper of his people. The fate of McIntosh was too recent, his own part in that tragedy too prominent to leave any doubt as to the result of a tampering by the few with the rights of the many. He saw the danger in which he was placed by the disclosure of a plan prompted by a foreign influence, doubtful in itself, and not yet matured. He knew as well as the accomplished jurist of Great Britain that popularity may be gained without merit, and lost without a fault—that the *people*, civilised or savage, are easily ruled, and as easily offended, and that, in the excited state of his tribe, the memory of his own services might be instantly obliterated by the slightest shadow cast upon the patriotism of his motives. He grew restless, and said to the interpreter, "Tell him he talks too much." Colonel McKenney replied, that the welfare and happiness of the Creeks was all that their Great Father at Washington sought in this interview, and if what had been said was that which they ought to know, their chief should take no exception to it. He hoped there was no impropriety in telling the truth, and having commenced a talk he should finish it, no matter what might be the consequence. The effect was electrical. A hum of voices was heard through the council, and it was manifest that Opothle-Yoholo, though he maintained the calmness of a warrior, saw that his life hung upon a thread. The commissioner, knowing that the Little Prince, head chief of the nation, whose power was absolute, was encamped in the neighbourhood, concluded his exposition by saying he should appeal to him, and if he spoke the language of that council, their talk would be reported to the President for his decision. The appeal to Cæsar gave a new direction to the thoughts of the savage assembly, and probably arrested the dissension that might have ensued. The commissioner, without waiting for a reply, left the council, followed by the whole body of the tawny warriors, who rushed towards him as he was about to mount his horse. Surprised by this sudden movement, he demanded to be informed of its object, and was answered, "We came to look at the man who is not afraid to speak."

The Little Prince was then stricken in years. The commissioner found him, in the primitive state of a forest chief, lying upon a blanket under a tree; near him was a fire and the preparations for cooking, and suspended from a bough over his head were the provisions that were to form his banquet. He was approached with great veneration; for in the history of the southern Indians there is not found a name of more sterling worth. His mind was enlightened on all matters that concerned his people; his spirit unflinching; his sense of justice keen and abiding. To

him the commissioner made known the whole matter, not
omitting the offensive interference of the Cherokee young
men.   It was this disclosure that Opothle-Yoholo feared.
He could manage his own chief, the Big Warrior, near
whom he was officially placed, and of whose ear he had
possessed himself, but he could not encroach upon the
authority of the Little Prince, who ruled the whole Creek
nation, uniting under his authority the Upper and Lower
towns.   The Prince heard the statement in silence;
although to his visitor he paid every becoming attention,
not a syllable of comment escaped him; not a look of
assent or disapprobation.   With that caution which marks
the whole tenor of the Indian's life, and especially governs
his intercourse as a public man, he withheld the expression
of any opinion until he could make up a decision which
should be sanctioned by deliberate reflection.   The commissioner, though well aware of this feature of the Indian
character, supposed from the apparent apathy with which
he was listened to, that he had only related what the chief
knew and approved, and concluded the brief interview by
saying, "I now leave you and your people.   I shall return
immediately to Washington, and report what I have seen
and heard."   They parted, the one to reflect on what had
passed, the other to seek repose for the night at the
agency at Fort Mitchell.

At midnight a runner, sent by the Little Prince, arrived
at the Fort.   "Tell the commissioner," was his message,
"not to go—in the morning the Little Prince will come to
him and make a treaty."   At daylight another messenger
came to say that the Little Prince's horse had strayed
away in the night, but that he would visit the commissioner early in the day.   About noon he arrived, attended by
several of his chiefs, but Opothle-Yoholo was not of the
number.   After the usual salutations, the chieftain said to

Colonel McKenney, "Take a paper, and write to the Cherokee chief, that if his young men (naming them) come among my people again I will kill them." This characteristic despatch—which shows, that in the crude diplomacy of the forest the last resort of civilised nations is the first appeal for justice—was written, the mark of the Little Prince affixed, and the missive sent. The transaction showed a suitable jealousy of a foreign influence over his people, and over the chief functionary of the Big Warrior, which probably led more than any other consideration to the decision to make the treaty which his meddling neighbours endeavoured to prevent. The treaty was prepared and agreed upon, a council was called which ratified the proceeding, and the important document signed, which gave peace to that frontier, and forever closed this exciting question.[12]

This direct and unusual exercise of authority, in opposition to the decision of Opothle-Yoholo, made but a few days before in open council, greatly weakened the influence of the latter. But the Little Prince dying about a year afterwards, Opothle - Yoholo regained a power which had been inferior only to that of head chief, that of the Big Warrior being merely nominal. The successor of the Little Prince was Nea Micco,[13] a dull, heavy man; and the Big Warrior having also departed soon after to the land of spirits, was succeeded by Tuskena, his son, a person of slender capacity. Opothle - Yoholo became therefore the principal man of the Creeks in fact though not in name, and has continued ever since to exercise over them the power of an absolute potentate. It is said that he might have been elected to the chieftainship on the demise of the Little Prince, but that he preferred his position as speaker, which, by bringing him more directly in contact with the people, gave him all the advantage of his address and eloquence.

During the late unhappy contest between the United States and the Seminole Indians, it was to be expected that the sympathies of the Creeks would be strongly excited in favour of the latter, who are wandering tribes, descended from the Creek nation.[14] Accordingly, in 1836, when the war grew hot, and the Seminoles were successful in several sanguinary engagements, the spirit of revolt spread through the Creek nation, and many of that people were urged, by the fatal destiny which seems to have doomed the whole race to extinction, into open war. Saugahatchee,[15] one of the towns of Opothle-Yoholo's district, was the first to revolt. The warriors, without a single exception, painted themselves for war ; the young men rushed out upon the highways and murdered all the travellers who fell in their way. Opothle-Yoholo, on hearing the intelligence, immediately placed himself at the head of the warriors of his own town, marched upon the insurgents, burned their village, and having captured some of their men, delivered them over to the military, by whom they were imprisoned. At the request of Governor Clay [16] of Alabama, he called a council of his warriors, at Kialegee,[17] and, having collected about fifteen hundred of them, proposed to lead them against the hostile Creeks. They consented, and within five days were encamped at Tallahassee,[18] the then headquarters of Major-General Jesup,[19] to whom a formal tender of their services was made. The offer was accepted, and Opothle-Yoholo appointed the commander of the whole Indian force, with the rank of Colonel. General Jesup marched the united regular and Indian army without delay to Hatchechubbee,[20] where the hostiles were assembled, and was about to attack them, when the latter, overawed by the superior

force and prompt action of the American General, surrendered themselves, and thus ended the contest.

We have not hesitated to speak freely of the causes
and conduct of the Indian wars that we have had occasion
to glance at in various parts of this work. They have
usually been provoked by the whites. Those alluded to
in this sketch were the result of frauds committed by land
speculators, who sought to enrich themselves at the
expense of those illiterate savages, and who have either
deceived the general and state governments, or committed
them by acts which, though they could not approve, they
have been obliged to sanction. This oppression, together
with a reluctance to emigrate on the part of some of the
Creeks, engendered that revengeful temper which has
thrown so many obstacles in the way of the attempts of
the Executive of the United States to separate the red and
white races.

The close of the disturbances rendering the further
services of Opothle-Yoholo and his warriors unnecessary,
and the time for their emigration having arrived, they were
ordered into encampments with a view to their immediate
removal, and shortly after left the land of their fathers
forever.

It is not to be inferred from the prompt support given
by Opothle-Yoholo to the American General, that his
sentiments had become favourable to emigration; on the
contrary, he remained inflexible in his aversion to that
measure. He was not only unwilling to leave his native
soil, but opposed especially to a removal to the lands
offered by the Government—perhaps because his people
would there be thrown into contact with the followers of
McIntosh, and he may have supposed it doubtful whether
they could live together in peace. He therefore, in 1834
or 1835, went to Texas to seek a home, and, having

explored the country, purchased a large tract, for which he was to give eighty thousand dollars; but the Mexican Government, jealous on account of the revolutionary movements then in progress, and unwilling to receive a population which would not probably make such subjects as it would desire, interposed to prevent the transfer, and there being also a doubt suggested as to the title to the land, the intention was given up, with a loss of twenty thousand dollars, which had been paid in advance.

The several parties of the Creek nation, unhappily divided by the contest relative to the sale of their country, are reunited in Arkansas,[21] and are said to be living in harmony. Opothle-Yoholo is popular, and is spoken of as principal chief of the united tribes. His competitor is Rolly McIntosh, brother of the murdered chief, General McIntosh.

Opothle-Yoholo is believed to have but one wife. Two of his daughters are said to be very beautiful. One son was educated at the Choctaw Academy, in Kentucky, and bears the name of the venerable patron of that institution, Richard M. Johnston.[22]

NOTES

1. This was the treaty concluded at Washington, March 24, 1832, and ratified April 4 following. Lewis Cass was the commissioner on behalf of the Government, and "Opothle-holo" was the first of the Creek signers.

2. See the biography of MENAWA, p. 178, this volume.

3. His name is properly *Hupuehelth Yaholo*, from *hupuewa*, "child," *he'hle*, "good"; *yahólo*, "whooper," "hallooer," an initiation title, often occurring in Creek personal names.

4. See Vol. I., p. 261, this work.

5. On this point consult Mooney in *Nineteenth Annual Report of the*

Bureau of American Ethnology, pt. 1, 1900, also Abel in *Report of the American Historical Association.*

6. See Vol. I., note 7, p. 271, this work.

7. The treaty of January 24, 1826, conducted by James Barbour, Secretary of War. "O-poth-le Yoholo" was the first Creek signer, and McKenney served as one of the witnesses. This treaty was confirmed, April 22. John Quincy Adams was President at this time. It was during this visit to Washington that the accompanying portrait of Opothle-Yoholo was painted by King, as noted in the Rhees *Catalogue* (see Introduction, Vol. I., p. xlix, No. 53) : " Opothle Yoholo, Principal Chief of the Creek deputation to Washington in 1825. King, 1825." The copy in the Peabody Museum of Harvard University, presumably by Inman, bears catalogue No. 28.211. His portrait was later (July, 1843) painted by Stanley.

8. For the instructions, see McKenney's *Memoirs,* pp. 60-61.

9. In the present Russell county, Alabama. Fort Mitchell was the seat of the Creek Agency.

10. See McINTOSH, Vol. I., p. 261, this work. McKenney barely mentions these negotiations in his *Memoirs* (p. 187).

11. The full Creek name of the "black drink" is *ássi-lupútski,* meaning "small leaves" and referring to the *Ilex cassine.* The decoction is also known among whites as "Carolina tea." It was in common use among the tribes bordering on the Gulf of Mexico for purposes of purification in connection with their ceremonies, notably the *búskita,* or *púskita,* commonly called "busk," an annual thanksgiving observance. The celebrated Osceola (*q.v.*), or Ossi-yoholo ("black-drink hallooer"), derived his name from this drink. Consult Gatschet, *Migration Legend of the Creek Indians,* Vol. II., 1888 ; Hawkins, *Sketch of the Creek Country,* 1848 ; Speck in *Memoirs of the American Anthropological Association,* Vol. II., No. 2, 1909, with authorities therein cited ; and Hale, *Ilex Cassine,* Washington, 1891.

12. As previously mentioned, this treaty of the Creek Agency, Fort Mitchell, Alabama, was concluded by McKenney and Agent Crowell, November 15, 1827, and was ratified March 4, 1828. The land ceded by this treaty comprised a strip ranging in width from about five miles to about seven miles, and extending from the intersection of Chattahoochee River with the western boundary of Georgia, northward for a distance of nearly seventy miles along the state border, or almost to the northern boundary of the present Haralson county, Georgia. Opothle-Yoholo's name is not signed to this treaty, while the name of the Big Warrior of Tukabatchi appears as "Tustmuggee Thlucco, *by proxy.*"

13. "Weah Micco" signed the treaty last referred to as a representative of Suoculo (evidently Sawokli) town.

14. The Seminole separated from the Creeks, as their name (Sim-a-no'-le, "separatist," "runaway") indicates. They were originally made up of immigrants from Lower Creek towns on Chattahoochee River, who moved down into Florida after the destruction of the Apalachee about the year 1705. They first became known as Seminole about seventy years later. In 1906 there were 2132 Seminole by blood and 979 Seminole freedmen in Indian Territory; in 1900 there were 358 Seminole in Florida. There is also a refugee band of Seminole negroes on the Rio Grande near Eagle Pass, Texas.

15. Saugahatchee, or Saugahatchie, was an Upper Creek settlement on an eastern branch of Tallapoosa River, ten miles below Eufaula, Alabama, evidently in Tallapoosa county.

16. Clement Comer Clay (1789-1866) served as Governor of Alabama from 1835 until 1837, when he was chosen to the United States Senate, in which body he served until 1841, when he resigned.

17. This is Kailaidshi, a former Upper Creek town on a small western tributary of the Tallapoosa River, near the northern boundary of Elmore county, Alabama. The name survives in that of the present town of Kowaliga.

18. Tallassee, or Talase, on the western bank of the Tallapoosa, in the south-eastern part of the present Elmore county, Alabama.

19. Thomas Sidney Jesup (not Jessup as in previous editions) was born in Virginia in 1788; died at Washington, D.C., June 10, 1860. He served with distinction in the War of 1812, being successively promoted from lieutenant to major; in recognition of his bravery at the battle of Chippewa he was promoted lieutenant-colonel by brevet in July, 1814, and colonel by brevet in the same month for services in the battle of Niagara, where he was severely wounded. Becoming full lieutenant-colonel in 1817, he was made adjutant-general with rank of colonel in 1818, and quartermaster-general with rank of brigadier-general in the same year. Ten years later he received the brevet of major-general. On May 20, 1836, General Jesup took command of the army in the Creek country, and in December succeeded General Richard K. Call in command of the army in Florida. Being wounded, January 24, 1838, in an action with the Seminole at Jupiter inlet, he was relieved by General Zachary Taylor.

20. Hatchichapa, meaning "half-way creek." This was a branch settlement of Kailaidshi (see note 17, above), between Coosa and Tallapoosa Rivers, Alabama. It was burned by the hostile Creeks in 1813, but was afterward rebuilt, and in 1832 had sixty-two families. The name survives in that of the town of Hatchechubbee, in Russell county, Alabama.

21. That is, Indian Territory, now Oklahoma.

22. See Vol. I., note 27, p. 103. With regard to the subsequent career of Opothle-Yoholo, Mr George W. Grayson, a member of the Creek tribe, says: "When General Albert Pike, at the beginning of the Civil War, visited the Creeks in a great council near the present town of Eufaula and urged them to treat with the Confederacy, Opothle-Yoholo exercised all his influence against the treaty, and when the council decided, after several days of debate and deliberation, to enter into the treaty, he withdrew with his following from the council. Later he withdrew from the Creek nation with about a third of the Creeks and espoused the cause of the Union. Fighting his way as he went, he retreated into Kansas, and later died near the town of Leroy." (*Handbook of American Indians*, pt. 2, 1910, p. 141.)

YOHOLO-MICCO

(A CREEK CHIEF)

YOHOLO-MICCO [1] was principal chief of the Eufalo town,[2] which lies between Tallassee and Oakfuskee, in the Creek nation, the Tallapoosa River running through it. In the war of 1813-14, he served with McIntosh against the hostile Indians, and shared largely and honourably in all the battles that were fought. His bravery was equalled only by his eloquence, which gained him great distinction. He was the speaker of the Creek nation, as Opothle-Yoholo was of the division called the Upper towns, and opened the councils on all occasions.

At the council called in 1827, by the Little Prince, to receive the propositions offered by the Government through Colonel McKenney, which we have noticed in another place, Yoholo-Micco explained the object of the mission in a manner so clear and pointed as not to be easily forgotten by those who heard him. He rose with the unembarrassed dignity of one who, while he felt the responsibility of his high office, was familiarly versed in its duties, and satisfied of his own ability to discharge it with success. He was not unaware of the delicacy of the subject, nor of the excitable state of the minds to which his argument was to be addressed, and his harangue was artfully suited to the occasion. With the persuasive manner of an accomplished orator, and in the silver tones of a most

YOHOLO-MICCO
A Creek Chief

flexible voice, he placed the subject before his savage audience in all its details and bearings—making his several points with clearness, and in order, and drawing out his deductions in the lucid and conclusive manner of a finished rhetorician.

The deportment of this chief was mild, his disposition sincere and generous. He advocated warmly the principles and practices of civilised life, and took so decided a part in favour of the plans to improve the condition of his people, proposed by the American Government and by individuals, that he became unpopular, and lost his place and influence in the general council and the chieftaincy of his tribe. His successor as principal chief of the Eufalo town is Octearche Micco.

Yoholo-Micco was amiable in his family relations, and brought up his children with care, giving them the best advantages in point of education which the country afforded. His sons were bred to the pursuits of civilised men. One of his daughters, named Lotti Yoholo, married a chief of the Eufalo town, and, following the example of her father, gave her children liberal educations.

This chief visited Washington in 1826, as one of the delegates from his nation.[3] He afterwards consented to remove to Arkansas, and fell a victim to the fatigues attending the emigration, in his fiftieth year, while on his way to the land of promise. His memory is honoured by the Indians, who, in common with all who knew this excellent person, speak of him as one of the best of men.

The word "Micco" signifies *king* or *chief*, and will be found forming a part of the names of many of the southern chiefs; while Yoholo, which signifies the possession of royal blood, is an aristocratic adjunct to the names of those who are well descended.[4]

NOTES

1. The name is little more than an official appellation, signifying " Hallooer Town-Chief."

2. There were several Eufaula towns at various periods, belonging to both the Upper Creeks and the Lower Creeks. The one here referred to was situated in the present Tallapoosa county, Alabama, west of Dadeville. Yoholo-Micco was therefore an Upper Creek, as stated farther on.

3. This was the occasion of the negotiation of the treaty of January 24, 1826, which was signed by thirteen Creek chiefs, headed by Opothle-Yoholo. McKenney was one of the witnesses. The Creeks reached Washington in November, 1825, and therefore remained at the capital several weeks. Current newspapers refer to the visit and speak of Yoholo-Micco as "the favorite orator of the nation." During this visit Yoholo-Micco's portrait was painted by King, as noted in the Rhees *Catalogue*, No. 27. The Inman copy in the Peabody Museum bears catalogue No. 280.212.

Yoholo-Micco was signer of the treaty of January 22, 1818. (See Vol. I., note 5, p. 270, this work.)

4. See note 1 above, and OPOTHLE-YOHOLO, note 3, p. 32, this volume.

MISTIPPEE

(SON OF YOHOLO - MICCO)

THIS is a son of Yoholo-Micco, who bears a name the origin of which would be discovered with difficulty by the most cunning etymologist ; and we are happy to have it in our power to solve a problem which might else, at some far distant day, cause an infinite waste of valuable time and curious learning. The parents of this youth, having decided on rearing him after the fashions of their white neighbours, bestowed upon him the very ancient and respectable appellation of Benjamin, from which soon arose the usual abbreviation of Ben and Benny, which the young chief bore during the halcyon days of infancy. To this familiar name, respect for his family soon prefixed the title of Mr, and, in the mouths of the Indians, Mr Ben soon became Mistiben, and finally Mistippee—the original Benjamin being lost in the superior euphony of that very harmonious word *mister*.

It is not improbable that the individual who bore this name when his portrait was taken may now be known by another, for, as we have remarked elsewhere, these designations are frequently changed ; and an Indian has usually as many names as there are remarkable events in his history. Those which they receive in infancy are entirely accidental, or are induced by the most trifling circumstances. *Litker*, the Swift, is the name of an active boy ; but if a

child is called *Isca,* the Ground Hog, or *Woodcoochee,* the
Raccoon, it is not to be presumed that he resembles that
animal, because he would be as likely to receive it from the
mere circumstance of being seen to play with the animal,
or to wear its skin, or to imitate some of its motions.   On
the other hand, *Minechee,* which signifies little, smart and
active, is the appropriate name of a female child.   These
names are retained during childhood, and until the youthful
character begins to show its bias, when others are given
which are supposed to be more descriptive ; and we
believe it is always usual, when a young man is admitted
into the war councils, to give him a name with reference
to his qualifications as a warrior.   For instance, a youth
who is modest and retiring may be called *Chofixico,* which
would be interpreted, "timid as the deer," yet the word is
a compound used chiefly as a proper name.   *Cho* is an
abbreviation of *echo,* a deer—*fix* is abbreviated from *fegee,*
which means life or spirit—and *ico* is a contraction of *sicco,*
gone—from all which we get the very poetical compound
above mentioned.   A bold and fearless spirit is called
Yaha Hadjo, the Crazy Wolf, from *yaha,* a wolf, and *hadjo,*
crazy.   Another class of names are given still later in life,
and are such as refer to some exploit or adventure by
which the individual became distinguished for the time,
as, " *He who stands and strikes,*" " *He who fights as he flies,*"
or " *The wolf killer.*"

Mistippee escaped having the name of an animal conferred upon him, in the manner we have seen, but spent
his boyhood, as is usual with the Indian children, in
practising with the blow-gun and bow, and in hunting the
smaller kinds of game.   The blow-gun[1] is a favourite
weapon among the boys of the southern tribes.   It is
simply a hollow reed of eight or ten feet in length, made
perfectly smooth within, from which a small arrow is blown

MISTIPPEE
Son of Yoholo-Micco

with much force by the breath. The arrow is made of
light wood, armed with a pin, or small nail, at one end, and
with thistle-down carefully wrapped round the other, in a
sufficient quantity to fill the reed, so that, when placed in
the end to which the mouth is applied, it is forced through
the reed with great swiftness, and, if well directed, with
the certainty of the rifle ball. At a distance of ten yards,
the little Creeks will snuff a candle, with one of these
arrows, four times out of five ; and as no noise attends the
discharge, they are quite successful in killing small birds
by means of this simple contrivance, which is called, in the
Creek tongue, *cohamoteker*. By these exercises the young
Indians not only develop their physical powers, but acquire
the cunning, the patience, the dexterity, and the fund of
sylvan knowledge that render them the most accomplished
hunters in the world. If one of these boys chances to kill
a deer with the bow and arrow, or to perform any exploit
above his years, he is marked as having a spirit which will
greatly distinguish him in after-life, or as being a lucky
person, which, in the estimation of the Indian, amounts
to about the same thing as the possession of superior
abilities.

In presenting the spirited likeness of this youth, we
may be permitted to take the occasion to repeat some
of the lessons which are taught the young Indian and
contribute to form his character. Among these is the
tradition of their origin, which is instilled into the infant
mind of the savage with a care similar to that bestowed by
Christian parents in teaching the great truths of Creation
and Providence. Perhaps the curiosity of a child in
relation to its own being would have a natural and
universal tendency to render this a first lesson ; and the
subject which, above almost all others, is veiled in obscurity,
is that which is attempted to be explained to the young

mind in the earliest stage of its development.   The tradition
of the Creeks is, that they came through the sea, from
some distant land.   To enable them to pass through the
deep waters with greater safety and certainty, they were
transformed into brutes; and the nation is now divided
into separate bands, which retain the names of the different
animals from which they are said to be descended.   Our
information with regard to the means used to perpetuate
this arrangement agrees with that of Mr Gallatin, who
remarks, " It has been fully ascertained that the inviolable
regulations by which these clans are perpetuated amongst
the southern nations were, first, that no man could marry
in his own clan ; secondly, that every child belongs to his
or her mother's clan." [2]

The peculiar economy of this clanship gives rise to
the practice, in their courtships, of applying first to the
maternal uncle of the girl who is to be asked in marriage,
for his consent—the father being of a different tribe from
his own daughter and her prospective offspring.   The
young men are said to be shy and bashful in these
adventures, and, having resolved to marry, conceal their
first overtures with great dexterity.   The uncle is easily
won by a present, and, when his assent has been gained,
the suitor is left to his own ingenuity to thrive as he
may with the object of his preference.   His intention
is conveyed secretly to the lady, through some confidential
channel : she is then supposed to be ready for the question,
which is decided without debate.   A deer is killed and
laid at the door of the wigwam ; if the present is received,
the lover is a happy man ; if it be suffered to remain
untouched, he may go and hang himself, or seek a more
willing fair one.   The latter is said to be the more usual
practice, as hanging for love is a procedure only known
in the more civilised conditions of society.   If the deer

be accepted, a rich soup is made of the head and marrow bones, and the lover is treated with this repast, in which there is supposed to be great virtue.

Not only are the youth instructed in their origin, and disciplined in their modes of courtship, but they are also taught the ceremonies of their religion—if the superstitions of a people, destitute of any adequate notion of the being and attributes of God, may be dignified with that name. The chief of these is the Green Corn Dance,[3] which is celebrated with great zeal and devotion, in the autumn. Wherever the Indian corn is raised it is a chief and favourite article of food—its productiveness, its nutritious qualities, and the variety of modes in which it may be used, giving it a preference over every other description of grain. Among the Indians who cultivate little else, the ripening of this crop constitutes an era in the year. The whole band is assembled to celebrate the annual festival. The fires of the past year are extinguished— not a spark is suffered to remain. New fire is produced artificially, usually by rubbing two sticks together. Sometimes the new fire thus obtained is sent from one band to another, and the present is received, like the New Year's gift among ourselves, as a token of friendship. Having kindled a cheerful blaze, they assemble around it, dancing, and singing songs. The latter are addressed to the fire—a custom which may have been borrowed from the worship of the sun, said to have been practised by the Nachez Indians. In these songs they express their gratitude to the Great Spirit that they have lived through the year, that they see the same faces and hear the same voices; they speak of the game they have taken, and of the abundance of their crops. But if the crop be short, or the hand of death has been busy among them, the notes of gratulation are mingled with strains of mourning, the national calamity is attributed to the crimes of the people, and pity and pardon are invoked. On this occasion they partake of the "black drink" which we have described in our sketch of the life of Opothle-Yoholo. The dance being finished, they feast upon boiled corn, the first fruits of the year; and the singing, dancing, and eating are kept up for several days. Should a culprit, whose life has been forfeited, have escaped punishment until this festive season, and be so fortunate or so dexterous as to make his way into the square during the dance, he is considered as being under the protection of the Great Spirit, to whose agency they attribute the circumstances of his previous escape and present appearance among them, and his pardon is secured.[4]

Of Mistippee there is little to tell. When at Washington, in 1826, he was a remarkably handsome boy, and in all respects prepossessing. His father gave him unusual advantages in regard to education, which he is supposed to have improved. When at maturity he wedded a comely woman of the Hillabee towns,[5] and soon after emigrated to the new home provided for his people, west of the Mississippi.[6]

NOTES

1. The use of the blow-gun in North America appears to have been confined to the south-eastern part of the country. The cane *Arundinaria macrosperma*, of which the weapons were made, grew only within that area.

2. Albert Gallatin, "Synopsis of the Indian Tribes of North America," in *Transactions and Collections of the American Antiquarian Society*, Vol. II., Worcester, Mass., 1836. The statement is correct, since among the Creeks descent is reckoned through the mother, and the tribe therefore had the clan rather than the gentile system.

3. The ceremony here referred to, known as *búskita*, or *púskita*, and popularly called "busk," is described in greater detail by Gatschet, *Migration Legend of the Creek Indians*, Vols. I. and II., Philadelphia, 1884, and St Louis, 1888; also Speck, "The Creek Indians of Taskigi Town," *Memoirs of the American Anthropological Association*, Vol. II., pt. 2, 1907. See OPOTHLE-YOHOLO, note 11, p. 33, this volume.

4. See Gallatin, (pp. 108-109) cited in note 2 above. The statements here given by McKenney and Hall refer, of course, to the Creeks. For further information regarding their social organisation, etc., consult the works of Gatschet and Speck, cited in note 3 above.

5. Hillabi, or Hillabee, town was on Koufadi Creek, a branch of Hillabee River, between Coosa and Tallapoosa Rivers, near the site of Ashland, Clay county, Alabama. Before Hawkins' time (1799) the Hillabi people had settled in four towns, known as the Hillabi towns, called Hlanudshiapala, Anatichapko, Istudshilaika, and Uktahasasi. The inhabitants suffered severely at the hands of General Jackson, November 18, 1813, when 316 of them were killed or captured and their settlement devastated.

6. As here stated, Mistippee accompanied his father to Washington in the winter of 1825-26, but there is no indication that he signed the treaty—evidently he was too young to serve as a delegate. His portrait, painted by King in 1825, bears No. 24 in the Rhees *Catalogue ;* a copy by the same artist (No. 176) is in the Redwood Library at Newport, Rhode Island; while the Inman copy in the Peabody Museum collection is numbered 28.213.

PADDY CARR

(A CREEK INTERPRETER)

THE name of this individual indicates his lineage. His father was an Irishman who married a Creek woman, and handed down to his son a name which, though neither euphonious nor dignified in our ears, is perpetuated with no little pride by the son of Erin. The young Paddy was born near Fort Mitchell, in Alabama, and in his infancy was taken into the family of Colonel Crowell, the Indian agent, and kindly reared in the habits of civilised life. He was very intelligent, acquiring with facility the language of his benefactors, yet retaining his own, so as to be able in after years to speak both with equal fluency. In 1826, he accompanied the delegation headed by Opothle-Yoholo, to Washington City,[1] in the capacity of interpreter; and although but nineteen years of age, he evinced a quick perception of the human character, which enabled him to manage and control the Indians with more success than many who were his seniors. His intuitive sagacity was such that, in rapidly interpreting the speeches of the Indian orators, even under the embarrassment of a public audience, while he faithfully repeated the thought expressed by the speaker, he often gave it additional vigour and clearness, by the propriety and force of the language in which he clothed it. As the substance of the harangues made

46

on such occasions by aboriginal diplomatists is usually
matured by previous consultation, he was probably well
advised of the whole ground that would be taken; but
those who know how much ability is employed in making
an accurate and spirited translation, will acknowledge the
merit of filling well so difficult an office as that of interpreter. He possessed the entire confidence of the whole
delegation, who regarded him as a youth of superior
talents.

Soon after his return from Washington, he married the
daughter of Colonel Lovett, a respectable half-breed, with
whom he received a portion which, with the property
accumulated by himself, furnished a capital sufficient to
enable him to go into trade. In a few years he amassed
a considerable property, and is now, in 1837, possessed of
from seventy to eighty slaves, besides landed property,
and a large stock of horses and cattle.

In 1836, he was drawn from the quiet pursuits of trade
and agriculture by the hostile attitude of a portion of the
Creeks, and, unwilling to remain inactive, he promptly took
the side of the Government. When Major-General Jesup,[2]
with an escort of about a hundred horsemen, attempted to
pass through a part of the revolted district, for the purpose
of joining and taking command of the Alabama forces,
Paddy Carr attended him as guide and interpreter. In a
part of the country where much of the land was low and
swampy, and where the roads were rendered passable by
causeways made of logs, these latter were found torn up,
and several straggling Indians were seen. Supposing these
to be the scouts of a large body, Paddy Carr expressed his
conviction that an army of eight hundred warriors was at
hand, and suggested that no time should be lost in getting
through these passes. The advice was taken, and, by
pushing boldly through, the danger was avoided. In

conducting the escort back a circuitous route was taken, by which the same body of Indians was again eluded, and a party of gallant volunteers were saved from the fatal catastrophe which befell the lamented Dade [3] and his unfortunate companions. This happy result has been attributed, and we suppose with some reason, to the sagacity of Paddy Carr, who was the successful guide.

He continued in the service as a guide and interpreter, and also as a leader of the Indian warriors, during the continuance of the troubles in the Creek nation, and was a general favourite with the army.

The Creek revolt being over, Paddy Carr marched to Florida as second in command of about five hundred Creek warriors, who volunteered their services to the Government. We understand that he ranks deservedly high, as well for his courage and skill as for his acceptable deportment in the social circle.

Paddy Carr has an innate passion for fine horses, and owns a large number of very valuable animals. He is fond of racing, and, when he has a trial of speed depending, if he cannot suit himself with a rider, he rides his own horse. He is of a liberal and generous disposition, hospitable to strangers, and kind to the poor. Many of the poorer class of Indians depend on him for support. He has three wives, one of whom is daughter of the ill-fated General McIntosh. [4] The two first-born of his children were twin girls, and Captain Crowell, the son of his early friend and patron, having a daughter named Ariadne, he called one of his twins *Ari* and the other *Adne*, thus evincing a sense of benefits received, which is in itself one of the highest evidences of a noble mind.

PADDY CARR
Creek Interpreter

NOTES

1. He was evidently present at the signing of the treaty, January 24, 1826, in the City of Washington, although his name does not appear in that document. The accompanying portrait was evidently painted during this visit to Washington, as it represents a young man of about the age mentioned. The original may have been by King, although the name of the artist is not given in the Rhees *Catalogue*, in which it bears No. 128. There is no copy of this portrait in the Peabody Museum collection.

2. See OPOTHLE-YOHOLO, note 19, p. 34, this volume.

3. See HALPATTER-MICCO, note 12, p. 15, this volume; and consult *The War in Florida* [by Woodburn Potter], Baltimore, 1836, p. 102.

4. See Vol. I., p. 261, this work.

TIMPOOCHEE BARNARD

(A YUCHI WARRIOR)

A CONSIDERABLE number of the persons who have risen to distinction among the southern Indians, within the last quarter of a century, have been the descendants of adventurers from Europe or the United States, who, having married Indian women, and adopted the savage life, obtained the confidence of the tribes, and availed themselves of that advantage to accumulate property. They were at first traders, who carried to the Indians such goods as they needed, and bought their peltries, but soon directed their means to the purchase of negro slaves, whom they employed in the cultivation of the soil, and the care of large numbers of cattle and horses. They lived in a state of semi-civilisation, engrafting a portion of the thrift and comfort of husbandry upon the habits of savage life, having an abundance of everything that the soil, or the herd, or the chase, could yield, practising a rude but profuse hospitality, yet knowing little of anything which we should class under the names of luxury or refinement. Their descendants formed a class which, in spite of the professed equality that prevails among the Indians, came insensibly into the quiet possession of a kind of rank. Although they were bred to the athletic exercises and sports of the Indian, they had a nurture superior to that

50

of the savage; the most of them received the rudiments
of an English education, and a few passed with credit
through college. The real Indian, while he despised and
spurned at civilisation when offered to himself or his
children, respected in others the practical advantages
which he saw it gave them; and thus the half-breeds,
having the Indian blood on the one hand, and the
advantage of property and education on the other, became
very influential, and, had they been permitted to form
governments, as was attempted in one instance, would
probably have concentrated in their own hands all the
property of the Indians. To this class mainly was confined the civilisation among the southern tribes so much
spoken of a few years ago.

Timpoochee Barnard was the son of a Yuchi woman.
His father was a Scotsman, said to be of gentle blood,
whose name was Timothy Barnard. It is supposed that
large estates may be in reversion for the descendants of
Timpoochee.

The Yuchees [1] were once a distinct and powerful people,
but were subdued by the Creeks upwards of a century
ago, and those who escaped the massacre, which usually
attends an Indian victory, were taken into the country of
the victors, and held in servitude. Being unaccustomed
to labour, they were probably of little value as slaves,
especially to a people who had no agriculture, and who
needed warriors more than servants. They gradually
became emancipated, and incorporated with the Creek
nation, with whom they have ever since remained in close
and cordial union, although, as is customary with the
Indians, they have preserved their identity as a tribe, and
retained their language. The latter is described by the
venerable and learned Mr Gallatin,[2] in his elaborate work,
just published, as "the most guttural, uncouth, and

difficult to express, with our alphabet and orthography, of any of the Indian languages within our knowledge." The Creeks do not attempt to speak it, although the Yuchees speak the Creek language as well as their own. Timpoochee's mother carefully imparted her own dialect to her son, while his father, though a practised interpreter of the Creek, never attempted to master the Yuchi.

The subject of this memoir was first known in public life in 1814, when he took part with the American forces against the hostile Creeks, and commanded about one hundred Yuchi warriors, with the commission of Major. He was at the battle of Callabee[3] under General Floyd, and distinguished himself by an act of gallantry. An attempt was made to surprise the American camp at night, and to cut off a detachment under General Brodnax encamped near the main body. Timpoochee Barnard discovering this movement, made a desperate onset upon the assailants, at the head of his Yuchi braves, and, after a severe loss, succeeded in driving back the enemy, or in opening the way for the detachment to join the main body. During the war he acquired a high reputation for skill and bravery. He was often honoured by being placed in the post of danger, and he did not in any instance disappoint the expectations of the commanding General. He took part in nearly all the battles in the south, during that war, and was twice wounded.

On the return of peace he rejoined his family, near the Creek Agency, on Flint River, in Georgia. His wife was a Creek, and is reported to have been remarkable for her good sense and propriety of conduct; while Major Barnard is said to have been domestic in his habits and devotedly attached to his children, of whom he had six.

TIMPOOCHEE BARNARD
A Yuchi Warrior

Of the latter, two were girls, who were extremely beautiful, and the family, taken together, was considered the handsomest in the Creek nation. One of the daughters fell a victim to a delicacy not often found in her race, nor in the women of any country where the practice of polygamy debases the marriage relation. She was overruled in her choice of a husband, and compelled to marry against her will; and, although her husband was a Creek chief of distinction, she could not brook the degradation, as she esteemed it, of being a second and subordinate wife, and put an end to her life by poison.

On his return from the Creek nation, in 1827, Colonel McKenney[4] brought to Washington with him two little Indian boys, one of twelve and the other nine years of age, with the intention of having them educated under his own care, at the expense of the Government. The elder of these was William, son of Timpoochee Barnard; the Indian name of the other was Arbor, but he was called Lee Compere, after the missionary of that name who lived in the Creek nation. After they had travelled about a hundred miles, at the beginning of their journey, Lee discovered some symptoms of discontent, and Colonel McKenney, having learned through William, who spoke a little English, that he was dissatisfied at being sent from home, requested the stage driver to stop his horses, and told Lee that he might return. The boy's countenance instantly brightened, and, seizing his bundle and his little blow-gun, he began to clamber out of the carriage. He was, of course, not permitted to go; but the anecdote is mentioned to show the fearlessness with which the young savage throws himself upon his own resources. They remained in Colonel McKenney's family about three years, and until his connection with the Indian Department ceased, when they were sent home. They went to school during

this period, and William made considerable progress, and
bade fair to become an honour to his name and country.
He was intelligent and docile, while Lee had all the Indian's
stubbornness of temper, impatience of restraint, and disin-
clination for sedentary pursuits.   The schools selected for
these boys was one of those at which, in imitation of the
discipline at West Point, the pupils were required to
perform martial exercises, and to submit to a military
police.   The young Indians were pleased with this routine,
which was in unison with their naturally martial dispositions.
The uniforms and the parades were precisely suited to gratify
their tastes, but neither of them liked the exact enforcement
of strict rules.   On one occasion Lee was ordered, for some
delinquency, to be placed under guard, during the hours
allotted for recreation.   He was accordingly confined in a
room, which was called the "black hole," and another boy
placed as a sentinel at the door.   Lee sat for a little time,
gazing wistfully at the boys who were playing on the outside, and at the sentinel who paced to and fro with a
musket on his shoulder, when, espying a bayonet in the
room, he seized it, and rushed upon the guard, who escaped
its point at first by dodging, and then by running away.
On finding himself at liberty, Lee threw down the weapon,
and deliberately walked home.

Those who have paid attention to the subject have not
failed to remark, that in the attempt to civilise the Indian,
a *little* learning is a dangerous thing, and that a half-educated
savage seldom becomes an useful man.   Such an individual,
thrown back upon savage life, is inferior to those who had
never quit it in their own arts, without bringing back much
that is valuable of the habits of civilised men.   Unless he
has the strength of mind to attach himself decidedly to one
side or the other, he is apt to vacillate between employments
of the white man and the Indian, inferior to both, and

respected by neither. We do not say that such was the case with William Barnard. We only know that his career has been unfortunate. Though but fifteen years old on his return home, he fell into a series of difficulties, with the precise nature of which we are not acquainted, but in course of which he killed several Indians, and he afterwards joined the Indian force sent to Florida under Paddy Carr to assist in the war against the Seminoles.

Thus did this worthy and highly respectable person reap his full share of those domestic afflictions which not infrequently embitter the last days of those who have been most exemplary in private life, and whose affections are garnered up in the holy and endearing joys of the domestic circle. Major Barnard had, however, the consolation to know that he had faithfully performed a parent's duty, gaining for himself the sincere attachment of those around him, and for his family the respect of the public.

A compliment paid to this individual by the late President of the United States, is too striking to be omitted. During the residence at Washington, of the two Indian boys already mentioned, they were taken by Colonel McKenney to see the President, who received them with the paternal kindness of manner which distinguished so remarkably the social intercourse of that eminent man. On hearing the name of William Barnard, he took the boy by the hand and asked him if he was the son of Major Timpoochee Barnard; the reply being in the affirmative, General Jackson placed his hand on the head of the youth, and said, "A braver man than your father never lived." There is no applause which savours less of flattery than the spontaneous homage which is paid by one brave man to the courage of another.

Timpoochee Barnard was one of the delegation chosen

to proceed to Washington[5] to remonstrate against the treaty of Indian Springs, at which time his portrait was taken.   After living in such affluence as his country afforded, distinguished for probity, benevolence, and hospitality, as highly as he was by valour and public spirit, he died near Fort Mitchell, in Alabama, aged about fifty-eight years.

NOTES

1. "Lower down on both sides of the Savannah were located the Uchi [Yuchi] tribe, which constituted a distinct linguistic stock (Uchean). The remnant of the tribe are now incorporated with the Creeks. They were probably identical with the 'Cofitachiqui' of De Soto's chroniclers, a tribe whose village is supposed by the best authorities to have been located at the site of Silver Bluff, on the Savannah, in Barnwell county, South Carolina, about twenty-five miles by water below Augusta." — Mooney, *Siouan Tribes of the East*, Washington, 1894, p. 83.   See also, Yuchi, p. 1003 *et seq.*, pt. 2, *Handbook of American Indians*, op. cit.; F. G. Speck, "Ethnology of the Yuchi Indians," in *Anthropological Publications of the University of Pennsylvania*, Vol. I., No. 1, 1909.

2. Albert Gallatin, "Synopsis of the Indian Tribes in North America," in *Transactions of the American Antiquarian Society*, Vol. II., Worcester, Mass., 1836.

3. Pickett, *History of Alabama*, Vol. II., pp. 336-337.—"At twenty minutes past five o'clock in the morning [January 27, 1814], the Red Sticks, who had secreted themselves in the swamp during the latter part of the night, sprung upon the Georgians like tigers, driving in their sentinels, and taking the whole army by surprise. In twenty minutes, the action became general, and the front right and left flanks of the Americans were closely pressed; but the enemy was met at every point. The front line was preserved by the steady fire of the artillery, under Captain Thomas, aided by the riflemen of Captain Adams. These troops suffered severely, for the enemy rushed within thirty yards of the cannon. Captain John Broadnax, who commanded one of the picket guards, maintained his post, until a party of Indians had cut off his retreat to the main army. In this desperate situation, his resolute band cut their way through to their friends, assisted by Timpoochy Barnard, a half-breed, at the head of some Uchees." At the beginning of this engagement the American troops were encamped on

the high lands along Calebee creek, which flows in a north-westerly direction through Macon county, Alabama.

4. See Introduction, Vol. I., p. xvi., this work.

5. This was during the winter of 1825-26. The portrait of "Major Timpoochy Barnard" was painted by King at that time (1825) and bears No. 135 in the Rhees *Catalogue.* A copy of the portrait was bequeathed by King to the Redwood Library, Newport, Rhode Island, where it is now preserved.

MAKATAIMESHEKIAKIAH, OR BLACK HAWK

(A SAUK BRAVE)

FEW Indians have obtained a celebrity so widely extended
as that of the individual now before us. Without being a
chief, or a person of remarkable abilities, he became
known to the American public as the principal person
engaged in the brief and hopeless war waged by a
fraction of the Sauk tribe against the United States.
Having been taken prisoner at the close of that contest,
he was conducted with a few companions to Washington,
and some other of our cities, where his fame and his
misfortunes excited so much curiosity that he was everywhere visited by crowds, while his propriety of deportment
was such as to sustain the reputation that had preceded
him. He was the greatest "lion" of the day; and the
public will probably be disappointed at the discovery that,
although a respectable person, he is by no means a hero.
The events of his early life we extract from a small volume
published at Cincinnati in 1833, and said to have been
dictated by himself, and which we know to be acknowledged by him as authentic. The Black Sparrow, or
as he is now called, Black Hawk, whose unpronounceable
Indian name we shall not attempt to repeat,[1] was born
at the principal village of his tribe on Rock River, in

Illinois, about the year 1767, and was the great-grandson of a chief called Nanamakee, or Thunder. At the early age of fifteen, having had the good fortune to wound an enemy of his nation, he was admitted to the rank of a brave, and allowed to paint himself and wear feathers. The chief of a neighbouring tribe coming to the Sauk town shortly after, to raise recruits for an expedition against their common enemy, the Osages, he was permitted, in company with his father, to join the war party. A battle was fought in which the Sauks and their allies were successful, and Black Hawk signalised his valour by killing and scalping a warrior. On the return of the party he was permitted, for the first time, to join in the "scalp dance." Having now established a reputation as a brave, he was enabled, a few months afterwards, to raise a party of seven young men, who went forth with him in search of adventure, and, falling in with a camp of a hundred Osages, he boldly attacked them, killed one of their warriors, and retreated without losing a man. This exploit gained him so much reputation, that when he next offered to lead a war party, a hundred and sixty braves placed themselves under his command. After a long march, they approached an Osage village with great caution, in the expectation of surprising it, but found it deserted; and the dissatisfied warriors, with the exception of five, abandoned their leader and returned home. The little remnant of the war party continued to pursue their enemies, determined not to return without a trophy; and, after some days, succeeded in killing a man and a boy, with whose scalps they marched back in triumph.

The defection of his braves on this occasion injured the standing of Black Hawk with his nation, who supposed him deficient in good fortune, or in conduct, and he was unable for some time afterwards to obtain a command.

At length, at the age of nineteen, he succeeded in raising a party of two hundred warriors, whom he led against the Osages, and, meeting with an equal number of the enemy, a desperate battle ensued, in which the Sauks were victorious, and slew a hundred of their enemies, with a loss on their side of but nineteen. Black Hawk says he killed five braves and a squaw, and took four scalps.

After this decisive battle, active hostilities with the Osages ceased, and the Sauks turned their arms against the Cherokees. Black Hawk accompanied a small party commanded by his father, who met the Cherokees near the Merrimac River,[2] the latter having the advantage in numbers. The Cherokees are said to have lost twenty-eight men, and the Sauks but seven. The father of Black Hawk being among the slain, he assumed the command, took possession of *the great medicine bag*[3] of the deceased, and led the party home. This expedition was considered so unfortunate, that our hero blacked his face, fasted, and for five years abstained from war, praying frequently to the Great Spirit, and engaging in no manly exercises but those of hunting and fishing.

After this period, the Great Spirit having taken pity on him, or in other words, his people believing that he had sufficiently atoned for his bad luck, he led out a small party against the Osages, but could only find six men, whom he captured and delivered up to the Spanish commandant at St Louis. In his next expedition he was more fortunate. At the head of a large party he surprised an encampment of forty lodges of the Osages, all of whom, without distinction of age or sex, were put to death, except two women, who were taken captive. He declared that in this battle he killed seven men and two boys with his own hand.

He then led an expedition against the Cherokees, to revenge his father's death; but finding only five of their people, he states, that having captured these, he afterwards released four and carried the other one home, being unwilling to kill so small a party. This assumption of mercy on an occasion when revenge was his sole object, succeeding so closely the narrative of an indiscriminate massacre, in which he killed two boys, is not easily reconciled. We give the story as we find it, leaving the reader to draw his own conclusions. The details of several other battles, in which Black Hawk describes himself as having borne a conspicuous part, we pass over.

The treaty made by Governor Harrison with the Sauks and Foxes in 1804,[4] by which they ceded their lands east of the Mississippi, is alluded to in this volume, as having been executed by a few chiefs, without the knowledge or consent of the nation. As we have not the means of deciding this question, we shall not enter upon it.

The erection of Fort Madison,[5] upon the Mississippi, is mentioned, the dissatisfaction of the Indians at this encroachment of the Americans, and an unsuccessful attempt which was made by the Sauks and Foxes to surprise and cut off the garrison. The visit of the enterprising traveller, Pike,[6] at Rock Island, is noticed, and we are told that when this officer presented them with an American flag, they received and hoisted it, but when he required them to pull down the British flag, they declined, as they "wished to have two Fathers."

At this time the Sauks and Foxes were in the practice of trading with the British posts on the northern Lakes, and Great Britain having adopted the policy of retarding the expansion of our settlements, much exertion was used by the officers of that power to conciliate the Indians, and to gain an influence over them.   The state of affairs on the Western frontiers of the United States was very unsettled.   The emigration to the valley of the Ohio had pushed the settlements into contact with numerous and warlike tribes of Indians, and although the latter had sold the lands that were now becoming occupied by the whites, they saw with jealousy the rapid increase of a population so essentially different from their own.   Occasions were sought to rescind or deny the treaties by which territory had been ceded, and the American Government, to avoid even the appearance of injustice, in various instances purchased the same tract of country over and over from the same tribe, and extinguished successively the conflicting titles of different tribes; while, on the other hand, intrusions were often inconsiderately committed on the hunting-grounds of the Indians.

For several years previous to 1811, the prospect of a war between the United States and Great Britain produced an irritable state of feeling on the frontier, and opened a wide field for the machinations of those persons who thought their own interests promoted by exciting the Indians to hostilities.   The British officers and traders, therefore, co-operated in their exertions to attach the Indians to their country, and to alienate them from the American people and Government.   Colonel McKee, Colonel Dixon, and Simon Girty were the most active agents in this unwise and unchristian warfare, and were busily employed for several years in holding talks with the Indians residing within the United States, supplying them with arms, making them liberal presents, and inciting them to make war upon the American settlements.   Several interviews were held with these officers by Black Hawk, and on one of these occasions we find him, for the first time, dignified with a title.   His own relation is as

follows :—"In the encampment, I found a large number
of Potawattimies, Kickapoos, Ottawas, and Winnebagoes.
I visited all their camps and found them in high spirits.
They had all received new guns, ammunition, and a variety
of clothing. In the evening a messenger came to me to
visit Colonel Dixon. I went to his tent, in which were
two other war chiefs and an interpreter. He received me
with a hearty shake of the hand, and presented me to the
other chiefs, who shook my hand cordially, and seemed
much pleased to see me. After I was seated, Colonel
Dixon said : 'General Black Hawk, I sent for you to
explain to you what we are going to do, and the reasons
that have brought us here. Our friend, La Gutrie, informs
us in the letter you brought from him, what has lately
taken place. You will now hold us fast by the hand.
Your English Father has found out that the Americans
want to take your country from you, and has sent me and
his braves to drive them back to their country. He has
likewise sent a large quantity of arms and ammunition,
and we want all your warriors to join us.

"About the same time a deputation from the Sauk
and Fox nation visited Washington,[7] and, on their return,
reported that President Madison had said to them, that, in
the event of a war with Great Britain, he wished them not
to interfere on either side, but to remain neutral. He did
not want their help, but wished them to hunt, and support
their families, and live in peace."

There seems to have been at this time a difference of
opinion among these Indians as to which side they should
take in the approaching war. Individual chiefs may have
had their predilections towards one side or the other ; but
most probably they hesitated only to ascertain which party
would offer them the most advantageous terms. When
the war actually broke out, a large party went to St Louis,

and offered the services of the tribe to the American Government. The offer was promptly declined, because our Government had resolved that they would not employ the savages. A small party claimed protection, and, separating from the nation, were sent to a new home provided for them on the Missouri, where they still live : but the great body of the Sauks and Foxes joined the British standard, and fought with their troops during the war.

An anecdote which Black Hawk relates as having occurred about this time, has probably many parallels in frontier history. A friend of his, who was old and crippled, had an only son, who had been adopted by Black Hawk, though he continued to live with his father. He had called to see his old friend on his way to join the British. Their next meeting was on his return, and is thus described :—"We were in the vicinity of our village, when I discovered a smoke ascending from a hollow in the bluffs. I directed my party to proceed to the village, as I wished to go alone to the place from whence the smoke proceeded, to see who was there. I approached the spot, and, when I came in view of the fire, saw a mat stretched, an old man sitting under it in sorrow. At any other time I would have turned away without disturbing him, knowing that he had come there to be alone, to humble himself before the Great Spirit, that he might take pity on him. I approached and seated myself beside him. He gave one look at me, and then fixed his eyes on the ground. It was my old friend. I anxiously inquired for his son, my adopted child, and what had befallen our people ? My old comrade seemed scarcely alive; he must have fasted a long time. I lighted my pipe and put it in his mouth. He eagerly drew a few puffs, cast up his eyes, which met mine, and recognised me. His eyes were glassy; he would again have fallen off into forgetfulness,

had I not given him some water, which revived him."
The wretched man who was thus mourning in solitude,
told the cause of his sorrow. His boy had gone out alone
to hunt. Night came and he did not return. The alarmed
parents passed a sleepless night. In the morning the
mother applied to the other lodges for assistance, and all
went in pursuit of the absent boy. There being snow on
the ground, they soon came upon his track, and after
following it some time, found also the trail of a deer which
he had been pursuing. They came to the place where he
had stood and fired, and found a deer which had been
skinned hanging upon a branch of a tree. But here
they found also the tracks of *white men.* They had
taken the boy prisoner. Their tracks led across the
river, and then down towards a fort; and after following the footsteps for some distance, the boy was
found dead. His body was shot and stabbed, and his
head scalped! The mother died soon after, and the old
Indian, left alone in the world, and, perhaps, destitute of
the means of subsistence, hied him to a solitary place
to die. This recital exhausted his strength, and Black
Hawk had only time to promise to avenge the murder of
his son, when the eyes of the old man closed in death.
Such are the atrocities of border warfare—when national
animosity becomes embittered by private injuries; the
invasion of dwellings, and the destruction of private
property plant the feeling of revenge deep in the heart,
and one deed of violence is retaliated by another, until
mercy and generosity are wholly forgotten.

Shortly after this occurrence, Black Hawk with a party
of eighteen warriors descended the Mississippi in canoes,
and landed near Cap au Gris, in Illinois. They struck
into the country, until they came to one of those rude
fortresses of logs which the settlers of the frontier erect

for their protection, near which they concealed themselves. Presently two white men riding on one horse approached, when the Indians fired and killed the horse and one of the riders, while the other escaped into the fort. The Indians retreated, but were immediately pursued by a party of mounted men, who surrounded them, and forced them into one of those funnel-shaped cavities which in this country are called sink-holes. Taking advantage of this position, the Indians threw themselves on the ground, and, being covered as by a breastwork, fired from the brink of the hole. The backwoodsmen were not to be thus foiled. A part of them retired, and soon returned with a large ox-cart, the body of which was tilted so as to be nearly perpendicular, and pushing this movable rampart forward to the edge of the cavity, they fired from behind it. Such was the ingenuity displayed mutually, that but one man was killed on each side at this spot; when, night coming on, the Americans retired to their fort, and the Indians retreated. The incident thus related by Black Hawk in his autobiography is substantially confirmed by a narrative repeated to us some years ago by one of the white men who was concerned in the affair, and who is now an affluent citizen of Illinois.

At the conclusion of the war between Great Britain and the United States, the Sauks and Foxes made peace with the American Government, and the latter soon after established a fort on Rock Island.[8] The planting of a military post so near their principal village was little relished by this warlike community, nor did they willingly give up a beautiful island which abounded in wild fruits and was much frequented by them in the summer. They believed that a good spirit had the care of it, who lived in a cave in the rocks, immediately under the place where the fort was built. He is said to have been often seen by the

Indians; and was white, with wings resembling those of a swan, but ten times larger. They were careful to make no noise in that part of the island which he inhabited, for fear of disturbing him. He has never been seen since the building of Fort Armstrong, and is supposed to have been driven away by the din of the drums and cannon, or by the boisterous mirth of a licentious soldiery.

A permanent peace was now established between these Indians and the Americans, which has not since been interrupted by any general war. But many causes of dissatisfaction occurred. The facilities afforded to an intercourse with the whites enabled the Indians to procure ardent spirits more frequently than in former times, and a train of evil consequences ensued. The treaty[9] by which the lands they still inhabited were ceded was a subject of bitter reflection; and, as the settlements of the whites expanded from year to year, they saw that the time was rapidly approaching when they must abandon their pleasantly situated village, and the delightful plains of Illinois. Collisions occurred between their hunters and the people of the frontier. The latter were in the habit of suffering their cattle and hogs to roam at large in the woods and over the prairies, and when any of these animals were lost, the Indians were suspected—in most instances we think unjustly—of having stolen them. On one occasion when Black Hawk was hunting near the settlements, a party of white men seized him, charged him with having killed their hogs, and beat him severely with sticks. At another time, an Indian having discovered a hive of wild bees, cut down the tree for the purpose of taking the honey, and, although trees were then considered of no value, but were constantly hewed down by any who pleased, this unfortunate Indian was pursued, and robbed of all the furs he had taken during a winter's hunting, under the pretence of compensation for the injury he was alleged to have committed.

It is believed that Keokuk[10] regarded these deeds of violence in the proper light, as the unauthorised acts of lawless individuals, who received no countenance from the American Government or people. This chief was now at the head of his nation, and, although a distinguished warrior, his policy was pacific, and his professions of friendship towards the Americans sincere. Black Hawk, who viewed him with dislike and jealousy, was at the head of a faction called the "British band," who continued to make annual visits to the British post at Malden, where they made their purchases, and received presents, while the majority of the tribe conformed to the regulations in regard to them made by the American Government, and traded at St Louis. This state of things continued for about twenty years after the war, with but little alteration.

In the meanwhile, the territory of Illinois had been formed into a state,[11] and the settlements which had commenced in the southern part of this delightful country were rapidly extending to the north. The Sauks and Foxes still occupied the most desirable part of the state, and around their village in every direction was an immense district of wilderness, over which they hunted. In the extreme north-western part of the state, at Fever River, a rich mineral region was discovered, and began to be occupied, and the flourishing town of Galena sprung into existence.

We shall now turn our attention to the war in which Black Hawk acted a conspicuous part. By a treaty made in 1804,[12] at St Louis, between Governor Harrison on the part of the United States, and certain chiefs of the united Sauk and Musquakee nation, the latter ceded all their lands in Illinois to the United States, under a reservation, however, contained in the following words : "As long as the lands which are now ceded to the United States remain their property, the Indians belonging to the said tribes shall enjoy the privilege of living and hunting upon them." This treaty was disclaimed by the Sauk and Fox nation, as having been made by persons who were not authorised to treat on that subject ; but it was afterwards confirmed by the treaty of Portage des Sioux in 1815,[13] and by another treaty made in 1816.[14]

The provision which allowed the Indians to occupy the ceded territory occasioned no inconvenience so long as the settlements in Illinois were confined to the southern part of that state ; nor would any have occurred, had the citizens of the United States been content to observe the simple and salutary regulations of their own laws. The statutory provisions for the protection of the Indians are numerous and ample. White men are strictly prohibited from purchasing or occupying the lands of the Indians, and from entering the Indian country for any purpose whatever, without a licence ; and the latter are only granted to a limited number of traders. The lands of the Indians are, therefore, in the eye of the law, sacred from intrusion, and the two races are so separated as to prevent any contact or collision which might be likely to disturb the harmony of either party. Not less guarded are the laws by which the lands of the Government, previous to their conversion into private property, are protected from intrusion. When a portion of the Indian territory is purchased, it becomes part of what is termed the public domain of the United States, and individuals are strictly prohibited from inhabiting, or in any manner occupying, or trespassing upon such lands, until they are regularly offered for sale. The practice of the Government has been to remove the Indians from the public lands previous to any measures being taken to

bring them into market.   A portion of the territory is then
surveyed, divided into tracts of a convenient size, by lines
corresponding with the cardinal points of the compass, and
the lands are then offered for sale.   By these cautious
enactments the Indians are not only protected in the enjoyment of their own lands, but after having ceded them, the
progressive steps by which the new population are admitted
oppose barriers which, if not broken down by lawless
violence, would effectually prevent the one race from
crowding oppressively upon the other.

Unhappily, however, these humane and wise provisions
have been but little regarded ; and the greater number of
our Indian wars have been incited by the impatience of
our own people to possess the hunting - grounds of the
receding savage.   The pioneers, or first settlers of our
country, are a hardy, erratic, adventurous race, uniting the
habits of the hunter and the farmer, and among them the
desire for new lands is a passion as strong as it is universal.
They delight in the wilderness.   A fertile uninhabited
tract combines the requisites which they deem necessary
to happiness : a virgin soil, fresh and luxuriant, which yields
an abundant harvest without laborious culture—a wide
range of natural pasture over which their cattle may roam
at large—and a country stocked with game.   Allured by
such advantages, thousands of individuals are constantly
in the practice of breaking through the wholesome restraints
to which we have alluded, and intruding not only on the
public domain, but the lands of the Indians.   Having found
a choice spot, the pioneer erects his cabin, as fearless of the
law as he is reckless of danger from the savage or the
wild brute, and takes quiet possession, in the confidence
that when the district shall be brought into market, an
indulgent Government will grant the right of pre-emption
to those who shall have settled within it in contravention

of its laws, or, that those who shall lawfully enter the country at a future day for the purpose of becoming purchasers, will be generous enough to refrain from buying a tract already occupied, and on which the tenant has expended his labour. However unreasonable such calculations may seem, they have seldom proved fallacious.

In the winter of 1827, when the Sauks and Foxes were absent from their town on Rock River, engaged in hunting, some evil-disposed persons, who were probably impatient to hasten their departure from the ceded territory, set fire to the vacant lodges, of which about forty were consumed. The Indians made no attempt to resent this outrage, but on their return quietly rebuilt their desolated village. In the following year, six or seven families of whites moved out and settled upon a choice tract of land adjoining the village. At that time nearly the entire northern half of Illinois was a wilderness, with a few scattered settlements, thinly dispersed at distant points, none of which were within fifty miles of Rock Island. There was, therefore, no reason founded upon necessity or inconvenience, nor any limitation of choice which confined the selection to that particular spot; millions of acres untrodden by the foot of civilised man, and blooming in all the luxuriance of Nature, afforded ample scope to the most fastidious choice. But, besides the violation of law and the infraction of a solemn treaty, this intrusion was fraught with the most ruinous consequences to the Sauks and Foxes. The Indians keeping no domestic animals but dogs and horses, make no fences round their corn fields, or at best, throw about them slight enclosures of brushwood. The intruders brought with them large herds of cattle, which were turned out to graze upon the open plain, and by which the patches of corn planted by the squaws were entirely destroyed. They even went so far as to extend their fences over the ground in the actual use of the Indians, on which corn was growing, and to plough up the latter in mere wantonness—for there could be no reason nor any apology for such an act, when the surrounding and contiguous country was all unoccupied except that the corn grounds of the Indians, being already under tillage, were prepared for the use of the farmer, without subjecting him to the labour of breaking the natural sod, as in the new lands. When some of the squaws, not aware of being guilty of any offence, clambered over the fences, thus unlawfully erected, they were beaten with sticks! All these wrongs and indignities were perpetrated by a handful of whites, in the midst of a warlike Indian nation; but so determined were the red men to keep at peace, and such the awe inspired by the overwhelming superiority of the American people, that they submitted without attempting any act of retaliation.

In 1829 the writer,[15] then occupying a civil office in Illinois, in company with a friend, who had recently filled a high post in the same state, visited Rock Island. The unhappy collision between the intruding whites and the Indians had then reached the most painful state of excitement, and we gathered from the Indian agent, the officers at Fort Armstrong, and the Indians, the particulars of this disastrous contest. Black Hawk, on hearing of the arrival of two strangers, who were as he supposed chiefs in their own country, came to relate to them the wrongs of his people. He spoke of the indignity perpetrated upon himself when, upon suspicion of an act that he would have scorned, he was beaten like a criminal, and, pointing to a black mark upon his face, said that he bore it as a symbol of disgrace. The customs of his nation, and their notions of honour, required that he should avenge the wrong he had received by shedding the blood of the aggressor; but he chose rather to submit for a season than involve his people in a war which must be fatal to them. And this was the only alternative; for such is the readiness with which offence is taken against the Indian, that if one of this race should kill, or even strike a white man, the act would be eagerly seized upon and exaggerated, the whole frontier population would rush to war, and the red men would be hunted from their homes like wild beasts. He spoke of the intrusion upon their fields, the destruction of their growing corn, the ploughing up of the graves of their fathers, and the beating of their women; and added: "We dare not resent any of these things. If we did, a great clamour would be raised; it would be said that the Indians were disturbing the white people, and troops would be sent to destroy us." We inquired: "Why do you not represent these things to our Government—the President is a wise and good ruler, he would protect you?" The reply was, "Our Great Father is too far off; he cannot hear our voice." "But you could have letters written and sent him." "So we could," said the old man, "but the white men would write letters and say that we told lies. Our Great Father would not believe an Indian in preference to his own children." This interview is alluded to in the biography already mentioned; and Black Hawk says of his visitors: "Neither of them could do anything for us; but they both evidently appeared very sorry. It would give me great pleasure, at all times, to take these two chiefs by the hand."

Under these circumstances, the Government required the removal of this nation from the ceded tract to their lands west of the Mississippi, and ordered the necessary surveys preparatory to the opening of a new land district; and, although by the treaty of 1804, the Indians had a right to occupy this country until it should be actually sold to individual purchasers, it was, perhaps, best for them that this right should not be insisted upon. The settlements were approaching so rapidly that their tenancy could be but brief.   At the end of two or three years, at most, they would be forced to retire.   The Government having determined to sell the lands, the only question was, whether they would insist on remaining during the period while the preparations for the sale should be going forward, or retire voluntarily before the pressure of the expected emigration should elicit new causes of dissatisfaction.   Keokuk, sustained by the majority of the nation, took the more prudent view of the subject and prepared to remove; while Black Hawk with the British band determined to remain.   It is due, however, to these unfortunate people, to state that while they decided to insist on a right guaranteed to them by a solemn treaty, they neither threatened violence nor prepared for war. They simply resolved to remain on the land during the whole term reserved to them, or until ejected by force.

In the spring of 1831, after the Indians had for a long while passively endured a series of insults and injuries from the intruding whites settled in their vicinity, and while the most profound peace existed on the frontier, a war was suddenly kindled by the same parties who had thus far been the aggressors.   The fences of the white people had, it seems, been thrown across a path which the Indian women had been accustomed to use, and the latter finding their way obstructed threw down the enclosure.   This trivial offence was eagerly seized upon by those who had long sought to bring about a war.   Letters were despatched to the interior in which it was alleged that the Indians were hostile, that measures had been taken to unite the Winnebagoes and Potawattimies with them in a league against the whites, that aggressions had been already committed upon the property of the settlers, and that the latter, wholly unprotected and in the power of merciless savages, were on the eve of abandoning their homes; and an express was despatched to the Governor of Illinois [16] formally communicating intelligence of a similar character. Upon this representation, a body of militia was ordered out by the Governor and marched immediately to Rock River. Fortunately for the peace of the frontier, General Gaines, [17] the commander of the western division of the army of the United States, was then at St Louis, and hastened to the scene of action, where his presence and conciliatory conduct soothed for a time the elements of discord. A council was held, in which these matters were discussed during several days; and it was finally agreed that the Sauks and Musquakees should retire to their own lands on the western shore of the Mississippi.

While this council was in session, General Gaines, observing that Black Hawk was seated among the chiefs and leading men who represented the Indian nation, and having heard his name often repeated as the most active of those who opposed the whites, inquired one day, " Who is Black Hawk? Is he a chief? By what right does he appear in council?" No reply was made. Black Hawk arose, gathered his blanket around him, and stalked out of the council room. On the following morning he was again in his seat. With the caution which marks the Indian character, he had refrained from making a reply while under the influence of passion, but had taken time to prepare himself. When the council was opened, he arose and said: "My Father, you inquired yesterday who is Black Hawk—why does he sit among the chief men? I will tell you who I am. I am a Sauk, my father was a Sauk—I am a warrior, so was my father. Ask those young men who have followed me to battle, and they will tell you who Black Hawk is! Provoke our people to war, and you will learn who Black Hawk is!" He then resumed his seat, and nothing more was said upon the subject.

The nation removed, agreeably to this treaty, to the western side of the river; but the State of Illinois continued to be agitated by rumours indicating a hostile disposition on the part of these Indians. Individuals among them were said to have visited the neighbouring tribes to incite them to war—a prophet was employed in dreaming and working spells—Black Hawk visited the British post at Malden, for the supposed purpose of procuring arms and ammunition—and the band attached to this leader were known to be discontented. It was confidently asserted, that a general league among the north-western tribes threatened the frontier with the desolation of the tomahawk and firebrand. However true these reports may have been in regard to the faction whose movements caused them, it is known that Keokuk and the majority of the nation were sincere in their pacific professions; and although Black Hawk was now mischievously disposed, it is not probable that, failing in his intrigues to implicate other tribes in the quarrel, he would have ventured upon any hostile demonstration with the small band under his own influence.

In the ensuing spring, while the public mind was thus excited, Black Hawk adopted the injudicious step of returning to Illinois, alleging that his band had been invited by the Potawattimies, residing on Rock River, to spend the summer with them, and plant corn on their lands. They crossed the Mississippi in open day, attended by their women and children, and carrying with them their lodges and travelling equipage; thus demonstrating that, whatever might have been their ulterior views, their immediate purpose was not hostile—for the Indian always strikes his foe suddenly, and by stealth, leaving behind him every encumbrance which might hinder a rapid retreat. A band of men trained to war, and well versed in its various incidents, could not be fairly suspected of the folly of making a hostile inroad upon the territory of a powerful people, under circumstances which must alike have rendered defeat certain and flight impracticable. But reason sleeps when fear and jealousy are awake. The dreadful experience of the horrors of Indian warfare, too familiar to our frontier population, has rendered them so keenly sensitive to its dangers, that the slightest rumour of such an incursion excites a universal alarm.

On hearing the intelligence of the invasion, as it was termed, of Black Hawk, the Governor of Illinois called out a large body of militia, and, placing himself at their head, marched to Rock Island. A singular state of things was now presented. Not a blow was struck. The Indians, after resting a few days at their village, pursued their march towards the country of the Potawattimies, without concealment or violence. Notwithstanding their merciless rule of warfare, which spares no foe who may fall into their hands, however helpless, they passed the isolated cabins in the wilderness, without offering the slightest outrage to the defenceless inhabitants. The property of the settlers, intruders upon the lands of these very Indians, remained untouched. Travellers between St Louis and Galena proceeded singly, or in small parties, through a wild region, now the reputed seat of war, without molestation, while an army was on its march to the frontier, and the newspapers were filled with reports of an Indian war in all its "pomp and circumstance." Matters did not remain long in this condition. A battalion of mounted militia, which had been sent in advance of the army, falling in with five or six Indians, who were approaching them with pacific signals, unhappily captured and put to death all except one, who made his escape, bearing the news of the slaughter of his comrades to the Indian camp, which was near. Black Hawk, who alleges that he was engaged in entertaining some visitors with a dog feast, immediately planned an ambuscade, into which the militia were enticed. On receiving the fire of the Indians they became panic struck, and fled in great disorder, with the loss of about fourteen men.

The Indians, finding that the war was commenced in earnest, now determined to do all the mischief in their power. Dividing their little force into numerous parties, they struck into the settlements which at that time were thinly scattered over an immense region of frontier, burning the huts of the settlers, and slaughtering such as fell in their way. In the course of a few weeks they committed much bloodshed and destruction. The whole State of Illinois became greatly excited. Two thousand additional militia were ordered out, and the citizens of every profession or calling were eager to participate in the campaign. It would be impossible for those who have never witnessed such scenes to realise the state of public feeling which pervaded the country at that period. The greater portion of the population of Illinois were emigrants from older Western States, and had either experienced the horrors of Indian warfare, or were the immediate descendants of those who had seen and felt the atrocities of savage barbarity. They had been accustomed from infancy to hear of the midnight conflagration and the slaughter of women and children, and to regard the Indian with fear and hatred. They thought of the red man only as one whose hand was ever ready to shed innocent blood; and there were few who could not tell of some friend or relative whose hearthstone had been desolated by the tomahawk. Although many years had rolled on in peace, and a new generation had grown up, the feuds of the border were not forgotten. With such feelings the whole population rose at the first alarm, and so popular was the war, that it was hardly creditable for any able-bodied man to remain at home. Farmers, lawyers, physicians, merchants, civil officers of every grade and department, were among the volunteers; and especially were all gentlemen who had any aspiration for political preferment, eager to signalise themselves in this field.

The plan of our work would not authorise a detailed account of this war.[18] It is enough to say that the little band of Black Hawk were soon compelled to fly before the immense force arrayed against them, directing their course north and west over the uninhabited waste lying between the head-waters of Rock River and the Mississippi. The army pursued with ardour, but under many disadvantages. Although the country was level and open, the Indians being the smaller party, were enabled to elude their pursuers, while the army, too numerous for the service allotted them, and encumbered with waggons, moved with heavy steps. After several weeks' laborious marching, and some skirmishes in which gallantry was displayed on both sides, the Indians were overtaken on the shore of the Mississippi, near the mouth of a stream called Bad Axe, and nearly the whole party slain or captured. Black Hawk was among the few who escaped; but he was delivered, a few days after, to General Street, the Indian agent at Prairie du Chien, by two Winnebagoes. Thus ended a war instigated by a few individuals to forward their own sinister views, but which cost the Government more than two millions of dollars, besides needlessly sacrificing many valuable lives. But while we condemn the beginning of this contest, we would award credit to those who afterwards became engaged in it. However unjustly a war may be brought about, it becomes the cause of our country whenever hostilities have commenced, and honour should be awarded to the citizen who draws his sword to repel an armed foe from our borders.

In the spring of 1833,[19] several of the captive leaders of the hostile band were conducted to Washington. Among these was the Prophet, who was supposed to have been the chief plotter; Neopope,[20] who was the active military leader; Black Hawk and his son, a fine-looking young man who was facetiously called by some of the editors of the day, Tommy Hawk. On their arrival at the Federal City, they were admitted to an audience with the President, to whom Black Hawk, on being presented said, " I am a man, you are another." Being informed by President Jackson that it was intended to hold them captive until the treaty made with General Gaines should be complied with, the Prophet made a speech, in which he remonstrated against this decision, and Black Hawk, after giving a history of the causes of the war, concluded a long address by saying : " We did not expect to conquer the whites. No, they have too many houses, too many men. I took up the tomahawk, for my part, to revenge injuries which my people could no longer endure. Had I borne them longer without striking, my people would have said, Black Hawk is a woman : he is too old to be a chief, he is no Sauk. These reflections caused me to raise the war whoop. I say no more on that subject; it is all known to you. Keokuk was once here; you took him by the hand, and when he desired to return home, you were willing. We hope you will treat us in the same way, and let us go."

The prisoners were conducted to Fortress Monroe, in Virginia, where they were kindly treated, and received every mark of consideration and attention. On their liberation, after a detention of about a month, Black

Hawk made a speech to General Eustis,[21] the commanding officer, of which the following is said to have been the substance :—

"Brother, I have come on my own part, and in behalf of my companions, to bid you farewell. Our Great Father has at length been pleased to permit us to return to our hunting-grounds. We have buried the tomahawk, and the sound of the rifle will hereafter bring death only to the deer and the buffalo. Brother, you have treated the red men very kindly. Your squaws have given them presents, and you have provided them with plenty to eat and drink. The memory of your friendship will remain until the Great Spirit says that it is time for Black Hawk to sing his death song. Brother, your houses are as numerous as the leaves upon the trees, and your young warriors like the sands upon the shore of the big lake which lies before us. The red men have few houses and few warriors, but they have hearts as warm as those of their white brethren. The Great Spirit has given us our hunting-grounds, and the skin of the deer which we kill there is his favourite, for it is white. This dress and these feathers are white : accept them, my brother. This present will remind you of Black Hawk when he is far away. May the Great Spirit preserve you and your children. Farewell."

Previous to their return to their own country, the captive warriors were conducted to the principal cities of the Atlantic states, and received everywhere the most marked attention and hospitality. They were invited to the theatres, museums, and other places of public resort ; and great pains were taken to show them the various objects which were considered worthy of their attention, or likely to excite their curiosity. At New York they witnessed the ascension of a balloon, which was about to rise into the air, as the steamboat which carried them to that city reached the wharf. On beholding the immense crowd which was assembled, and hearing the cheers of the multitude, they were at first alarmed, supposing those cries to be the war whoop of enemies ; but when the real cause of the tumult was pointed out, they expressed the highest admiration. When the silken globe ascended gracefully into the air, and the aeronaut waved his flag, Black Hawk exclaimed, "That man is a great brave, but I do not think he will ever get back." When the balloon had attained so great a height as to be scarcely visible, he said, "I think he can go to the heavens, to the Great Spirit" ; and another of the party added, "I should think he could see the Great Spirit now."

After a tour of about two months, during which they visited Baltimore, Philadelphia, New York, Albany, Boston, and other towns of less note, they returned, by way of the northern lakes, to Fort Armstrong. Major Garland, of the army, under whose charge they had travelled, being instructed to secure for them a kind reception from their nation previous to their enlargement, sent a messenger to advise Keokuk of their arrival. That chief was encamped on the opposite shore of the river, about twenty miles below; and although these persons were his enemies, and had especially contemned his authority in bringing about the recent disastrous war, he determined, with the dignity which usually marks his conduct, to give them a respectful and cordial reception. A message was sent immediately to announce his intention ; and at noon the following day the dull, monotonous sound of the Indian drum proclaimed the approach of the chief. He led the cavalcade, with two large canoes lashed together, and shaded by a canopy, under which, with his three wives, he sat in state. About twenty canoes followed, each containing six or eight braves, who sung their wild songs as they plied the paddle. They ascended the river slowly until they came abreast of the fort, and then landed on the right bank, where they remained about two hours, engaged in painting themselves and arranging their dresses. They then crossed the river, and, on landing, Keokuk said to his followers, "The Great Spirit has sent our brothers back; let us shake hands in friendship." On reaching the spot where Black Hawk and his companions were encamped, they found these unfortunate braves seated in front of their tent, silent and motionless, as if absorbed in sorrowful reflection —doubtful, perhaps, of the reception that awaited them. Keokuk extended his hand to Black Hawk and then to the rest of the newly returned party, without speaking; his followers imitated his example; the salutation was reciprocated with apparent cordiality, and then the whole company seated themselves on the ground. No one spoke, each waiting until the chief should break the silence. After an interval of fifteen minutes, Keokuk asked Black Hawk how long he had been on the road, adding that he had been expecting him, and was on the way to meet him when he heard of his arrival. Pipes were then introduced, and a general conversation ensued; after which the parties separated, Black Hawk and his party remaining in their camp at Fort Armstrong, while Keokuk with his band returned to the western shore of the river, where they spent the night in singing and dancing.

A council was held the next day, in a large room in the fort. Keokuk came attended by a hundred braves, decked in their savage finery, and singing their wild songs, until they reached the fort, which they entered in silence. Keokuk seated himself with Pashepahaw [22] on one side, and Wapella [23] on the other. The braves sat behind, and maintained a profound silence during the whole interview. Black Hawk with his party entered afterwards, and were seated opposite, facing the rest of the tribe. The chiefs rose and shook hands with them. Black Hawk and his son appeared dejected; they had unwillingly consented to attend this council, which to them could be no other than a scene of public humiliation. He had parted from his people in anger and rebellion, stigmatising them as cowards, and heaping, especially upon Keokuk, the most abusive epithets, because they would not rashly plunge into a war with a nation which could crush them at any moment. Keokuk had predicted the event of such a contest, and Black Hawk, who had brought it on his followers by imprudently entering the country of an incensed enemy, now stood before his people a ruined man, owing his life to the clemency of his captors—his reputation for prudence and conduct blighted, his followers nearly all slaughtered, his long-nursed scheme of superseding Keokuk blasted forever.

Major Garland was the first to speak. He expressed his gratification at the friendly reception which had been extended to Black Hawk and his companions, and hoped that the nation would now live at peace. He reminded them of a speech made to the prisoners by the President, in which the red men were dissuaded from war and domestic broils, and caused that address to be interpreted at full length. Keokuk arose and said : " The heart of our Great Father is good ; he has spoken like the father of many children. The Great Spirit made his heart big in council. We receive our brothers in friendship, our hearts are good towards them. They once listened to bad advice, now their ears are closed against evil counsel. I give them my hand. When they shake it, they shake the hands of all. I will shake hands with them, and then I have done."

They were then told by Major Garland, that the President considered Keokuk the principal chief of the nation, and desired he should be acknowledged as such; he expected Black Hawk would listen, and conform to this arrangement; he hoped the dissensions in the tribe would cease, that he should hear no more of two bands, but that all would unite in living together as one nation. From some mistake of the interpreter, Black Hawk understood that he was *ordered* to submit to the advice of Keokuk, and became greatly excited. Losing all command of himself he arose, trembling with anger, and exclaimed : "I am a man—an old man. I will not obey the counsels of anyone! I will act for myself—no one shall govern me! I am old, my hair is grey. I once gave counsels to young men—am I to be ruled by others ? I shall soon go to the Great Spirit, where I shall be at rest! What I said to our Great Father at Washington, I say again—I will listen to him. I am done !"

This address caused a momentary excitement throughout the assemblage. It was an unusual departure from the decorum which ordinarily prevails in an Indian council, and was not expected from so old a man—still less from one who had recently been severely punished for giving way to his passions. The offensive remark was explained : he was told that the President had not commanded, but advised him, to submit himself to the chief of his people. He made no reply. His galled spirit had been touched; he had given loose to feelings which had long been restrained, and he now sat in moody silence. Keokuk, in a low tone, said to him : "Why do you speak thus before white men ? You trembled—you

did not mean what you said. I will speak for you."
The old man consented, and Keokuk arose:

"Our brother, who has lately come back to us,"
said he, "has spoken, but he spoke in anger. His tongue
was forked. He did not speak like a man, like a Sauk.
He felt that his words were bad, and trembled like a
tree whose roots have been washed by many rains. He
is old—let us forget what he said. He says he did not
mean it. He wishes it forgotten. What I have said are
his words, not mine. Let us say that our brother spoke
in council to-day, and that his words were good. I have
spoken."

Conciliatory remarks were made by Colonel Davenport,
the commanding officer at Rock Island, and by Major
Garland, after which Black Hawk requested that if his
words had been written down, a black line might be
drawn over them.

Wapella said: "I am not in the habit of talking—I
think — I have been thinking all day. Keokuk has
spoken; he spoke for us all. I am glad to see my
brothers. I will shake hands with them. I have done."

After the council had closed, Major Garland invited
the principal chiefs, with Black Hawk, to spend the
evening at his quarters, in the hope of cementing the
reconciliation which had been effected. The pipe was
circulated, and the Indians treated to a glass of spark-
ling champagne, which they relished highly. Pashepahaw,
after shaking hands with the whole company, made a
speech:

"We met this morning," said he, "I am glad we have
met again. That wine is very good; I never drank any
of that kind before. I have thought much of our meeting
to-day; it was one that told us we were brothers, that we
were all Sauks. We had just returned from a buffalo

hunt, and thought it was time for our brothers to be here, as our brothers at St Louis told us they would come in this moon. We started before sunrise to meet you; we have met, and taken our brothers by the hand in friendship. They always distrusted our councils, and, forsaking the trail of the red men, went where there were no hunting-grounds, nor friends—now they have returned to find the dogs howling around their wigwams, and wives looking for their husbands. They said we counselled like women, but they have found our counsels were sound. They have been through the country of our Great Father. They have been to the wigwams of the white men. They received them kindly, and made their hearts glad. We thank them: say to the white people that Keokuk and Pashepahaw thank them. Our brother has promised to listen to the counsels of Keokuk. What he said in council to-day was like the fog of the Mississippi—the sun has shone and the day is clear, let us forget it. His heart is good, but his ears have been open to bad counsels. He listened to them, and closed his ears to the voice which came across the great waters. He now knows that he ought to listen to Keokuk. We told our Great Father that all would be quiet, and asked him to let our brother go. He opened his dark prison and let him see the rising sun; he gave him to his wife and children, who were without a lodge. Our Great Father made straight the path of our brother. I once took prisoner a great chief of the Osages. I heard the cries of his women and children. I took him out to the rising sun, and put him upon the trail to his village. Go, said I, and tell your people that Pashepahaw, chief of the Sauks, sent you. We thank our Great Father. Say to him that I reach out my right hand; he is a great way off, but I now shake him by the hand. Our hearts are good towards him. I hope to see him before I lie down in peace. May the Great Spirit be in his counsels. What our brother said to-day, let us forget. I am done."

Keokuk arose and said : " We feel proud that you have invited us here this evening to drink with you. The wine which we have drank we never tasted before. It is the wine which the white men make, who know how to make everything. I will take another glass, as I have much to say. To-day we shook hands with our brothers. We were glad to see them—we often thought of our brothers. Many of our nation said they would never return ; their wives and children often came to our wigwams, which made us feel sad. What Pashepahaw said is true. I talked to our young braves, who had the hearts of men ; I told them that the Great Spirit was in our counsels, and they promised to live in peace. Those who listened to bad advice and followed our brothers, have said that their ears are closed—they will go to war no more. I sent their words to our Great Father, whose ears were open. His heart had been made sad by the conduct of these our brothers, whom he has now sent home. We thank him. Say to him, Keokuk thanks him. Our brothers have seen the great villages of the white men ; they travelled a long road, and found the Americans like grass. Many years ago I went through the villages of our Great Father ; he had many that were broad like the great prairies. He has gone ; another is our Father ; he is a great war chief. I want to see him ; I shall be proud to take him by the hand. I have heard much of him ; his head is grey. Tell him as soon as the snow melts from the prairie I will come. What I have said I wish spoken to him, before it is put upon paper, so that he shall hear it as I said it. What our brother said in council to-day let us forget. He told me to speak ; I spoke his words. I have spoken."

MA-KA-TAI-ME-SHE-KIA-KIAH
or " BLACK HAWK "
A Sauk Brave

Black Hawk then rose with a calm but dejected air. "I feel," said he, "that I am an old man; once I could speak, but now I have little to say. We have met many of our brothers to-day; we were glad to see them; we have listened to them; their hearts are good. They have behaved like Sauks since I left them; they have taken care of my wife and children, who had no wigwam; I thank them for it. The Great Spirit knows I thank them. Before the sun gets behind the hills to-morrow I shall see them. When I left them I expected to return soon. I told our Great Father at Washington I would listen to his counsels; I say so to you. I will listen to Keokuk. I shall soon be far away, where I shall have no village, no band; I shall live alone. What I said in council to-day I wish forgotten. Say to our Great Father, and Governor Cass, I will listen to them. Many years ago I met Governor Cass in council,[24] far across the great prairies towards the rising sun. His advice was good, but my ears were shut. I listened to the Great Father far across the big waters. My father, whose band was large, also listened to him. My band was once large—now I have no band. I and my son, and all our party, thank our Great Father for what he has done. He is old, I am old; we shall soon go to the Great Spirit and be at rest. He sent us through his great villages. We saw many of the white men, and were kindly treated. We thank them. Say to them, we thank them. We thank you for travelling with us—your path was long and crooked. We never saw so many white men before; but when with you we felt as safe as if among friends. When you come to the Mississippi again you shall come to my lodge—now I have none. On your road home you will pass where our village once was. No one lives there now—all are gone. I give you my hand; we may never meet again, but we

shall remember you.   The Great Spirit will be with you,
and your wives and children.   I will shake hands with
my brothers here, and then I am done."

Thus ended the brief but disastrous contest brought
about by the rapacity of a few of our citizens.   But
although this was the immediate cause of the war, it must
not be denied that there were other latent sources of
disquiet which had predisposed a portion of the Sauks to
such a measure.   The rivalry between Black Hawk and
Keokuk was of long standing, and had occasioned much
heart-burning.   The former was the older man, and was
descended from the chiefs, but was deficient in talent, and
inferior to his rival in popularity; the latter, having
energy, address, conduct, and eloquence, gradually rose to
the head of the tribe.   The division would probably have
been healed long since but for an unfortunate interference.
After the war between the United States and Great
Britain, in which the Sauks and Foxes took part with the
latter, a formal peace was made, in 1815, in which those
tribes acknowledged themselves to be under the protection
of the American Government.[25]   For this reason, and
because their lands were within the boundaries of the
United States, Keokuk at once admitted the propriety of
trading and negotiating entirely with the American agents
and traders, and made his annual visits accordingly to St
Louis.   Black Hawk, from mere perverseness at first, but
afterwards from interest, continued to resort to the
British post at Malden, and to receive protection from the
British authorities, or, as he expressed it, " to listen to the
Great Father across the big waters."   Those who recollect
the late unhappy war with Great Britain, have not
forgotten that it occasioned, especially upon the frontier,
a bitterness of feeling akin to that created by a civil war,
and which continued to rankle for years after the contest

was over. The visits, therefore, of Black Hawk to Canada were not likely to produce on his part a disposition friendly to the United States. It was on such occasions that he received the bad advice alluded to by the chiefs in their speeches.

Black Hawk was one of the party which attended Keokuk in his journey to Washington in 1837.[26] He was, however, not one of the delegates, but was taken with them to prevent him from engaging in their absence in intrigues which might disturb the harmony of the tribe. He accompanied them to all public places, and was treated as a friend and equal, but did not sit in council, except as a spectator. At their first interview with the Secretary of War, where we happened to be present, Keokuk rose and said : "There is one here who does not belong to the council, but he has been accustomed to sit with us at home, and is our friend. We have brought him with us—we hope he will be welcome."

This noted individual is now old, and is frail and broken in his appearance. His stature is small, and his figure not striking; nor do his features indicate a high grade of intelligence. The strongest evidence of his good sense is found in an assertion contained in his autobiography, that he has never had but one wife.

NOTE.—Since the foregoing was written, the papers announce the death of Black Hawk. He died at his village on the Des Moines River on the 3rd of October, 1838. His body was disposed of, at his special request, after the manner of the chiefs of his tribe. He was placed upon the ground in a sitting posture, his hands grasping his cane. A square enclosure made of saplings is all the monument that marks the spot where rest the remains of this far-famed chief.[27]

NOTES

1. The name, according to the late Dr William Jones, is Ma'kata-wimeshekä'käa, from *ma'katäwi*, "it is black," *mishi*, "big," *kä'kä*, "chest," the name referring to the description of a bird, or sparrow-hawk.

2. Evidently the Merrimec River, between Jefferson and St Louis counties, Missouri; it empties into the Mississippi about forty miles below the mouth of the Missouri.

3. Such bags, carried generally by warriors and priests, or "medicine-men," contained sacred objects of various kinds, especially the parts of animals, which were supposed to represent the magic power possessed by the animal or other object to which they pertained, and to impart this power to the owner.

4. The treaty was signed at "Saint Louis," in the district of Louisiana, November 3, 1804.

5. The site of the present city of Fort Madison, in Lee county, Iowa.

6. Maj. Z. M. Pike, U.S.A., *An Account of Expeditions to the Sources of the Mississippi, and through the Western Parts of Louisiana*, Philadelphia, 1810. The expedition to the upper Mississippi left St Louis, August 9, 1805, and reached the Sauk village, at the head of the rapids, August 20. On the following morning Pike spoke to the assembled chiefs and warriors.

7. See Vol. I., p. 315, note 2, this work.

8. Fort Armstrong, Iowa, across the Mississippi River from Rock Island, Illinois.

9. Treaties were made separately with the two tribes. The treaty of "peace and friendship" with the Sauk was signed September 13, 1815, and that with the Foxes the following day. The transactions took place at Portage des Sioux, on the Mississippi, ten miles above the mouth of the Missouri.

10. See biography of KEOKUK, p. 115, this volume.

11. Illinois was admitted as a State, December 3, 1818.

12. See note 4, above.

13. See note 9, above. Portage des Sioux, where the treaties were signed, is one of the oldest French settlements in the Mississippi valley; it is situated on the right bank of the Mississippi about ten miles above the Missouri. The legendary account of the event which gave Portage des Sioux its name was thus related by an old French inhabitant of the place: "During the latter part of the eighteenth century, a Sioux war-party came down the Mississippi to attack a settlement of the Omaha, situated on the Missouri a short distance above the mouth. The Sioux learning that the Omaha knew of their approach, and were in ambush near the mouth of the Missouri, changed their course, and, instead of continuing down the Mississippi, portaged to the Missouri, less than one mile distant. Embarking on the Missouri, the Sioux soon reached the Omaha village; this they destroyed, while the Omaha warriors were some miles away, near the mouth of the Missouri." From this event the name Portage des Sioux was derived.

14. "A treaty of peace and friendship" was concluded at St Louis, May 13, 1816, between the Government commissioners and "chiefs and warriors of the Sacs of Rock River and the adjacent country." The commissioners who signed this treaty were William Clark, Ninian Edwards, and Auguste Chouteau.

15. Hall is here referred to; he was at that time (1829) living at Vandalia, then the capital of Illinois.

16. General Atkinson, then at Fort Armstrong, wrote from that post, April 13, 1832, to Governor John Reynolds: ". . . The band of Sacs under Black Hawk, joined by about one hundred Kickapoos, and a few Pottawatamies, amounting in all to about five hundred men, have assumed a hostile attitude. They crossed the river at the Yellow Banks, on the 6th instant, and are now moving up on the east side of Rock River towards the Prophet's village. . . .

"The regular force under my command. is too small to justify me in pursuing the hostile party. To make an unsuccessful attempt to coerce them would only invite them to acts of hostility on the frontier, sooner than they probably contemplate. Your own knowledge of the character of these Indians, with the information herewith submitted, will enable you to judge of the course proper to be pursued. I think the frontier is in great danger, and will use all the means at my disposal to co-operate with you, in its protection and defence."

Soon after receiving this communication, the Governor, then at Belleville, issued the following proclamation:—

"To the Militia of the North-Western Section of Illinois.

"Fellow Citizens: your country requires your services. The Indians have assumed a hostile attitude, and have invaded the State, in violation of the treaty of last summer. 'The British band' of Sacs, and other hostile Indians, headed by Black Hawk, are in possession of the Rock River country, to the great terror of the frontier inhabitants.

"I consider the settlers on the frontiers in immediate danger. I am in possession of the above information from gentlemen of respectable standing, and from Gen. Atkinson, whose character stands so high in all classes.

"In possession of the foregoing facts and information, I hesitate not as to the course I should pursue. No citizen aught to remain quiet when his country is invaded, and the helpless part of the community is in danger. I have called out a strong detachment of militia, to rendez-vous at Beardstown, on the 22nd instant; provision for the men and corn for the horses will be furnished in abundance. I hope my country-men will realise my expectations, and offer their services, as heretofore, with promptitude and cheerfulness in defence of their country.

"JOHN REYNOLDS,
"*Commander-in-Chief.*"

(Wakefield, *History of the Black Hawk War*, Caxton Club Reprint, Chicago, 1908, p. 35 *et seq.*)

17. See TUSTENNUGGEE EMATHLA, note 6, p. 177, this volume.

18. A great deal has been written on this so-called "war." One of the most authentic accounts is the *History of the War*, by John A. Wakefield, Jacksonville, Ill., 1834, reprinted by the Caxton Club, Chicago, 1908, under the title: *The Black Hawk War*, by Frank E. Stevens, Chicago, 1903. See also, *The Sauks and the Black Hawk War*, by Perry A. Armstrong, Springfield, Ill., 1887; *Autobiography of Ma-ka--tai-me-she-kia-kiak, or Black Hawk*, also *A History of the Black Hawk War*, by J. B. Patterson, Oquawka, Ill., 1882.

19. The five captives reached Washington, April 22, 1833, where they remained four days, during which time they met President Jackson. From Washington they were conducted to Fortress Monroe, Virginia, but they were soon released from captivity, leaving the fortress June 5, 1833, and after a very eventful journey reached their homes on the Mississippi about two months later. (*Cf.* KEOKUK, p. 140, this volume.) *The Aboriginal Races of North America*, by Samuel G. Drake, 15th edition, N.Y. [1880], p. 660.

20. Drake (*op. cit.*, p. 661) quotes the following as the names of the captives: Mac-cut-i-misk-e-ca-cac, Black Hawk; Na-she-escuck, his son, Loud Thunder; Wa-be-ke-zhick, the Prophet, Clear Day; Pamaho, Prophet's brother, Fish Fin; Po-we-zhik, Prophet's adopted son, Strawberry; Napope, the Warrior; Strong Soup.

21. Abraham Eustis, born Petersburg, Va., March 28, 1786; died Portland, Me., June 27, 1843.

22. See biography of PASHEPAHAW, Vol. I., p. 194, this work.

23. See biography of WAPELLA, p. 99, this volume.

24. As Lewis Cass negotiated many treaties with various tribes of Indians, it is highly probable that Black Hawk met him on several occasions. However, this particular reference may be to the gathering of many tribes at the "Rapids of the Miami" in September, 1817, although the Sauk and Foxes were not represented officially.

25. The treaties of Portage des Sioux; see note 9, above.

26. See KEOKUK, p. 140, this volume. During this visit, in 1837, the portrait of " Much-a-tai-me-she-ka-kaik, Black Hawk," was painted by King; it bears No. 133 in the Rhees *Catalogue.* A portiait in the Redwood Library, Newport, Rhode Island, one of the collection bequeathed to that institution by King, is thought to be a painting of Black Hawk. It is entirely different from the portrait reproduced in this volume, as it represents a much younger, robust man. It may be a portrait of Black Hawk made many years before 1837. A portrait of Black Hawk painted in 1833 by R. M. Sully is in possession of the Wisconsin Historical Society; while another, by J. W. Ford, hangs in the State Library at Richmond, Virginia. George Catlin made a portrait of Black Hawk while the latter was detained at Jefferson Barracks, a few miles below St Louis on the Mississippi, subsequent to the war and before he was conducted to Washington (see note 19, above). The portrait is reproduced in Catlin's *Letters and Notes*, London, 1841, Vol. II., fig. 283, facing p. 211.

27. During the month of July, 1839, his grave was opened and the remains stolen and carried to St Louis. Later the bones were sent to Quincy, Illinois, for articulation. On the protest of Governor Lucas, of Iowa Territory, the bones were restored and were soon afterward removed to the collections of the Burlington Geological and Historical Society, but in 1855 the building in which they were deposited was destroyed by fire and they were lost.

KISHKEKOSH

(A FOX BRAVE)

AMONG the Fox braves who appeared at Washington in 1837,[1] on the occasion to which we have already alluded, was Kishkekosh, or *The man with one leg*, whose name, however, is not descriptive of his person[2]; for we discovered no deficiency in the limbs of this individual. At the council which we described in the life of Keokuk,[3] where the Sauks and Foxes were confronted with the Sioux, Kishkekosh appeared in the same hideous head-dress which is exhibited in the picture, and the attention of the spectators was strongly attracted by this novel costume. The buffalo horns and skull upon the man's head would have rendered him conspicuous in a grave assembly collected for a serious purpose, in the presence of a numerous and polished audience; but this was not sufficient for Kishkekosh, who, when his party were all seated, stood up on a bench behind them, so as to display his full stature, and attract the special notice of all eyes. It was seen that this exhibition was not lost upon the Sioux, who whispered, exchanged glances, and were evidently disturbed. Those who were merely spectators, and who knew nothing of the personal history of the strange beings before them, were amused at what they supposed to be a piece of savage buffoonery, and could not help smiling at the ludicrous contrast between the

KISH-KE-KOSH
A Fox Brave

uncouth figure perched up against the wall, and the silent, motionless group of grave warriors who sat before him, arrayed in all the dignity of barbarian pomp.

We learned afterwards that the intrusion of the buffalo head was not without its meaning. It seems that on a certain occasion, when some skirmishing was going on between these hostile tribes, Kishkekosh, with a single companion, charged suddenly upon the Sioux, rushed into their ranks, killed several of their warriors, and retreated in safety, bringing off as a trophy this buffalo head, which Kishkekosh tore from the person of one of the slain. Such exploits, which are not uncommon among the Indians, resemble some of the deeds of antiquity, or those of the knights errant of a later age. Acts of desperate valour, leading to no practical advantage, but undertaken in mere bravado, must often occur among a people who follow war as their main employment, and who place a high value on military glory. Among savages especially, or any rude nation whose warfare is predatory, and made up chiefly of the exploits of individuals or small parties, such deeds are estimated extravagantly, not only on account of the courage and conduct shown in them, but because they afford themes for biting sarcasm and triumphant boasting over their enemies. Such, doubtless, was the light in which this deed of Kishkekosh was viewed by his tribe; and when they were to meet their enemies in a public council, at which a large number of persons were present besides the hostile parties, they tauntingly displayed this trophy with the deliberate purpose of feeding their own hatred and insulting their foemen.

NOTES

1. "Kish-kee-kosh" was the last of twenty-three members of his tribe to sign the treaty, the first being "Kee-o-kuck, The Watchful Fox, principal chief of the confederated tribes." The treaty was signed at the City of Washington, October 21, 1837. During this visit to Washington, the portrait of "Kis-te-kosh" was painted by Cooke. It bears No. 120 in the Rhees *Catalogue*.

2. The name signifies "He With a Cut Hoof," according to the late Dr William Jones, who states that it might apply to a one-legged person.

3. See biography of KEOKUK, p. 115, this volume.

WAPELLA

(CHIEF OF THE FOXES)

WAPELLA,[1] whose name signifies the *Prince*, or the *Chief*, is the head man of the Musquakee, or Fox tribe. He was one of the delegation led by Keokuk to Washington in 1837, and made a favourable impression by the correctness of his deportment on that occasion.[2] In stature he is shorter and more heavily built than most of the Indians, and has the appearance of great strength and activity.

In the council held by the Secretary of War, for the purpose of reconciling the Sioux with the Sauks and Foxes, Wapella spoke next after Keokuk, and acquitted himself well. Although he possessed not the fine form and striking manner of Keokuk, many thought his speech not inferior to that of the principal chief. It was well digested, sensible, and pertinent. We remarked that, in the opening of his harangue, the authority of Keokuk was distinctly recognised as well as the identity of interest of the tribes represented respectively by these two chiefs. "My Father," said Wapella, "you have heard what my chief has said. He is the chief of our nation. His tongue is ours. What he says we all say—whatever he does we will be bound by it."

Having concluded their visit at Washington, the delegates were conducted to several of the principal cities of the Atlantic states, where they excited much curiosity

and, we are happy to say, were treated with uniform kindness and hospitality. Unfortunate as are the relations
between our Government and the Indians, imposed by
a train of circumstances for which, as a people, we are
not accountable, there is evidently no lack of generous
sympathy towards that race in any part of our country.

The reception of these Indian delegates at Boston was
conducted with more ceremony than at any other place,
and must have been highly gratifying to them, as well as
interesting to numerous assemblages of citizens, most of
whom saw for the first time the American savage in his
native costume. It is said that so great a multitude was
never assembled in that city to witness a public spectacle.
In the morning, from ten to twelve, the chiefs held a levee
at Faneuil Hall, for the reception of ladies exclusively,
when it might doubtless have been said of the Boston
ladies, as a New England poet wrote, long ago,

"All longed to see and touch the tawny man";

for we are told that this ancient hall was crowded in every
part, floor and gallery, by the fair citizens.

At noon the chiefs and warriors were conducted to the
State House, where the Governor, the members of the
Legislature, and other dignitaries, were prepared to receive
them. Governor Everett,[3] whose celebrity as a scholar,
statesman, and philanthropist would have naturally placed
him in a conspicuous position at this exhibition of civic
hospitality, independently of his office, addressed them in a
bland and spirited manner. The chiefs replied separately.
As usual, Keokuk spoke first, and after him Wapella.
The remarks of the latter were as follows :—

" I am very happy to meet my friends in the land of
my forefathers. When a boy, I recollect my grandfather
told me of this place, where the white man used to take

WA-PEL-LA, *or* " THE PRINCE "
Chief of the Foxes

our fathers by the hand. I am very happy that this land has induced so many white men to come upon it; by that I think they get a living on it, and I am pleased that they content themselves to stay on it. (Great applause.) I am always glad to give the white man my hand and call him brother. The white man is the eldest of the two; but perhaps you have heard that my tribe is respected by all others, and is the oldest among the tribes. I have shaken hands with a great many different tribes of people. I am very much gratified that I have lived to come and talk with the white man in this house, where my fathers talked, which I have heard of so many years ago. I will go home and tell all I have seen, and it shall never be forgotten by my children."

When the speaking was concluded, the Governor and the chiefs repaired to the balcony of the State House, which overlooks a beautiful and extensive open square, where presents were distributed to the Indians. Keokuk received a splendid sword and a pair of pistols; his little son a pretty little rifle. The principal chiefs were presented with costly swords, and others of less value were given to the warriors. Black Hawk had a sword and pistols. Shawls, calico, and trinkets were given to the women. "During this ceremony," says one of the Boston editors, "a mass of at least fifteen acres of people stood below, filling the streets and the common. The chiefs were escorted to the common by the cadets, and began their war dance. The crowd very patiently kept outside the lines, leaving a space of many acres, in the centre of which were the Indians. Their war exercises were not very striking. One beat a drum, to which they hummed monotonously, and jumped about grotesquely. This lasted half an hour, when they moved off in carriages to their lodgings."

At Philadelphia, the delegations were taken to Cooke's splendid circus, and witnessed the equestrian exercises, which were probably more to their taste than any exhibition with which they were gratified during their tour. At New York they visited Mr Catlin's extensive gallery of Indian portraits, and are said to have borne testimony to the fidelity of the likenesses of their acquaintances in that valuable collection.[4]

Perhaps the most amusing incident of this tour was that which occurred at the Washington Theatre, to which the several Indian delegations had access every evening during their stay in the metropolis. Their conduct on these occasions did not evince the apathy usually attributed to them, but struck us rather as characterised by the habitual decorum and gravity of this singular people, mingled with an indifference resulting from their indistinct understanding of the subject. There were exceptions from this general deportment. They sometimes whispered to each other, with an appearance of interest, and more than once laughed heartily at some stroke of buffoonery. But the occurrence alluded to was of a more decided character. Miss —— was acting the part of a sylph, which she did very charmingly. The merit of the performance consisted in her graceful attitudes, and in movements so light and easy that they seemed to be effected by means of mere mental volition, independently of the vulgar locomotive machinery commonly used by mortals. The Sioux occupied a stage box, and were so much delighted that, in the midst of the performance, one of them rose, and, taking a dressed buffalo robe from his shoulders, threw it at the feet of the actress, with a speech, which, according to the established phraseology, should doubtless be called an *appropriate address;* another threw a head-dress, a third something else, until the whole company had each given a token of his approbation. Though taken by surprise, the sylph showed great presence of mind; indeed, if there is anything for which a woman is never wholly unprepared, it is admiration. Gathering up the unexpected tribute, she threw the articles over her arm, and continued to act in character, until showers of Indian finery became so thick that she was obliged to seek assistance to remove them. After a momentary absence she reappeared with a sheaf of ostrich feathers, which she distributed among the warriors—with an *appropriate* address.

We may mention, in connection with the foregoing anecdotes, the conduct of some Pawnee and Otto chiefs and warriors who visited the Cincinnati Theatre on their way to Washington, during the same season. The Ravel family were exhibiting their wonderful feats of strength and agility, and the Indians evidently shared the universal admiration excited by these surprising performances. They confined themselves, however, to the ordinary expressions of pleasure, until the lad who was called the " Infant Hercules " exhibited a feat which displayed great muscular power, when the whole band evinced their admiration by loud shouts.

NOTES

1. According to the late Dr William Jones, the name is derived from Wapana, signifying " He of the Morning."

2. " Wa-pella " was a signer of the treaty of Washington, October 21, 1837. His portrait, bearing No. 106 in the Rhees *Catalogue,* was painted by King during this visit to Washington. The name of this chief is attached to the following treaties: Fort Armstrong, September 3, 1822, signed " Wapulla "; Prairie du Chien, July 15, 1830, signed " Wapalaw, the prince"; Fort Armstrong, Rock Island, Illinois, September 21, 1832, signed " Wau-pel-la "; Dubuque county, Wisconsin Terr., opposite Rock Island, September 28, 1836, as " Wa-pella "; Washington, D.C., October 21, 1837, as " Wa-pella."

3. Edward Everett (1794-1865), Governor of Massachusetts from 1835 to 1839.

4. Catlin remained in New York until the autumn of 1839, when he took his entire collection to England. He had already been in communication with the Hon. C. A. Murray, master of Her Majesty's household, whom he had met during the latter's travels in America. Arriving in London, Catlin exhibited his collection of more than six hundred portraits and other paintings in Egyptian Hall, Piccadilly.

AP-PA-NOO-SE
A Sauk Chief

APPANOOSE

(A SAUK CHIEF)

THIS individual is one of the peace chiefs, and presides over a village of the Sauks. His name[1] signifies "*A chief when a child*," and indicates that his station was inherited. He was one of the delegation sent to Washington in 1837,[2] and, when at Boston, was said to have made the most animated speech, both in manner and matter, that was delivered by the chiefs. He said :—

"You have heard just now what my chief has to say. All our chiefs and warriors are very much gratified by their visit to this town. Last Saturday they were invited to a great house (Faneuil Hall), and now they are in the great council house. They are very much pleased with so much attention. This we cannot reward you for now, but shall not forget it, and hope the Great Spirit will reward you for it. This is the place which our forefathers once inhabited. I have often heard my father and grandfather say they lived near the sea-coast, where the white man first came. I am glad to hear all this from you. I suppose it is put in a book, where you learn all these things. As far as I can understand the language of the white people, it appears to me that the Americans have attained a very high rank among the white people. It is the same with us, though I say it myself. Where we live, beyond the Mississippi, I am respected by all people, and they consider me the tallest among them. I am happy that two great men meet and shake hands with each other." As he concluded, Appanoose suited the action to the word by extending his hand to Governor Everett, amid the shouts of applause from the audience, who were not a little amused at the self-complacency of the orator.

The newspaper account, from which we gather some of these facts, concludes with the following remark: "We have taken pains to give the speeches of the Indian chiefs with verbal accuracy, as a matter of high intellectual curiosity. History, romance, and poetry, have embodied the Indian character to our perceptions from childhood. It is pleasant, therefore, to see the original, and find how accurate the picture has been. The language, ideas, and style of these Indians are precisely such as have been ascribed to their race. There is much to admire in the simple and manly manner in which they convey their ideas. He must be but a churl who does not associate with their visit here, objects of philanthropy and protection to their race."

NOTES

1. Apenos[a], "dear child," or "little child," is the true interpretation of the name according to Dr Jones.

2. "Appan-oze-o-ke-mar, The Hereditary Chief (or He who was a Chief when a Child)," is the form of the name attached to the treaty of Washington, signed October 21, 1837. The portrait of Appanoose was painted by Cooke at that time, as recorded in the Rhees *Catalogue* (No. 39) under the form "Ap-pa-noose-o-ke-maw."

TAIOMAH

(A FOX BRAVE)

THE name of this brave,[1] when interpreted, signifies "*The bear whose voice makes the rocks to tremble.*" He is of the Musquakee [Fox] tribe, and has always borne a good character, especially in reference to his uniform friendship and good faith towards the United States. He is at the head of a secret society which has long existed among the Sauks and Foxes, and may be considered as a national institution. The meetings of this body are held in a spacious lodge, erected for the purpose, the entrance to which is guarded by a sentinel, who admits none but the initiated. They are understood to have a ceremony of initiation which is solemn and protracted, and a secret that may not be divulged without fatal consequences. Candidates for admission are subjected to careful trial and scrutiny, and none are received but such as give undoubted evidence of courage and prudence. Women are eligible to membership; but as those only are admitted who are exemplary for discretion, and have sustained characters wholly unblemished through life, we regret to say that the number of females who have attained this honour is very small. They have a peculiar dress and mode of painting, and, like our Freemasons, from whom the institution may have been derived, exhibit themselves to the public in costume on certain great occasions. Taiomah is also called "*The medicine man,"* in virtue of his office as the presiding functionary of this society, by means of which he is supposed to have acquired some valuable occult knowledge. The members are all considered as more or less expert in such information, and are called medicine men.   When a young man proposes to join this society, he applies to a member to propose and vouch for him.   The application is communicated to the head man of the Order, who, in a few days, returns an answer, which is simply affirmative or negative, without any reason or explanation.   If accepted, the candidate is directed to prepare himself.   Of this preparation we have no knowledge, but we are informed that a probation of one year is imposed previous to initiation.   The society is sometimes called the Great Medicine of the Sauks and Foxes : it is said to embrace *four roads* or degrees—something is to be done or learned to gain the first degree, a further progress or proficiency leads to the second, and so on.   Admission is said to cost from *forty* to *fifty* dollars, and every subsequent step in the four roads is attended with some expense.   There are few who have attained to the honours of the fourth road.   These particulars have been gathered in conversation with intelligent Indians, and embrace all that is popularly known, or rather believed, on this curious subject.   The traders have offered large bribes for the purpose of obtaining information in regard to the mysteries of the society ; but these temptations and the promises of secrecy failed alike to lead to any disclosures.   Many of the tribes have similar institutions.

Taiomah was one of the delegation led to Washington in 1824,[2] by General William Clark, and signed the treaty of that year.   He was then in very inferior health, as his portrait indicates, and died soon after his return to his people, as is believed, of consumption.

TAI-O-MAH
A Fox Brave

NOTES

1. Taiomah is derived, according to the late Dr William Jones, from Täimä, and signifies "Sudden crash (of thunder and lightning)." He belonged to the Thunder clan. The name of this Indian is preserved in that of a county and a town (Tama) in Iowa.

2. Taiomah was a signer of the following treaties : Fort Armstrong, September 3, 1822, signed "Themue"; Washington, August 4, 1824, signed "Faimah, or the bear"; Prairie de Chien, August 19, 1825, signed "Ti-a-mah, the Bear that makes the rocks shake." No. 48 in the Rhees *Catalogue* is the portrait of "Tia-mah, the bear whose scream makes the rocks tremble—Fox Chief." The artist's name does not appear, but the painting was probably by King.

NOTCHIMINE

(AN IOWA CHIEF)

THIS individual is a village chief, or peace chief, of the Iowas, and resides at Snake Hill, on the Missouri, about five hundred miles above the confluence of that river with the Mississippi. He was about forty years of age when this portrait was taken [1] in 1837. His brief history, like many others contained in this series, was taken from his own recital through the medium of an interpreter, and adds another to the many evidences afforded in these volumes of the sameness of the tenor of an Indian warrior's life. Whatever may have been his vicissitudes, his joys or his sorrows, he tells only of his warlike exploits. The touching episodes of domestic life, which in the auto-biography of a civilised man afford such varied and agreeable pictures of human thought and experience, have scarcely a place in the narrative of the savage. He may have a relish for home, and a strong love for those who surround his camp fire—friendship and paternal love and conjugal affection may have interwoven their tendrils with the fibres of his heart, and his bosom may have often throbbed in joy or in sorrow, but he is silent in regard to all such emotions. Whatever may have been his experience, he has not observed attentively the lights and shadows of domestic life, or scorns to

narrate them, but delights in depicting the storms that
he has braved in the chase or on the war-path.

Notchimine, or *No Heart*, remembers that when a boy
he killed squirrels and other small game with the bow
and arrow, and that when he grew to be a young man
he used a gun, and pursued the deer and the elk.   While
yet a youth he joined a war party, and went against
the Ottos, but the expedition was unsuccessful.   His
next adventure was with a party under The Orator,[2] when
the only trophy gained was the scalp of an old Indian.
Again he went, against the Osages,[3] with a large war
party, of which his father, Mauhawgaw, was leader, and
Wanathurgo was second in command : they killed ten
Osages, of whom Notchimine, though still a boy, scalped
one.   The next time he went under his brother, the
White Cloud, against the Sioux.   Having discovered
an encampment of the enemy, who were sleeping around
four fires, they crept stealthily upon them, spending
the whole night in watching and approaching the foe.
At daybreak they rushed with sudden onset and loud
yells upon the encampment, Notchimine being mounted
on the same horse with White Cloud.   A lad about his
own age struck down with a club the first of the enemy
who fell.   The Sioux scattered themselves over the prairie,
and the fight became general.   The White Cloud, abandoning his horse, dashed into the battle on foot, and took a
woman   prisoner.   This expedition was undertaken to
revenge the death of the father of White Cloud, who had
been killed by the Sioux.

Notchimine now took command of a party of twenty-
five warriors, and went against the Osages, but did not
succeed in meeting with any of the latter.   An
unsuccessful war party is always dangerous to friend
or foe; disappointed in their purposes of revenge or

plunder, they become more than ordinarily ferocious, and wreak their fury upon any helpless wanderers who may fall in their way. It was so with this party. Meeting two Kansas,[4] a man and his wife, they murdered them; the leader taking upon himself the distinguished honour of killing with his own hand the woman, who was very handsome. The spoil gained by this exploit was six horses, of whom they killed four, and retained the others. Nor did the gallant adventures of this courageous band end here. Five years previously the Omahas had killed a son of the Crane, an Iowa leader, who had marched against them, and now, finding an Omaha squaw at the house of a trader, they endeavoured with pious zeal to appease the spirit of the dead by whipping her; and again, by killing a Pawnee squaw, who was so unfortunate as to fall into their hands. These facts throw a strong light upon the principle, or rather impulse, of revenge which constitutes so prominent a feature in the Indian character, and in the history and policy of the savage tribes. If it was a sense of honour, a desire to wipe out an insult, or any other feeling usually comprehended under the term chivalric, which stimulated the Indian to the pursuit of vengeance, the lives of women and children would be secure from his resentment. But we find that the Indian, when seeking revenge, and especially when foiled in an attempt upon the primary object of his hatred, becomes possessed of an insatiate and insane thirst for blood, which impels him to feed his passion, not only with the carnage of the helpless of the human race, but even by the slaughter of domestic animals.

Still prosecuting the ancient feud with the Osages, our hero was subsequently one of a party of twelve who went against that tribe under Totanahuca, the Pelican. They captured fifty-six horses. Then he went against

NOT-CHI-MI-NE, *or* " NO HEART "
An Iowa Chief

the Omahas, and, on this occasion, distinguished himself
by rushing into a lodge, in which were horses as well
as people, and capturing seven horses, three of which
he carried home, leaving four that were of little value.
His next expedition against the Osages was bloodless,
eventuating in the capture of a few horses.

Two years ago he endeavoured unsuccessfully to make
peace with the Omahas, whose village he visited for
that purpose. He afterwards went to St Louis[5] to effect
the same object, through the intervention of General
Clark, when it was arranged that he should visit
Washington.

He says that the practice of his people has been,
previously to going to war, to send out hunters to kill
a deer, which is eaten, and a prayer for success made
to the Great Spirit. On such occasions he has had
dreams, and, according to the belief of his fathers, put
full faith in them. Previous to going out as leader of
a party he dreamed of taking two prisoners; in the event,
one of the enemy was taken, and one killed, which he
deemed a sufficient fulfilment. In some instances,
possibly, the wanton cruelty of the Indians, displayed
in the slaughter of women, or of chance captives not
taken in battle, may be the result of a desire, or a fancied
necessity, to fulfil a dream. The faculty of dreaming
is in many respects so important to the leader of an
ignorant and superstitious band, and is so frequently exerted
for the purpose of quelling or directing the savage mind,
that the chiefs have a strong inducement to bring about
events in accordance with their real or pretended visions.

This chief has but one wife and three children living.
Since killing the Pawnee woman he has inclined to peace,
and has been friendly towards the whites.

NOTES

1. No. 103 of the Rhees *Catalogue*: "Nau-che-wing-ga, No Heart—Ioway. King, 1837." Catlin likewise made a portrait of a chief of this name which is reproduced as fig. 129, facing p. 22, of Vol. II., *Letters and Notes*, London, 1841. Catlin wrote regarding him: "The present chief of this tribe [Iowa] is Notch-ee-ning-a (the White Cloud, plate 129), the son of a very distinguished chief of the same name, who died recently, after gaining the love of his tribe, and the respect of all the civilised world who knew him. . . . [The] son of White Cloud, who is now chief, and whose portrait I have just named, was tastefully dressed with a buffalo robe, wrapped around him, with a necklace of grizzly bear's claws on his neck; with shield, bow, and quiver on, and a profusion of wampum strings on his neck." In Catlin's *Notes of Eight Years' Travels and Residence in Europe*, London, 1848, Vol. I., p. 273, being a catalogue of his paintings; the portrait of "Notch-ee-ning-a" bears No. 256, with this inscription: "No Heart, called White Cloud; Chief of the tribe; necklace of grisly bear's claws, and shield, bow and arrows in his hand."

The principal chief of the "Fourteen Iowa Indians" who visited Europe in 1843 was "Mew-hu-she-kaw, the White Cloud." It is difficult to say whether this "White Cloud" and the one previously mentioned by Catlin were one and the same, or in what manner he or they were connected with "Nan-che-wing-ga" painted by King in 1837. They may, however, have been brothers, as suggested by a passage in the biography of Notchimine.

2. That is, "Watchemonne, or The Orator." See his biography, p. 164, this volume.

3. The Osage, or correctly Wazhazhe, lived at that time in the southern part of Missouri, south of the Missouri River. They are living in Oklahoma, and numbered 2056 in 1912.

4. The Kansas, or Kansa, a Siouan tribe living at that time northwest of the Osage, on Kansas River. In 1912 the population was only 158, less than half of whom were full-bloods. They reside in Oklahoma.

5. A treaty of minor importance was concluded at St Louis, November 23, 1837, between Joshua Pilcher, representing the Government, and four Iowa chiefs, representing their tribe. "Non-che-ning-ga" was the first Indian signer. His name is attached also to other treaties: Fort Leavenworth, September 17, 1836, signed "Nau-che-ning, or no heart"; Great Nemowhaw sub-agency, October 19, 1838, signed "Non-gee-ninga, or No Heart."

KEOKUK[1]

(CHIEF OF THE SAUKS AND FOXES)

THE Sauks[2] and Musquakees, more usually called the Sauks and Foxes,[3] having for many years resided together, form now a single community, divided only by certain internal regulations, by means of which each portion keeps up its distinctive name and lineage. The individuals and families adhere carefully to certain customs, which distinguish them, and have thus far prevented them from being merged, the one in the other. They have separate chiefs, who, at the sittings of councils, and on other occasions of ceremony, claim to be recognised as the representatives of independent tribes; but they are in effect one people, and Keokuk, who is the head man of the Sauks, is the ostensible and actual leader of the united nation.

There is reason to believe that these two tribes were originally one. They both acknowledge a common descent from the great Chippeway[4] stock, although the tradition which has preserved this fact retains no trace of the progressive steps by which they acquired a distinct language and became a separate people. The word Sauk is derived from the compound *asawwekee*, which signifies *yellow earth*, while Musquakee comes from *mesquawee*, or red earth— showing a similarity of name which strongly indicates an identity of origin.[5] Nor is it difficult to imagine that such a separation may have occurred, without leaving any

decisive remembrance of the rupture.   In the predatory
and erratic life led by the Indians, it is not uncommon for
a party to become disunited from the main body of the
nation, and in process of time to form a distinct tribe.
The separation becomes the more complete in consequence
of the want of a written language, to fix and preserve the
common tongue of the dispersed members of a nation;
and as the Indian dialect is, from this cause, continually
fluctuating, the colony soon loses one of the strongest
ties which would otherwise bind it to the mother nation.
Numerous as are the dialects spoken by the various tribes
in North America, Mr Gallatin[6] has very successfully
traced them to a few sources.

The former residence of the Sauks was on the banks
of the St Lawrence, whence they were driven by the Six
Nations, with whom they carried on a long and bloody
war.   As they retired towards the West, they became
embroiled with the Wyandots, and were driven further
and further along the shores of the lakes, until they found
a temporary resting place at Green Bay.   Here they were
joined by the Musquakees, who, having been so greatly
reduced by war as to be unable to maintain themselves
as a separate people, sought refuge among their kindred.
La Hontan,[7] under the date of 1689, speaks of " the villages
of the Sakies, the Potawattimies, and the Malhominies,"
on Fox River, and of a house or college established there
by the Jesuits; and Hennepin,[8] in 1680, speaks of the
Outagamies, or Foxes, who dwelt on the Bay of Puants,
or Green Bay.   The Sauks soon removed to the portage
between the Fox and Wisconsin Rivers, and afterwards to
the left bank of the Mississippi, below the Wisconsin.   It
is probable that they gained useful experience in the
hard school of adversity.   In the long series of hostile
operations in which they had been engaged against superior

KEOKUK
Chief of the Sauks and Foxes

numbers, they had become very warlike, and they now prepared to act upon the offensive.

The delightful plains of Illinois were inhabited at that time by a numerous people called the Illini, or, as we find it elsewhere written, Linneway, or Minneway.[9] The former reading is that of Joutel,[10] a French officer, who visited the country in 1683, and the fact that the territory inhabited by that nation received from the earliest French explorers the name of Illinois, seems to be decisive in favour of that orthography. In the interpretation of the word, however spelled, we find no disagreement, the name being uniformly translated "men," or "perfect men." This nation was divided into various bands, the principal of which were, the Kaskaskias, Cahokias, and Tamarois, in the southern part of the territory; the Michigamies, near the mouth of the Des Moines, and probably on the right bank of the Mississippi; the Piankeshaws, near Vincennes; the Weas, on the Wabash above Vincennes; the Miamis, towards the lakes; the Peorias, on the Illinois River; and the Mascos, or Mascoutins, called by the French "Les Gens des Prairies," on the great central plains between the Wabash and Illinois Rivers. All these used the language which is now spoken by the Miamis[11]; and, though scattered over a wide expanse of country, considered themselves as one people.

Against this nation the Sauks and Musquakees, in league with the Chippeways, the Ottowas, and the Potawattimies turned their arms; while the Choctaws and Cherokees at the same time invaded the Illinois country from the south. A bloody war ensued, which lasted many years. It was probably an unequal contest between the inhabitants of these rich plains and the more hardy barbarians of the north, accustomed to the rigours of an inhospitable climate, and to the vicissitudes of continual warfare. The tribes of Illinois were nearly exterminated. Of a population which must have exceeded fifty thousand, not more than five hundred remain. The Miamis and Weas, who abandoned the country, number about four hundred. A larger number of the Kaskaskias, protected by the French at the village which bears their name, escaped that war, but many of them were afterwards slaughtered by the Kickapoos, and intoxication has since reduced them to about forty souls. Of the Piankeshaws but forty or fifty, and of the Peorias not more than ten or fifteen, are left.[12] The Sauks defend the exterminating policy pursued by them and their allies in this war, by alleging that the Illini were more cruel than other Indians, and always burned their prisoners; and that in retaliation they adopted the practice of delivering over such of the Illini as fell into their hands, to the women, to be tortured to death.

During this contest an incident occurred which may be mentioned in illustration of the uncompromising character of savage warfare. On the shore of the Illinois stands a singular rock,[13] rising perpendicularly from the water's edge and inaccessible on three sides, while on the fourth its summit, which is level, may be reached by a very narrow pathway. A party of the Illini, hotly pursued by their enemies, took refuge on this rock with their women and children. They were discovered and besieged; and such was the vigilance of their adversaries, that, although certain death by starvation awaited them within their fortress, they were unable to effect a retreat. They even stationed sentinels in canoes upon the river, by day and by night, to defeat any attempt of the besieged to procure water by lowering vessels into the stream; and the wretched garrison, having no stores, nor means of supply, began soon to be tortured by the pangs of hunger and thirst. They resolved to die rather than

surrender ; and, for a while, consoled themselves by hurling
defiance and scoffs at their foes.   At length they ceased to
appear upon the ramparts, and their voices were no longer
heard.   The besiegers, cautious to the last, and secure of
their prey, delayed making any attempt to enter the fortress
until so long a time had elapsed as to render it certain that
famine had performed its deadly office.   When at last they
ascended to the summit of the rock, but one soul was found
lingering among the carcasses of the dead—an aged squaw
was still breathing, and lived many years in captivity, the
last of her tribe.   The "Starved Rock" is still pointed
out by the inhabitants as the scene of this heartrending
adventure.

Having possessed themselves of the country, the
invaders continued to pursue, with unrelenting hostility,
the scattered remnants of the once powerful Illini, who
lingered for protection about the settlements of the French
and Spaniards.   Their last attempt to destroy this unhappy people was in 1779, when they approached St Louis
with fifteen hundred braves, in search of a small band of
Peorias, supposed to be lurking in that vicinity.   The
Spanish Governor turned a deaf ear to the representations
of the inhabitants, who believed their village to be in danger ;
and the latter, unable to prevail upon him to put the place
in a posture of defence, sent an express to the American
Colonel, George Rogers Clark, who was then at Kaskaskia,
to solicit his protection.   Clark instantly marched with five
hundred men, and encamped on the left bank of the river,
opposite St Louis.   The Governor, convinced at last of the
hostile intentions of the Indians, who, not finding the Illini,
were marching upon St Louis, became panic struck, and
offered to deliver over the colony to Clark.   The latter
declined an offer which he had no authority to accept, but
remained in his camp prepared to assist the inhabitants if

required.   An attack was made.   Clark immediately crossed the river with a party of his men, but the Indians, on seeing the "Long-Knives," as the Virginia troops were called by them, hastily retreated, having previously killed about seventy of the Spaniards.[14]   Colonel Clark afterwards sent a detachment of one hundred and fifty men, who scoured the country far above the Sauk village, and returned without molestation; the Indians, awed by the boldness of this measure, declaring that, if so few dared to invade their country, they were prepared to fight with desperation.

There was a small tribe of Iowas in the Illinois country at the time of the irruption by the northern Indians, who were probably themselves intruders.   Being too weak to oppose the invaders, they received them hospitably, and remained at peace with them.

Having conquered the country, the Musquakees established themselves on Rock River, near its junction with the Mississippi; the Sauks soon followed them, and this spot became the principal seat of the united nation.   The whole of this region is fertile and picturesque beyond description. It is a country of prairies—of magnificent plains, spreading out in every direction as far as the eye can reach, and whose beautifully undulating surface is clothed with a carpet of the richest verdure, studded with splendid groves, giving to the extended landscape an air of ornate elegance and rich embellishment such as is seldom beheld in the scenery of the wilderness.

The Mississippi, which below its junction with the Missouri is a turbid stream, meandering through low grounds and margined by muddy banks, is here a clear and rapid river, flowing over beds of rock and gravel, and bordered by the most lovely shores.   Nothing of the kind can be more attractive than the scenery at the Upper

Rapids, in the vicinity of the Sauk and Fox village. On the western shore a series of slopes are seen commencing at the gravelly margin of the water, and rising one above another with a barely perceptible acclivity for a considerable distance, until the background is terminated by a chain of beautifully rounded hills, over which trees are thinly scattered, as if planted by the hand of art. This is the singular charm of prairie scenery : although it be a wilderness, just as Nature made it, it has no savage nor repulsive feature—the verdant carpet, the gracefully waving outline of the surface, the clumps, the groves, and the scattered trees, give it the appearance of a noble park, boundless in extent, and adorned with exquisite taste. It is a wild but blooming desert, that does not awe by its gloom, but is gay and cheerful, winning by its social aspect, as well as by its variety and intrinsic gracefulness. The eastern shore is not less beautiful. A broad flat plain of rich alluvion, extending from the water's edge, is terminated by a low range of wooded hills. A small collection of Indian lodges stood on this plain when the writer last saw it ; but the principal village of the Sauks and Foxes was about three miles distant, on Rock River. In the front of the landscape, and presenting its most prominent feature, as viewed from an ascending boat, is Rock Island, on the southern point of which, elevated upon a parapet of rock, stands Fort Armstrong. The surrounding region is healthy, and amazingly fruitful. The grape, the plum, the gooseberry, and various other native fruits abound ; the wild honeysuckle gives its perfume to the air, and a thousand indigenous flowers mingle their diversified hues with the verdure of the plain.

These prairies were formerly covered with immense herds of buffalo, and abounded in game of every description. The rivers furnished excellent fish ; and the whole region, in every respect so rich in the bounties of Nature,

must have formed that kind of paradise of which alone
the Indian has any conception.   If ever there was a spot
on earth where scenic beauty, united with fecundity of
soil and salubrity of climate, could exert a refining influence
upon the human mind, it was here ; and those who claim
for the savage an Arcadian simplicity of character, or who
suppose the human mind may become softened by the
genial influence of climate and locality, might reasonably
look here for effects corresponding with such opinions.
Blessed with abundance, there could have been no necessity for any intrusion upon the hunting-grounds of others,
and the causes of war, other than the lust for carnage,
must have been few.   Surrounded by the choicest beauties
of Nature, it would seem that a taste for the picturesque,
a sense of the enjoyment of home and comfort, and an
ardent love of country, would have been implanted and
fostered.   But we find no such results.   The Sauks of
Illinois presented the same character half a century ago
which they now exhibit.   They are savages as little
ameliorated by place or circumstances as the Osages and
the Camanches of the farther West, or the Seminoles of
Florida, and are in no respect more assimilated to civilised
men than the wretched Chippeway who wanders over the
bleak and sterile shores of Lake Superior.

The office of chief, among the Sauks, is partly elective
and partly hereditary.   The son is usually chosen as the
successor of the father, if worthy ; but if he be passed over,
the most meritorious of the family is selected.   There are
several of these dignitaries, and in describing their relative
rank, they narrate a tradition, which we suppose to be
merely figurative.   They say that, a great while ago, their
fathers had a long lodge, in the centre of which were
ranged four fires.   By the first fire stood two chiefs, one
on the right hand, who was called the Great Bear, and

one on the left called the Little Bear. These were the village or peace chiefs. They were the rulers of the band, and held the authority that we should describe as that of chief magistrate—but not in equal degree, for the Great Bear was *the* chief, and the other, next in authority. At the second fire stood two chiefs, one on the right called the Great Fox, and one on the left called the Little Fox. These were the war chiefs or generals. At the third fire stood two braves, who were called respectively the Wolf and the Owl; and at the fourth fire were two others, who were the Eagle and the Tortoise. The last four were not chiefs, but braves of high reputation, who occupied honourable places in the council, and were persons of influence in peace and war. The lodge of four fires may have existed in fact, or the tradition may be merely metaphorical. It is quite consonant with the Indian character to describe events by figures, and the latter, in the confusion of bad translations, are often mistaken for facts. The chiefs actually rank in the order pointed out in this legend; and the nation is divided into families, or clans, each of which is distinguished by the name of an animal. Instead, however, of there being but eight, there are now twelve.

The place of peace chief, or head man, confers honour rather than power, and is by no means a desirable situation, unless the incumbent be a person of popular talents. He is nominally the first man in the tribe. He presides at the councils; all acts of importance are done in his name; and he is saluted by the patriarchal title of Father. But his power and influence depend entirely upon his personal weight of character; and when he happens to be a weak man, the authority is virtually exercised by the war chiefs. He is usually poor. Whatever may be his skill or success as a hunter, he is compelled to give away his property in hospitality or benevolence. He is expected to be affable and generous, must entertain his people occasionally with feasts, and be liberal in giving presents.   He must practise the arts of gaining popularity, which are much the same in every state of society, and among which a prodigal hospitality is not the least successful.   If anyone requires to borrow or beg a horse on any emergency, he applies to the chief, who cannot refuse without subjecting himself to the charge of meanness.   Not infrequently the young men take his horses, or other property, without leave, when he is perhaps the only individual in the tribe with whom such a liberty could be taken with impunity.   He is the father who must regard with an indulgent eye the misdeeds of his children, when he is himself the injured party, but who must administer inflexible justice when others are aggrieved.   A person of energetic character may maintain a high degree of influence in this station, and some who have held it have been little less than despotic ; but when a man of little capacity succeeds to the hereditary chieftaincy, he becomes a mere tool in the hands of the war chiefs, who, having command of the braves and young men, control the elements of power, and readily obtain the sway in a community essentially martial, where there is little law, and less wealth.   The principal war chief is often, therefore, the person whose name is most widely known, and he is frequently confounded with the head man.   The station of war chief is not hereditary, nor can it properly be said to be elective ; for, although in some cases of emergency a leader is formally chosen, they usually acquire reputation by success, and rise gradually into confidence and command.   The most distinguished warrior, especially if he be a man of popular address, becomes by tacit consent the war chief.

Whether the eight fires, or families, mentioned above comprised at any period the whole tribe, we cannot determine. The Sauks are now divided into twelve families, and the Musquakees into eight[15]; and, although great care is taken to preserve this distinction, we may readily suppose that a name sometimes becomes extinct, and that a distinguished man may found a new family.

There is another division peculiar to this tribe which is very singular. Every male child, shortly after its birth, is marked with *white* or *black* paint, the mother being careful to use the two colours alternately, so that if her eldest son be marked with black, the second will be distinguished by white. Thus, if there be an even number of males in a family, the number marked with each colour respectively will be equal, and the whole nation will be nearly equally divided. The colours thus given are appropriated to the individuals unchangeably through life, and in painting themselves upon any occasion, those of the one party use white, and those of the other black, in addition to any other colours they may fancy, all others being free alike to the whole nation. The object of this custom is to create a continual emulation between the two parties. At the public ball playing, and all other games, the whites play against the blacks. In the dances of ceremony they endeavour to outdo each other; and in war, the scalps taken by each party are numbered against those of the rival division.

The chiefs have the sole management of the public affairs, but the braves are consulted as advisers, and have great influence. In the councils a question is not usually considered as decided unless there is an unanimous voice. The discussions are deliberate and grave, seldom disturbed by inflammatory appeals, or distracted by flippant or unadvised counsels. The speakers, in general, prepare themselves carefully beforehand. Their style is sententious and figurative, but their speeches are weakened by the frequent repetition of the same idea. One circumstance in regard to their public speaking, which we have never seen noticed, has struck the writer forcibly on several occasions. The same etiquette which, in the parliamentary bodies of civilised nations, forbids the speakers to allude to each other by name, prevails among them. We do not pretend to say that the practice is invariable ; but whenever we have attended their councils, we noticed that, in commenting on each other's speeches, they used expressions such as "the chief who has just spoken," "the chief who spoke first," "one of my brothers has said," with other circumlocutions, which were obviously the result of a guarded intention to avoid a more direct allusion. They are, however, fond of speaking in the third person, and in doing this the orator often uses his own name.

The laws of this nation are few and simple. Debts are contracted but seldom, and no method of enforcing payment is known. The obligation is merely honourable. If the party is unable to fulfil his engagement at the stipulated time, that is a sufficient excuse, and the failure, under any circumstances, is considered as a trivial affair. This arises not so much from want of integrity as from the absence of definite notions of property, and of the obligations consequent upon its possession.

Civil injuries are settled by the old men who are friendly to the parties. A murder, when committed by one of the nation upon another, is seldom punished with death. Although the relatives of the deceased may, as in all the Indian tribes, take revenge, this mode of reparation is discouraged, and it is more usual to accept a compensation in property. If the parties cannot agree, the old men interfere, and never fail to effect a compromise. We are not aware of any offence which is considered as against the peace and dignity of the public, or is punishable as a national affair, except aiding or assisting their enemies, unless it be some dereliction connected with military duty, which always receives a prompt and contemptuous rebuke. A sentinel, for instance, who neglects his duty, is publicly flogged with rods by the women. The traders consider the Sauks and Foxes perfectly honest, and feel safe among them, seldom locking their doors by day or night, and allowing them free access. They are humane in the treatment of their prisoners. Young persons taken in war are generally adopted into the family of one of the slain. Other prisoners are bought and sold as such; but if, after having gained the confidence of their masters, they choose to go to war and kill an enemy of the nation, they become free, and are entitled to all the rights of a native. The women taken in war are received into the families of those who capture them, either as wives or servants, and their offspring become members of the tribe. One who knew the Sauks and Foxes intimately for many years, informs us that he never knew of their burning a prisoner, except in the war with the Menominies, and in this instance they alleged that their enemies commenced the practice. An instance occurred in which a Sauk brave having died, a favourite male slave was slain by his relatives and buried with him, in order that his spirit might wait on that of his master in the other world.

The individual whose history we are about to relate is now the head of the Sauk nation, and is one of the most distinguished of his race. His public career commenced in early life, and has been eminently distinguished through a long series of years. In his first battle, when quite young, he killed a Sioux warrior by transfixing him with a spear, under circumstances which rendered the exploit conspicuous, the more especially as he was on horseback ; and the Sioux being considered greatly superior in horsemanship, the trophy gained on this occasion was esteemed a matter of national triumph. A feast was made by the tribe in honour of the incident. They requested of the chiefs that Keokuk should be put in his father's place, or, in other words, that he should be admitted to the rank of a brave, and all the rights of manhood, notwithstanding his youth. It was also allowed that on public occasions he might appear on horseback. He continues to enjoy this singular mark of respect ; and even when all the rest of the tribe appear on foot, in processions and other ceremonious occasions, he has the privilege of being mounted, and may be often seen riding alone and proudly among his people.

Shortly after this event, and while Keokuk was yet too young to be admitted to the council, a rumour reached the village that a large body of American troops was approaching to attack it. So formidable was this enemy considered, that, although still distant, and the object of the expedition not certainly ascertained, a great panic was excited by the intelligence, and the council, after revolving the whole matter, decided upon abandoning the village. Keokuk, who stood near the entrance of the council lodge, awaiting the result, no sooner heard this determination than he stepped forward and begged to be admitted. The request was granted. He asked permission to address the council, which was accorded ; and he stood up for the first time to speak before a public assemblage. Having stated that he had heard with sorrow the decision of his elder brethren, he proceeded with modesty, but with the earnestness of a gallant spirit, to deprecate an ignominious flight before an enemy still far distant, whose numbers might be exaggerated, and whose destination

was unknown. He pointed out the advantages of meeting
the foe, harassing their march, cutting them up in detail,
driving them back, if possible, and finally of dying honourably in defence of their homes, their women and their
children, rather than yielding all that was dear and
valuable without striking a blow. " Make me your leader,"
he exclaimed ; " let your young men follow me, and the
pale faces shall be driven back to their towns ! Let the
old men and the women, and all who are afraid to meet
the white man, stay here ; but let your braves go to
battle ! I will lead them." This spirited address revived
the drooping courage of the tribe. The warriors declared
their readiness to follow Keokuk. The recent decision
was reversed, and Keokuk was appointed to lead the
braves against the invaders. The alarm turned out to be
false ; and after several days' march it was ascertained
that the Americans had taken a different course. But the
gallantry and eloquence of Keokuk in changing the
pusillanimous policy at first adopted, his energy in
organising the expedition, and the talent for command
discovered in the march, placed him in the first rank
among the braves of the nation.

The entire absence of records by which the chronology
of events might be ascertained, renders it impossible to
trace, in the order of their date, the steps by which this
remarkable man rose to the chief place in his nation, and
acquired a commanding and permanent influence over his
people. We shall, therefore, without reference to the
order of the events, present such facts as we have collected
with great care, partly from personal observation, and
partly from the testimony of gentlemen whose statements
may be relied on as authentic.

Possessing a fine person, and gifted with courage,
prudence, and eloquence, Keokuk soon became the chief

warrior of his nation, and gradually acquired the direction
of civil affairs, although the latter continued for many years
to be conducted in the name of the hereditary peace chief.
The most daring and graceful rider of his nation, he was
always well mounted, and has no doubt owed much of his
popularity to his imposing appearance when equipped for
war or ceremony, and to his feats of horsemanship. From
a natural pride, or from policy, he has always made the
most of this advantage by indulging, at great expense, his
love of fine horses, and costly caparisons, and exhibiting
himself in the best manner on public occasions.

Keokuk is, in all respects, a magnificent savage. Bold,
enterprising, and impulsive, he is also politic, and possesses
an intimate knowledge of human nature, and a tact which
enables him to bring the resources of his mind into prompt
operation. Successful in his undertakings, yet there is a
freshness and enthusiasm about him that throw a tinge of
romance over many of his deeds, and would indicate a
mind acting for effect rather than from the dictates of
policy, if there were not abundant proofs of the calm
judgment which forms the basis of his character.

Keokuk is fond of travelling, and of paying visits of
state to the neighbouring tribes. On these occasions he
always goes in an imposing style, which cannot fail to make
a favourable impression. The mild season of autumn,
so peculiarly delightful in the prairie region of Western
America, is the time chosen for these excursions, that being
the period of the year when game and forage are abundant.
A band of forty or fifty of the most active and finest-looking
young men are selected to accompany the chief, all of
whom are well mounted and completely equipped. The
chief, especially, spares no expense in his own outfit. The
most superb horse that can be procured, the most showy
Spanish saddle and housings, arms of faultless workman-

ship, a robe elaborately wrought with all the combined taste and skill of his six wives, and a pipe of state, are duly prepared. A runner is sent forward to announce his intention ; and in this style he visits some one of the tribes with whom he is at peace—either the Osages, the Ottoes, the Omahas, the Winnebagoes, or the Iowas. The honour is properly appreciated, and ample provision made for the entertainment of so illustrious a guest. Food and tobacco are laid up in store against his coming, and especially, if it be at all attainable, is there a supply procured of the *Christian's fire water*. The guests are received hospitably, and with every mark of ostentatious ceremony that may be afforded by the circumstances of the parties. The time is spent in a round of hunting, feasting, athletic sports, and a variety of games. Horse racing, ball play, foot races, and gambling with dice, form the amusements ; while dancing, which may be considered rather as a solemnity than a recreation, fills a due portion of the time. Keokuk is a great dancer, and has been an overmatch for most of his contemporaries at all athletic sports.

The warlike exploits of this chief have been numerous ; but few of them are such as would interest our readers. On one occasion, while engaged with a body of his warriors in hunting on the great plains which lie between his nation and their mortal enemies, the Sioux, a war party of the latter came suddenly upon them. Both parties were mounted ; but the Sioux, being the superior horsemen, and fully armed for battle, had the advantage, for the plain afforded no coverts to which the Sauks, who excel them in fighting on foot, could retreat. A less prompt leader than Keokuk would have sacrificed his band, either by an attempt at flight, or a desperate effort to resist an unequal foe. His resolution was instantaneously adopted. Forming his horses in a compact circle, the dismounted band were placed within, protected from the missiles of the enemy, and placed in a condition to avail themselves of their superiority as marksmen. The Sioux charged with loud yells, and were received with a well-directed fire, which compelled them to fall back. The attempt was repeated, but with the same result which usually attends a charge of horse upon well-posted infantry. The horses could not be forced upon the muzzles of guns which poured forth fire and smoke, and, after several ineffectual efforts, the assailants retreated with loss. On this occasion the promptitude of Keokuk was not more praiseworthy than the military sagacity by which he estimated the peculiarities of his own force and that of the enemy, and the accuracy of judgment with which he opposed the one to the other.

At another time, during a temporary peace between these tribes, the Sauks had gone to the prairies to hunt the buffalo, leaving their village but slightly guarded, and Keokuk with a small party approached a large encampment of the Sioux. By accident he learned that they were painted for war, and were preparing a numerous party, destined against his village. His own braves, widely scattered, could not be hastily collected together. He adopted the bold expedient of a daring and generous mind, and threw himself between his people and danger. Advancing to the encampment of his treacherous foes, he left his party hard by, and rode alone into the camp. The war pole stood in the midst of the lodges, the war dance was going on, and all the fierce excitements by which the Indians lash themselves into fury, and stir up the storm of vengeance in each other's bosoms, were in full practice. Revenge upon the Sauk was the burthen of their song. At such a moment Keokuk, mounted as usual on a fine horse, rode boldly in among them, and demanded to see their chief. "I have come," said he, "to let you know that there are traitors in your camp. They have told me that you are preparing to attack my village. I knew they told me lies, for you could not, after smoking the pipe of peace, be so base as to murder my women and children in my absence. None but cowards would be guilty of such conduct!" The Sioux, who, for a moment, were abashed by the audacity of their enemy, now began to crowd about him, in a manner that showed a determination to seize his person; and they had already laid hold of his legs, on either side, when he added, in a loud voice, "I supposed they told me lies; but if what I heard is true, then know that the Sauks are ready for you!" So saying, he shook off those who were attempting to seize him, plunged the spurs into his horse's flanks, and dashed away through the crowd. Several guns were fired at him ineffectually, and a number of warriors, instantly mounting, followed him in rapid pursuit. But they had lost their prey. Keokuk was now in his element. Yelling the dreadful war whoop, brandishing the tomahawk, and taunting his foes as he fled before them, he continued on his way gallantly, until he came in sight of his own little band. The Sioux, fearing some stratagem, then halted, and Keokuk deliberately joined his people, while the Sioux retired. He took measures to call in his braves, and returned hastily home; but the Sioux, finding their design discovered, did not attempt to put it into execution.

The talents of Keokuk as a military chief and civil ruler, are evident from the discipline which exists among his people. We have seen no other tribe so well managed. In 1837,[16] when deputations from a number of tribes visited Washington, a striking contrast was observed; for, while all the other Indians strutted about in blue coats and other absurd finery, which they had received as presents, the Sauks and Foxes appeared in their native dress, evincing a dignity and good taste which attracted general notice. Another anecdote is illustrative of the same habitual good order. A few years ago a steamboat, ascending the Mississippi, touched for a few minutes at Rock Island. A number of the Indians sauntered to the shore to gaze at it, and a passenger, expecting to see a scramble, held up a whisky bottle, and beckoned to the savages, who took no notice of his motions. He stepped on shore, again showed the enticing bottle, and made signs, but without effect. Supposing the Indians to be bashful, or afraid, he placed the bottle on the ground, pointed to it and returned to the boat, which now shoved off, while his fellow-passengers laughed loudly at his want of success. No sooner did the boat leave the shore than the Indians ran from the top of the bank where they had been standing down to the water's edge, and the passenger beholding, as he supposed, the expected scramble, exulted in the success of his experiment; but, to his astonishment, the Indians picked up the bottle and threw it, with symptoms of great glee, after the boat, into the water, at the same time clapping their hands, laughing and evidently exulting in the disappointment of the passenger.

In the year 1829, the writer[17] made an excursion up the Mississippi, and having passed beyond the settlements, stopped one day at a cabin on the shore, inhabited by a respectable farmer from Pennsylvania, who had been enticed by a fine tract of land to sit down in the wilderness, more than fifty miles from any neighbour. While enjoying the hospitable fare that was kindly spread before us, we inquired if these dwellers in the blooming desert were not afraid of the Sauks and Foxes, whose hunting grounds extended around them. They said they had felt much alarm until after a circumstance which occurred

shortly before our visit. They one day saw canoes
ascending the river, and small parties of Indians passing
along the shore, and in the evening the main body arrived
and encamped in the neighbourhood. At night a warrior
of very prepossessing appearance came to the house, and
by signs asked permission to sleep by the fire. This they
dared not refuse ; and resolving to make the best of what
they considered an awkward predicament, they spread a
good meal for their self-invited guest, having despatched
which he took up his lodging upon the floor. The good
people were much alarmed ; the more so as some Indians
were seen lurking about during the night. In the morning
early their guest departed, but shortly after sent a person,
who spoke English, to explain that the tribe had been to
St Louis to receive their annuities, and having been
indulged in the use of ardent spirits, were not under the
control of their usual discipline. Fearing that, under these
circumstances, some depredation might be committed upon
the property of the backwoodsman, a war chief had taken
post in his house, and sentinels had been placed around
it ; and the farmer was assured, that if, hereafter, any
injury should be discovered to have been committed during
that night by the Indians, the chief would pay for it when
he next came that way. Whether Keokuk was the
person who slept in the settler's cabin, we had not the
means of learning, but as he was undoubtedly at the head
of the band, the anecdote shows him desirous to avoid
giving offence to the whites, and exhibits a careful attention to the discipline of his tribe.

Keokuk is an able negotiator. He has several times
made peace with the Sioux, under the most unpromising
circumstances, and they have as often broken the treaties.
One of his achievements in this way displays his skill and
eloquence in a remarkable manner. Some of his warriors

falling in with an encampment of unarmed Menominies in sight of Fort Crawford, at Prairie du Chien,[18] wantonly murdered the whole party. The Menominies, justly incensed at an unprovoked and cowardly murder, declared war; and their friends, the Winnebagoes, who were previously hostile to the Sauks, were also highly indignant at this outrage. To prevent a sanguinary war, General Street, the agent of the United States at Prairie du Chien, invited the several parties to a council. They assembled at Fort Crawford, but the Menominies positively refused to hold any negotiation with the offending party. When Keokuk was informed of this resolution, he told the agent confidently that it made no difference, that he would make a treaty with the Menominies before they separated—all he asked was to be brought face to face with them in the council house. The several tribes were accordingly assembled, each sitting apart; but when the ceremony of smoking, which precedes all public discussions, was commenced, the Menominies refused to join in it, sitting in moody silence, while the other tribes exchanged this ordinary courtesy. The breach between the Winnebagoes and the Sauks and Foxes was talked over, explanations were mutually made, and a peace cemented. Keokuk then turned towards the Menominies and addressed them. They at first averted their faces, or listened with looks of defiance. The commencement of a speech without a previous smoking and shaking of hands was a breach of etiquette, and he was, besides, the head of a tribe who had done them an injury that nothing but blood could atone for. Under all these disadvantages the Sauk chief proceeded with his harangue, and such was the power of his eloquence, even upon minds thus predisposed, that his hearers gradually relaxed, listened, assented—and when he concluded by saying proudly, but in a conciliatory tone,

" I came here to say that I am sorry for the imprudence of my young men—I came to make peace. I now offer you the hand of Keokuk—who will refuse it ?" they rose one by one, and accepted the proffered grasp.

In the year 1831, a faction of the Sauk tribe, formerly called the British band, but latterly known as Black Hawk's band, became engaged in a war with the whites, some account of which is given in our sketch of Black Hawk.[19] Keokuk, with the majority of the Sauk and Fox nation, remained at peace with the United States; but it required all the influence, firmness, and tact of this chief, to keep his people in a position so little consonant with their habits and feelings. Their natural fondness for war, their love of plunder, their restless dispositions, their dislike towards the whites, and the injustice with which they had been treated, all conspired to enlist their sympathies with their countrymen and relatives who were engaged in hostilities. To preserve them from temptation, as well as to give assurance of his pacific intentions, Keokuk, who had removed from the eastern side of the Mississippi, which was the theatre of war, to the western side of that river, requested the agent of the American Government to send to his camp a white man who could speak the Sauk language, and who might witness the sincerity with which he was endeavouring to restrain his band. A person was sent. The excitement in the tribe continued and increased —a moody, vindictive, and sensitive state of feeling pervaded the whole mass. Keokuk stood on a mine ready for explosion. He knew not at what moment he might be sacrificed. The slightest spark dropped upon materials so inflammable would have fired the train; and the chief who had restrained the passions of his people would have been denounced as the friend of the whites, and doomed to instant death. He remained calm and unawed, ruling his turbulent little state with a mild, parental, yet firm sway, and keeping peace at the daily and hourly risk of his life. One day an emissary arrived from the hostile party; whisky was introduced into the camp, and Keokuk saw that the crisis was at hand. He warned the white man, who was his guest, of the impending danger, and directed him to seek safety by concealing himself. A scene of wild and tumultuous excitement ensued. The emissary spoke of blood that had been shed; of a little gallant band of their relatives who were at that moment chased over their own hunting grounds by an overwhelming force of well-armed troops; of recent insults, and of long cherished injuries inflicted by the white man. He hinted at the ready vengeance that might be taken, at an exposed frontier, defenceless cabins, and rich booty. These exciting topics were passed and exaggerated from mouth to mouth —ardent spirits were circulated, and the long smothered rebellion began to fester in the inflamed bosoms of the savage horde. The braves assembled about the war pole to dance the war dance, and to smear their faces with the hideous symbols of revenge. Keokuk watched the rising of the storm, and appeared to mingle in its raging. He drank, listened to all that was said, and apparently assented to the inflammatory appeals made to the passions of his deluded people. At length the warriors cried aloud to be led to battle, and the chief was called upon for his opinion —he was asked to lead them. He stood forward and addressed them with that eloquence which never failed him in the hour of need. He sympathised in their sense of wrong, their hatred of the white race, and their lust for vengeance. He won their confidence by describing and giving utterance to the passions which they felt, and echoing back their own thoughts with the skill of a master spirit. Having thus secured their attention, he considered

briefly the proposition to go to war—alluded rapidly to the
numbers and power of the American people, and the utter
hopelessness of a contest so unequal.   But he told them
he was their chief, whose duty it was to be at their head
in peace or war—to rule them as a father if they chose to
remain at home, to lead them if they determined to go to
battle.   He concluded by telling them, that in the proposed
war there could be no middle course; the power of the
United States was such, that, unless they conquered that
great nation, they must perish ; that, therefore, he would
lead them instantly against the whites on one condition,
which was, that they would first put all their women and
children to death, and then resolve that, having crossed
the Mississippi, they would never return, but perish among
the graves of their fathers, rather than yield them to the
white men.   This proposal, however desperate it may
seem, presented the true issue.   It poured the oil of reflection upon the waves of passion.   It held up the truth that
a declaration of war against the United States must be
either a mere bravado, or a measure of self-destruction.
The tumult of passion and intoxication subsided, subordination was restored, and the authority of Keokuk became
firmly re-established.

The Black Hawk faction, always opposed to Keokuk,
have regarded him with increased aversion since the
disastrous termination of the war into which they madly
rushed against his judgment, and in contravention of his
authority; and so active have been their intrigues, that
at one time they had nearly effected his downfall.   Having
for many years exercised the sole power of chief, a fate
like that of Aristides had like to have befallen him.
Some of his people became tired of the monotony of an
uninterrupted rule, and longed for a change.   His enemies
complained of his strictness.   They objected that the

power of the other chiefs was swallowed up in his single
voice, and they insinuated that he was exercising a
usurped sway in defiance of the usages of the nation. The
matter was at last brought to a formal discussion; the
voice of the nation was taken, and a young chief was
raised to the place of head man. In this trying crisis
Keokuk discovered his usual good sense and address.
He made no public opposition to the measures taken
against him, but awaited the result with dignified calmness. When the choice of his successor was decided, he
was the first to salute the young chief by the title of
Father; and it was an affecting sight to behold this
distinguished man, now nearly sixty years of age, extending his hand, with every appearance of cheerfulness and
respect, to a youth who was to supersede him in authority.
He did more. He led the newly elected chief to the
agent of the United States, who was then at Rock Island,
introduced him with every demonstration of profound
respect as "his chief and his father," begged that he might
be recognised as such, and solicited, as a personal favour,
that the same regard and attention which had been paid
to himself should be transferred to his successor. The
sequel may be readily supposed. The people saw their
error. Keokuk as a private individual was still the
first man in the nation. His ready acquiescence in the
decree which reduced him from the highest station to
the level of the people, won their sympathy; and he rose
silently but rapidly to the place from which he had
been removed, while the person who had been chosen
to supersede him sunk quietly to his former insignificance.

The writer had the gratification of seeing this distinguished man at Washington, in the autumn of 1837, when
the delegates from several tribes assembled in that city,
at the invitation of the Secretary of War. Some of

the councils held on that occasion were exceedingly interesting. One of them especially attracted our notice. The
Secretary of War, Mr Poinsett, proposing to effect a
reconciliation between the Sioux and the Sauks and Foxes,
caused them to be brought together in council. The
meeting took place in a church, at one end of which a
large stage was erected, while the spectators were permitted to occupy the pews in the remainder of the
house. The Secretary, representing the President of the
United States,[20] was seated on the centre of the stage,
facing the audience, the Sioux on his right hand, and
the Sauks and Foxes on his left, the whole forming a
semicircle. These hostile tribes presented in their appearance a remarkable contrast—the Sioux appearing tricked
out in blue coats, epaulettes, fur hats, and various other
articles of finery which had been presented to them,
and which were now incongruously worn in conjunction
with portions of their own proper costume—while the
Sauks and Foxes, with a commendable pride and good
taste, wore their national dress without any admixture,
and were studiously painted according to their own notions
of propriety. But the most striking object was Keokuk,
who sat at the head of his delegation, on their extreme
left, facing his mortal enemies, the Sioux, who occupied
the opposite side of the stage, having the spectators upon
his left side, his own people on his right, and beyond
them the Secretary of War. He sat as he is represented
in the picture which accompanies this sketch,[21] grasping
in his right hand a war banner, the symbol of his station
as ruling chief. His person was erect, and his eyes fixed
calmly but steadily upon the enemies of his people. On
the floor, and leaning upon the knee of the chief, sat his
son, a child of nine or ten years old, whose fragile figure
and innocent countenance afforded a beautiful contrast

to the athletic and warlike form, and the intellectual
though weather-beaten features of Keokuk.   The effect
was in the highest degree picturesque and imposing.

The council was opened by smoking the pipe, which
was passed from mouth to mouth.   Mr Poinsett then
briefly addressed both parties in a conciliatory strain,
urging them in the name of their Great Father, the
President, to abandon those sanguinary wars by means of
which their race was becoming exterminated, and to
cultivate the arts, the thrift, and the industry of white men.
The Sioux spoke next.   The orator, on rising, first stepped
forward and shook hands with the Secretary, and then
delivered his harangue, in his own tongue, stopping at
the end of each sentence until it was rendered into
English by the interpreter, who stood by his side, and
into the Sauk language by the interpreter of that tribe.
Another and another followed, all speaking vehemently,
and with much acrimony.   The burthen of their harangues
was—that it was useless to address pacific language to
the Sauks and Foxes, who were faithless, and in whom
no confidence could be placed.   "My Father," said one
of them, "you cannot make those people hear any good
words, unless you bore their ears with sticks."   "We
have often made peace with them," said another speaker,
an old man, who endeavoured to be witty, "but they
would never observe any treaty.   I would as soon think
of making a treaty with that child," pointing to Keokuk's
little boy, "as with a Sauk or a Musquakee."   The Sioux
were evidently gratified and excited by the sarcasms of
their orators, while their opponents sat motionless, their
dark eyes flashing, but their features as composed and
stolid as if they did not understand the disparaging
language that was used.

We remarked a decided want of gracefulness in all

these speakers. Each of them, having shaken hands with
the Secretary of War, who sat facing the audience, stood
immediately before and near him, with the interpreter at
his elbow, both having their backs to the spectators, and
in this awkward position, speaking low and rapidly, but
little of what they said could be understood, except by
the persons near them. Not so Keokuk. When it came
to his turn to speak, he rose deliberately, advanced to the
Secretary, and having saluted him, returned to his place,
which being at the front of the stage, and on one side of it,
his face was not concealed from any of the several parties
present. His interpreter stood beside him. The whole
arrangement was judicious, and, though apparently
unstudied, showed the tact of an orator. He stood erect
in an easy but martial posture, with his robe thrown over
his left shoulder and arm, leaving the right arm bare, to
be used in action. His voice was fine, his enunciation
remarkably clear, distinct, and rapid. Those who have
had the gratification of hearing a distinguished senator[22]
from South Carolina, now in Congress, whose rapidity of
utterance, concentration of thought, and conciseness of
language are alike peculiar to himself, may form some idea
of the style of Keokuk, the latter adding, however, an
attention to the graces of attitude and action, to which the
former makes no pretension. He spoke with dignity, but
with great animation, and some of his retorts were excellent. "They tell you," said he, "that our ears must be
bored with sticks; but, my Father, you could not pene-
trate their thick skulls in that way—it would require hot
iron." "They say they would as soon think of making
peace with this child as with us—but they know better;
for when they made war with us they found us men."
"They tell you that peace has often been made, but that
we have broken it. How happens it, then, that so many

of their braves have been slain in our country ?   I will tell
you.   They invaded us—we never invaded them—none of
my braves have been killed in their country.   We have
their scalps, and can tell where we took them."   We shall
speak further of this council in some of the other sketches
of the Sauks and Foxes.   It produced no effect unless
that of widening the breach between these tribes.

The following letter, which was published in the
Illinois newspapers about the time of its date, is said to
have been sent by Keokuk to the Governor of that state.
It was, of course, written by some white man, at his
dictation.   The "village criers" mentioned were the editors
of newspapers, and the reports alluded to were circulated
shortly after the close of the Black Hawk war.

" Raccoon Fork of Des Moines River, November 30, 1832.

" To the Great Chief of Illinois :

"My Father—I have been told by a trader that several
of your village criers have been circulating bad news,
informing the whites that the Indians were preparing for
war, and that we are dissatisfied.   My Father, you were
present when the tomahawk was buried, and assisted me
to place it so deep that it will never again be raised
against the white children of Illinois.

"My Father—Very few of that misguided band that
entered Rock River last summer remain.   You have
humbled them by war, and have made them friendly by
your generous conduct to them after they were defeated.
Myself, and the greater part of the Sauks and Foxes, have
firmly held you by the hand.   We followed your advice,
and did as you told us.   My Father, I take pity on those
of my nation that you forgave, and never mention the
disasters of last summer.   I wish them to be forgotten.

"I do not permit the criers of our village to proclaim any bad news against the whites, not even the truth. Last fall an old man, a Fox Indian, was hunting on an island, a short distance below Rock Island, for turkeys to carry to Fort Armstrong. He was killed by a white man. We passed it over—we have only spoken of it in whispers. Our agent has not heard of it. We wish to live in peace with the whites. If a white man comes to our camp or village, we give him a share of what we have to eat, a lodging if he wants it, and put him on the trail if he has lost it.

"My Father—Advise the criers of your villages to tell the truth respecting us, and assist in strengthening the chain of friendship, that your children may treat us friendly when they meet us; and be assured that we are their friends, and that we have feelings as well as they have.

"My Father—This is all I have to say at present.

"KEOKUK,
" Chief of the Sauk Nation."

Keokuk is a large and finely formed man. His manners are dignified and graceful, and his elocution, as well in conversation as in public speaking, highly energetic and animated. His flow of language and rapidity of utterance are remarkable; yet his enunciation is so clear and distinct that it is said not a syllable is lost. His voice is powerful and agreeable, and his countenance prepossessing. It is not often that so fine a looking man is seen as this forest chieftain, or one whose deportment is so uniformly correct.

As much of the history of Keokuk is interwoven with that of Black Hawk, we have endeavoured to avoid repetition, by omitting many particulars which will be found in our sketch of the latter.

NOTES

1. The name "Keokuk" is derived from *Kiyo‘kag*ᵃ, "one who moves about alert," according to Dr Jones.

2. Sauk (*Osa-kiwĭg*, "People of the Outlet," or, possibly, "People of the Yellow Earth," in contradistinction to the *Muskwakiwuk*, "Red Earth People," a name of the Foxes).

3. Foxes (translation, in plural, of *wagosh*, "red fox," the name of a clan). An Algonquian tribe, so named, according to tradition recorded by Dr William Jones, because once while some Wagohugⁱ, members of the Fox clan, were hunting, they met some Frenchmen, who asked who they were; the Indians gave the name of their clan, and ever since the whole tribe has been known by the name of the "Fox clan."

4. The Algonquian linguistic stock included the majority of the tribes from Virginia to the St Lawrence, and from the Atlantic to the Mississippi. The Chippewa or Ojibwa, and likewise the Sauk and Foxes, are of this stock.

5. See notes 2 and 3, above.

6. Albert Gallatin, "Synopsis of the Indian Tribes of North America," in *Transactions of the American Antiquarian Society*, Vol. II., Worcester, Mass., 1836.

7. "The villages of the Sakis, the Pauteouatamis, and some Malominis, are seated on the side of that [Fox] River, and the Jesuits have a House or College built on it."—Lahontan, *New Voyages to North America*, London, 1703, Vol. I., p. 104, written in 1689. As early as 1670 the Jesuits had established the Mission of St Mark on Fox River. See J. G. Shea, *Catholic Church in Colonial Days*, New York, 1886, p. 274.

8. Hennepin wrote in September, 1679: "Nous arrivames á une Isle située a l'entrée de la Baye des Puans, a quarante lieües de Missilimakinak. Elle est habitée par des Sauvages de la Nation nommee Poutaüatamis." (*Nouvelle Découverte*, Utrecht, 1697, p. 140.)

9. The aboriginal form is *Iliniwek*, from *ilini*, "man"; *iw*, "is"; *ek*, the plural termination, changed by the French to *ois*.

10. *Journal of the Last Voyage Perform'd by Monsr. de la Sale*, London, 1714.

11. That is, they all spoke dialects of the Algonquian language.

12. In 1912, various tribes, including the remnant of Piankashaw, consolidated under the name Peoria-Miami, numbered 359, of whom not one was of pure blood.

13. This refers to the noted rock on Illinois River, near Peoria Lake, on the summit of which, in 1680, La Salle erected Fort Crevecœur. See Tonti, *An Account of Monsieur de la Salle's Last Expedition*, London, 1698, p. 72; and for further information consult Parkman, *The Discovery of the Great West*, Boston, 1869, p. 165.

14. Winsor (*Narrative and Critical History of America*, Vol. VI., p. 737) gives a list of sources of information on this point of history, and continues: "On May 26, 1780, a raid was made on the Spanish post of St Louis by a party of fifteen hundred Indians and a hundred and forty English and Canadian traders, fitted out by Lieutenant-Governor Sinclair, of Michilimacinac, and led by a Sioux chief named Wabasha. The affair lasted only a few hours, and no assault was made on the fortified enclosure; but a considerable number of persons found on their farms or intercepted outside of the palisades were shot or captured. A portion of the party crossed the Mississippi and made a similar raid on Cahokia. They all left for their northern homes as rapidly as they came, some by way of the Wisconsin and Fox Rivers, and others by way of the Illinois River to Chicago, where Sinclair had two vessels awaiting them. This affair has been the occasion of many conflicting statements as to the time it occurred, and the number of persons killed and captured, and how it happened that so large a body of Indians in the British service came so far and did so little which was warlike. It has been often asserted, and as often denied, that George Rogers Clark, at the request of the Spanish commandant, was at St Louis at the time of the incursion, or so near as to render efficient service."

15. The following references to the Sauk are quoted from the *Handbook of American Indians* (pt. 2, p. 478):—"Society was rather complex. In the days when the tribe was much larger there were numerous gentes. There may be as many as fourteen gentes yet in existence. These are: Trout, Sturgeon, Bass, Great Lynx or Fire Dragon, Sea, Fox, Wolf, Bear, Bear-potato, Elk, Swan, Grouse, Eagle, and Thunder. It seems that at one time there was more rigid order of rank both socially and politically than at present. For example, chiefs came from the Trout and Sturgeon gentes, and war chiefs from the Fox gens; and there were certain relationships of courtesy between one gens and another, as when one acted the rôle of servants to another, seen especially on the occasion of a gens ceremony. Marriage was restricted to men and women of different gentes, and was generally attended with an exchange of presents between families of the pair.

"Besides the grouping into gentes, the tribe was further divided into two great social groups or phratries: Kishko[a] and Oshkash[a]. The painting colour of the first was white clay, and that of the second was charcoal. A child entered into a group at birth. Sometimes the father, sometimes the mother, determined which group. The several groups engaged one another in all manners of contests, especially in athletics. The Sauk never developed a soldier society with the same degree of success as did the Foxes, but they did have a buffalo society; it is said that the first was due to contact with the Sioux, and it is reasonable to suppose that the second was due to influence also from the Plains."

The following, from the same work (pt. 1, p. 473), pertains to the Foxes:—

"The Fox gents gentes are the Bear, Fox, Wolf, Elk, Big Lynx, Buffalo, Swan, Pheasant, Eagle, Sea, Sturgeon, Bass, Thunder, and Bear-potato."

16. During this visit to Washington the important treaty of October 21, 1837, was concluded by Carey A. Harris, Commissioner of Indian Affairs, and representatives of the Sauk and Foxes. By virtue of Article 1 of this treaty the tribes ceded to the United States a tract of land containing 1,250,000 acres. " Kee-o-kuck, The Watchful Fox, principal chief of the confederated tribes," was the first signer. Other treaties signed by him were: Fort Armstrong, September 3, 1822, signed " Keeocuck "; Washington, August 4, 1824, signed "Kee-o-kuck "; Prairie du Chien, August 19, 1825, signed " Ke-o-kuck "; Prairie du Chien, July 15, 1830, signed " Kee-o-cuck."

17. This was Hall, who was then living in Illinois. See Introduction, Vol. I., p. xxv., this work.

18. At the mouth of Wisconsin River, in the state of Wisconsin.

19. See p. 74, this volume.

20. Martin Van Buren, of New York, President, 1837-41.   Joel Roberts Poinsett, of South Carolina, was Secretary of War, 1837-41.

21. No fewer than three portraits of Keokuk are noted in the Rhees *Catalogue*. The first, bearing No. 33, does not include the date or the name of the artist; No. 77 is attributed to King, 1829. (A copy by Inman of the 1829 portrait is in the Peabody Museum, No. 28.263.) No. 144 is attributed to King, 1827. (See Introduction, Vol. I., pp. xxxix, xlviii, l, liii, and liv.) It is suggested by the text of this article that the original painting, of which the illustration in this volume is a reproduction, was made during Keokuk's visit to Washington in 1837. The illustration shows Keokuk and his son, which agrees with the description of Rhees' No. 144: "Keokuk, Watchful Fox: and Mu-se-wont, son of Keokuk, Long-haired Fox " ; hence it would appear that this portrait (No. 144) was made in 1837, not in 1827.   A portrait of Keokuk, by King, was bequeathed by the artist to Redwood Library, Newport, Rhode Island. The earliest recorded portrait of this cele-

brated chief is that by Lewis, painted at Prairie du Chien in 1827, and forming the ninth plate in his *Portfolio*.

Another portrait of Keokuk was painted by Stanley in May, 1846, "on the Kansas River where he [Keokuk], with his people, were temporarily residing after their removal from the Desmoines River [Iowa]."

In 1834 Catlin visited Keokuk's village, sixty miles above the mouth of Des Moines River, and while there made a full-length portrait of the chief, which is reproduced as plate 280, facing p. 210, of Vol. II., *Letters and Notes of the Manners, Customs and Conditions of the North American Indians*, London, 1841. Plate 290 of the same volume shows Keokuk mounted on his favourite horse. Another portrait by Catlin, dated 1836, belongs to the Museum of the University of Pennsylvania.

22. John Caldwell Calhoun.

NEOMONNI

(AN IOWA CHIEF)

THIS is the fifth chief, in grade, in the Iowa tribe.[1] In attempting to describe his own age, he said that he was born when his tribe made war, the first time, upon the Osages, and that, he believed, was about forty years ago. This is as near as the Indians usually approach to accuracy in regard to their own ages. He describes himself as having had a pacific disposition in childhood, and as having no desire to kill anything until he was ten years old. At that time a great flight of wild pigeons covered the country, and he went out with other boys to kill them. Having been employed for some days in this way, he became fond of the sport, and then killed a squirrel. After that his brothers offered him a gun, of which at first he was afraid, but being induced to receive it, he went out and shot a turkey. He remembers that, while yet a boy, being one day in the village, some warriors returned from an expedition, shouting and making a great noise. The people collected around them, while the warriors sung and danced, and exhibited the scalps they had taken. His father took him by the hand, and said to him : " Son, listen to me. Look at those scalps, and at those great warriors! This is what I like to see. Observe those braves, and learn to follow their example. Go to war and kill too, and the chiefs will look upon you as a brave man." Such

150

teaching would not be lost upon a boy, and least of all upon the Indian lad, whose first lesson inculcates the shedding of blood, and whose innate destructiveness, practised in the beginning upon the lesser animals, is rapidly developed and improved as his strength increases, by the strongest incentives, until it attains its maximum in the great exploit of manslaughter.   He was soon after permitted to accompany a war party, and, being too young to bear arms, was employed in carrying the cooking utensils and other burthens.   It is thus that the Indian boys, like the pages and squires of chivalry, are trained for the business of war.   He was in the rear when an onset was made upon a camp of the Kansas, and running eagerly forward to indulge his curiosity, witnessed the killing of a woman, struck his knife into the expiring victim, and had the fortune to seize upon two children, who became his prisoners, and were afterwards given up by him to General Clark, the Superintendent of Indian Affairs, at St Louis.

When about seventeen, he was at a hunting lodge with a small party, under his uncle, the Hard Heart, who left them for a short time to go to procure powder and lead. While lounging about the camp he espied an Omaha, who was peeping at him, and endeavouring at the same time to avoid observation.   Neomonni called the stranger to him, and invited him to spend the night at the lodge.   The Omaha, who probably could not readily escape, came to them, and they watched him all night.   His death was resolved upon, but as the Indian seldom acts except by stratagem, the tragedy was deferred until morning.   At the dawn they began to move their camp.   While on the march, one of the party shot the Omaha, and Neomonni, after he had fallen, discharged an arrow into his body and scalped him.   An old man of the party, whose son had been killed by the Omahas, exclaimed, "Now, I'll be captain!" by which he meant, that having a cause for revenge against the Omahas, he had the best right to take the lead in the savage gratification of exulting over a fallen enemy.

As our readers would not probably be edified by a particular detail of the sanguinary deeds of this chief, we shall not pursue the minute recital with which he was good enough to favour us. However interesting such adventures might be to the spectators of a war dance, or the grave members of a council, we fear they might not be equally pleasing to civilised ears, and shall, therefore, abridge a narrative which contains but a repetition of such deeds as those already repeated.

"*The cloud out of which the rain comes*"—for such is the signification of the compound word Neomonni—is a warrior of repute. In one of his adventures he accompanied the celebrated Otto chief Ietan [2] to the river Platte; and when shown the portrait of that warrior, in a former number of this work, he immediately recognised his old comrade. In summing up his various exploits, he claims to have taken three scalps of the Kansas, two of the Omahas, one of the Missouris, one of the Sioux, one of the Sauks, and two of the Osages. In the reputable business of horse stealing he has been engaged thirteen times, and has taken forty horses. On four expeditions he has acted as captain; and he has presented sixty-seven horses and twenty rifles, on different occasions, to individuals or tribes other than his own. These acts of liberality are recounted with much complacency, because, while they show on the one hand a wealth gained by daring and successful stratagem, they evince on the other a generosity, public spirit, and zeal for the honour of the tribe, highly becoming the character of a great chief.

NE-O-MON-NI
An Iowa Chief

NOTES

1. "Ne-o-mon-ni" was the first of the four Iowa chiefs to sign the treaty of St Louis, November 23, 1837, the third article of which states: "The expenses of this negotiation and of the chiefs and delegates signing this treaty to the City of Washington and to their homes to be paid by the United States." The chiefs who signed this treaty and later went to Washington were: Ne-o-mon-ni, Non-che-ning-ga, Wat-che-mon-ne, and Tah-ro-hon, the portraits of all of whom were painted by King in 1837, as recorded in the Rhees *Catalogue*, entry No. 101 being "Ne-o-mon-ne, Walking Rain." "Neu-mon-ya (Walking Rain)" is given as one of the party of Iowa Indians who visited Europe in 1843. (*Cf.* note 1, p. 114, under NOTCHIMINE, this volume.)

2. That is, Shaumonekusse, or L'Ietan. See Vol. I., p. 156, this work.

KEESHESWA

(A FOX CHIEF)

THE medicine men were formerly held in high repute among the Indians[1]; but in some of the tribes the faith in them has lately been much shaken. Imposture, however ingenious, exercises over the human mind a precarious sway, which is constantly liable to detection; and the influence of the medicine men is based on a combination of imposture and superstition. They who practise the art are alike deceivers and deceived. To a certain extent they believe in the efficacy of their own spells; but as the fallacy of these practices becomes obvious to themselves, they are driven to ingenious contrivances to keep up the delusion, and sink into insignificance, or become artful impostors, just as they may happen to be cunning and successful, or the reverse.

There are medicine men among all the tribes. Their ordinary business is to cure diseases, and their remedies are chiefly spells, although most of them resort also, in plain cases, to their knowledge of the qualities of medicinal plants. But the latter branch of their practice is limited by the acquaintance which the Indians generally possess of simple remedies, and by their habit of using them when occasion requires. The medicine men are also dreamers, and interpreters of dreams, employing, in this part of their profession, much the same degree of intellect and cunning which are practised by the fortune-tellers who practise

154

upon the credulity of the vulgar in more civilised communities. Sometimes they rise to a higher proficiency in their art, and assume the name of prophets, mingling in the political affairs of their tribes, and assuming rank in the councils, in virtue of their supposed favour with the gods and prescience of events.

Keesheswa,[2] *The Sun*, is a medicine man of some note in the Musquakee tribe, and, so far as we can judge from appearances, is a devout believer in his science. Although in good health, and apparently a sound sleeper, he dreams very often, and very much to the purpose. He adheres firmly to all the ancient superstitions of his people, and is a stickler for the usages of his forefathers. He is especially discreet and observant of form in his smoking, and never puts the pipe into his mouth without due solemnity, nor omits any of the little proprieties which should accompany this ceremony. While he enjoys his pipe with the complacency of a true lover of the weed, no one who has witnessed the initiatory forms with which he lights it, would suspect him of smoking for mere enjoyment. He goes through it with a seriousness which shows that he considers it a matter of no small moment; and that, however agreeable may be the sedative effect of the tobacco, the act of inhaling the smoke is closely connected with his religious opinions. He is a sincere and honest smoker.

The reputation of Keesheswa as medicine man is not so great as it was a few years ago. The more intelligent of the Sauks and Musquakees, in consequence probably of their intercourse with the whites, have become sceptical in regard to the efficacy of spells; and, except when under strong excitement, treat their medicine men with an indifference amounting almost to levity. When threatened by danger, or blinded by passion, superstition regains its sway; but as a general fact, the juggler is less esteemed than formerly.

Keesheswa is much respected as an individual. His deportment is inoffensive, and he is believed to be sincere in his own belief of the efficacy of his spells—which we suppose to be true of but few of his class. At all events, it is a pleasure to see him smoke his pipe, and quite impossible to treat with levity an occupation in which he engages with a truly devout and edifying gravity of demeanour.

NOTES

1. "In every Indian tribe there were, and in some tribes still are, a number of men, and perhaps also a number of women, who were regarded as the possessors of supernatural powers that enabled them to recognise, antagonise, or cure disease; and there were others who were better acquainted with actual remedies than the average. These two classes were the 'physicians.' They were oftentimes distinguished in designation and differed in influence over the people as well as in responsibilities. Among the Dakota one was called *wakan witshasha,* 'mystery man,' the other *pejihuta witshasha,* 'grass-root man'; among the Navaho one is *khathali,* 'singer,' 'chanter,' the other *izéélini,* 'maker of medicines'; among the Apache one is *taiyin,* 'wonderful,' the other simply *izé,* 'medicine.'

"The mystery man, or thaumaturgist, was believed to have obtained from the deities, usually through dreams, but sometimes before birth, powers of recognising and removing the mysterious causes of disease. He was 'given' appropriate songs or prayers, and became possessed of one or more powerful fetishes. . . . He was feared as well as respected. . . .

"The ordinary procedure of the medicine-man was about as follows: He inquired into the symptoms of dreams, and transgressions of tabus of the patient, whom he examined, and then pronounced his opinion as to the nature (generally mythical) of the ailment. He then prayed, exhorted, or sang the last perhaps to the accompaniment of a rattle; made passes with his hand, sometimes moistened with saliva, over the part affected; and finally placed his mouth over the most painful spot and sucked hard to extract the immediate principle of the illness. This result he apparently accomplished, often by means of sleight-of-hand, producing the offending cause in the shape of a thorn, pebble, hair, or other object, which was then thrown away or destroyed; finally

KEE-SHES-WA, *or* "THE SUN"
A Fox Chief

he administered a mysterious powder or other tangible medicine, and perhaps left also a protective fetish. There were many variations of this method, according to the requirements of the case, and the medicine-man never failed to exercise as much mental influence as possible over his patient. For these services the healer was usually well compensated."—Hrdlicka in *Handbook of American Indians*, pt. 1, 1907, pp. 838-839.

2. According to the late Dr William Jones, the name is Ki'shesw*, "Sun." His portrait was painted by King, but no date is given in the Rhees list, in which it bears No. 37, "Kee-sheswa—The Sun—Fox warrior." Keesheswa may have accompanied the party of his tribe to Washington in 1837, when the important treaty was signed October 21 of that year.

TAHROHON

(AN IOWA WARRIOR)

THIS is an Iowa warrior [1] who lives at the village on the
Missouri above Fort Leavenworth. One of his earliest
adventures was in a expedition against the Osages. They
arrived in the vicinity of an Osage village, situated on the
bank of a river; but the latter ran between them and their
enemies, and was filled with ice. They were hungry, and
chilled with cold. They heard the Osage drum beat, and
supposing a dance or a feast was going on, were the more
anxious to partake of their good cheer. But the captain
could not prevail on any of his men to go into the water,
until he came to Tahrohon, the youngest of the party, who
consented without hesitation, and immediately stepped into
the stream. A few others followed him, and, on reaching
the opposite shore, he said, "Come, let us go to the man
who sings so well, and is beating the drum," when a dog
barked, and they feared they were discovered, but, after a
short consultation, determined to get into the village and
kill an enemy. The brother of Tahrohon checked his
impetuosity, thinking it imprudent to risk an attack at that
time; but breaking away from his companions, he rushed
to the nearest lodge, and there found an Osage woman
marked all over, indicating her birth, and distinguishing
her as one of a family of note,[2] whom he shot, and, suddenly
retreating, recrossed the river. Satisfied with this achieve-

ment, the party returned home, where the announcement of their exploit filled the village with joy; for the Osages, having killed an uncle and two sisters of Tahrohon, it was considered that he had taken revenge in a very happy and appropriate manner, the more especially as the feat was consummated in the midst of the enemy's camp.

The leader of the band then proclaimed that, having been so lucky in one expedition, they ought to proceed immediately upon another, while their good fortune continued to attend them, and proposed to lead a party to steal horses from the Osages. Fourteen warriors, of whom Tahrohon was one, agreed to follow him. Arriving near the Osage village, they remained concealed until night, then hid their guns, and cautiously proceeded towards the scene of action, sending Tahrohon forward as a scout, to seek their prey. Not succeeding in finding horses, they began to cast round them in search of food, for they had eaten nothing for two days, and were almost famished with hunger. But they could find no corn, and returned dispirited to the spot where they had deposited their guns. Tahrohon then proposed to go again in quest of horses, believing he should find some near a creek not far distant. Groping his way in the dark, with that sagacity which renders daylight almost superfluous to the Indian, he discovered an Osage lodge, and regretted that he had left his gun. While hesitating what course to pursue, the tall grass rustled near him, and he sat down. Presently all was still. He cautiously approached the camp, and discovered a piece of buffalo meat hanging at the opening of a lodge, barely visible in the dim light thrown upon it by an expiring camp fire. He determined to steal it, but remained for some time wistfully gazing at the spoil, and endeavouring to measure the danger to be encountered against the chances of success. Approaching nearer by degrees, he was at length in the act of reaching up to seize the spoil, when he discovered something on the ground, which he supposed to be two sacks of corn, a prize too tempting to be resisted, and stooping down he grasped— not a bag of food—but the nether limbs of an old woman, which, being wrapped in large leggings, presented, in the deceptive light of the decaying embers, the appearance which deceived the hungry prowler.   When his hand rested on a human being, he sprang back terrified, and was about to run off, when he reflected that if he turned his back he would probably be shot by the warriors occupying the camp; and, drawing his knife, he boldly stepped forward to meet the danger, and slay the first who should oppose him.   It turned out that the encampment comprised but one lodge, the sole occupant of which was an old squaw.

As this party returned home they discovered a trail, such as is made by dragging over the grass the kind of sled on which the Indians carry off their wounded.   As the track led towards their village, they followed it, and overtook a party of their own people, headed by Wahumppe, who had had a fight with the Osages and Kansas.   Though surprised and surrounded by superior numbers, but one of the Iowas was killed.   Hard Heart was wounded three times, and it was he who was drawn on the sled.

Ten days after, another war party went out to revenge the death just mentioned; for thus in savage life one deed of violence leads to another; and whether we pursue the annals of a tribe or the biography of an individual, the tale is but a series of assaults and reprisals.   But although the Osages were the offending party in this instance, it was determined to wreak their vengeance upon the Sioux, probably because the latter were most likely to be unprepared for such a visit.   When they reached the Sioux

TAH-RO-HON
An Iowa Warrior

country, spies were sent out. The leader made a talk to his warriors, and concluded by inviting them to tell their dreams, upon which two individuals said they had dreamed that they had gone through a great country, and had seen many people, but no one molested them. This was considered a good dream. Presently the spies came in and reported that they had discovered fifteen lodges of the Sioux. This intelligence made them cautious, and they concealed themselves for twenty-four hours to consult and feel their way. Then the horses were hoppled, a guard put over them, and the main body marched to the attack. To avoid being discovered, as well as to prevent anyone from straying off and being taken for an enemy, they moved in a close body, each man touching his fellow. The constraint imposed by this unusual movement displeased Tahrohon, who determined, by a trick, to anticipate his companions, and strike the first blow. Accordingly he stepped aside from the main body, and threw himself on the ground, pulling down with him an Indian, who was his relative, and who, like himself, had been displeased by some neglect. These two, determining to seek honour in their own way, remained still until the war party passed, and then rushed into the village of the enemy by the point at which it was supposed the inhabitants when alarmed would attempt to retreat. But the spies, with the true Indian craft, after communicating the truth to the leader of the band, had spread a false report among his followers, and our adventurers entered a deserted place, while the enemy was flying in an opposite direction. Thus disappointed, and placed in an equivocal position, they determined to return home and to frame some plausible excuse for their desertion. They had not travelled far when they came suddenly upon a Sioux camp, composed of several skin lodges that were new and white, and upon

which the moon was shining clearly.   Here was a chance
to do something.   "Let us take a smoke," said one to the
other; and sitting down among the tall grass they lighted
a pipe, and began to consider what act of mischief might
be perpetrated upon the sleeping inmates by two desperate
marauders bent on distinguishing themselves at any hazard.
After smoking and peeping awhile, they found a horse;
and their spirits being raised by this success, they groped
about actively and soon discovered four more, which they
led to a grove in a bend of the river, where they hid them,
for they were not satisfied with what they had done.   But
before they could return to the lodges the day dawned, and
a prophet was heard singing, shaking his gourd, and
praying for the relief of a sick person.   A Sioux Indian
came to the river for water, and our hero stepped forward
to kill him, but just as he was about to fire, his companion
exclaimed, "Look, there is our army!"   The young men
stood for a moment stupefied with surprise and terror; for
the danger now was that the Iowa band, rushing forward
upon the Sioux lodges with loud yells, would not recognise
these youths found thus in the enemy's camp; nor was it
likely they could make themselves known in the noise and
smoke of the onset.   They sprang, therefore, down the
bank of the river, and attracted the attention of the
prophet, who called to his people, who had not yet discovered the advancing Iowas, to fire on them.   But at
that instant the Iowas raised the war-whoop, and rushed
forward.   The two young men, in danger from both sides,
attempted to mingle in the fight, but found the missiles of
both parties hurled at them.   At length our hero, seeing
the two Sioux surrounded by several Iowas, who were
pushing each other aside in their eagerness to strike a foe,
rushed through the circle and shot one of the Sioux.   He
then mingled in the fight, and felt like one relieved from

the horrors of a disagreeable dream, when he found himself fairly reinstated among his friends. In this fight
twelve Sioux were killed, and four were taken prisoners.

NOTES

1. "Tah-ro-hon" was the fourth and last signer of the treaty of
St Louis, November 23, 1837. He later went to Washington, and at this
time his portrait was painted by King; it bears No. 38 in the Rhees
Catalogue. Cf. note 1, under NEOMONNI, p. 153, this volume.

2. This no doubt refers to the Osage custom of tattooing, which was
practised by both men and women, but the significance of the markings,
which are probably cosmical in their nature, is not yet definitely known.

WATCHEMONNE

(AN IOWA CHIEF)

WATCHEMONNE, or *The Orator.* the third chief of the Iowas, was born at the old Iowa village on Des Moines River, at this time occupied by Keokuk,[1] and is now, in 1838, about fifty-two years of age. In recalling his earliest recollections, he tells, as the Indians mostly do, that he began in boyhood to kill small game with the bow and arrow. When he became big enough to use fire-arms, he procured a fowling-piece, or, as the phrase is upon the border, a shot-gun—a weapon considered of far inferior dignity to the more deadly rifle. But such was the awe inspired in his mind by the effects of gunpowder, that he was at first afraid to discharge his gun, and threw a blanket over his breast and shoulder before he ventured to level the piece. His first experiment was upon a wild turkey, which he killed, and after that he hunted without fear. This occurred before he was thirteen, for at that age he killed deer with his gun. At sixteen he went to war, killed an Osage, and took a piece of a scalp. His leader on that occasion was Wenugana, or *The man who gives his opinion.* After a long time he again went out with a war party under Notoyaukee, or *One rib.* Approaching a camp of the Missouris, some of their swiftest young men went forward, dashed into the camp, despatched three men, and returned, saying

164

they had killed all. He was in the same affair with
Notchimine,[2] when the eleven were killed, and remembers
that among the slain was a great chief. He slew none
himself, but struck the dead and took three scalps, which
is regarded as the greater exploit.

After these events, The Orator had the misfortune
to lose a brother who was slain by the Osages, and whose
death it became his duty as a warrior and a man of spirit
to avenge. On such occasions the Indian does not act
upon the principle of the civilised duellist, whose chief
aim seems to be to vindicate his own courage by making
a show of resentment. His object is to appease the spirit
of his deceased friend by the death of the slayer, and,
if that be not practicable, by shedding the blood of some
other enemy of his family or tribe; and he prepared
himself for the exploit with every care and solemnity
which is conceived necessary to ensure success. Every
aid suggested by superstition is invoked, while a studied
attention is given to every circumstance indicated by
the more rational sagacity and experience of the warrior,
as tending to render the meditated blow swift and fatal.
He accordingly fasted and prayed a long time; then he went
out and killed a deer and a bear, and made a feast in honour
of the Great Spirit, to which all the warriors of his village
were invited. He now became very angry, and professed
to mourn greatly for his brother, whose spirit was very
unhappy, and could find no rest so long as the murderer
lived to boast in triumph over him. He called upon his
friends who were willing to follow him, and all warriors who
loved the war-path, and all young men who thirsted for
distinction, to gather around his war pole; and when
the volunteers were collected, he sang for them, and
they danced—he recounting the virtues of the deceased,
and imprecating vengeance, and they responding by

grunts of approbation, and yells of passion. Then he sang to the women, who also danced—and all united in hoping the Great Spirit would prosper his praiseworthy undertaking. Finally he told his party, that at the end of thirteen days he would lead them out to seek the foe—that in a dream he had seen an old man, and was told that if he succeeded in killing him he would also slay many others. He believed the vision, and accordingly they had not gone far when they met an aged Missouri, who was very bald; and as he was recognised as one who had slain many Iowas, they attributed his baldness to the numerous murders he had committed. Him they slew, but the rest of the dream was not fulfilled, though The Orator comforted himself with the belief that it would prove true in the end. He therefore called his young men together again; but they were dispirited by his former ill-success, and only one agreed to follow him. With this companion he went to the west fork of Grand River, and having collected some of his tribe whom he met by the way, found himself at length at the head of twenty-two men. Meeting with a party of Osages, they attacked them and killed one man, which seems to have been considered satisfactory by the living, if not by the dead, for the party returned in good spirits. He states that, previous to his going out on this expedition, it was understood that if an enemy was killed he was to be considered as a general or leader, and he accordingly received his present name, Watchemonne, which signifies *War leader*, or, as we should say, General. The title of Orator, by which he is known more commonly, was given him by the whites, because he speaks well in council, and is usually appointed to receive visitors and deputations.

On one occasion, when this warrior was engaged in

an expedition against the Sioux, he conceived that he should not have luck *to kill*, and quitting his companions he wandered off by himself in search of adventure. His object seems to have been to fall in with some individual of the enemy, whom he could slay either by stealth or courage, so that by shedding blood his evil destiny might be changed. The notions of the Indians on these subjects are so confused that they do not give any very distinct account of their superstitions ; but we apprehend that on occasions like this they imagine there are bad spirits who may be propitiated by bloodshed, and that it matters not how the victim is slain. The only Sioux that he met with was a little girl. Had it been a boy he would have killed him, but he captured the girl and made her a present to his captain, who in return gave him a string of wampum.

Besides these warlike incidents we are happy to record other anecdotes which we have received of this chief. The first one he calls *the beginning of his making presents*. The Sauks had killed two Iowas, and to avert the accustomed vengeance on the part of the latter, a deputation was sent to offer a compensation for the injury. The deputies, fearful that they might not be well received, halted near the Iowa village, sent for The Orator to come to them, and solicited his interposition. Having consented to become the peacemaker, he made a present of seven Mackinaw blankets to the Iowa chief, and then gave the Sauks a keg of whisky to revive their spirits, and enable them to enter the village without fear.

The Iowas being at war with the Osages, one of the war parties of the former nation, returning home from an unsuccessful expedition, passed an American settlement on the frontier of Missouri, and with that desperate propensity for mischief which the Indian always evinces under those circumstances, they stole four horses. The danger of such an act arose not out of the value of the property taken, but from the alarm the outrage would create, and the retribution that the men of the frontier would be sure to visit upon what they would consider the preliminary act of an Indian war. The chief, therefore, desired the young men to return the horses ; but this they declined, and Watche-monne immediately bought them, and sent them back to the owners. This act gained him great credit among the people of the border, who have ever since treated him with confidence and spoken in his praise. After that a number of the Sauks came on a visit of ceremony to the Iowas— probably on one of the occasions alluded to in the life of Keokuk [3]—when The Orator, for the credit of his tribe, presented them with two horses. At another time, an Otto paying him a visit, he gave his guest at his departure a horse and a fine chief coat, such as the Government distributes annually among the leading men of the tribes ; and he has always, when it was in his power, displayed this kind of liberality to those who visit him.

This chief says he has no knowledge of any tradition of his tribe beyond Lake Pepin [4]—that is, before they crossed that lake—a very expressive form of speech, indicating the migratory character of the people, and their own conviction that they are strangers in the land they inhabit. He only knows that on the shores of that water dwelt his nation before it had become divided into the Winnebago,[5] the Omaha, the Missouri, and the Iowa tribes, and this he was told by his father, who derived it through eight preceding ancestors. It was the will of the Great Spirit that they should not be stationary, but travel from place to place, cultivating different ground ; and they believe that they will only continue to have good crops and healthy children so long as they obey this law of their nature.

WAT-CHE-MON-NE, *or* "THE ORATOR"
An Iowa Chief

They had better corn, and were more prosperous before the division of their nation than since. They have a secret among them about the Great Spirit which it would be unlucky to tell. They have a number of medicine bags, containing the herbs and other articles used in juggling and in propitiating the Great Spirit, and other spirits, which they keep in a lodge that is usually shut up, and that no woman is permitted to enter. Before they go to war they engage for four days in religious ceremonies, during which time they practise entire abstinence. A deer or a bear having been provided beforehand, a feast is made, when the fasting is over, and a general invitation given to all who choose to attend. The old men are invited to pray. Those who are going out to war engage frequently in secret prayer; and they believe that those who pray insincerely will have bad luck. When any disagreement occurs in the tribe, a similar feast is made for the purpose of effecting a reconciliation, and the chief offers to the parties between whom the quarrel exists, a pipe filled with a mixture of dried herbs, which they call the *Great Spirit's tobacco.* It is believed that death would speedily follow a refusal to smoke the pipe thus tendered. A singular example of superstition occurred in this tribe recently. A man having lost three children by sickness, thought it his duty to go to war and shed blood, in order to change his luck. The chief, White Cloud's brother, assembled the people of his band, and endeavoured to prevail on the unfortunate person to smoke the pipe of peace, by which he would be pledged to forgo his sanguinary purpose. Finding him obstinate, and fearing perhaps that the tribe would be involved in a war by the infatuation of one individual, he presented the bereaved father with seven horses as a compensation for his loss. Still the pipe was refused; and a few days afterwards the poor man lost his wife, in consequence, as the tribe believed, of his non-compliance with an ancient usage; but in punishment, as he thought, of his having delayed to shed the blood of an enemy. He went out, therefore, and killed an Omaha, and was satisfied. They consider themselves authorised, and sometimes constrained, to avenge the death of friends who die a natural death.

This chief is a cousin of White Cloud, whose biography was given in a former number. He was a good man, and greatly beloved by his tribe; and Watchemonne was much struck with our picture of him, which he declared to be an excellent likeness. When a copy of that portrait was sent to the tribe, they were grieved so much that they could not bear to look at it. Even the children remember him well, although four years have elapsed since his death, and he is still mourned. They have never been accustomed to pictures of their friends, and are pained to see those they loved thus exhibited.

Shortly after the death of a chief it is usual to hold a meeting for the purpose of consoling the surviving family. The whole company is formally seated, the chiefs in one place, the braves in another, and the relatives of the deceased in a third, while the women and children of the tribe form a circle around. Presents are then made to the family, one giving a horse, another a blanket, and so on; after which the chiefs and braves speak of the virtues of the departed, and narrate his exploits, each speaker rising in turn, and the whole auditory listening with great decorum. The one who pronounces the most satisfactory eulogy is treated to something to drink. Two or three such meetings have been held in honour of the White Cloud. Watchemonne relates that after his brother, the Crane, died, when he thought they had mourned long enough, he led the warriors to the grave, and seated them around it. He told them they had mourned long enough, and that it was time to rub the black paint off their faces and to resume the red paint. He then distributed red paint among them, and afterwards liquor.

This chief has but one wife, and several children. One of his sons, now about nineteen years of age, has been for six years at the Choctaw Academy[6]; and a daughter, whose Indian name signifies the *Rainbow*, is under the care of the missionaries, who call her Mary.

NOTES

1. That is, the village on Des Moines River, sixty miles above its mouth, where Catlin painted Keokuk's portrait.

2. See biography of NOTCHIMINE, p. 110, this volume.

3. See p. 131, this volume.

4. Lake Pepin is formed by the broadening of a stretch of the Mississippi between Minnesota and Wisconsin.

5. The Winnebago, Omaha, Missouri, and Iowa are Siouan tribes. Regarding the question here mentioned we quote from the *Handbook of American Indians*, pt. 2, 1910, p. 577 :—
"According to tradition the Mandan and Hidatsa reached the Upper Missouri from the north-east, and, impelled by the Dakota, moved slowly upstream to their present location. Some time after the Hidatsa reached the Missouri, internal troubles broke out, and part, now called the Crows, separated and moved westward to the neighbourhood of Yellowstone River. The Dakota [or Sioux] formally inhabited the forest region of southern Minnesota, and do not seem to have gone out upon the plains until hard-pressed by the Chippewa, who had been supplied with guns by the French. According to all the evidence available, traditional and otherwise, the so-called Chiwere tribes—Iowa, Oto, and Missouri—separated from the Winnebago or else moved westward to the Missouri River from the same region. The five remaining tribes of this group—Omaha, Ponca, Osage, Kansa, and Quapaw—which have been called Dhegiha by J. Owen Dorsey, undoubtedly lived together as one tribe at some former time, and were probably located on the Mississippi. Part moving farther down became known as 'downstream people,' *Quapaw*, while those who went up were the 'upstream people,' *Omaha*. These latter moved north-westward along the river and divided into the Osage, Kansa, Ponca, and Omaha

proper.   As to the more remote migrations that must have taken place in such a widely scattered stock, different theories are held."

6. The Choctaw Academy was established, about 1825, near Georgetown, Kentucky, and was supported by the Choctaw nation. However, a clause was inserted in the Creek treaty of November 15, 1827, appropriating $5000 to be "applied under the direction of the President of the United States towards the education and support of Creek children at the school in Kentucky known by the title of the 'Choctaw Academy.'"

TUSTENNUGGEE EMATHLA

(A CREEK CHIEF)

THIS is a fine-looking man, six feet and one inch in height, of manly and martial appearance, and great physical strength, who seems well calculated to command the respect of a band of savage warriors. Our brief sketch of him is framed from memoranda taken from his own lips. He is a full-blooded Creek, and was born on the Tallapoosa River, about the year 1793, which would make him forty-five years old at the period to which we bring down his biography. He is most generally known by the familiar name of Jim Boy, but is properly entitled to that which we have placed at the head of this article, Tustennuggee, meaning *Warrior*, and Emathla, which signifies *Next to the warrior*.

When the war broke out in 1811, between the Creeks and the American people, he was too young to wield the tomahawk, but was permitted to follow the warriors of his nation to the field ; and he thus witnessed the capture of Fort Mims,[1] a fortress which the Indians surprised at the commencement of hostilities, and where they basely massacred all who fell into their hands, without regard to age or sex. He was also present at the battle of Cahawba,[2] but took no further part in that war. He afterwards accompanied General Jackson, under the command of McIntosh, towards Florida, but was not in any fight.

When the Creek nation became divided into two parties, one of whom were friendly to the American people and Government, and disposed to yield to the settled and inevitable policy which demanded their entire separation from the white race, and the other hostile to our country and unwilling to emigrate, Tustennuggee Emathla attached himself to the former party. He has continued, since he reached the years of maturity, the undeviating friend of the Americans; and it affords us great pleasure to recognise, in the steady attachment of this individual and many others, the most intelligent and best disposed of their race, some proof that, whatever abuses may have corrupted and disgraced our intercourse with that unfortunate people, the general policy of our Government towards them has been of a kind and liberal character.

In the present war in Florida, Tustennuggee Emathla seems to have rendered some service. General Jesup [3] sought his services to lead a party against the Seminoles, and he accordingly raised a band of seven hundred and seventy-six warriors, whom he conducted to the seat of war. He descended the Chattahoochee to Tampa Bay, [4] having instructions from General Jesup not to engage in hostilities against the Seminoles until he should first have endeavoured, as a mediator, to induce them to abandon the bloody and fruitless contest in which they were unhappily engaged. In this attempt he was not successful; and we find him, soon after his arrival at Tampa, joining the camp of Colonel Lane, by whom he was sent, with two hundred of his warriors, to look after the Seminoles. He fell in with a party of the latter, and drove them into a swamp, from which they opened fire and wounded several of his men. He was then sent to meet Governor Call, [5] and arrived at the spot where General Gaines [6] was surrounded, soon after that officer had been relieved. On the following day he joined Governor Call, and proceeded to Fort Drane. Thence they moved on one of Acee-Yoholo's towns, called Weecockcogee, or Little River, about sixty miles from Fort Drane, where the Seminoles, though numerous, refused them battle, fled, and were pursued. The Creeks were unable to overtake them; but the Tennessee horse fell in with them on the following day, and a fight ensued, in which several were killed on each side.

Tustennuggee and his party joined the army again at Fort Dade, and the Seminoles being in a swamp hard by, an attack was planned, in which the Creeks were invited to go foremost, an honour which they promptly declined, while they cheerfully agreed to advance side by side with the white men. In this fight the Creeks lost four men, besides one who was accidentally killed by the whites; but the Seminoles were beaten. He was afterwards sent to a place towards Fort Augustine for provisions, and was in several skirmishes not worth recording.

This chief states that he joined our army under a promise made by the commanding general, that in the removal of the Creeks to the west of the Mississippi, which was about to take place, his family and property should be attended to, and that he should be indemnified for any loss that might happen in consequence of his absence. These stipulations he alleges were broken by the removal of his women and children while he was absent in the service of the Government, whereby his entire property was destroyed. Nor was this the worst of his misfortunes. His family, consisting of a wife and nine children, were among the unfortunate persons who were on board the steamboat *Monmouth* when that vessel was sunk by the mismanagement of those to whose care it was entrusted; and two hundred and thirty-six of the Creeks, including four of the children of Tustennuggee Emathla, were drowned. Melancholy as such an occurrence would be under any circumstances, the catastrophe is infinitely the more deplorable when happening to an ignorant people while emigrating unwillingly under the charge of our public agents, and to a people whose whole intercourse with the whites has tended to render them suspicious of the faith of civilised men. The more intelligent among them will doubtless attribute the misfortune to culpable negligence, if not design, while the ignorant will see in it, with superstitious awe, another link in the chain of fatal events entailed upon the red men by their contact with the white race. So far as the chief before us has any claim upon the justice or benevolence of our country, there can be no doubt that the Government will maintain its faith inviolate. Whatever may be thought of our policy towards the Indian tribes, as such, we are not chargeable, as a people, with any backwardness in the discharge of our obligations to individual claimants.[7]

NOTES

1. The massacre at Fort Mims occurred August 30, 1813. For a full account of this disaster consult Pickett, *History of Alabama*, 1851, Vol. II., p. 264 ; John Henry Eaton, *Life of Andrew Jackson*, 1824, p. 33; also note 32, p. 400, Vol. I., this work.

2. During the winter of 1813-14, several minor skirmishes occurred near the " Cahawba Old Towns," a group of Choctaw settlements in the present Perry county, Alabama.

3. See OPOTHLE-YOHOLO, note 19, p. 34, this volume.

4. Of course he could not have entered Tampa Bay from the Chattahoochee. Probably he went down the Chattahoochee and Apalachicola Rivers to the Gulf of Mexico, thence crossed to Tampa Bay, a distance of more than 200 miles.

5. Richard Keith Call, born near Petersburg, Virginia, 1791 ; died at Tallahassee, Florida, 1862. He was a volunteer aid to General

TUSTENNUGGEE EMATHLA, *or* "JIM BOY"
A Creek Chief

Jackson in April, 1818, and became member of the legislative council of Florida in 1822. In January, 1823, Call became brigadier-general of the West Florida militia, and the same year was chosen delegate to Congress, which position he retained until 1825. He was Governor of Florida from 1835 until 1840; commanded the army in the Seminole war from December 6, 1835, until December 6, 1836, and was again Governor of Florida, 1841-44.

6. Edmund Pendleton Gaines (1777-1849) advanced from second lieutenant in 1799 to the rank of brigadier-general in 1814; August 15, 1814, received the brevet of major-general "for his gallantry and good conduct in defeating the enemy at Fort Erie, N.C.; received the thanks of Congress, November 3, 1814, for gallantry and good conduct in defeating the enemy at Erie on the 15th of August." At the time of the Seminole war, 1835, the United States was divided into two military departments by a line drawn from the north-western angle of Lake Superior to the southern extremity of Florida. Major-General Scott was in command of the eastern section, and Major-General Gaines of the western. At the beginning of hostilities, General Scott was in Washington, while General Gaines had left his headquarters at Memphis, Tennessee, on a tour of inspection. The latter, learning of the uprising in Florida, hastened to the scene of action, not knowing that General Scott had already taken the field.

7. The portrait of Tustenugge-Emathla is evidently No. 36 in the Rhees *Catalogue*, the name appearing as "Wea-Matla," painted by King, 1826. His portrait was later painted by J. M. Stanley, June, 1843. In the *Guide to the Smithsonian Institution*, 1861, p. 43, is a brief reference to the man. "He is and always has been a firm and undeviating friend of the whites; he led a party of 776 warriors to Florida, and endeavoured, first as mediator, to induce the Seminoles to abandon the bloody and fruitless contest in which they were engaged, but was unsuccessful."

MENAWA

(A CREEK WARRIOR)

THIS chief is a half-blooded Creek, of the Oakfuskee towns,[1] which lie on the Tallapoosa River, in Alabama. He was formerly called Hothlepoya, or *The crazy war hunter*, in consequence of his daring feats as a marauder upon the frontiers of Tennessee, at an early period in the settlement of that state. He was in the habit of passing over annually to the Cumberland River, for the purpose of stealing horses, or, as the fierce clansmen of Scotland would have phrased it, driving cattle. The great modern novelist has designated treason a gentlemanly crime, and border warriors, of whatever race, have, in like manner, considered the occupation of transferring each other's horses, either by stealth or violence, as a reputable martial employment. Hothlepoya was widely known and feared by the new settlers along the border, as a bold and successful adept in this species of warfare, which he practised with the least possible breach of the public peace—seldom shedding blood if unresisted, but fighting with desperation when opposed. Various are the adventures attributed to him while thus engaged, in some of which he is represented as pursuing his object with daring audacity, and in others obtaining it by ingenious trickery. On one occasion,

> " As bursts the levin in its wrath,
>   He shot him down the winding path.
>   Rock, wood, and stream, rung wildly out,
>   To his loud step and savage shout ";

while again the honest farmer, bereaved of his noblest steed, suspected not the felonious deed until *The crazy war hunter* was far beyond the reach of pursuit.

The stories told of this individual are so numerous as to warrant the inference that his celebrity in the peculiar species of horse-jockeyship to which he devoted his attention, induced those who suffered injury at his hand to give him credit, not only for his own exploits, but those of his various contemporaries, as the Greeks attributed to their deified Hercules the deeds of numerous heroes who bore that name. Some of these adventures are too marvellous to be readily believed; many, that seem plausible enough, want confirmation, and but few have reached us, in detail, in such an unquestionable shape as to be worthy of repetition. We pass them over, therefore, with the single remark, that while enough is known to establish the character of Hothlepoya as an adroit and bold taker of the horses of his civilised neighbours, we are unable to give so minute a detail of these enterprises as would be edifying to the public, or instructive to the youthful aspirant after similar honours.

One incident is well vouched for, which shows that our marauder could emulate the liberality of the famous Robin Hood. Returning once from a successful excursion, he fell in with a tired pedestrian, trudging along the trail that in those days led from Augusta to the Tombigbee. The latter was a white man, who had lost his good nag; whether like Fitz James,

> " ———— touched with pity and remorse,
> He sorrowed o'er the expiring horse,"

we are not told, but we learn that he was on foot, in a cheerless wilderness, with no other companion than a hound, who,

> " With drooping tail and humbled crest,"

followed the fallen fortunes of his master. Had Hothlepoya encountered this traveller mounted upon a good
horse, the probability is that he would, either by stratagem
or force, have despoiled him of the animal. As it was, he
gave him a fine steed worth two hundred dollars, which
he had just stolen at the hazard of his life, and received
in exchange the stranger's hound—not as an equivalent,
for the dog was of little value, but as a something to
stand in place of the horse, and to be shown as a trophy
on his return home. The acquisitive propensity of so
heroic a person is not excited by the value of the thing
stolen, but by the glory of the capture.

When Tecumthe [2] visited the southern Indians, about
the year 1811, for the purpose of endeavouring to unite
them with the northern tribes in a general conspiracy
against the whites, the subject of this notice was second
chief of the Oakfuskee towns, and had acquired the name
of Menawa, which means *The Great Warrior;* and the
politic Shawanoe leader distinguished him as one of those
whose co-operation would be necessary to the accomplishment of his purpose. He made a special visit to Menawa,
and formally communicated his plan, in a set speech,
artfully framed to foment the latent hatred of the Creek
chief towards the whites, and to awaken the ambition
which he well knew must form a prominent feature in a
character so daring and restless. Menawa heard his
illustrious visitor with deep attention, for he loved war,
and was not unwilling to strike the pale-faced enemy of
his race. War is always a popular measure among the
Indians, and the chiefs readily indulge their followers in a
propensity that diverts their attention from domestic
affairs, and keeps up the habit of subordination in these
wild and factious bands, who are at all times ruled with
difficulty, but more especially when peace brings its

ME-NA-WA
A Creek Warrior

season of idleness, intemperance, and licence. Another reason which, doubtless, had a powerful though secret influence upon the mind of the Oakfuskee chief, was his jealousy of the growing power of McIntosh,[3] whom he disliked, and who was known to favour the whites. A murder had recently been committed upon some white men, in the direction of the Oakfuskee towns, in revenge for which the people of Georgia, charging the crime upon Menawa's band, had burnt one of his villages. It was secretly rumoured, and believed by Menawa, that McIntosh, who feared to attack him openly, and perhaps had no plausible pretence for a public rupture with his rival, had instigated the murder and had then caused it to be charged to the Oakfuskee band, for the express purpose of exposing the latter to the vengeance of the Georgians; and he was soured alike at the whites, who had chastised his people without a cause, and at McIntosh, who was the supposed author of the injury. The proposed war had, therefore, the additional recommendation, that as McIntosh would most probably join the whites, he would be converted from a secret enemy, protected by rank and position, into an open foe, leagued with the oppressors of his race.

We have already spoken of the Creek war, and we now recur to it to detail the part acted by Menawa, who engaged in it with great alacrity. Although he was the second chief of his band, his reputation for valour and military skill placed him foremost on occasions when danger threatened, or when enterprise was required. The principal chief was a medicine man, who relied more on his incantations than upon the rifle or tomahawk—a peaceable person, who probably inherited his station and owed his elevation to good blood rather than a meritorious character. He wore around his body a number of gourds, containing the herbs and other articles which constituted

his medicine, and which he believed had power to repel
the bullets of the enemy, to preserve his own life, and give
success to his party.   Menawa, though a man of vigorous
intellect, was slightly infected with the superstition of his
people, and from habit venerated the character of his chief;
but the miracles which were said to have followed the visit
of Tecumthe, and which we alluded to elsewhere, so far
outshone the gourds of the Oakfuskee juggler, as to create
some little contempt, and perhaps distrust towards the
spells of the latter.   But the faith of the principal chief
only waxed stronger and stronger, and he continued to
juggle without intermission, and to prophesy with confidence, while the Indians, partaking of his fanaticism,
generally believed in him, and relied upon his power.

Thus incited by the blind zeal of fanaticism, added to
the many existing causes of hatred against the whites, and
to the belief that a general war to be waged under supernatural guidance was about to afford the opportunity for
ample revenge, the Creeks proceeded in earnest to actual
hostilities.   We pass over a number of engagements that
occurred in this war, in several of which Menawa acted a
leading part, sparing our readers from the mere details of
bloodshed, which could afford them but little interest, and
passing on to the great battle of the Horseshoe,[4] wherein
it was the fate of this chief to act and suffer as became the
military head of a gallant people.   The scene of this
disastrous conflict has already been described in another
part of our work; and we shall only repeat here, that the
Indians were posted on a small tongue of land, surrounded
by the Tallapoosa River on all sides but one, where it was
joined to the mainland by a narrow isthmus, across which
they had thrown a strong breastwork of logs.   The Oakfuskee prophet, after performing certain incantations,
informed his followers that the impending assault would

be made in the rear of their position, which was swept by
the river ; and by presumptuously assuming to predict the
plan which would be adopted by his enemy, unintentionally
misled the Indians, who, instead of trusting to their own
natural sagacity, arranged their defences in reference to
an imaginary plan of assault.   General Jackson, who, to
an inflexible firmness of purpose united a vigorous judgment, perceived the impregnable nature of the points the
Indians had prepared to defend, and conceived the bold
as well as judicious step of assailing the breastwork that
extended across the isthmus.   The movement of the
American General was so rapid, that its object was not
discovered until his cannon were planted in front of the
entrenchment.   But when the battery was opened upon
this point, when the Tennesseans were seen rushing
forward with impetuous valour, and it was discovered
that the main force of the American army was about to
be precipitated upon the breastwork, Menawa, enraged at
his chief, whose juggling had betrayed the Indians into a
fatal error, flew at the unfortunate prophet, and, aided by
others alike incensed, slew him upon the spot.   He then
placed himself at the head of the Oakfuskee braves, and
those of the neighbouring towns, and uttering, with a voice
of unusual compass, a tremendous war-whoop, leaped the
breastwork and threw himself in the midst of the assailants.
A Greek or Roman leader, who had thus slain his chief,
assumed the command, and abandoning the shelter of
his fortifications, plunged into the thickest ranks of the
enemy, to conquer or die for his people, would have been
immortalised in classic story; while in the American
savage such conduct will only be remembered as among
the evidences of the extraordinary ferocity of his race.

The comrades of Menawa followed him into the battle,
and fought at his side with desperate valour, until nearly

all were slain, and he fell wounded by seven balls. The whole fight was of the most desperate character. The waters of the Tallapoosa River were red with blood. The ferocity with which the Indians fought may be attributed in part to their custom of not suffering themselves to be taken as prisoners, while their position cut them off from retreat, and still more perhaps to the fact that the ground of the Horseshoe was a consecrated spot, where they considered themselves protected by friendly spirits and were nerved to desperation by a faith like that which excites the frantic valour of the Mahometan. Of nine hundred warriors led into that sanguinary fight by Menawa, only seventy survived, and one only, who fled at the first discharge of cannon, escaped unwounded.

When the storm of the battle subsided, Menawa remained on the field, lying in a heap of the slain, devoid of consciousness. Recovering his senses, he found himself weltering in blood, with his gun firmly grasped in his hand. The battle had ceased, or swept by, but straggling shots announced that the work of death was not over. Raising himself slowly to a sitting posture, he perceived a soldier passing near him, whom, with a deliberate aim, he shot, but at the same moment received a severe wound from a bullet, which, entering his cheek near the ear, and carrying away several of his teeth, passed out on the opposite side of the face. Again he fell among the dead, retaining, however, so much of life as to feel the victors treading upon his body as they passed over it, supposing him to be slain. When night came he felt revived, and the love of life grew strong in him. He crawled cautiously to the bank of the river, and descending to its margin found a canoe, which he entered, and by shaking it from side to side loosed it from the shore. The canoe floated down the river until it reached the neighbourhood of a swamp at Elkahatchee, where the Indian women and children had been secreted previous to the battle. Some of these wretched beings, who were anxiously looking out for intelligence from the scene of action, espied the canoe, and upon going to it, discovered the mangled chief lying nearly insensible in its bottom.

Menawa was removed to a place of rendezvous which had been appointed on the Elkahatchee creek, where he was joined by the unhappy survivors of that dreadful battle. For the purpose of brooding over their grief, mourning for the dead, and deciding upon the measures necessary to be adopted in consequence of the recent disaster, a silent council was held, that lasted three days, during which time these moody warriors neither ate, nor drank, nor permitted their wounds to be dressed. At the expiration of the third day it was determined that the Indians should return to their respective homes, submit to the victors, and each man make his own peace as best he might. Their wounds were then dressed by the women, who usually officiate as surgeons, as did the ladies of Europe in the days of chivalry. The Indians are said to display under such circumstances a remarkable tenacity of life, and to recover rapidly from the effects of the most serious wounds, in consequence, probably, of their active and abstemious habits, rather than of the absence of physicians. They soon dispersed, and all of them surrendered formally to the American authorities, except Menawa, whose wounds prevented him from leaving his retreat until after the close of the war. As soon as he was able to travel he sought his home, at the Oakfuskee towns, but found neither shelter nor property. The desolating hand of war had swept all away. Before the breaking out of hostilities, Menawa was among the richest of the Indians of the Upper towns. Like many of his nation, of the mixed blood, he had partially adopted the habits of the white man, keeping large herds of cattle which he exchanged for merchandise, and bartering the latter with his own people for the products of the chase. He had entirely abandoned the predatory habits of his early life, was the owner of a store, and of more than a thousand head of cattle, an equal number of hogs, and several hundred horses. He carried on a brisk trade with Pensacola, and was known to load, at one time, a hundred horses with furs and peltries. Like the famous Rob Roy, he was by turns a chieftain, a drover, and a marauder, a high-mettled warrior, and a crafty trader; and like him, his propensity for war was unfortunately stronger than his prudence. All his earnings were now destroyed. He found his village burned; not a vestige remained of all his property—houses, cattle, and merchandise, had alike disappeared. The Oakfuskee chief was as poor as the most abject individual of his band, and has lived in poverty ever since that fatal campaign. He could never be prevailed upon afterwards to revisit the battle ground at the Horseshoe. It is believed that he entertained a superstitious dread of the spot, at which he supposed a malign influence existed, fatally hostile to his people and himself. This is not improbable, and is entirely consistent with the Indian character. But this aversion may be attributed to a more natural cause. Men of high spirit are liable to strong prejudices and obstinate antipathies, and Menawa may have felt an unconquerable reluctance to revisit a spot so replete with humiliating recollections—the scene of signal defeat and mortification to himself, as a man and as a chieftain. Napoleon, bereft of imperial power, would have taken no pleasure in retracing the road to Moscow.

Menawa regained his health, resumed his authority

over the remnant of the Oakfuskee band, and became
an influential person in the Creek nation. In the conflict
of opinion which for many years distracted this unfortunate people, he acted with those who resisted the
encroachments of the whites, refused to sanction further
cessions of territory, and opposed every measure which
would lead to the compulsory emigration of his people.
McIntosh,[5] as we have seen, espoused the opposite side,
and when that chief was sentenced to death for having
signed a treaty of cession in violation of the known wishes
of the majority, Menawa was selected to execute the
fatal decree. Between these leaders there had never
existed any friendly feeling, nor is it supposed that
Menawa would have been seduced into the imprudent
measure of taking up arms against the American Government, but for the spirit of rivalry mutually entertained
and the belief of the one that he had been deeply injured
by the other. The knowledge of these facts, as well
as their confidence in the firmness and bravery of Menawa,
may have led the Creeks to select him as the executioner
of their sentence. He at first declined the office, and
requested the council to entrust it to a more impartial
hand; but that body adhering to their choice, he accepted
the trust, and discharged it in the manner we have related
in our sketch of McIntosh.

The subject of this notice was one of the delegation
sent by the Creeks to Washington, in 1826,[6] to remonstrate
against the treaty of the Indian Springs, and to effect
some compromise which should quiet the troubles that
preceded and ensued the death of McIntosh. His
conduct on that occasion was calm and dignified, and the
force of his character was felt in all the negotiations which
took place at the seat of Government. He was decidedly
opposed to the emigration of the entire Creek people, but

was willing to sell the country, reserving certain lands to be parcelled out to such individuals as might choose to remain, to be held by them severally in fee simple. By this plan the entire sovereignty and jurisdiction of the country would have been yielded, the Creeks as a nation would have retained nothing, but any individual choosing to continue within the ceded territory would have had a tract of land granted to him in perpetuity, which he would hold under the State Government. None would have accepted these conditions but such as proposed to subsist by agriculture, or some of the kindred arts, and were willing to submit to the restraints of law. The untamed Indian who preferred his own savage mode of life, would have sought a home more congenial to his taste in the forests and prairies of the West. This plan is more consonant with justice than any other that has been suggested ; whether it would have satisfied the people of Georgia, or have ultimately promoted the happiness of the Indians, we do not pretend to decide. Failing in this proposition, he succeeded in getting a provision inserted in the treaty, by which it was agreed that patents should be issued after five years to such Indians as might choose to occupy land. As it turned out eventually, this provision afforded no benefit to himself, for by an arbitrary mode adopted of making the allotment, the tract on which he had resided—his *home*—was given to another, and the land offered to himself not being acceptable, he sold it, and purchased other land in Alabama.

Menawa was not only brave and skilful, but was a gentleman in appearance and manners. Although he was a savage in the field, or in the revel, he could at any moment assume the dignity and courtesy proper to his high station. Not long after his return from Washington, a gentleman to whom we are indebted for some of the incidents related in this memoir, called upon this chief. He found him surrounded by his braves, engaged in a deep carouse; but Menawa had too much tact to receive his visitor under such circumstances. As the gentleman approached the house in which the Indians were carousing, he was met by an *aide* of the chief, who directed him to another house, where he was requested to remain until the next morning. The hint was taken. In the morning early Menawa was seen approaching well mounted, and in the full uniform of a general officer, from chapeau to spurs— being the dress presented to him at Washington at the conclusion of the treaty. At the door of the house at which his visitor was lodged he reined up his steed, and gracefully dismounted. Advancing with his chapeau under his arm, and bowing to the stranger, he desired to know the business of the latter which had induced his call. Being informed, he said promptly : "I am now engaged with my people in a frolic. I must return to them, but will see you to-morrow, and attend to your business." Whereupon he remounted, bowed, and galloped off. Punctual to his promise, he returned on the following morning and adjusted the matter of business.

Notwithstanding the hostility of Menawa towards the whites, and the injuries he had received, he remained inviolably faithful to the treaty he had made, and the pacific policy to which he was pledged. He said that when at Washington he had smoked the pipe of peace with his Great Father, and had buried the tomahawk so deep that he never again could dig it up. When, therefore, in 1836, the temporary successes of the Seminoles kindled a contagious spirit of insurrection among the Creeks, Menawa was among the first to tender his services to the authorities of Alabama; and his offer being accepted, he collected his braves and led them to the field, in combination with those of Opothle-Yoholo.[7]   On this occasion he was dressed in a full suit of American uniform, and affected the conduct of a civilised leader, whose sole object was to prevent the effusion of blood.   In addition to his own services, he sent his oldest son to Florida, to aid in the defence of the country against the Seminoles.   Under these circumstances he had reason to expect that he should be gratified in his ardent wish to spend the remnant of his days in his native land, and lay his bones with those of his forefathers.   He paid a visit to the Catawba Indians,[8] in North Carolina, to see how they prospered under the laws of that state ; and having satisfied himself that there was no insurmountable objection to such a mode of life, used every exertion to be excluded from the emigrating party. He was at last, in consideration of his recent services, gratified with the promise of being permitted to remain. But this act of justice had scarcely been conceded to him when, by some strange inadvertence, or want of faith, he was ordered to join the emigrating camp.   We hope and believe that this, with many other wanton acts of injustice towards the Indians, are not chargeable to our Government. The complicated relations with the tribes are necessarily entrusted to numerous agents, acting far from the seat of Government, and vested with discretionary powers which are not always discharged in good faith ; nor is it easy for the Executive to arrive at the truth in reference to such transactions, where some of the parties are interested, some unprincipled, and the majority both lawless and illiterate.

On the eve of his departure, this veteran chief said, to a highly reputable gentleman, who is our informant, presenting him at the same time with his portrait—a copy of the one which accompanies this sketch : " I am going away.   I have brought you this picture—I wish you to

take it and hang it up in your house, that when your
children look at it you can tell them what I have been. I
have always found you true to me, but great as my regard
for you is, I never wish to see you in that new country to
which I am going—for when I cross the great river, my
desire is that I may never again see the face of a white
man!"

When it was suggested to him that many supposed his
repugnance against emigrating arose from the apprehension
that he would meet in Arkansas the hostility of the
McIntosh party, who had preceded him, he shook his head
and said : "They do not know me who suppose I can be
influenced by fear. I desire peace, but would not turn my
back on danger. I know there will be bloodshed, but I
am not afraid. I have been a man of blood all my life;
now I am old, and wish for peace."

Before he took a final leave of the land of his fathers,
he requested permission to revisit the Oakfuskee town,
which had been his favourite residence. He remained
there one night. The next morning he commenced the
long-dreaded journey towards the place of exile. After
crossing the Tallapoosa he seemed for some time abstracted
and uneasy. His conduct was that of one who had forgotten something, and under this supposition it was
proposed to him to return for the purpose of correcting the
omission. But he said, "No! Last evening I saw the sun
set for the last time, and its light shine upon the tree-tops,
and the land, and the water, that I am never to look upon
again. No other evening will come, bringing to Menawa's
eyes the rays of the setting sun upon the home he has left
forever!"

The portrait of this distinguished chief, in the gallery of
the War Department,[9] which we copy, was taken in 1826,
when he was supposed to be about sixty years of age. It

is one of the most spirited of the works of that gifted artist, King, and has been often recognised by Menawa's country-men, who on seeing it, have exclaimed, "Menawa!" and then, fired by the remembrance of the deeds which gained him the name of *The Great Warrior*, they have gone on to recount them.   If this extraordinary person be yet living, he is far from his native land and all the scenes of a long and most eventful career, and is forming new associations at a period of life beyond the three score and ten allotted to man.

NOTES

1. A former Upper Creek town on both sides of Tallapoosa River, Alabama, about thirty-five miles above Tukabatchi, possibly on the southern boundary of Cleburne county, where a village of the same name now stands.   The Oakfuskee Indians on the eastern bank of the river came from three villages: Chihlakonini, Huhlitaiga, and Chukah-lako.   In 1799 Oakfuskee, with its 180 warriors and seven branch villages on the Tallapoosa (with 270 warriors), was considered the largest com-munity of the Creek confederacy.   The seven villages were Atchinaalgi, Imukfa, Ipisogi, Niuyaka, Sukaispoka, Tallahassee, Tukabatchi, and Tukhtukagi.

2. While Tecumseh did visit many tribes in person, he nevertheless sent agents to the distant tribes to make known his ideas and desires. But before his plans were consummated the disastrous battle af Tippe-canoe was fought, November 7, 1811.   Consult Pickett, *History of Alabama,* Vol. II., p. 240.

3. See Vol. I., p. 261, this work.

4. The battle of the "Horseshoe," fought March 27, 1814, at Great Bend of the Tallapoosa River, Alabama, was the last important battle of the Creek war.   The Creeks, numbering 1000 warriors, were defeated by the Americans and the Cherokee allies under General Jackson.   The Creeks left 557 dead on the field.   Consult Pickett, *History of Alabama,* Vol. II., p. 341.

5. See Vol. I., p. 265, this work.

6. The treaty concluded at the City of Washington, January 24, 1826, and ratified April 22 of the same year, was made " to remove the difficulties" arising from the treaty of Indian Springs, signed February 12, 1825.   "Menawee" was the fourth of thirteen Creek signers.   James

Barbour, Secretary of War, represented the Government, and McKenney was the first witness.

7. See biography of OPOTHLE-YOHOLO, p. 17, this volume.

8. The Catawba (probably from Choctaw *Katápa,* "divided," "separated," "a division"—Gatschet). The most important of the eastern Siouan tribes. Comparatively little is known of their early history, but they probably lived somewhere in eastern South Carolina at the time of their first contact with European colonists. In 1763 their possession of the reservation on Catawba River, within the present York and Lancaster counties, South Carolina, was confirmed. In 1826 nearly the whole reservation was leased by white settlers, and soon afterward the Catawba removed to the Eastern Cherokee, in North Carolina; but becoming again dissatisfied they returned to their reservation.

9. The portrait bears No. 23 in the Rhees *Catalogue,* but neither the name of the artist nor the date of the painting is recorded. The entire entry in the catalogue reads : "Menawee—a great Warrior and Creek Chief. This chief commanded the party that killed General McIntosh, and was one of the few that saved themselves from the defeat at the Horseshoe, by swimming the river, after being badly wounded in the head."

WABAUNSEE[1]

(A POTAWATOMI CHIEF)

In the portrait which accompanies this sketch we are happy to have it in our power to exhibit an excellent likeness of a very distinguished man. It is to be regretted that so few anecdotes of him have been preserved; but his general character, which is well known, is that of a warrior of uncommon daring and enterprise, and a chief of great intelligence and influence. His tribe take pride in recounting his numerous feats in war; and the agents of our Government who have met him in council speak in high terms of his capacity for business. Though cool and sagacious, he was a bold orator, who maintained the interests of his people with untiring zeal and firmness. He was the principal war chief of the Potawattimies of the Prairie, residing on the Kankakee River, in Illinois.[2]

The following anecdote, while it marks the daring spirit of this chief, is more especially characteristic of his race, and is one of the numerous instances of individual exploit with which the traditionary lore of the frontier abounds. Some years ago a small hunting party of Potawattimies, having wandered far to the West, were discovered by a band of Osages,[3] who surprised them and slew two or three of their number. It seems almost marvellous that such transactions should so frequently occur in the story of Indian life—that in a country of such

immense breadth, with a savage population so comparatively small, and with the melancholy proofs before their
eyes of a decrease in numbers so rapid as to threaten a
speedy extermination of the race, the individuals of
different tribes seldom meet without bloodshed. The propensity for carnage seems to be an innate and overmaster-
ing passion, which no reflection can chasten, nor the
saddest experience eradicate. Even their dread and
hatred of the white man, and the conviction of the common
fate which impends over the whole race, in consequence of
the superior numbers of those who are daily usurping their
places, has no restraining effect upon their wanton pro-
digality of blood. Although it is obvious, even to themselves, that the most fruitful source of their rapid decay is
to be found in their own unhappy dissensions, their
destructive habits continue unrestrained; and so many are
their feuds, so keen their appetite for blood, so slight the
pretence upon which the tomahawk may be lifted, that
two hunting parties from opposite directions can scarcely
meet in the wilderness without suggesting a stratagem, and
leading to the spilling of blood.

But common as such deeds are, they do not pass off
without important consequences. Although murder is an
everyday occurrence in savage life, the Indian resents it as
a crime, and claims the right to avenge the death of his
friend. On the occasion alluded to, one of the slain was
the friend of Wabaunsee, and he determined to revenge
the violence. It was long, however, before an opportunity
offered, the distance between the lands of the Potawattimies and Osages being so great, that the individuals
of the respective tribes seldom came in collision. But no
interval of time or distance cools the passion of revenge in
the Indian bosom. At length, while on one of his hunting
expeditions, Wabaunsee heard that some Osages were

expected to visit one of the American military posts not far distant, and thither he bent his steps, intent upon the completion of his purpose. On his arrival, he found the Osages there, and they met coldly, as strangers, without friendship and without feud. But smothered fires burned under that exterior apathy. Wabaunsee was determined to imbrue his hand in the blood of the tribe in whose lodges the scalp of his friend was hung; and the Osages no sooner learned the name of the newly arrived visitor than they guessed his purpose, and took counsel with each other how they might avert or anticipate the blow. Wabaunsee pitched his camp without the fort, while the Osages sought to secure their safety by sleeping within the fortress. But neither breastworks nor sentinels afford security from the hand of the savage, who is trained to stratagem, who finds no impediment in the obscurity of the thickest darkness, and can tread the forest with a step so stealthy as not to alarm the most vigilant listener. In the night Wabaunsee crept towards the fort, and evading the sentries, scaled the ramparts, and found admission through an embrasure. Alone, within a military post, surrounded by men sleeping on their arms, he glided swiftly and noiselessly about, until he found his victim. In an instant he despatched one of the sleeping Osages, tore the scalp from his head, and made good his escape before the alarm was given. As he leaped from the wall a trusty companion led up his horse, and the triumphant chief mounted and dashed off, followed by his little band; and before the sun rose they had ridden many miles over the prairie, and shouted often in exultation and derision over this bold but impudent exploit.

In the war of 1812 this chief and his tribe were among the allies of Great Britain, and were engaged in active hostilities against the United States. But at the treaty

WA-BAUN-SEE
A Potawatomi Chief

held at Greenville,[4] in 1814, he was one of those who, in the Indian phrase, took the Seventeen Fires by the hand, and buried the tomahawk. He has ever since been an undeviating friend of the American Government and people.

He was one of the chiefs who negotiated the treaty of the Wabash, in 1826.[5] At the close of the treaty, while encamped on the bank of the river, near the spot where the town of Huntingdon now stands, he engaged in a frolic, and indulged too freely in ardent spirits. A mad scene ensued, such as usually attends a savage revel, in the course of which a warrior, who held the station of friend, or *aide*, to Wabaunsee, accidentally plunged his knife deep in the side of the chief. The wound was dangerous, and confined him all winter; but General Tipton, the agent of our Government in that quarter, having kindly attended to him, he was carefully nursed, and survived. His sometime friend, fearing that he might be considered as having forfeited that character, had fled as soon as he was sober enough to be conscious of his own unlucky agency in the tragic scene. Early in the spring General Tipton was surprised by a visit from Wabaunsee, who came to announce his own recovery, and to thank the agent for his kindness. The latter seized the occasion to effect a reconciliation between the chief and his fugitive friend, urging upon the former the accidental nature of the injury, and the sorrow and alarm of the offender. Wabaunsee replied instantly: "You may send to him and tell him to come back. A man that will run off like a dog with his tail down for fear of death, is not worth killing. I will not hurt him." We are pleased to be able to say that he kept his word.

At the treaty held in 1828,[6] at which he assisted, one of the chiefs of his tribe, who was thought to be under the

influence of a trader, after the treaty had been agreed
upon by the chiefs and braves, refused to sign it unless
the commissioners would give him a large sum of money.
Wabaunsee was very indignant when he heard of this
circumstance. "An Indian," said he, "who will lie, is
not worthy to be called a brave. He is not fit to live.
If he refuses to sanction what we agreed to in council,
I'll cut his heart out." It was with some difficulty that
he was prevented from putting his threat into execution.

In 1832,[7] when the faction of Black Hawk disturbed
the repose of the frontier, it was feared that the Winnebagoes and Potawattimies would also be induced to take
up the hatchet, and it is supposed that they were tampered
with for that purpose. They were too sagacious to listen
to such rash counsels; and Wabaunsee relieved his own
conduct from doubt by joining the American army with
his warriors.

In 1833[8] the Potawattimies sold their lands in Illinois
and Indiana to the United States, and accepted other
territory west of the Mississippi, to which they agreed to
remove; and in 1835[9] he visited the City of Washington
for the purpose, as he said, of taking his Great Father by
the hand. The next year he led his people to their new
home, near the Council Bluffs on the Missouri, where he
is now living.

NOTES

1. According to Dr William Jones, the name is probably connected
with *Wâbanishi*, "he lives through the winter."

2. In the present Kankakee county, Illinois, about forty miles
south-west of Lake Michigan.

3. See NOTCHIMINE, note 3, p. 114, this volume.

4. Two treaties were signed at Greenville : the first was " Done at Greenville, in the territory of the United States north-west of the river Ohio," August 3, 1795 ; the second, " Done at Greenville, in the state of Ohio," July 22, 1814. Ohio was admitted as a state, February 19, 1803, and Greenville is now the county seat of Darke county, in the western part of the state, bordering on Indiana. The treaty of 1795 was " To put an end to a destructive war, to settle all controversies, and to restore harmony and a friendly intercourse between the said United States and Indian Tribes. . . ." The second treaty was made by the United States for the purpose of gaining certain tribes as allies in the pending war with Great Britain.

5. By the " treaty made and concluded near the mouth of the Mississinewa, upon the Wabash, in the state of Indiana," October 16, 1826, the Potawatomi ceded to the United States their lands in Indiana. " Waupsee " was one of sixty-two members of his tribe to sign. Lewis Cass, J. Brown Ray, and Thomas Tipton were the commissioners for the Government.

6. This was the treaty " concluded at the Missionary Establishments upon the St Joseph, of Lake Michigan, in the Territory of Michigan," September 20, 1828. Lewis Cass and Pierre Menard were the Government commissioners, and " Wa-ban-see " was one of the many members of his tribe to sign the treaty.

7. The Black Hawk War began early in the spring of 1832. See biography of BLACK HAWK, p. 58, this volume.

8. The treaty was signed at Chicago, September 26, 1833. George B. Porter, Thomas J. V. Owen, and William Weatherford were the United States commissioners, and the " United Nation of Chippewa, Ottowa, and Potawatamie " were represented by many members of their tribes. By virtue of the treaty, the tribes ceded to the United States all their lands in the vicinity of Lake Michigan, and accepted other grants west of the Mississippi.

9. It was during this visit to Washington that his portrait was painted by King; it bears No. 105 in the Rhees *Catalogue*, with this entry : " Wah-bawn-see, Causer of Paleness—Principal Chief of the Potawotamies." The original was among the collection bequeathed by King to the Redwood Library, Newport, Rhode Island (see Introduction, Vol. I., p. liii). In the illustration accompanying this sketch, Wabaunsee is shown wearing a head-dress, and a military coat with epaulets, etc.; these have been added to the original portrait as painted by King.

" Wa-bon-seh, or The White Sky," was also painted by Stanley in June, 1843. He was described as the " Principal Chief of the Prairie Band of Potawatomies, residing near Council Bluffs. This chief is a bold and sagacious warrior, but possesses no merit as an orator; his will is submitted to his people through his speaker, a man possessed of great powers of oratory. . . ." (*Portraits of North American Indians, painted by J. M. Stanley*, Washington, Smithsonian Institution, December, 1852, p. 27.)

CHITTEE-YOHOLO
A Seminole Chief

CHITTEE-YOHOLO

(A SEMINOLE CHIEF)

CHITTEE-YOHOLO, or *The snake that makes a noise*, is a Seminole of some note, although but twenty-eight years of age. He was born in Florida, in that region of inaccessible swamps which our gallant troops have found to be anything but a land of flowers. His complexion, which is of a darker hue than that of our other Indians, marks his descent; and there is an expression of fierceness in the countenance indicative of a race living in perpetual hostility. Such has been the history of the Seminoles, who are, as their name indicates, wanderers, or outcasts, from other tribes.[1] A few restless individuals, who separated themselves from the southern nations, either from dislike against the modified habits introduced into those communities by their contact with the whites, or from impatience of the restraints even of savage life, strayed off to the wilds of Florida, and connected themselves with some feeble remnants of the ancient population who lingered in that remote region. While that province remained in possession of the Spaniards,[2] the jealousy of that Government, as well as the peculiar character of the country and the savage nature of the people, rendered it comparatively inaccessible to American curiosity or enterprise; and we knew little of the savage tribes within its limits, except from their occasional depredations upon our frontier, and

from the protection afforded by them to runaway slaves
from the southern states.   These evils became enhanced
during the late war with Great Britain, and one of the
chief inducements to the purchase of Florida by our
Government, was the hope of either taming or driving
away such troublesome neighbours.   We merely touch
the subject in this place for the purpose of showing what
we suppose to be the main cause of the ferocious and
obstinate character of the hostilities that have recently
rendered that region a scene of widespread desolation.
In the history of wars of aggravated malevolence, it will
generally be found that some ancient grudge, festering in
the passions of the frontier population, gives a secret
rancour to the dispute which it could scarcely have
attained from the political differences that are alone
apparent to the public eye.

The first occasion on which Chittee - Yoholo was
engaged, was when General Gaines [3] was surrounded by
the Seminoles; he was one of the hostile party, and
declares that he fought hard, and tried his best to kill the
white men.   Soon after, he was engaged in another fight,
in which he killed a white man, and taking the scalp, he
carried it to the council house of his tribe and threw it at
the feet of an aged warrior—thus invoking the approbation of one who was experienced in the wiles and dangers
of warfare.   The men of the village assembled, danced all
night, recounted their recent adventures, especially that
which they were now celebrating, and, instead of honour-
ing the "lion" of the occasion with a toast, and requiring
a speech in return, as we should have done, they gave him
a new name, Chewasti Emathla—Emathla meaning, *next
to the warrior*, and Chewasti being a kind of surname,
thrown in for euphony.   After that he killed and scalped
another white man, carried in the bloody trophy, and

again the warriors danced in honour of his success; and now they called him Olocta Tuscane Hadja, which means, *The blue crazy warrior;* and again, on bringing in another scalp, they danced round it all night, and called him Olocta Tustennugge, *The Blue Warrior.*[4] All these were stealthy feats performed in the night. The Indians regard such with peculiar gratification, from the high estimate which they place on achievements conducted with cunning and won without exposure. He was constantly out, and usually without companions, stealing upon the sleeping inmates of the cabin, or waylaying the straggler in the forest; so that we may infer that the *Snake that makes a noise,* like the reptile whose name he bears, crouched in silence until the moment when he was about to spring upon his prey.

He was lying in the coverts around Fort Mellon[5] while Paddy Carr[6] was there with the friendly Indians, of whom he counted one hundred and twenty, as he gazed at them from his lurking place. After he had watched a whole night, he joined an assailing party of his people, who fired upon the fort in the morning, and of whom ten were killed; he received a spent ball in his hand, and being unable to manage his gun, retired. He was in a battle with the Tennessee volunteers, in which three Seminoles were killed, whose bodies were dragged to the nearest bushes and hidden, as there was not time to bury or to carry them off. He participated in the battle of Wahoo Swamp, where the Indians lost two warriors and killed several of the whites. The next day the whites came again, and a skirmish ensued. Acee-Yoholo was present in all these fights. On one occasion Chittee-Yoholo drove off a hundred cattle from the settlements of the white people; and he tells of various other battles that he was engaged in, in addition to those we have mentioned.

Having stated that he had seen and recognised "Jim Boy" at the head of the Indians friendly to the whites, he was asked why he had not killed that chief, whose unusual height made him a conspicuous object. He replied that it was not the will of the Great Spirit; and added that he had been in many battles, and not having lost his life, he concluded he should die of sickness, and he supposed that "Jim Boy" would die in the same way. The allusion to the latter was made in consequence of his being present at this conversation.

After the adventures related, and many others, this chief listened to the overtures of the Creek Indians, who invited him to a council, and gave him, as he expresses it, a good talk. He accompanied them to St Augustine, and gave himself up to the commanding officer, by whom he was kindly treated. He has a wife and two children in Arkansas.

NOTES

1. See OPOTHLE-YOHOLO, note 14, p. 34, this volume.

2. See HALPATTER-MICCO, note 2, p. 13, this volume.

3. See TUSTENNUGGEE EMATHLA, note 6, p. 177, this volume. This evidently refers to the battle on the Othlacoochee, fought March 28-29, 1836. It was estimated that 1500 Indians were engaged in the action. General Gaines received a wound in the mouth.

4. The name is probably identical with " Holato-Micco, Blue King, Seminole War Chief," whose portrait, painted by King in 1826, bears No. 107 in the Rhees *Catalogue.* A copy by Inman, in the Peabody Museum, is numbered 28.283.

5. Fort Mellon, on the shore of Lake Monroe, Florida.

6. See biographical sketch of PADDY CARR, p. 46, this volume.

METEA[1]

(A POTAWATOMI CHIEF)

THE strongly marked features of this individual are indicative of his decisive character, and the original cast of his mind. Metea was distinguished as an orator and as a warrior. He was a Potawattimie of unbounded influence in his tribe, and was esteemed by all who knew him as a man of commanding talents. He resided on the little St Joseph's River, about twelve miles from Fort Wayne, in Indiana.

We know little of Metea previous to the unfortunate war between Great Britain and the United States, which commenced in 1812, when his name was prominently connected with one of the most tragic scenes of that conflict. The employment of savages, in the hostilities against our frontier settlements, led to many outrages, but to none more afflicting than the massacre at Chicago.[2] At this solitary spot, far in the wilderness, and entirely detached from any of the populous parts of our country, a small fort had been established, and a few families, supported chiefly by the Indian trade, formed a little village in its vicinity. Captain Heald,[3] the commander, having received orders from General Hull[4] to abandon the post, and retire to Detroit, left the property which could not be moved under charge of a few friendly Indians, and marched out with the garrison, consisting of about fifty regulars. In his train were some females and children belonging to the garrison, and several families of the village, who were unwilling to remain at this solitary and exposed point after the withdrawal of the military. They had scarcely left their fortress when a band of Indians, who had been watching the motions of this ill-fated party, rushed upon them and commenced the work of extermination. Twenty-five of the regulars, and nearly all of the defenceless persons under their charge, were slain. A few of the soldiers were made prisoners, and a few escaped by means of some of those miraculous chances so common in border warfare. Captain Heald and his wife, who accompanied him, were both wounded. We have seen an accomplished lady—at that time, though married, in the prime of her youth—who was a participator in the horrors of that dreadful scene. She concealed herself for a time by plunging into the lake, on whose borders the bloody tragedy was acted, and at last escaped by placing herself under the protection of a young Indian, whom she knew, and who with some difficulty extricated her from the scene of slaughter, and conducted her, after many days of perilous and toilsome wandering in the wilderness, in safety to Detroit. Metea was a conspicuous leader in this affair.

When General Harrison [5] marched to Fort Wayne, in the autumn of 1812, for the purpose of raising the siege of that post, Metea led a party of his tribe to meet and obstruct the advance of the American army. Having posted his men advantageously in a swamp, five miles east of the fort, through which the army of Harrison must pass, he advanced some distance in front of them for the purpose of reconnoitring, and concealed himself behind a tree. General Harrison, who was well skilled in the stratagems of Indian warfare, had thrown his scouts out

in front and on the flanks of his line of march; and as one
of these was silently picking his way through the bushes,
the right arm of Metea, exposed from behind the trunk of
a large tree, caught his eye. To throw his rifle to his
shoulder, to aim with unerring precision at the only part
of his enemy which was visible, and to fire, required but
an instant; and the Potawattimie chief, with his arm
broken, retreated, closely pursued, to his men, who, being
discovered, raised their ambuscade and retired. When
narrating this anecdote, afterwards, to the gentleman from
whom we received it, Metea remarked that he found great
difficulty in escaping his pursuers, and saving his gun.
He was asked why he did not throw away his gun, to
which he replied, "I would rather have lost my life. Had
I returned from the battle without my gun, I should have
been disgraced; but if I had fallen with my face towards
the enemy, my young men would have said that Metea
died like a brave."

Metea was a prominent speaker at the council held at
Chicago, in 1821,[6] and afterwards at the treaty of the
Wabash, in 1826,[7] and on both occasions gave decisive
evidence of talent as a debater. Our informant, who was
for many years a member of Congress, and who saw this
individual on these and various other public occasions,
remarked that he had heard many bursts of eloquence
from him, such as were seldom exceeded by any public
speaker.

There is an interesting account of this chief in the
narrative of *Long's Second Expedition*,[8] performed in 1823,
from which we extract the following paragraphs, descriptive of an interview with him at Fort Wayne, where the
party halted to collect information in regard to the
Potawattimies.

"In order to afford the party an opportunity of obtaining the best information, General Tipton sent for one of the principal chiefs in that vicinity, with whom they conversed two days. The name of this man was Metea, which signifies in the Potawattimie language, *Kiss me.* He was represented to us as being the greatest chief of the nation; we had, however, an opportunity of ascertaining afterwards that he was not the principal chief, but that he had, by his talents as a warrior, and his eloquence as an orator, obtained considerable influence in the councils of his nation. He may be considered as a partisan, who, by his military achievements, has secured to himself the command of an independent tribe. He resides on the St Joseph, about nine miles from Fort Wayne, at an Indian village called Muskwawasepeotan, *The town of the old red wood creek.* Being a chief of distinction, he came accompanied by his brother, as his rank required that he should be assisted by some one to light his pipe, and perform such other duties as always devolve upon attendants. Metea appears to be a man of about forty or forty-five years of age. He is a full-blooded Potawattimie; his stature is about six feet; he has a forbidding aspect, by no means deficient in dignity. His features are strongly marked, and expressive of a haughty and tyrannical disposition; his complexion is dark. Like most of the Potawattimies whom we met with, he is characterised by a low, aquiline, and well-shaped nose. His eyes are small, elongated, and black; they are not set widely apart. His forehead is low and receding; the facial angle amounts to about eighty. His hair is black, and indicates a slight tendency to curl. His cheek-bones are remarkably high and prominent, even for those of an Indian; they are not, however, angular, but present very distinctly the rounded appearance which distinguishes the aboriginal American from the Asiatic. His mouth is large, the

ME-TE-A
A Potawatomi Chief

upper lip prominent. There is something unpleasant in
his looks, owing to his opening one of his eyes wider than
the other, and to a scar which he has upon the wing
of his nostril. On first inspection his countenance would
be considered as expressive of defiance and impetuous
daring, but upon closer scrutiny it is found rather to
announce obstinate constancy of purpose and sullen
fortitude. We behold in him all the characteristics
of the Indian warrior to perfection. If ever an expression
of pity or of the kinder affections belonged to his countenance, it has been driven away by the scenes of bloodshed
and cruelty through which he has passed. His dress was
old and somewhat dirty, but appeared to have been
arranged upon his person with no small degree of care.
It consisted of leather leggings, buttoned on the outside,
a breechcloth of blue broadcloth, and a short checkered
shirt over it; the whole was covered with a blanket,
which was secured round his waist by a belt, and hung
not ungracefully from his shoulders, generally concealing
his right arm, which is rendered useless and somewhat
withered from a wound received during the late war,
when he attacked, with a small party of Indians, the force
that was advancing to the relief of Fort Wayne. His
face was carefully painted with vermilion round his left
eye. Four feathers, coloured without taste, hung behind,
secured to a string which was tied to a lock of his hair.
In our second interview with him he wore a red and white
feather in his head, that was covered with other ornaments
equally deficient in taste. Mr Seymour [9] took a likeness of
him, which was considered a very striking one by all
who knew Metea.

"The chief was accompanied by his brother, who
is much younger, and resembles him, but whose features
indicate a more amiable and interesting disposition. We

observed that during the interview the latter treated
Metea with much respect, always preparing and lighting
his pipe, and never interfering in the conversation unless
when addressed by the chief. On entering the room
where the gentlemen of the party were, Metea shook
hands with the agent, but took no notice of the rest
of the company, until General Tipton had explained to
him, through his interpreter, the nature of the expedition,
the object of his Great Father, the President, in sending
it among the Indians, and the information which would
be expected from him. He informed him likewise that
his time and trouble would be suitably rewarded. The
chief then arose from his seat, shook hands with all who
were present, told them that he would very willingly reply
to all their questions, but that, according to usage, he
was bound to repeat to his nation all the questions that
should be asked and the replies that he would make;
that there were certain points, however, on which he
could give no information without having first obtained
the formal consent of his community; that on these
subjects he would remain silent, while to all others he
would reply with cheerfulness; and that after they should
have concluded their inquiries, he would likewise ask
them some questions upon points which he thought
concerned his nation, and to which he trusted they would
in like manner reply. He then resumed his seat, and
answered with much intelligence, and with a remarkable
degree of patience, all the questions that were asked of
him."

This minute narrative is not only graphic in relation to
the appearance and deportment of Metea, but is highly
descriptive of the decorum, the caution, and the gravity of
the Indian character.

After the war Metea was in the habit of visiting

Malden annually to receive pay, as he expressed it, for his arm, from his British Father. It is probable that he received presents whenever he visited the British posts.

In the latter part of his life, Metea became a warm advocate for educating the youth of his tribe; and in 1827, having collected a number of boys, he took them to the agent at Fort Wayne, who sent them to the Choctaw Academy [10] in Kentucky.

General Tipton, formerly an agent in the Indian Department, and now a senator in Congress, to whom we are indebted for the greater part of this sketch, describes Metea as possessing many noble traits of character. He was ambitious and fond of power, but he was brave and generous, giving freely to his friends, and never betraying the littleness of any selfish propensity. He devoted much of his time, and all his care, to the interests of his nation, and was an able and faithful chieftain. With all these good qualities he was the victim of that fatal passion for ardent spirits which has brought such swift destruction upon his race. The last council he attended was at Fort Wayne, in 1827,[11] when several days were spent in a difficult negotiation, during which he attracted attention by the dignity and propriety of his bearing. When the business was concluded he remarked that he must have a frolic, and the agent permitted him to receive a small bottle of spirits; by some secret means he procured more, and unhappily became intoxicated. In a state of frenzy he roamed through the village, demanding liquor; and at last is supposed to have taken a bottle of aqua fortis from the window of a shop, and swallowed the contents, which, in about half an hour, caused his death.

NOTES

1. Metea, according to the late Dr William Jones, is derived from *Metawä*, " he sulks."

2. The massacre at Fort Dearborn, situated on the south-western corner of Lake Michigan, the site of the present City of Chicago, Illinois, occurred August 15, 1812.

3. Nathan Heald, of New Hampshire, died 1832.

4. General William Hall (1753-1825), in 1805 appointed Governor of the Territory of Michigan.

5. William Henry Harrison (1773-1841), ninth President of the United States, elected 1840. He entered the army in 1791 ; in 1799 he was chosen a delegate to Congress from the North-West Territory, and was appointed Governor of Indiana Territory in 1801. On November 7, 1811, he commanded at the battle of Tippecanoe. He became a major-general in the regular army in 1813.

6. " Treaty made and concluded at Chicago, in the state of Illinois, between Lewis Cass and Solomon Sibley, Commissioners of the U.S., and Ottowa, Chippewa, and Pottawatamie Nations of Indians, Aug. 29, 1821." Mee-te-ay was the second of the Potawatomi signers, of whom there were fifty-five, thus showing the importance of the man.

7. See WABAUNSEE, note 5, p. 199, this volume.

8. *Narrative of an Expedition . . . under the Command of Stephen H. Long, Major U.S.T.E.*, by W. H. Keating, Philadelphia, 1824, Vol. I., p. 88 *et seq.*

9. Samuel Seymour accompanied the expedition as " landscape painter and designer." The portrait of Metea, drawn by Seymour and engraved by J. Hill, appears on plate 3, facing p. 90, Vol. I., of the work cited above.

10. See WATCHEMONNE, note 6, p. 172, this volume.

11. A treaty was concluded at St Joseph, Michigan, September 19, 1827, but Metea does not appear to have been a signer. However, his name was attached to the following treaties : " At the foot of the Rapids of the Miami of Lake Erie," September 29, 1817, signed " Metea," the first of his tribe to sign ; St Mary's, Ohio, October 2, 1818, signed " Metea " ; Chicago, August 29, 1821, signed " Mee-te-ay " ; at the Wabash, October 16, 1826, signed " Metea."

THAYENDANEGEA,[1] OR BRANT

(THE GREAT CAPTAIN OF THE SIX NATIONS)

THERE are few names in Indian history so conspicuous as that of Thayendanegea, or, as he was more commonly called, Joseph Brant. He was for many years the scourge of the frontier settlements of New York and Pennsylvania, whose inhabitants associated with him, in their excited imaginations, all that was fierce and relentless in the savage character. That they had ample reasons for the dread and hatred connected with his name, is but too well attested by the many deeds of rapine and slaughter which stand inseparably united with it upon the pages of history; and notwithstanding the able and benevolent attempt which has recently been made to erase those stains from his memory, it will be difficult for any American ever to look back upon the sanguinary catalogue of his military achievements without a shudder. In the hasty sketch that we shall give, we shall avail ourselves freely of the valuable labours of Mr Stone,[2] whose voluminous life of that chief, recently published, contains all the facts which are necessary for our purpose, and to whose kindness we are indebted for the use of the admirable portrait from which our engraving was taken. But while we compile the facts from that authentic source, and make the due acknowledgment, candour requires us to say that, differing materially from that ingenious writer in our estimate of the character of his hero, we must be held solely responsible for so much of this sketch as is merely matter of opinion.

The parents of Brant were Mohawks, residing at the Canajoharie Castle,[3] in New York ; but he is said to have been born on the banks of the Ohio, in 1742, during an excursion of his parents to that region.   He was not a chief by birth, although his family seems to have been one of some consideration ; and it is affirmed that he was the grandson of one of the five chiefs [4] who visited England in 1710, during the reign of Queen Anne.

In his youth, Brant became a favourite and protégé of Sir William Johnson,[5] the most celebrated of all the agents employed by the British Government in the management of their Indian affairs ; and who, by his talents, his conciliatory manners, and his liberality, enjoyed an unbounded popularity among the native tribes.   A well-known circumstance in the history of this gentleman, is thus related by Mrs Grant, of Laggan,[6] in her very agreeable *Memoirs of an American Lady:* "Becoming a widower in the prime of life, he connected himself with an Indian maiden, daughter to a sachem, who possessed an uncommonly agreeable person, and good understanding ; and whether ever formally married to him according to our usage or not, continued to live with him in great union and affection all his life."   Mary Brant, or, as she was called, *Miss Molly*, was the person here alluded to.   She was the sister of the subject of this notice, and to that union he owed the patronage of Sir William Johnson, and the favour of the British Government, which placed him in the road to promotion.   The successful manner in which he availed himself of these advantages is attributable to his own abilities.

At the age of thirteen he is said to have been present

with Sir William Johnson at the battle of Lake George,[7] in which the French were defeated, and their commander, the Baron Dieskau, mortally wounded. He served under Sir William in 1756, and again in 1759, when that commander gained a high reputation by a brilliant campaign.

Among the facts most honourable to the memory of Sir William Johnson, was the attention which at that early day he paid to the moral improvement of the Mohawks. The political agents of European Governments have seldom concerned themselves further in the affairs of the Indians than to use them in war, or make them a source of profit. Sir William selected a number of Mohawk youths and sent them to an Indian missionary school,[8] which was established at Lebanon, in Connecticut, under the direction of the Rev. Doctor E. Wheelock, afterwards President of Dartmouth College, which grew out of this small foundation. Thayendanegea, the promising brother of *Miss Molly*, was one of the lads thus selected, and the only one who is known to have derived any benefit from the discipline of the school-room, except Samson Occom,[9] who became a preacher and an author. The date of this transaction is not known, but it is supposed with reason to have immediately ensued the campaign of 1759. One of these lads, being directed by Doctor Wheelock's son to saddle his horse, refused, on the ground that he was a gentleman's son, and not obliged to do a menial office. "Do you know what a gentleman is?" inquired young Wheelock. "I do," replied the aboriginal youngster; "a gentleman is a person who keeps race horses, and drinks Madeira wine, which neither you nor your father do—therefore saddle the horse yourself."

The education of Brant must have been quite limited, for in 1762 we find him employed as an interpreter, in

the service of Mr Smith, a missionary who visited the
Mohawks in that year; and a war breaking out shortly
after, he engaged eagerly in a pursuit more consonant
with his taste and early habits.   He probably served one
campaign, and returned in 1764.   In the following year,
he was living at Canajoharie,[10] having previously married
the daughter of an Oneida chief, and here he remained
peaceably for three years.   "He now lives in a decent
manner," said a writer of that day, "and endeavours to
teach his poor brethren the things of God, in which his
own heart seems much engaged.   His house is an asylum
for the missionaries in that wilderness."   Being frequently
engaged as an interpreter by the missionaries, his opportunities for acquiring religious instruction were considerable, and he is supposed to have assisted Doctor Barclay,
in 1769, in revising the Mohawk Prayer Book.[11]   About
the year 1771, he was frequently employed by Sir William
Johnson, both at home and upon various distant missions.
He also assisted Doctor Stuart[12] in translating the Acts
of the Apostles into the Mohawk tongue.

In 1772 or 1773, Thayendanegea became the subject of
serious religious impressions.   He attached himself to the
Church, and was a regular communicant; and from his
serious deportment and the great anxiety he manifested
for the introduction of Christianity among his people,
hopes were entertained that he would become a powerful
auxiliary in that cause.   In a brief space those impressions
were erased, and Brant resumed the trade of war, with all
its savage horrors, with the same avidity with which the
half-tamed wolf returns to his banquet of blood.

Sir William Johnson died in 1774, when the storm of
the American Revolution was lowering in the political
horizon, and on the eve of bursting.   He was succeeded
in his title and estates by his son, Sir John Johnson, and

in his official authority as Superintendent of the Indian Department, by his son-in-law, Colonel Guy Johnson, neither of whom inherited his talents, his virtues, or his popularity.   They continued, however, with the aid of Brant, and "Miss Molly," who was a woman of decided abilities, to sway a considerable influence over the Six Nations, and in connection with Colonel John Butler, and his son, Colonel Walter N. Butler, became leaders in some of the darkest scenes of that memorable epoch.[13]

We are not permitted to enter minutely upon the complicated intrigues of these individuals, nor to detail the atrocities committed under their auspices.   Through their active agency the Indians within the sphere of their influence were not only alienated from the American people, but brought forward as active parties in the war. The American Congress and the authorities of New York endeavoured in vain to dissuade the Johnsons from enlisting the Indians in this unhappy contest; but they persisted, with a full knowledge of the horrors attendant on the warfare of savages; and it is now ascertained that Sir Guy Carleton gave the sanction of his great and worthy name to this unnatural and dishonourable form of hostility.   The consequence was that the Indians were turned loose upon the frontiers, and that a war of the most cruel and exterminating character ensued between those who had once been neighbours.

These outrages were the more to be deplored, as they might, to a great degree, have been prevented.   The American Revolution was not a sudden ebullition of popular fury, nor were the leaders mere adventurers reckless of consequences.   It resulted from the deliberate resolves of a whole people, seeking the redress of grievances, and who desired to purchase political freedom with the smallest possible expenditure of human life.   It was directed throughout by men of the highest character for talents and moral worth—men who risked everything in the contest, and who had too much reputation at stake to be careless of public opinion.   They knew that a civil war, under the best auspices, is usually fruitful of scenes of private revenge and vindictive outrage; and from the first they endeavoured, by their counsels and example, to exclude from this conflict all unnecessary violence, and to give it a tone of magnanimity and forbearance.   Especially did they deprecate the employment of the savage tribes, whose known rule of warfare is extermination without regard to age or sex—who acknowledge none of those humane regulations which, in modern times, have disarmed war of many of its horrors; and who, having no interest in the event of this contest, would only increase the effusion of blood without strengthening the hands or gaining the friendship of either party.   While, therefore, they declined the assistance of the Indians, they earnestly besought the British authorities to pursue a similar policy. It is greatly to be deplored that other counsels prevailed. The British officers, in the zeal of their loyalty, and from contempt for those whom they considered as traitors, were by no means choice in the measures they adopted to suppress the rebellion; and not being inhabitants of the colonies, having neither property nor families exposed to violence, they did not feel the same personal interest which the colonists felt, in the prevention of lawless outrage.

About the year 1776, Thayendanegea became the principal war chief of the confederacy of the Six Nations— it being an ancient usage to confer that station upon a Mohawk.[14]   He had not at that time greatly distinguished himself as a warrior, and we are at a loss to account for his sudden elevation, unless we suppose that he owed it, in some degree at least, to the patronage of the Johnsons, and the peculiar circumstances in which he was placed. It was deemed important by the British to secure the alliance of the Six Nations. Little Abraham, the chief of the Mohawks, was friendly to the colonists; other of the older warriors may have felt the same predilection, while Brant, whose ambition was equal to his ability and address, may have been less scrupulous in regard to the service that would be expected from the partisan who should lead the Indian forces. With the office of leader he acquired the title of "Captain Brant," by which he was afterwards known.

Mr Stone, in his *Life of Brant*,[15] remarks, in reference to this appointment :—"For the prosecution of a border warfare, the officers of the Crown could scarcely have engaged a more valuable auxiliary. Distinguished alike for his address, his activity, and his courage; possessing, in point of stature and symmetry of person, the advantage of most men even among his own well-formed race—tall, erect, and majestic, with the air and mien of one born to command—having, as it were, been a man of war from his boyhood—his name was a tower of strength among the warriors of the wilderness. Still more extensive was his influence rendered, by the circumstance that he had been much employed in the civil service of the Indian Department, under Sir William Johnson, by whom he was often deputed upon embassies among the tribes of the confederacy, and to those yet more distant, upon the great lakes and rivers of the north-west, by reason of which his knowledge of the whole country and people was accurate and extensive."

Immediately after receiving this appointment, Brant made his first voyage to England,[16] and his biographer suggests that this visit may have resulted from a hesitation

on the part of the chief, in regard to committing himself
in the war with the colonies.   A portion of the confederacy
inclined to the colonial side of the controversy, others were
disposed to be neutral.   Brant and some of his friends
favoured the British, while some brilliant successes recently
gained by the Americans " presented another view of the
case which was certainly entitled to grave consideration."
By making the voyage he gained time, and was enabled
to observe for himself the evidences of the power and
resources of the King, and to judge how far it would be
wise to embark his own fortunes on the side of his ancient
ally.   He was well received in England, and admitted to
the best society.   Having associated with educated men
all his life, and having naturally an easy and graceful
carriage, it is probable that his manners and conversation
entitled him to be thus received, and as he was an " Indian
King," he was too valuable an ally to be neglected.   Among
those who took a fancy to him was Boswell, "and an
intimacy seems to have existed between him and the
Mohawk chief, since the latter sat for his picture at the
request of this most amiable of egotists."   We can imagine
that a shrewd Indian chief would have been a rare "lion "
for Boswell.   He also sat to Romney [17] for a portrait for
the Earl of Warwick.

After a short visit, during which he received the hospitality of many of the nobility and gentry, and was much
caressed at Court, he returned to America, confirmed in
his predilection for the royal cause, and determined to
take up the hatchet against the Americans, agreeably to
the stipulations of a treaty which he had made with Sir
Guy Carleton.   He landed privately, somewhere in the
neighbourhood of New York, and pursued his journey
alone and secretly through the woods to Canada, crossing
the whole breadth of the State of New York, by a route

which could not have embraced a shorter distance than three hundred miles.

The determination of the Mohawk chief to take up arms caused great regret in the neighbouring colonies, where every exertion had been made to induce the Six Nations to remain neutral; and many influential individuals continued to the last to use their personal efforts to effect that desirable object. Among others, President Wheelock interfered, and wrote a long epistle to his former pupil, in which he urged upon him as a man and a Christian, the various considerations that should induce him to stand aloof from this contest between the King and his subjects. "Brant"—we quote again from Mr Stone—"replied very ingeniously. Among other things, he referred to his former residence with the Doctor—recalled the happy hours he had spent under his roof—and referred especially to his prayers, and the family devotions to which he had listened. He said he could never forget those prayers; and one passage in particular was so often repeated, that it could never be effaced from his mind. It was among other of his good preceptor's petitions, 'that they might be able to live as *good subjects*—to fear God and *honour the King.*'"

The first occasion on which we find Brant conspicuously mentioned as a commander, is at "The Cedars," a post held by Colonel Bedell, with three hundred and ninety provincials, which was assailed by Captain Forster, with six hundred British troops and Indians, the latter led by Brant. The American commander could easily have defended his position, but was intimidated by a threat from the enemy, "that should the siege continue, and any of the Indians be slain, it would be impossible, in the event of a surrender, for the British commander to prevent a general massacre"; and were induced by "these deceptive and unjustifiable means," as they are correctly termed by

General Washington, to surrender. Brant is praised by his biographer for having exerted himself, after the surrender, to prevent the massacre of the prisoners, and particularly for rescuing from torture Captain John McKinstry, whom the Indians were preparing to burn. We confess that we see nothing to approve in the whole transaction. The British and Indian commanders were both bound by the capitulation to protect the prisoners— they were bound by the plainest dictates of humanity, as well as by the code of military honour—and we cannot afford to praise men for doing merely a duty, the neglect of which would have covered them with infamy. The allegation that the Indians could not be controlled, which we find repeated on many occasions, was well characterised by the pure and high-minded Washington, as "deceptive," for there are no troops whose leaders exercise over them a more absolute control. But there can be no apology offered for the employment of savages who could not be restrained from the murder of prisoners; and Sir Guy Carleton, in using this species of force, has left an indelible blot on his name. Nor can we excuse Brant for deliberately engaging in such a warfare. He had received the education of a civilised man, had read the Scriptures, and professed to be a disciple of Christ, and he knew that the atrocities practised by the Indians were unjustifiable. The Mohawks had no interest in this quarrel; it was wholly indifferent to them whether the Government should be royal or republican; and they engaged in it as mercenaries, employed by a distant Government to fight against their own neighbours. The principle involved was beyond their comprehension: Brant might have had some idea of it, but if he had any actual knowledge on the subject, he must have known that neither party acknowledged the Indians as having any rights at stake. They could have had no inducement to take either side but the lust for blood and plunder. We must clearly, therefore, draw a broad line of distinction between such men as Philip, Pontiac, and Tecumthe, who fought in defence of their native soil, animated by a high-toned patriotism, and Thayendanegea, who was hired to fight in a quarrel in which he had no interest.

Among the various efforts made to induce the Indians to remain neutral, and to soften the horrors of this war, by excluding the dreadful agency of the tomahawk and firebrand, was a conference with Brant, sought by General Herkimer.[18] The latter was a substantial citizen, residing on the Mohawk River, near the Little Falls, and in that part of the country most exposed to the incursions of the Six Nations. He was a man of sagacity and courage, whose abilities had recommended him to his countrymen as a leader in their border wars; and having taken up arms in the sacred cause of liberty, and in defence of the firesides of his neighbours, he was chosen a general officer. He had been the friend and neighbour of Brant, and now sought a meeting with that chief for the purpose of using his personal influence to detach him from the war; or perhaps to drive him from the equivocal position he then occupied, by bringing out his real views, so that he might be trusted as a friend or treated as an enemy.

They met near Unadilla. The parties were encamped two miles apart, and about midway between them a temporary shed was erected, sufficiently large to shelter two hundred persons. It was stipulated that their arms were to be left at their respective encampments. Here they met, each attended by a few followers, and a long conversation ensued, in the course of which Brant became offended at some remark that was made, "and by a signal to the warriors attending him at a short distance, they ran back to their encampment, and soon afterwards appeared again with their rifles, several of which were discharged while the shrill war whoop rang through the forest." What means were used by Herkimer to counteract this treachery, we are not told, but it appears that the parties separated without bloodshed.

A singular version is given of the meeting between these leaders, which occurred on the following morning, by appointment. General Herkimer, we are told, selected a person named Waggoner, with three associates, to perform "a high and important duty." "His design, the General said, was to take the lives of Brant and his three attendants, on the renewal of their visit that morning. For this purpose he should rely on Waggoner and his three associates, on the arrival of the chief and his friends within the circle, as on the preceding day, each to select his man, and at a concerted signal to shoot them down on the spot. There is something so revolting—so rank and foul —in this project of meditated treachery, that it is difficult to reconcile it with the well-known character of General Herkimer." Had the author from whom we quote narrated the simple facts, without the comment so injurious to the memory of a venerated patriot of the Revolution, there would have been no difficulty in reconciling them with the character of a brave soldier; for in the sequel no attempt was made on the life of Brant, and the orders of Herkimer —if such orders were ever given—were doubtless precautionary, and intended only to be executed in defence of himself and his companions. Herkimer sought the friendship of Brant, not his life. His mission was peaceful: he sought to conciliate the Indians, not to irritate them by an act of rash violence. He was met in an overbearing spirit by the savage chief, who, having already hired out his tribe to the officers of the King, had not the

candour to admit that he was no longer free to treat with
the King's enemies, but endeavoured, like the wolf in the
fable, to fix a quarrel on his proposed victim. He came
to the meeting on the second day, as on the first, followed
by his warriors, in violation of the express terms of the
conference. "I have five hundred warriors with me," said
he, "armed and ready for battle. You are in my power,
but as we have been friends and neighbours, I will not take
advantage of you." "Saying which," continues his biographer, "a host of his armed warriors darted forth from
the contiguous forest, all painted and ready for the on-
slaught, as the well-known war whoop but too clearly
proclaimed." The interview ended without bloodshed.
We are wholly at a loss to find any evidence upon which
to throw the slightest blame upon Herkimer, or to palliate
the conduct of Brant, who evidently sought to provoke a
quarrel which might afford a pretence for bloodshed.

From this time we contemplate with less pleasure the
character of the highly gifted Mohawk, who, from the lofty
and noble eminence on which he had placed himself, as an
example and teacher of civilisation, descended suddenly
into a common marauder. Throwing aside all profession
of neutrality, he now attended a council held by British
commissioners, and pledged himself and his people to take
up the hatchet in His Majesty's service.

"From that day," says his biographer, Mr Stone,
"Thayendanegea was the acknowledged chief of the Six
Nations, and he soon became one of the master-spirits of
the motley forces employed by Great Britain in her attempts
to recover the Mohawk Valley, and to annoy the other
settlements of what then constituted the North-Western
frontier. Whether in the conduct of a campaign, or of a
scouting party, in the pitched battle or the foray, this
crafty and dauntless chieftain was sure to be one of the

most efficient, as he was one of the bravest, of those engaged. Combining with the native hardihood and sagacity of his race the advantages of education and civilised life—in acquiring which he had lost nothing of his activity and power of endurance—he became the most powerful border foe with whom the provincials had to contend, and his name was a terror to the land. His movements were at once so secret and so rapid, that he seemed almost to be clothed with the power of ubiquity."

One of his earliest military movements was a descent upon the defenceless settlement of Cherry Valley,[19] undertaken for the purpose of killing and capturing the inhabitants, and devastating their property. An accident saved them, for that time, from the blow. It happened, that as Brant and his warriors were about to issue from a wood in which they lurked, to attack a private house, the residence of Colonel Campbell, some children, who had formed themselves into a military corps, were seen parading with their wooden guns in front of the mansion, and the Indians mistaking them for real soldiers, retired. Balked of their prey they slunk into the wood, and lay concealed, brooding over their schemes of malevolent mischief. Unhappily at this moment a promising young American officer, Lieut. Wormwood, travelling on horseback, with one attendant, reached the spot, and was shot down by the Indians, and *scalped by Brant's own hand.* His biographer adds, that the chief "lamented the death of this young man. They were not only acquaintances, but friends." Yet he took the scalp with his own hand.

A most melancholy illustration of the wickedness of employing savages in war is afforded in the tragic fate of Miss McCrea—a lovely young woman, engaged to a British officer, and on her way to meet and be united with him, when she was captured, murdered, and mangled in the

most shocking manner, by the Indians attached to the
British army.   This occurred on the northern frontier, and
at about the period to which we have brought this sketch.
About the same time an Indian secretly entered the house
of the American General Schuyler,[20] for the purpose of
assassinating that illustrious person, whose life was saved
by the fidelity of his servants.

We notice these events merely to show the character of
the war which was waged upon the frontiers, and in
which Brant was a conspicuous man—an unsparing
warfare against private individuals and private property.
But we cannot in a brief outline like this, enter upon a
minute narrative of the exploits of that chieftain, who was
constantly in the field, sometimes with the British forces,
but more frequently leading parties of Indians and Tories
against the settlements.   His most important service about
this period was at the battle of Oriskany, where General
Herkimer,[21] with a small body of provincials, came into
conflict with an Indian force led by Brant.   The latter had
selected a position with admirable skill, and formed an
ambuscade in a defile, through which the Americans were
to pass, and fell suddenly upon the troops while they were
crossing a ravine.   The Americans were thrown into
irretrievable disorder, but fought with courage.   General
Herkimer was desperately wounded early in the engagement, but caused himself to be seated on his saddle, at the
foot of a tree, against which he leaned for support, and in
this position continued to direct the battle with unabated
coolness and judgment.   The conflict was fierce and the
slaughter great.   The Tories and savages, superior in
numbers, closed around the Americans, fighting hand-to-
hand, and the gallant little army of Herkimer seemed
doomed to destruction, when a violent storm bursting
suddenly upon them, separated the combatants for about

an hour. The Americans availed themselves of this respite to prepare to renew the action, and in the event effected a masterly retreat, under the orders of their intrepid commander, who was brought off on a rudely constructed litter. Of this brave and excellent man it is told, that during the hottest period of the battle, while sitting wounded upon his saddle, and propped against a tree, he deliberately took a tinder box from his pocket, lighted his pipe, and smoked with perfect composure; and when his men, seeing him exposed to the whole fire of the enemy, proposed to remove him to a place where there would be less danger, he said, "No, I will face the enemy." He did not long survive the battle. Both parties claimed the victory. It was a well-fought field, in which Brant showed himself a consummate leader.

At the opening of the campaign, in 1778, Mr Stone relates that "Thayendanegea returned to his former haunts on the Susquehanna, Oghkwaga, and Unadilla. He soon proved himself an active and dreaded partisan. No matter for the difficulties or the distance, whenever a blow could be struck to any advantage, Joseph Brant was sure to be there. Frequent, moreover, were the instances in which individuals and even whole families disappeared, without any knowledge on the part of those who were left, that an enemy had been there. The smoking ruins of the cabins, the charred bones of the dead, and the slaughtered carcasses of domestic animals, were the only testimonials of the cause of the catastrophe, until the return of a captive, or the disclosure of some prisoner taken from the foe, furnished more definite information. But there is no good evidence that Brant was himself a participator in secret murders, or attacks upon isolated individuals or families; and there is much reason to believe that the bad feelings of many of the loyalists induced them to perpetrate greater enormities themselves, and prompt the parties of Indians whom they often led, to commit greater barbarities than the savages would have done had they been left to themselves."

We have given the whole of the above paragraph—fact and inference—in order that the character of Brant may have the full benefit of the defence set up by his biographer. Negative proof is, at best, unsatisfactory; and it would not be strange if there were in fact no evidence of the leader in deeds so secret as those alluded to. That he was the master-spirit of the predatory warfare waged against the frontier settlements of New York, is distinctly asserted in the commencement of the paragraph, and that warfare consisted almost entirely of "secret murders, and attacks upon private individuals or families." And we see no reason for drawing a distinction between himself and the Johnsons and Butlers, who directed the measures of the loyalist inhabitants of that region. The sin and the shame of these men consisted in warring at all upon the homes of the peasantry—in carrying the atrocities of murder and arson to the firesides of the inhabitants—in turning loose bands of savages, whether red or white, to burn houses, devastate fields, and slaughter women and children. There can be no apology for such inhuman deeds; and it is in vain to attempt by nice distinctions to discriminate between the heads that planned and the brutal hands that per-petrated, schemes so fraught with horror—unless it be to pronounce the heavier malediction on the former—upon those who originated the plan with a full knowledge of the fearful outrages which must attend its execution, and who persevered in such a warfare after having witnessed, even in one instance, its direful effects.

We have not room to enter into a detailed account of the murders and burnings of this energetic marauder; a general statement from the pages of the biographer already quoted will be sufficient for our purpose. "The inhabitants around the whole border, from Saratoga north of Johnstown, and west to the German Flats, thence south stretching down to Unadilla, and thence eastwardly crossing the Susquehanna, along Charlotte River to Harpersfield, and thence back to Albany—were necessarily an armed yeomanry, watching for themselves, and standing sentinels for each other in turn; harassed daily by conflicting rumours; now admonished of the approach of the foe in the night by the glaring flames of a neighbour's house; or compelled suddenly to escape from his approach, at a time and in a direction the least expected. Such was the tenure of human existence around the confines of this whole district of country, from the spring of 1777 to the end of the contest in 1782."

The destruction of the settlement of Wyoming,[22] by a British force under Colonel John Butler, of three hundred regulars and Tories, and five hundred Indians, has been recorded in the histories of the Revolution, and rendered immortal in the verse of Campbell. It was signalised by cruelty and perfidy such as have never been excelled; and although it now appears that many exaggerations were published in relation to it, the melancholy truths that remain uncontradicted are sufficient to stamp this dark transaction with everlasting infamy.

The participation of Brant in this expedition is denied by Mr Stone, who says: "Whether Captain Brant was at any time in company with this expedition, is doubtful; but it is certain, in the face of every historical authority, British and American, that so far from being engaged in the battle, he was many miles distant at the time of its occurrence. Such has been the uniform testimony of the British officers engaged in that expedition, and

such was always the word of Thayendanegea himself."
He also alludes to a letter written after the death of Brant
by his son, to the poet Campbell, in which the younger
Brant is said to have "successfully vindicated his father's
memory from calumny," and to one received by himself
from a Mr Frey, the son of a loyalist, who was engaged
in that atrocious affair.

We do not think the point placed in issue by this
denial of sufficient importance to induce us to spend
much time in its examination. The character of Brant
would not be materially affected by settling it one way
or the other, for the massacre at Wyoming differs in no
essential particular from a number of sanguinary deeds in
which that chief was the acknowledged leader; and it was
part of a system which unavoidably led to such cruelties.
It is not improbable that Brant himself took this view
of the question, for although he lived thirty years after that
affair, during the whole of which time he was mentioned
by British and American writers as one of its leaders,
and the chief instigator of the cruelties committed, he
does not appear to have ever publicly disclaimed the
connection with it imputed to him. "Gertrude of
Wyoming," one of the noblest monuments of British genius,
was familiarly known wherever the English language was
spoken, and the American people were soothed by the
circumstance that the "Monster Brant" and his deeds
were denounced by an English bard of the highest standing.
Campbell undertook to spurn from the national character
the foul stain of those dastardly and wicked murders, and
to place the opprobrium on the heads of certain individuals
—and none denied the justice of the decree. Brant was
an educated man, who mingled in the best provincial
society, and corresponded with many gentlemen in Europe
and America. He certainly knew the position in regard

to public opinion which he occupied, and had the means to rectify the wrong, if any existed. It would be a singular fact, too, if "*every* historical authority, British and American," concurred in a statement which the "*uniform* testimony of the British officers engaged in the battle" contradicted, and "that such was always the word of Thayendanegea himself," and yet that no formal refutation should have been attempted in the lifetime of the chief, nor until forty-five years after the event. The testimony of the British officers would have been satisfactory; but we apprehend that the mere hearsay evidence of two of the sons of the actors in these events, will hardly be received now in opposition to the unanimous and uncontradicted statements of contemporary writers.

The destruction of the delightful settlement of the German Flats, in 1778, was the admitted exploit of Brant. The inhabitants, providentially advised of his secret march upon them, were hastily gathered together—men, women, and children—into two little forts, Herkimer and Dayton. The chief crept upon them with his usually stealthy pace, "unconscious that his approach had been notified to the people in season to enable them to escape the blow of his uplifted arm. Before the dawn he was on foot, and his warriors sweeping through the settlement, so that the torch might be almost simultaneously applied to every building it contained. Just as the day was breaking in the East, the fires were kindled, and the whole section of the valley was speedily illuminated by the flames of houses and barns, and all things else combustible." Such is the account of the writer who contends "that there is no good evidence that Brant was himself a participator" in such transactions. There were burned on this occasion sixty-three dwelling-houses, fifty-seven barns, three grist-mills, and two saw-mills. What the fate of the inhabitants would have been had they remained in their houses, as Brant supposed them to be when he ordered the firebrands to be applied, our readers may readily imagine. It does not appear that the forts were molested, nor does Brant seem on this occasion to have sought collision with armed men. The marauders retired, chagrined, "that neither scalps nor prisoners were to grace their triumph"; "and the settlement, which but the day before for ten miles had smiled in plenty and beauty was now houseless and destitute."

In the same year Cherry Valley was again ravaged, and those enormities repeated, of which we have perhaps already related too many. Among the numerous murders perpetrated on this occasion were those of the whole family of Mr Wells, except a boy [23] who was at school, at Albany, and who afterwards became a distinguished member of the Bar. "The destruction of the family of Mr Wells was marked by circumstances of peculiar barbarity. It was boasted by one of the Tories that he had killed Mr Wells while engaged in prayer—certainly a happy moment for a soul to wing its flight to another state of existence; but what the degree of hardihood that could boast of compassing the death of an unarmed man at such a moment! His sister Jane was distinguished alike for her beauty, her accomplishments, and her virtues. As the savages rushed into the house, she fled to a pile of wood on the premises, and endeavoured to conceal herself. She was pursued and arrested by an Indian, who, with perfect composure, wiped and sheathed his dripping knife, and took his tomahawk from his girdle. At this instant a Tory, who had formerly been a domestic in the family, sprang forward and interposed in her behalf, claiming her as a sister. The maiden too, who understood somewhat of the Indian language, implored for mercy

—but in vain. With one hand the Indian pushed the Tory from him, and with the other planted his hatchet deep in her temple!"

In the valley where these atrocities were committed there was a small fort, defended by a few men, but the Indians, "being received by a brisk fire of grape and musketry from the garrison, avoided the fort, and directed their attention chiefly to plundering and laying waste the village, having sated themselves in the outset with blood." Such is the warfare of the Indian—cool, patient, and brave, when compelled to face danger; but always, when acting from choice, shunning the contest with armed men, and seeking out the weak and unprepared.

In the biography of Brant, from which we select these facts, we find an attempt to vindicate his conduct on this occasion. It is said that he was "not the commander of this expedition, and if he had been it is not certain he could have compelled a different result. But it is certain that his conduct on that fatal day was neither barbarous nor ungenerous. On the contrary, he did all in his power to prevent the shedding of innocent blood." We are at a loss to know what blood was shed on that occasion that was not *innocent* blood. The expedition was not directed against any military post, nor any body of armed men, but against the homes of peaceful farmers, whose houses and barns were burnt, and whose wives and children were slaughtered. "The torch was applied *indiscriminately to every dwelling-house,* and in fact, to every building in the village." The country was desolated for miles around; and human life was extinguished without regard to the form in which it existed, however reverend, or beautiful, or innocent. Those of the inhabitants who were not slain, were driven away like a herd of beasts. At night they were huddled together, under the charge of sentinels, and forced to lie half-naked on the ground, with no cover but the heavens. Of two of these unfortunate beings the following heartrending anecdote is told. "Mrs Cannon, an aged lady, and the mother of Mrs Campbell, being unfitted for travelling by reason of her years, the Indian having both in charge despatched the mother with his hatchet, by the side of her daughter. Mrs Campbell was driven along by the uplifted hatchet, having a child in her arms eighteen months old, with barbarous rapidity, until the next day, when she was favoured with a more humane master."

These are but a few of a long list of similar atrocities which, in our apprehension, were both barbarous and ungenerous. Butler and Brant each endeavoured subsequently to cast the stigma of these cruelties on each other, the one alleging that he was not the commander in the enterprise, and the other that the crafty Mohawk had secretly instigated his people to these excesses to advance his own ends; but impartial history will not attempt to trace the imaginary line of distinction between the leader in such an inroad and the second in command—in a case, too, where both were volunteers, and neither had any legal or actual control over the other. Neither of them were natives of Great Britain—both were mercenaries, serving occasionally for the emolument, or the gratification to be earned in that service. The murder of women and the devastation of fields formed their chosen path of honour —the smoking ruins of cottages and the charred bones of infants were the monuments of their warlike deeds. Nor can we admit the validity of the often repeated apology for Brant—that he could not control his warriors. There are no troops in the world that are more completely under the command of their leaders than the Indians. Their discipline is exact and uncompromising. From infancy

the Indian is taught self-control, and obedience to his
superiors; and death on the spot, by the hand of the leader,
is the usual punishment of contumacy. But Brant and
Butler knew when they set out on these enterprises that
the sole object was to burn dwellings, to fire barns, to
slaughter unarmed men, women, and children; and if it
was true, that having turned loose their savages to the
work of blood they could no longer control them, we do
not see what they gain by this excuse. The savages did
the work which had been planned for them; and we fancy
there is little room for casuistry to scan nicely the degrees
of barbarity which marked the conduct of the different
actors.

In an action near Minisink,[24] in 1779, in which his
opponents were armed men, Brant deserved the credit of
having adroitly planned and boldly executed an attack.
The usual cruelties, however, were perpetrated, and
seventeen wounded men, who were under charge of a
surgeon, perished by the tomahawk.

Brant fought again at the battle of the Chemung[25]
in the same year, where fifteen hundred Tories and
Indians, commanded by himself, the Butlers, and the
Johnsons, were beaten by the Americans under General
Sullivan.

It was during the campaign of Sullivan that Red
Jacket first made his appearance as a conspicuous man
among the Indians, and a feud commenced between him
and Brant which continued throughout their lives. Brant
accused Red Jacket[26] not merely of cowardice, but also of
treachery, and asserted that he had discovered a secret
correspondence between the latter and the American
General. Red Jacket, it was said, was in the habit of
holding secret councils with a number of young warriors,
and with some timid and disaffected leaders, and at length

sent a runner with a flag to General Sullivan, to advise
him that a spirit of discontent prevailed among the Indians.
Brant, who was confidentially informed of these proceedings, privately despatched two warriors to waylay and
assassinate the runner, which being effected, put an end
to the intrigue.

In 1780, Brant led a party of forty-three Indians and
seven Tories against the settlement of Harpersfield, which
was surprised and destroyed; and he then bent his steps
towards Scoharie, which he supposed to be undefended.
On his way he encountered Captain Harper and fourteen
men, who were making sugar in the woods, of whom
three were killed and the remainder taken. Harper, a
brave man, famed for more than one hardy exploit, determined to save the settlement of Scoharie from the dreadful calamity of a visit from Brant, and on being questioned
as to its defences, coolly stated that three hundred
continental troops had just been stationed there, and
persisted in this story until the Indians were induced to
retrace their steps to Niagara. On their way they fell in
with an old man and his two youthful grandsons, who
were also captured; but finding the old man unable to
keep pace with the party, he was put to death, and his
scalp added to the trophies of the expedition. It was
intended that on the arrival of the party at Niagara the
prisoners should be subjected to the barbarous torture of
running the gauntlet, but Brant frustrated this plan by
sending a message secretly to the commander of the fort
at that place, in consequence of which they were received,
on their arrival at the outposts, by a party of regulars, who
took possession of them. We cheerfully accord the praise
due to this act of humanity.

We shall not pursue the Mohawk chief through all
the windings of his crafty and sanguinary career. He

continued until the close of the war in 1782 to harass the settlements by such incursions as we have described. Those who delight in recitals of tragic interest may find a series of such events well told in Mr Stone's work. They are too numerous to be related at length in such a sketch as this, and too much alike in their general outlines to be abridged with advantage. In perusing this history the heart sickens at the oft-repeated tale of domestic agony—the tearing of husbands, wives, and children from each other's embrace—the captivity of delicate females—the driving of half-clad and bare-footed women and children through the wilderness, exposed to all the vicissitudes of climate—the torture of prisoners— the thousand varieties of savage cruelty. All these deeds, which we contemplate with comparative composure when told of untaught savages stung to rage by the invasion of their hunting grounds, awaken a lively sensation of horror when we behold them deliberately planned and executed under the flag of a great nation, by persons of European descent, and by a sagacious chief who had felt and acknowledged the advantages of civilisation, who had reaped honour and advantage through an intercourse with the whites, which, previous to this unhappy war, had been characterised by mutual confidence and kindness. Brant had no wrongs to avenge upon the American people—he had nothing to gain by the part he acted but the pay of a mercenary and the plunder of a marauder, while the effect of these hostilities upon his tribe was demoralising and destructive of that reform which he professed to be endeavouring to introduce among them.

It is not to be denied that this dark picture is occasionally relieved by acts of mercy on the part of the Mohawk chief. But we are not inclined to accord much praise to isolated acts of generosity, that glimmer at distant intervals through a long career of brutal violence. The miser who devotes all his life to the hoarding of gold, gains no applause for an occasional freak of generosity; nor does the savage who pauses in the midst of a prolonged series of murders to spare a woman, or a trembling child, deserve the laurel of the hero. We estimate the character of a man by his general conduct, and while we forgive the little errors of a good man, we must on the same principle pass over the accidental departures of a depraved mind from its habitual wrongdoing. It is a common but sound objection against fictitious writings, that characters essentially bad are tricked out in a few redeeming virtues which recommend them to the thoughtless reader; and with still stronger reason should this grave argument of the moralist be applied to the personages of history, whose habitual crimes should not be lost sight of amid the lustre of a few bright actions.

In 1785, the war being over, Brant made another visit to England, where he was well received. On being presented to the King he declined kissing His Majesty's hand, but observed that he would gladly kiss the hand of the Queen. The Bishop of London, Fox, Boswell, Earl Percy, Earl Moira, and other distinguished persons admitted him to their society; and it is no small proof of his talent and address that he sustained himself well in the best circles of the British metropolis. The Prince of Wales is said to have taken delight in his company, and sometimes took him, as the chief afterwards remarked, "to places very queer for a prince to go to." It is also asserted that the scenes of coarse dissipation which he witnessed at the Prince's table, and the freedom with which the leading Whigs spoke of the King, had the effect of greatly weakening his respect for royalty, as well as his regard for the King's person.

The ostensible object of Brant's visit was to obtain for his tribe some remuneration for their services during the war; but as the Canadian authorities had already made them a large grant of land in Upper Canada, to which they removed, and where they still reside, it is probable that his mission had relation chiefly to another subject. After the war, Great Britain retained possession for several years of certain military posts, south of the lakes, and within the limits of the United States. The tribes at war with the United States made these posts their rallying points, and received from them constant supplies. The British Ministry, who had never formed any adequate judgment of the extent of this country, or of the enterprise and energy of the people, vainly supposed that Great Britain, by uniting with the savage tribes, might restrain the Americans from extending their settlements beyond the Ohio and Mississippi Rivers, and by possessing herself of that region and ultimately of the whole Mississippi plain, acquire an ascendancy on the continent which would enable her to recover her lost colonies. The crafty and intriguing character of Brant rendered him a willing and an able actor in these schemes; and he passed frequently from Canada to the North-Western Territory, to hold councils with the Indians. But as the British Government did not avow these proceedings, and the Indians might have been doubtful how far the agents who tampered with them were authorised, it was desirable that some more direct communication should be had with the Ministry; and the chief purpose of Brant's visit was to ascertain whether, in case of a general war between the Indians and the United States, the former might rely upon the support of Great Britain. Such is the clear import of numerous letters collected in Mr Stone's work, some of which are published for the first time, and which throw light upon points of this history which have been obscure. The British Government, however, would not commit itself on so delicate a matter, and Brant was referred to the Governor of Canada, with general assurances of His Majesty's friendship.

While in London, Captain Brant attended a masquerade, at which many of the nobility and gentry were present— appearing in the costume of his tribe, with one side of his face painted. A Turk who was of the company, was so much struck with the grotesque figure of the chief, and especially with his visage, which he supposed to be formed by a mask, that he ventured to indulge his curiosity by touching the Mohawk's nose; but no sooner did he make this attempt, than the chief, much amused, but affecting great rage, uttered the terrific war-whoop, and drawing his tomahawk flourished it round the head of the astonished Turk, creating a panic which sent the ladies screaming for protection in all directions.

He translated the Gospel of Mark into the Mohawk [27] language during this visit; and as the Prayer Books given to the Indians had mostly been lost or destroyed during the war, the Society for the Propagation of the Gospel in Foreign Parts chose the opportunity to bring out a new edition under his supervision, including the Gospel of Mark as translated by him. The book was elegantly printed in large octavo, under the patronage of the King, and embellished with a number of scriptural scenes engraved in the best style of that day. The date of his return is not exactly known, but his visit was not prolonged beyond a few months, as he was at home in July, 1786.

Brant was now placed in a position which required the exercise of all his address. The Mohawks had withdrawn into Canada, and were under the jurisdiction of Great Britain; the other five of the Six Nations resided in the United States; yet the confederacy remained unbroken, and Thayendanegea continued at its head. The Mohawks were embittered against the American people, to whom their recent cruelties had rendered them justly odious, while some of the other tribes were decidedly friendly. It required all his attention to keep together a confederacy thus divided. He is supposed, and with little doubt, to have been at the same time engaged in extensive conspiracies against the peace of the American frontiers, and is known to have been frequently in council with the hostile Indians. But while thus engaged he sought every opportunity of professing his love of peace, his friendship towards the United States, and his desire to heal the existing differences. The mantle of Christianity, which had been thrown aside during the war, was again assumed; and the chief was now engaged in correspondence on religious and benevolent subjects with several distinguished Americans. He affected an earnest desire to civilise his own tribe, and to teach them the Gospel; but there is too much reason to believe that his real sentiments accorded with those of his friend the Duke of Northumberland, who had served in America as Lord Percy, and having been admitted as a warrior into the Mohawk tribe, wrote to Brant, in 1806, as follows: "There are a number of well-meaning persons here, who are very desirous of forming a society to better (as they call it) the condition of our nation, by converting us from warriors and hunters into husbandmen. Let me strongly recommend it to you, and the rest of our chiefs, not to listen to such a proposition. Let our young men never exchange their liberty and manly exercises to become hewers of wood and drawers of water. If they will teach our women to spin and weave, this would be of use, but to endeavour to enervate our young men by doing nothing but tilling the earth, would be the greatest injury they could do the Five Nations."

But such was the reputation of Brant for abilities, and such the confidence in his professed desire "to accomplish the desirable end of civilisation and peacemaking," that the Government of the United States earnestly sought his mediation with the hostile tribes. A correspondence was opened in which he was appealed to as a man of high-toned benevolence, and as a friend of the red race, to save them from the inevitable destruction to which their perseverance in unnecessary wars must bring them. His replies show that his judgment approved these sentiments, and in them he repeatedly promised to do all in his power to make peace. The war,[28] however, continued for several years longer, the Indians becoming more and more audacious in their hostilities and unreasonable in their demands.

Besides a number of lesser engagements, several battles were fought, the most disastrous of which was the defeat of St Clair[29] by a large Indian force, aided by several hundred Canadians. "Their leader, according to the received opinion," says Mr Stone, "was Meshecunnaqua, or *Little Turtle*, a distinguished chief of the Miamis. He was also the leader of the Indians against General Harmer, the year before. It is believed, however, that though nominally the commander-in-chief of the Indians on this occasion, he was greatly indebted both to the counsels and the prowess of another and an older chief. One hundred and fifty of the Mohawk warriors were engaged in this battle; and General St Clair probably died in ignorance of the fact that one of the master-spirits against whom he contended, and by whom he was so signally defeated, was none other than *Joseph Brant—Thayendanegea.* How it happened that this distinguished chief, from whom so much had been expected as a peacemaker, thus suddenly and efficiently threw himself into a position of active hostility, unless he thought he saw an opening for reviving his project of a great north-western confederacy, is a mystery which he is believed to have carried in his own bosom to the grave."

We do not doubt that Mohawk braves were engaged in this battle, nor that Brant, during the whole of this unhappy war, so distressing to the frontier settlements and so ruinous to the deluded savages, was secretly engaged in fomenting discord, while affecting the character of a peacemaker. But we cannot suppress our scepticism as to his alleged participation in the battle of November 4, 1791, now first announced upon the authority of his family. We do not undertake to prove a negative, but we aver that the whole weight of the evidence contradicts this novel assumption. It is barely possible that he was there, and if so his counsels would doubtless have had great influence. But we think it altogether improbable that a leader of such distinction could take part in a general engagement, so important and so decisive, and the fact remain concealed for near half a century—especially under the circumstances connected with that disastrous event. The defeat of St Clair caused great excitement, and led to keen inquiry, and its circumstances were investigated by a military court. Subsequently the scene of the battle, and the lands inhabited by most of the tribes engaged in it, have become settled by Americans. Treaties have been made with those tribes. They have become dependent on the American Government, whose agents have been planted among them constantly, from a period immediately succeeding the battle of Wayne[30] in 1794.

There has been constant intercourse between our people and all the tribes of that region during the entire period that has elapsed since that war; and many Americans who were prisoners among those Indians at the time of the battle, as well as before and since, have, on their return home, communicated a variety of minute information touching an affair which caused even a greater excitement among the Indians than among us. It was a great and an unexpected triumph, the honour and spoils of which were divided among many tribes, who would each discuss all the circumstances and claim their portion of the glory. It is hardly possible that if Brant was present his name could have been concealed, or that all the individuals of all the tribes engaged should have concurred in yielding to Little Turtle the laurels that belonged to Thayendanegea. No one but himself could have been interested in keeping such a secret, while the fact, if it existed, must have been known to many—to Canadians, British officers, and the chiefs and warriors of various tribes, besides the one hundred and fifty of his own people who were in the engagement. We deem it an act of justice to the memory of Brant to suggest these objections, for although we, as Americans, have little reason to admire his military career, we are aware that much might be said, and indeed much has been said, in defence of his conduct while at open war with us which could not avail in regard to hostilities committed by him while professing to be at peace.

He continued, after the events just related, to correspond with the officers of the American Government, in the character of a mediator, keeping up without interruption the intercourse commenced before St Clair's campaign, and still professing his ardent desire "to accomplish the desirable end of civilisation and peacemaking." These sentiments accorded so well with the pacific views of the President,[31] and were received with such confidence, that he was several times invited in urgent and complimentary terms to visit the Government at Philadelphia; and after declining more than once, he at last, in June, 1792, commenced a journey to the metropolis of the United States. It is creditable to the moral character of our people that, although he passed through the Mohawk Valley, whose inhabitants had been so severely scourged by his hand, and although threats of vengeance were thrown out by indiscreet individuals, he was unmolested. He was kindly and respectfully received at Philadelphia. The true causes of the war with the western Indians were explained to him; and great pains were taken by the President and Secretary of War to impress upon his mind the sincere desire of the United States to cultivate the most amicable relations with all the Indian tribes and to spare no exertions to promote their welfare. In the end he was induced to undertake a mission of peace to some of the tribes, and was furnished with full powers for that purpose. But, however sincere were his intentions, they were changed on his return home; and the auspicious results anticipated fron his mediation were never realised. The United States, wearied out by ineffectual attempts to make peace, were at last compelled to prosecute the war with vigour, and found in General Wayne a negotiator who soon brought the enemy to terms.

We turn with pleasure to a more agreeable part of the life of this remarkable person. After the campaign of 1794 he was not again engaged in war, and devoted his attention to the interests and moral improvement of his tribe. He was not in the slightest degree tinctured with the habitual indolence of his race, and did not sink into mere apathy when sated with bloodshed. He laboured for years to get a confirmation of the title of his tribe to the land granted them on Grand River, which proved a source of vexation to him during the remainder of his life. He claimed for his tribe a complete right to the land, with power to sell and grant titles in fee simple; while the Government alleged the title to be imperfect, giving to the Indians only the right of occupancy, and reserving the pre-emption. "Council after council was holden upon the subject, and conference after conference; while quires of manuscript speeches and arguments, in Brant's own hand, yet remain to attest the sleepless vigilance with which he watched over the interests of his people, and the zeal and ability with which he asserted and vindicated their rights." Two deeds were successively framed and offered to the Mohawks, and rejected, and the land continued to be held by the same tenure by which the Indians in the United States occupy their territory.[32]

Before their removal from the Mohawk Valley some of the tribe had turned their attention to agriculture. Brant himself cultivated a large farm near the residence of General Herkimer. No man ever estimated more truly the advantages of civilisation, and had he been sincere in his professions upon that subject, and avoided all connection with the wars of England and America, his tribe would probably have afforded the earliest and most complete example of Indian civilisation. His own attainments were considerable; he spoke and wrote the English language correctly, and his compositions are highly respectable in point of thought and style. He was a close observer, and had made himself well acquainted with the arts and customs of the whites.

In his own house Brant was a hospitable and convivial man, and those who visited him were kindly received. He erected a spacious dwelling in Upper Canada, where he lived in handsome style, and his children were all well educated, two of them under the charge of President Wheelock, son of the preceptor of Brant. One son, Isaac, fell a victim to the besetting vice of his race; in a fit of intoxication he assaulted his father, and the stern chief, drawing a dirk, inflicted a wound upon his own son which proved mortal.

A mutual dislike existed between this chief and Red Jacket. They were rival politicians; each was the leading man among his own people, and as the Senecas and Mohawks were the principal tribes of the confederacy, each sought the first place in the nation. Their claims were nearly balanced, and they appeared to have gained the superiority in turn. In the year 1803 Red Jacket succeeded in procuring the deposition of Brant from the chieftainship of the confederacy, in consequence of some alleged speculations in land, by which it was thought the chief had advanced his own personal interest at the expense of his nation, but at a subsequent council Brant procured the reversal of this sentence. Both were artful and eloquent men; but Brant had the advantages of education and travel, while Red Jacket was superior in genius and in devotion to his people. Neither of them was scrupulous as to the means employed to compass his ends; but the one was selfish, while the other was ambitious. Brant sought to advance himself by means of his people, and was ever regardful of his private interests, while Red Jacket, though he claimed the first place among the Senecas, neglected his private interests and laboured incessantly for his tribe. Brant was an able warrior; he was cool, sagacious, and bold, but he was also cruel, vindictive, and rapacious; Red Jacket, though not a coward, disliked war, and abhorred bloodshed. They differed as much in policy as in character. Brant

THAYENDANEGEA, *or* BRANT

The Great Captain of the Six Nations

delighted in the society of civilised and even refined persons. Red Jacket sternly adhered to the language and customs of his own people, and shunned and discountenanced any familiar intercourse with the whites. The latter considered that the Indians could only be free so long as they remained savages—that every art and custom of civilisation which they adopted weakened the line of separation, while it introduced a new want to be supplied by the labour or the charity of white men, and increased the dependency of the Indians. Brant maintained through life a friendly intercourse with the English, and favoured the introduction of agriculture and the useful arts. He professed in early life to be converted to the Christian faith, and though he afterwards departed widely in practice from the meek and merciful deportment of a true believer, he always favoured the teaching of the Word, and an outward support to religion in his public capacity. Red Jacket opposed the missionaries, the Christian religion, and everything that emanated from the oppressors of his race. On the whole, Brant was one of the most remarkable men of his time; a person of brilliant parts, of great vigour and strength of intellect, full of energy and perseverance, and exceedingly subtle in compassing any object he had in view.

He died in November, 1807, at the age of nearly sixty-five years, at his own house, near Burlington, on Lake Ontario, and was buried at the Mohawk village on Grand River, by the side of the church he had built there. His last words to his adopted nephew were, "Have pity on the poor Indians: if you can get any influence with the great, endeavour to do them all the good you can." [33]

NOTES

1. "Thayendangea (Thayĕñdanē'kĕⁿ, 'He sets or places together two bets,' referring to the custom of fastening together the articles of approximate value placed as wagers by two phratries in tribal contests. The elements are *t* for *te*, 'two'; *ha*, 'he-it'; *yenda*, 'a wager'; nē'kĕⁿ, 'set side by side iteratively')."—Hewitt in *Handbook of American Indians*, op. cit., pt. 2, p. 791.

2. William L. Stone, *Life of Joseph Brant (Thayendanegea)*, 2 vols., Albany, 1864.

3. Canajoharie (Kă-nă-'djo'-'ha-reʻ, "it, the kettle, is fixed on the end of it"). An important Mohawk village, known as Upper Mohawk Castle, formerly situated on the east bank of Otsquago creek, nearly opposite Fort Plain, Montgomery county, New York.

4. See Vol. I., p. 189, note 3, and consult "*The Four Kings of Canada. Being a Succinct Account of the Four Indian Princes lately Arriv'd from North America* . . . London, Printed: And sold by John Baker, at the Black Boy in Pater-Noster-Row. 1710." Reprinted by J. E. Garratt & Co., London, 1891.

5. Sir William Johnson, born about 1715; died in New York in 1774. See his *Life and Times*, by William L. Stone, Albany, 1865.

6. Mrs Anne Grant, of Laggan (1755-1838), an accomplished Scottish writer, whose *Memoirs of an American Lady* was published in 1808.

7. September 8, 1755. The French commander, Dieskau, however, was not mortally wounded; he died near Paris in 1767.

8. Eleazar Wheelock, D.D., born near Windham, Connecticut, 1711; died 1779.
The precise year in which he [Brant] was thus placed under the charge of Dr Wheelock cannot now be ascertained. The school itself was opened for the reception of Indian pupils, avowedly as an Indian missionary school, in 1748; the first Indian scholar, Samson Occom, having been received into it five years before. It has been asserted that Joseph [Brant] was received into the school in July 1761, at which time he must have been nineteen years old, and a memorandum of his preceptor to that effect has been quoted."—Stone, *op. cit.*, p. 21.

9. Samson Occom was a Christian convert, called "the pious Mohegan," born in 1723. Converted to Christianity under the influence of Rev. E. Wheelock in 1741, he received in the family of that minister a good education, learning to speak and to write English and obtaining some knowledge of Latin and Greek, and even of Hebrew. Owing to ill-health he did not complete the collegiate instruction intended

for him. He was successively a school teacher in New London, Conn.
(1748); preacher to the Indians of Long Island for some ten years;
agent in England (1766-67) for Mr Wheelock's newly established
school, where he preached with great acceptance and success; minister
of the Brotherton Indians, as those Mahican were called who removed
to the Oneida country in the state of New York (1786). He was
ordained to the ministry in 1759. On his death at New Stockbridge,
N.Y., in 1792, Occom was greatly lamented. He is said to have been
an interesting and eloquent speaker, and while in England delivered
some 300 sermons. A funeral sermon on Moses Paul, a Mahican
executed for murder in 1771, has been preserved in printed form.
Occom was the author of the hymn beginning " Awaked by Sinai's Awful
Sound," and of another, " Now the Shades of Night are Gone," which
gave Bishop Huntington delight that the thought of an Indian was made
part of the worship of the Episcopal Church; but it was omitted from
the present hymnal. It was through his success in raising funds in
England that Mr Wheelock's school was transferred from Lebanon,
Conn., to New Hampshire, where it was incorporated as Dartmouth
College. As a man, Occom exhibited the virtues and the failings of
his race. He was a regularly ordained minister, having been examined
and licensed to preach by the clergymen of Windham county, Conn.,
and inducted in 1759 by the Suffolk presbytery, Long Island. His later
years were marred by drunkenness and other vices, but on the whole
his life was one of great benefit to his race, though Schoolcraft (*Indian
Tribes*, v., 518, 1855) praises him perhaps too highly. See J. Edwards,
Observations on the Language of the Muhhekaneew Indians, 1789; W. De
Loss Love, *Samson Occom and the Christian Indians of New England*, 1899.—
(Chamberlain in *Handbook of American Indians*, pt. 2, 1912.)

10. See note 3, above.

11. " The / Morning and Evening Prayer. / The Litany, and Church
Catechism. / Ne / Orhoengene neoni Yogaraskagh / Yondereana-
yendaghkwa, / Ne Ene Niyoh Raodeweyena, neoni / Onoghsadogeaghtige
Yondadderighwanondoentha" was printed at Boston by Richard and
Samuel Draper in 1763. "It may have been printed at the instance
of the Rev. Dr Eleazar Wheelock, or by the Boston Commissioners
of the (Scotch) Society for Propagating Christian Knowledge, for the
use of the missionaries and school-masters sent from New England
to the Six Nations." The revision referred to found publication as:
"The Order / For Morning and Evening prayer, / And Administration
of the / sacraments, /" etc., by William Andrews, Henry Barclay, and
John Ogilvie, printed at New York by W. Weyman and Hugh Gaine
in 1769. The following note on the history of the book, by Rev. W. M.
Beauchamp, is extracted from Pilling, *Bibliography of the Iroquoian
Languages*, 1888, pp. 4-5 :—
" In 1762, with a prospect for continued peace, Sir William Johnson

turned his attention more directly to the improvement of the Six Nations. He was earnest in helping all efforts for their conversion and education, and his position and long experience gave him practical insight into measures affecting their welfare. Most of the Mohawks, and some of the Oneidas and Tuscaroras, could now read, and he often furnished them suitable books. As knowledge spread among them, the need of a new edition of the Indian Prayer-book attracted his attention, and he undertook its publication at his own expense, securing the Rev. Dr Barclay to superintend the work. With a copy of the old edition he sent translations of the singing psalms, the communion office, that of baptism, and some prayers, which he desired added. When completed the book was an octavo of 204 pages.

"But it was not printed at once, and the causes of the delay were both interesting and curious. Mr William Weyman, of New York, commenced the work in 1763, and soon encountered difficulties of which he has left us full accounts. He had a good font of type for printing English, but was soon 'out of sorts' in this new language. Let him tell his own story: 'We are put to prodigious difficulty to print such language (in form) in North America, where we have not the command of a *letter maker's* founding-house to suit ourselves in ye particular sorts required, such as *g's*, *k's*, *y's*, etc., etc., when, had it been in ye English tongue, we could make much greater dispatch— but at present 'tis absolutely impossible—I having been obliged to borrow sundry letters from my brother printers, even to complete this present half sheet.'

"Rev. Dr Barclay died in 1764, and his long sickness and death hindered, and for a time actually stopped, the work on the new edition, as there was then no one in the city of New York who could revise or correct it but him. He found that the copy sent was very erroneous, and spent much time in correcting it; while, at the same time, it was so long since he had used the Mohawk language, that he was distrustful of his own ability. During his illness he suggested that Mr Daniel Claus, afterward Indian agent in Canada, was better able to do it than himself, but he was then away. Mr Weyman, therefore, sent the copy back to be transcribed clearly, under Sir William's own eye, agreeing to 'follow copy' when it was returned.

"Two years later, Mr Weyman wrote that 'the Indian Common Prayer-Book still lies dead.' He suggested that Rev. Mr Ogilvie, then of Trinity Church, New York, and late missionary to the Mohawks, might undertake its correction, if Johnson doubted his 'sticking close to a legible copy.' His own death, in 1768, caused further delay, and Hugh Gaine finished the work early in 1769. The little volume of 204 pages had been only six years in course of publication. On the title-page it is said to have been prepared under direction of Rev. Messrs Andrews, Barclay, and Ogilvie, formerly missionaries to the Mohawks."

12. Rev. John Stuart (spelled Stewart in previous editions of McKenney and Hall) was born at Harrisburg, Pa., February 24, 1740, and died at Kingston, Upper Canada, August 15, 1811. He was married in England, returned to Philadelphia about 1770, and for seven years officiated as a missionary among the Indians of the Mohawk Valley, for whom he made a translation of the New Testamen into the Mohawk language (Drake). According to Rev. W. M. Beauchamp (*Church Eclectic*, Vol. IX., p. 432, Utica, N.Y., 1881), Mr Stuart was largely instrumental in the preparation of the *Book of Common Prayer, in Mohawk*, London, 1787. See Pilling, *Bibliography of the Iroquoian Languages*, 1888, pp. 158-159.

13. This refers chiefly to the "Wyoming Massacre" of July 3, 1778, when the British troops and their Indian allies were commanded by Major John Butler. Mr J. N. B. Hewitt (in *Handbook of American Indians*, pt. 2, p. 742), however, denies that Brant was present at the massacre of Wyoming, as has been charged.

14. This statement is an error. There was no such chieftaincy among the Iroquois. When the several tribes were in council, any individual of sufficient personal influence would naturally become its spokesman, and by reason of his intelligence and experience Brant naturally assumed this position, but he was never elected chief of the Six Nations.

15. See note 2, above.

16. He sailed for England late in the year 1775, reached London early in 1776; he remained there several months. In May, 1776, we find him allied with the British troops in the battle of "The Cedars," above Montreal.

17. This portrait is reproduced as the frontispiece to Vol. I. of his *Life* by Stone, *op. cit.* See note 33, below.

18. General Nicholas Herkimer, of the New York militia (*ca.* 1715-77).

19. November 11, 1778.

20. Philip John Schuyler, born at Albany, N.Y., November 22, 1733; died in the same place, November 18, 1804. He served with distinction in the French and Indian War, and in June 1775 was given rank of major-general with command of the northern department of New York. He was superseded in August, 1777, by General Horatio Gates, and owing to jealousy and intrigue he resigned from the army, but his resignation was not accepted by Congress on the ground that his services were invaluable. He was a member of the Continental Congress in 1777, and was elected a member of Congress in 1778, serving until 1781. He was state senator of New York from 1780 to 1784, from 1786 to 1790, and from 1792 till 1797. From 1789 to 1791 he was U.S. Senator, and, succeeding Aaron Burr, held that office from 1797 to January, 1798, when he resigned on account of illness. See Lossing, *Life and Times of Philip Schuyler*, 2 vols., New York, 1860-62.

21. Stone (*op. cit.*, Vol. I., p. 234 *et seq.*) gives a vivid description of this engagement, which was fought August 6, 1777. General Nicholas Herkimer was severely wounded early in the action, and after the battle was conveyed to his home near the Mohawk River, thirty-five miles away, where he died ten days later.

22. July 3, 1778.

23. The "boy" was the future Judge John Wells of New York, whose father was Robert Wells.

24. The battle was fought July 20, 1779. Regarding the town of Minisink, Stone (*op. cit.*, Vol. I., p. 415) wrote: "Minisink, for an inland American town, is very ancient. It is situated about ten miles west of Goshen, in the county of Orange (N.Y.), on the Navisink River, and among what are called the Shawangunk Mountains. It is bordered on the south-west by the States of New Jersey and Pennsylvania. The Wallkill also rises in this town. Its history, previous to the war of the Revolution, is full of interest. A severe battle was fought with the Indians in Minisink, July 22, 1699, the bloody horrors of which yet live in the traditions of that neighbourhood."

25. August 29, 1779. General Sullivan commanded the American troops, while Brant and Colonel John Butler led the Indians and regular troops and rangers. The Americans gained a decisive victory.

26. See biography of RED JACKET, Vol. I., p. 5, this work.

27. See: "The Gospel according to St Mark," translated into the Mohawk Tongue, by Captain Brant, in *Book of Common Prayer, in Mohawk*, pp. 176-311, London, 1787, 12°.

See also: *The Gospel according to St Mark*, translated into the Mohawk Tongue, by Captain Brant. As also several portions of the Sacred Scriptures, translated into the same language. New York. Published by the New York District Bible Society. M'Elrath & Bangs, Printers. 1829. 12°, 239 pp., alternate English and Mohawk.

28. Some years ago, the late Professor Enrico H. Giglioli, of Florence, Italy, obtained from a dealer in Paris a stone gouge-shaped implement, made of granite and of American origin. Attached to it is a label, so old and discoloured that only part of the writing can be deciphered. It reads: "Hache des Indiens qui sous la conduite de leur chef Brant, en 1790, massacrerent et precipiterent dans l'Hudson 25 personnes sous le commandment." . . . See Bushnell in *American Anthropologist*, Vol. VIII., p. 253, 1906.

29. The disastrous defeat of Major-General Arthur St Clair, in command of the American troops, by the Indians, occurred November 4,

1791, at a point about six miles distant from the Miami village, in Ohio. By one authority the number of troops engaged on the American side is given as 1200, half of whom were killed or wounded during the battle. See also, *A Narrative of the Manner in which the Campaign Against the Indians, in the Year One Thousand Seven Hundred and Ninety-one, was Conducted under the Command of Major-General St Clair*, Philadelphia, 1812.

30. Major-General Anthony Wayne. The engagement was fought August 20, 1794, "on the banks of the Miamis, in the vicinity of the British port and garrison at the port of the Rapids," in the present State of Ohio. The Indians were defeated. The Americans sustained a loss of 133 killed and wounded.

31. This was during Washington's first term, and Philadelphia was the seat of the National Government.

32. See "Land tenure," in *Handbook of American Indians*, op. cit., pt. 1, p. 756.

33. In regard to the portraits of Brant: The frontispiece of Vol. II. of Stone's work (*op. cit.*) is a portrait of Brant, to which is attached the inscription: "Painted by G. Catlin from the original of E. Ames." This corresponds in all details with the illustration in the present work, and appears to have been the original from which the coloured plate was made. Another portrait, by Peale, is in the old State House at Philadelphia. The portrait by Romney, painted while Brant was in England, early in 1776, and contained in the collection of the Earl of Warwick, is reproduced as the frontispiece to Vol. I. of his *Life* by Stone. A "*large and fine mezzotint by J. R. Smith after G. Romney, size* 19⅞ *by* 13⅞ *in., with inscription margins,* 1779. *Brilliant impression in first state*," is among the rare engravings (portraits) in the Catalogue (No. 271) of Maggs Brothers, 109 Strand, London, W.C., issued October, 1911. This mezzotint portrait of "Tayadaneega (Joseph Brant, 1742-1807)" is No. 276 of the Catalogue, and is accompanied with a half-tone reproduction. "The inscription margin had been removed, but has now been carefully refixed to the plate," but this is not evident in the reproduction. The print is listed at £21.

AHYOUWAIGHS

(CHIEF OF THE SIX NATIONS)

THAYENDANEGEA, chief of the Mohawks, and head of the Iroquois confederacy,[1] was married three times. By his first wife he had two children, by his second none, and by the third seven. His widow, Catherine Brant, was the eldest daughter of the head of the Turtle family—the first in rank in the Mohawk nation; and, according to their customs, the honours of her house descended to either of her sons whom she might choose. By her nomination, her fourth and youngest son, John Brant, Ahyouwaighs, became the chief of the Mohawks, and virtually succeeded his father in the office, now nominal, of chief of the Iroquois or Six Nations.

This chief was born on the 27th September 1794; he received a good English education, and is said to have improved his mind by reading. In the war of 1812-15 between the United States and Great Britain, he espoused the cause of the latter, and participated in the dangers of the earlier part of the contest, but had not the opportunity to acquire distinction.

After the war, John Brant and his sister Elizabeth took up their abode at the family residence, at the head of Lake Ontario, where they lived in the English style; their mother having, after the death of Thayendanegea, returned to the Mohawk village, and resumed the customs

AHYOUWAIGHS
Chief of the Six Nations

of her fathers.   Lieutenant Francis Hall,[2] of the British
service, who travelled in the United States and Canada,
in 1816, visited "Brant House," and described John Brant
as a "fine young man, of gentleman-like appearance, who
used the English language correctly and agreeably, dressing
in the English fashion, excepting only the moccasins of his
Indian habit."   He says, in reference to Thayendanegea,
"Brant, like Clovis, and many of the early Anglo-Saxons
and Danish Christians, contrived to unite much religious
zeal with the practices of natural ferocity.   His grave is
seen under the walls of his church.   I have mentioned one
of his sons; he has also a daughter living, who would not
disgrace the circles of European fashion.   Her face and
person are fine and graceful: she speaks English not only
correctly, but elegantly, and has, both in her speech and
manners, a softness approaching to Oriental languor.   She
retains so much of her native dress as to identify her with
her people, over whom she affects no superiority, but
seems pleased to preserve all the ties and duties of
relationship."

This family is also favourably mentioned by James
Buchanan, Esq.,[3] British Consul for the port of New York,
who made a tour through Canada in 1819.   He describes
the same young lady as "a charming, noble-looking Indian
girl, dressed partly in the native, and partly in the Indian
costume"; and adds, "the grace and dignity of her movements, the style of her dress and manner, so new, so
unexpected, filled us with astonishment."

In 1821, John Brant visited England for the purpose
of settling the controversy in regard to the title of the
Mohawks to their land, which had cost his father so much
vexation.   The Duke of Northumberland, son to him who
was the friend of the elder Brant,[4] espoused his cause, as
did other persons of influence, and he received assurances

that the Government would grant all that was asked.
Instructions, favourable to the demands of the Mohawks,
were transmitted to the Colonial Government; but difficulties were thrown in the way by the provincial authorities
and no redress has yet been granted.

During this visit the young Brant addressed a letter to
the poet Campbell, in which he remonstrated against the
injustice alleged to have been done to his father's character,
in "Gertrude of Wyoming." The stanzas complained of,
purport to form a part of a speech uttered by an Oneida
chief, who came to warn a family that the forces of Brant
and Butler were at hand.

> " 'But this is not the time,'—he started up
>   And smote his heart with woe-denouncing hand—
> 'This is no time to fill the joyous cup,
>   The mammoth comes—the foe—the monster Brant—
>   With all his howling desolating band;—
>   These eyes have seen their blade and burning pine,
>   Awake at once, and silence half your land—
>   Red is the cup they drink, but not with wine:
>   Awake and watch to-night, or see no morning shine.
>
> " 'Scorning to wield the hatchet for his tribe,
>   'Gainst Brant himself I went to battle forth.
>   Accursed Brant! he left of all my tribe
>   Nor man nor child, nor thing of living birth—
>   No! not the dog that watched my household hearth
>   Escaped that night of blood upon our plains!
>   All perished—I alone am left on earth,
>   To whom nor relative, nor blood remains,
>   No! not a kindred drop that runs in human veins!' "

The appeal made to Campbell, by a son who was
probably sincere in the belief that his father had been
misrepresented, touched his feelings, and induced him to
write an apologetic reply, which is more honourable to

his heart than his judgment. The only objection to the stanzas, in our opinion, is the bad taste of the plagiarism upon the speech of Logan, contained in the last three lines. No one who has read the melancholy fate of the Wells family, can hesitate to acquit Campbell of injustice; nor is there the slightest doubt that the same language would be true of numerous scenes in the life of that bold desolater of the fireside, Thayendanegea. Chief Justice Marshall, who is above all reproach as a historian and as a gentleman of pure and elevated sentiments, was not convinced by the letter of John Brant, but in his second edition of the *Life of Washington*,[5] which was published several years after the appearance of that letter, reiterates the account of the massacre at Wyoming, in which Brant is stated to be the leader of the Indians.

On his return from England, the Mohawk chief seems to have given his attention to the moral condition of the tribe, which had been greatly neglected during the war between Great Britain and the United States; and in the year 1829, the "New England Corporation," established in London, by charter, A.D. 1662, for the civilisation of the Indians, presented him with a splendid silver cup, bearing an inscription, purporting that it was given, "In acknowledgment of his eminent services in promoting the objects of the Incorporation."

In 1832, John Brant was returned a member of the Provincial parliament, for the county of Haldimand, which includes a portion of the territory granted to the Mohawks. The election was contested upon the ground that the laws of Upper Canada require a freehold qualification in the voters, and that many of those who voted for Brant held no other titles to real estate than such as were derived from the Indians, who had no legal fee; and the seat of John Brant was vacated. It was not long after this decision that Brant and his competitor, Colonel Warren, both fell victims to the cholera.

Elizabeth Brant, the youngest daughter of Thayendanegea, was married, some years ago, to William Johnson Kerr, Esq., a grandson of Sir William Johnson, and resides at the family mansion at the head of Lake Ontario.

The widow of Thayendanegea, upon the death of her favourite son,[6] John, conferred the title of chief upon the infant son of her daughter, Mrs Kerr, and died on the 24th of November, 1837, thirty years, to a day, after the death of her husband, at the good old age of seventy-eight years.

NOTES

1. See THAYENDANEGEA, note 14, p. 253, this volume.

2. *Travels in Canada and the United States, in* 1816 *and* 1817, by Lieut. Francis Hall, London, 1818.

3. *Sketches of the History, Manners, and Customs of the North American Indians,* by James Buchanan, London, 1824.

4. It will be recalled that James Smithson (*ca.* 1754-1829), founder of the Smithsonian Institution at Washington, was a natural son of Sir Hugh Smithson, first Duke of Northumberland.

5. *The Life of George Washington,* by John Marshall, second edition, Philadelphia, 1834. See THAYENDANEGEA, note 14, p. 253, this volume.

6. The last survivor of the Brant children was Catherine B. Johnson, who died in 1867.

NEAMATHLA

(A SEMINOLE CHIEF)

THE war between the United States and the Florida Indians having given an increased interest to the history of those tribes, we propose to treat that portion of our subject with some degree of minuteness should we succeed in procuring the requisite materials. Our information in regard to them is not sufficiently precise to enable us to attempt this at present, and in presenting the valuable portrait which accompanies this sketch, we shall confine ourselves to a few general remarks.

The Spanish conquerors and discoverers, if we may place any confidence in their reports, encountered numerous and warlike tribes in the region which they were pleased to describe as the land of flowers; but they may have indulged in the poetic licence as greatly in regard to the number of inhabitants as in reference to the luxuries of the soil and climate. It is certain that but few of the ancient inhabitants remain ; and these are divided into small hordes, who neither exhibit the appearance nor retain the recollection of any former greatness. A new people has been added to them, who now form the great majority of the savage population of that country, and whose character has become impressed upon the whole mass.

The Seminoles,[1] or "Runaways," are descended from the Creeks and Cherokees, and perhaps from other of the southern tribes, and derive their name from the manner of their separation from the original stocks. While Florida belonged to Spain it afforded a place of refuge for the discontented individuals belonging to the tribes within the United States, as well as for fugitive negro slaves ; and of this mixed population were formed the various tribes now known under the common name of Seminoles. From the swamps and hammocks of Florida, they have been in the habit of annoying the frontiers of the adjacent states, and these injuries have been rendered the more galling by the protection afforded by those savages to runaway slaves, and by the ferocities practised by the latter under the influence of revenge and the fear of recapture. It is not to be denied, nor is it surprising, that these Indians have, under such circumstances, suffered much injustice, for the spirit of retaliation is never limited by moderation ; and it was a wise as well as a humane policy of the Government which decreed the separation of the exasperated parties, by the removal of the Seminoles to a territory more distant from the white settlements. Nor could the former, with any propriety, plead the territorial rights and local attachments so strongly urged by their parent nations ; for they were mere intruders, or at best but recent inhabitants, of the lands from which it was proposed to eject them.

Neamathla, who has been one of the most distinguished of the Seminoles, and was at one time their head man, or principal chief, was by birth a Creek. At what time he emigrated to Florida, or by what gradations he rose to authority, we are not well informed, and as we propose to make these sketches strictly authentic as far as they go, we pass over those details that have reached us with no better evidence than mere rumour. Mr Duval,[2] Governor of Florida, in a despatch to the Government at Washington, dated in March, 1824, describes him as a man of uncommon abilities, of great influence with his nation, and as one of the most eloquent men he ever heard. At a subsequent date in the same year, he writes thus: "Neamathla is a most uncommon man, and ought to be induced to remove with his people. This chief you will find perhaps the greatest man you have ever seen among the Indians: he can control his warriors with as much ease as a colonel could a regiment of regular soldiers." Again, we find the hospitality and manly feelings of this chief, and his great energy of character, spoken of in terms of high respect. When these opinions were expressed, hopes were entertained that Neamathla could be induced to second the views of the American Government in regard to the removal of the Seminoles to the land appropriated to them west of Arkansas[3]; but in the summer of that year it was found that instead of promoting that desirable measure, he was exerting his influence to defeat it, and Governor Duval deposed him from the chieftaincy. This is a curious instance of the anomalous character of the relation existing between our Government and the Indians; for while the latter are for many purposes considered as independent nations and are treated with as such, they are in all essential respects regarded and governed as subjects, and the Government has on several occasions sanctioned the creation and removal of chiefs.

There is some reason to believe that the reluctance of Neamathla to remove from Florida was the result of a natural attention to his own interest. By a previous treaty,[4] the United States with a view to conciliate this respectable chief, now advanced in years, set apart for his private use a tract of land, remote from the residence of the main body of the nation. The tenure of such reservations is that of occupancy only, and as Neamathla could not sell the land, he of course desired to enjoy its use, and was unwilling to remove to a distant wilderness. In another view of the subject, the liberality of the Government to this chief proved injurious, as it gave him a home remote from the villages of his people, among whom his influence was unbounded, and left them exposed to the intrigues of the mercenary individuals whose interest it was to promote dissension. That Neamathla desired to be at peace with the United States was apparent from the whole tenor of his conduct since the war which closed in 1815. He had maintained a strict discipline in his tribe, punishing the offences of his people, especially those committed against the whites, with uncompromising severity. His people feared, while they loved and respected him. The removal of such a man from among them was injudicious. It was proposed, therefore, to permit him to sell his reservation, under the expectation that he would convert the proceeds into cattle and horses, and be willing to remove with his people to the fertile lands provided for them. The arrangement was, however, not effected; and the influence of Neamathla being used in opposition to the views of the Government, and of that which was esteemed the best interests of the Seminoles, he was deposed, upon which he abandoned the Seminoles and returned to the Creek nation. That he was well received by the Creeks, and recognised as a person of consideration, appears from the fact that he sat in council with their principal men assembled to treat with the United States in 1827.[5]

We have received from an authentic source an anecdote of this chief which is highly characteristic of his race, and exhibits a remarkable coincidence in the opinions of Neamathla with those of other distinguished Indians. Pontiac, Red Jacket, Little Turtle, Tecumthe, and a few other of the master-spirits among the red men, uniformly opposed all attempts to introduce the civilisation and arts of the

NEA-MATH-LA
A Seminole Chief

European race among the Indians, under the plausible argument that the Great Spirit had created the several races for different purposes, and had given to each the arts proper to its destination.   These sagacious men saw that as the Indians adopted the habits of white men they acquired new wants, which could only be supplied by an intercourse with civilised people, upon whom they thus became dependent.   They felt that they were the weaker party in number, and the inferior in ingenuity; and as they knew of no contact between nations but that in which one must gain at the expense of the other, they believed that all intercourse between the white and red races must tend to the disadvantage of the latter.   There can be no question as to the correctness of this reasoning, nor any doubt that every advance made by the Indians towards civilisation contributes to destroy their independence.   We may think that they would be better off without such savage freedom, and in the enjoyment of the comforts that we possess; but they reason differently, and while they admit the advantages of our condition, they are not willing to purchase them at the expense of their national integrity. Their most sagacious men have, therefore, always viewed with jealousy our attempts to introduce our religion and our arts among them, and have considered the arms of the white man far less dangerous to their existence as a separate people than the education by which we would win them over to our customs.

By the sixth article of the treaty of Moultrie Creek, in the territory of Florida, concluded September 18th, 1823, it was provided, among other things, that the sum of one thousand dollars per annum, for twenty years, should be applied by the United States to the support of a school at the Florida agency, for the education of the children of the Indians.   In carrying the provisions of the treaty into effect, the commissioner for Indian Affairs at Washington received no information for some time touching that one for the establishment of the school, and supposed it to have been overlooked, when on inquiry it was found that the Indians declined receiving it. The delicate office of communicating this decision to the Governor of Florida was confided to Neamathla, or assumed by him as the head man of the Seminoles. The Indians are ceremonious in the mode of conducting their public affairs, and in refusing to receive the proffered liberality of the Government, the chief delivered his reasons at length in a speech, of which the following is a translation.

"My Father, we have listened to the message of our Great Father at Washington, who has taken pity on his red children, and would teach us to speak on paper like the children of the white men. It is very good to know all those things which the white people know, and it is right for them to teach them to their children. We also instruct ours in our own way : we teach them to procure food by hunting, and to kill their enemies. But we want no schools, such as you offer us. We wish our children to remain as the Great Spirit made them, and as their fathers are, Indians. The Great Spirit has made different kinds of men, and given them separate countries to live in ; and he has given to each the arts that are suited to his condition. It is not for us to change the designs of the Great Master of Life. If you establish a school, and teach our children the knowledge of the white people, they will cease to be Indians. The Great Spirit wishes no change in his red children. They are very good as he made them ; if the white man attempts to improve, he will spoil them.

"Father, we thank you for your offer; but we do not wish our children to be taught the ways of your people.

"Listen, Father, and I will tell you how the Great Spirit made man, and how he gave to men of different colours the different employments that we find them engaged in. After the world was made it was solitary. It was very beautiful; the forests abounded in game and fruit; the great plains were covered with deer and elk, and buffalo, and the rivers were full of fish; there were many bears and beaver, and other fat animals, but there was no being to enjoy these good things. Then the Master of Life said, we will make man. Man was made, but when he stood up before his maker, he was *white!* The Great Spirit was sorry: he saw that the being he had made was pale and weak; he took pity on him, and therefore did not unmake him, but let him live. He tried again, for he was determined to make a perfect man, but in his endeavour to avoid making another white man, he went into the opposite extreme, and when the second being rose up, and stood before him, he was *black!* The Great Spirit liked the black man less than the white, and he shoved him aside to make room for another trial. Then it was that he made the *red man;* and the red man pleased him.

"My Father, listen—I have not told you all. In this way the Great Spirit made the white, the black, and the red man, when he put them upon the earth. Here they were—but they were very poor. They had no lodges nor horses, no tools to work with, no traps, nor anything with which to kill game. All at once, these three men, looking up, saw three large boxes coming down from the sky. They descended very slowly, but at last reached the ground; while these three poor men stood and looked at them not knowing what to do. Then the Great Spirit spoke and said: 'White man, you are pale and weak, but I made you first, and will give you the first choice; go to the boxes, open them and look in, and choose which you will take for your portion.' The white man opened the boxes, looked in, and said : 'I will take this.' It was filled with pens, and ink, and paper, and compasses, and such things as your people now use. The Great Spirit spoke again, and said : 'Black man, I made you next, but I do not like you. You may stand aside. The red man is my favourite, he shall come forward, and take the next choice ; red man, choose your portion of the things of this world.' The red man stepped boldly up and chose a box filled with tomahawks, knives, war-clubs, traps, and such things as are useful in war and hunting. The Great Spirit laughed when he saw how well his red son knew how to choose. Then he said to the negro : 'You may have what is left, the third box is for you.' That was filled with axes and hoes, with buckets to carry water in, and long whips for driving oxen, which meant that the negro must work for both the red and white man, and it has been so ever since.

"Father, we want no change; we desire no school, and none of the teaching of the white people. The Master of Life knew what was best for all his children. We are satisfied. Let us alone."

This is a happy instance of the mode of illustration by parable, which, being the most simple and natural method of explanation, seems to have been adopted by all rude nations. The leading idea in the harangue of Neamathla was not original with him, but was the commonly received notion among the Indians, from the earliest times of which we have any account. The vast difference between them and the Europeans, both physical and moral, naturally suggested the idea that they were distinct races, created for different purposes; and the unhappy results of the intercourse between them, and of every attempt to unite them, gave additional strength to the opinion. The chiefs who, like all other politicians knew how to avail themselves of a popular prejudice, saw at once the great advantage of encouraging a belief which perpetuated their own authority, by excluding the foreign influences, that would have destroyed alike the national character of the savages, and their existing forms of subordination. The wealth, the arts, and the numbers of the invading race alarmed their jealousy; for they had the sagacity to perceive that if amicable relations and an unrestricted familiar intercourse should be established with a people possessing such ample means of conquest, the latter must inevitably, either by force or ingenuity, obtain the complete ascendancy. The fiction employed by Neamathla, to convey the ideas entertained by his people, is of his own invention, and is creditable to his ingenuity. It is a fair specimen of the Indian style of eloquence. They do not attempt what we would call argument; mere abstract reasoning is beyond their comprehension. But they are expert in the employment of figures, by which the familiar objects around them are made to represent their ideas. They have no theories nor traditions in regard to the creation which seem to have been derived from any respectable source, or to be venerated for their antiquity, nor any, indeed, which have much authority among themselves. Every tribe has its legends, fabricated by the chiefs or prophets to serve some temporary purpose; the most of which are of a puerile and monstrous character. Few of them are of much antiquity; and, being destitute alike of historical and poetic merit, they are soon forgotten.[6]

NOTES

1. See OPOTHLE-YOHOLO, note 14, p. 34, this volume.

2. William P. Duval, appointed Governor of the Territory of Florida by President Monroe in 1822, and continued in office until 1834.

3. By the treaty of Fort Gibson, March 28, 1833, a certain number of the Seminole chiefs agreed, " on behalf of the Seminole nation," to their removal to lands west of the Mississippi. Other chiefs and members of the tribe were strongly opposed to the plan. Among the former was Neamathla. On the general subject, consult Abel, Annie H., " History of Events resulting in Indian Consolidation West of the Mississippi," in *Annual Report of American Historical Association for* 1906, Vol. I., pp. 238-438.

4. " Nea Mathla " signed the treaty of Moultrie Creek, in the Territory of Florida, September 18, 1823, being the first of the thirty-two members of his tribe to sign. In the additional article of the treaty, " Neo Mathla " was recognised as one of the " principal Chiefs of the Florida Indians," and was allowed to remain in the district where he was then living, a tract of land "two miles square, embracing the Tuphulga village, on the waters of Rocky Comfort Creek," having been set apart for him and his connections. Thirty men and undoubtedly their families remained with him, and he was also allowed the sum of five hundred dollars as compensation for the improvements abandoned by him and to enable him to settle on a new site.

5. This evidently refers to the gathering of representatives of the United States Government and of the Creek nation at the Creek agency which resulted in the conclusion of the treaty signed November 15, 1827. The subject of this sketch was not, of course, a signer of the treaty.

6. Since this paragraph was written much information has been gained respecting the myths and traditions of the various tribes of North American Indians, and the literature of the subject is very voluminous. For a brief summary, consult the article on Mythology in *Handbook of American Indians*, Bulletin 30, pt. 1, Bureau of American Ethnology, Washington, 1907.

MARKOMETE

(A MENOMINEE BRAVE)

THIS is the first specimen we have presented of a small though very interesting tribe. The Menominees,[1] or Folles Avoines, inhabit the country between the lakes and the Mississippi River, their principal residence being west of Lake Michigan, whence they stray into the country of the Winnebagoes, who are their friends. Their language is peculiar, and difficult to be learned by white men. Charlevoix[2] says they were not numerous in his time, and they are now reduced to a few thousand souls. The early writers all speak of them in favourable terms, not only as "very fine men, the best shaped of all Canada," but as possessing an agreeable personal appearance, indicative of more neatness, and of a greater taste for ornament than that of any other of our north-western Indians. But they are now greatly degenerated, as we have remarked in our historical introduction, in consequence of their intercourse with the whites, and their fatal propensity for ardent spirits.

They are of a lighter complexion than the Indians around them, from whom also they differ in being less fierce and warlike. Though brave, they are peaceable, subsisting chiefly on the wild rice[3] or *false oats*, from which they derive their French designation, and avoiding, either from indolence or a dislike of war, the quarrels in which their neighbours are continually engaged. The women are patient, obedient, and laborious, and when introduced into the families of the traders residing in the wilderness, are preferred as domestics to those of the other Indian tribes.

We know little of the history of this people. The whites as well as the Indians respect them for their inoffensive habits, but all admit that, when engaged in war, they have always borne themselves with exemplary courage. However their pride may be subdued by circumstances, it is not less than that of the kindred tribes of their race; and evinces itself in the same contempt of danger which marks the conduct of all the aborigines. It is the singular boast of this tribe, that no other nation holds a Menominee as a slave or prisoner. Their invariable rule has been to prefer death to captivity, and when accidentally taken alive, to provoke their captors by the grossest insults to despatch them on the spot.

Markomete, if still alive, is about seventy years of age. His name, which signifies *Bear's oil*, may not seem, to our ears, to be appropriate or in good taste; but as the fat of the bear is esteemed a great delicacy among the Indians, when used as food, besides being valuable for other purposes, the designation may be as honourable in their estimation as to us are those of Cæsar or Napoleon. He has been well known as a warrior of excellent repute, a successful hunter, and a man of fair character. He was one of a deputation of his people who visited Washington a few years ago,[4] and, though not a chief, was a person of influence.

MAR - KO - ME - TE
A Menominee Brave

NOTES

1. "Menominee (*meno*, by change from *mino*, 'good,' 'beneficent';
min, a 'grain,' 'seed,' the Chippewa name of the wild rice. Full
name *Menominiwok ininiwok*, the latter term signifying 'they are men').
An Algonquian tribe, the members of which, according to the late
Dr William Jones, claim to understand Sauk, Fox, and Kickapoo far
more easily than they do Chippewa, Ottawa, and Potawatomi, hence it
is possible that their linguistic relation is near to the former group of
Algonquians."—*Handbook of American Indians*, pt. 1, p. 842.

2. Charlevoix, *Journal of a Voyage to North America*, London, 1761,
Vol. II., p. 61 (written July, 1721):

"After we had advanced five or six leagues, we found ourselves
abreast of a little island, which lies near the western side of the bay,
and which concealed from our view, the mouth of a river, on which
stands the village of the Malhomines Indians, called by our French
Folles Avoines or Wild Oat Indians, probably from their living chiefly on
this sort of grain. The whole nation consists only of this village, and
that too not very numerous. 'Tis really great pity, they being the
finest and handsomest men in all Canada. They are even of a larger
stature than the Poutewatamies. I have been assured that they had
the same original and nearly the same language with the Noquets
[*i.e.*, the Bear gens of the Chippewa] and the Indians at the Falls
[the Chippewa residing near the Sault Ste Marie]. But they add that
they have likewise a language peculiar to themselves, which they never
communicate. I have also been told several stories of them, as of a
serpent which visits their village every year, and is received with much
ceremony, which makes me believe them a little addicted to witchcraft."

3. *Zizania aquatica*.

4. A large deputation of the Menominee were in Washington early
in 1831, and an important treaty was signed there, February 8.
Markomete was probably one of this party, although his name does not
appear in the treaty. The portrait of "Mar-ko-me-ta, Bear's Oil,"
bears No. 96 in the Rhees *Catalogue*, but neither the name of the
artist nor the date of its execution appears ; however, it was evidently
painted during his visit to Washington in 1831.

AMISQUAM

(A WINNEBAGO BRAVE)

ALTHOUGH we shall scarcely infer the fact from his name, Amisquam, or the *Wooden Ladle*, is a very noted leader of the Winnebagoes,[1] a fierce and restless tribe of the Upper Mississippi. His mother was a woman of that nation, and his father a Frenchman named Descarrie, by which name also the subject of this notice is known. He is a fine-looking man,[2] of large stature and commanding mien, whose influence over the entire mass of the warriors of this numerous tribe is very great. He has led many war parties against the Chippeways, and has always been successful, returning laden with spoil and scalps.

The leader of such parties seldom engages in the fight as a common brave, nor does he usually even carry a gun. The systematic and cautious tactics of Indian warfare, and the inevitable disgrace which results from defeat, imposes upon him a responsible office; and, like the general in the army of a civilised people, he is expected rather to direct the efforts of others, than to fight with his own hand. The plan of the enterprise is often the subject of a council, in which all who are of sufficient age may speak, and the decision is usually unanimous; for we know of no instance among the Indians in which questions are decided by majorities. When the leading features of the scheme are agreed upon, the execution

274

A-MIS-QUAM, *or* " WOODEN LADLE "
A Winnebago Brave

is left to the war chief, who may rely on the secrecy
as well as the implicit obedience of his well-trained
followers. On the eve of a battle he gives his orders
to his captains, or, if the party be small, to the whole
band; and during the fight he is engaged in overlooking
and directing the whole operation. Occasions may occur,
as in all military enterprises, where it may be proper
for the leader to place himself at the head of his men,
and go foremost into battle; and in all cases when the
fight thickens so that braves meet hand to hand, the
leader is thrown into personal contact with the enemy;
but the general practice is as we have stated.

The Wooden Ladle was a general, or war chief, who
led large parties of his people, and gained reputation by
the sagacity with which he directed these military enterprises. He usually assembled his braves at Prairie du
Chien[3]; and before going out always adorned himself with
a string of beads, which he wore round his neck. This
was to be the prize of the first warrior who should kill
an enemy and bring his head to the leader, and the
trophy was always given on the spot.

NOTES

1. The tribe belongs to the Siouan linguistic family. The Winnebago
have been known to the whites since the French penetrated the
western country in 1634, at which time they were living on Green
Bay, the western part of Lake Michigan. The name Winnebago is
derived from the Algonquian, signifying "people of the filthy or bad-
smelling water." (See WATCHEMONNE, note 5, p. 171, this volume.)

2. The portrait of "Am-eiquon, Wooden Ladle," bears No. 6 in
the Rhees *Catalogue*. Although it is there attributed to Lewis, copied
by King in 1826, it does not appear in the Lewis *Portfolio*. (See
Introduction, Vol. I., p. xlvii., this work.)

3. At the mouth of Wisconsin River, the site of Fort Crawford.

STUMANU

(A FLATHEAD BOY)

THE Chinooks[1] are a tribe of Indians inhabiting the shores
of the Columbia River, near the Pacific Ocean. They
practise the savage custom of flattening the foreheads of
their infants by means of a board applied to that part,
whence they are called Flatheads by the whites, as others
are called *Nez Percés*, Pierced Nose Indians, although
neither of these terms are used among themselves. Most
of those Indians who flatten the head also pierce the nose.
These singular customs were found by the first discoverers,
among the savages on the shores of the Atlantic[2]; but they
seem to have become extinct in our country, except in the
distant region of the Columbia. The name Flathead
having been arbitrarily given, some explanation is necessary
to avoid confusion.

The term "Flathead" was formerly applied vaguely to
all the Indians inhabiting the unexplored regions about the
Rocky Mountains, except the Blackfeet; but as the country
became better known, the name was confined to a small
nation, who still bear it, and are not recognised among us
by any other, and who live chiefly in the gorges of the
mountains and on the plains on either side. They do not,
however, flatten the head, nor have they any term in their
language to express this idea. Beyond them, on the
Columbia River, are numerous tribes who pierce the nose

276

and flatten the forehead, who are mostly included under the name of Nez Percés—but the name Flathead is not commonly used in reference to them.

The nation to which our hunters and trappers apply the name of Flathead—the Flatheads of the Rocky Mountains—are a very interesting people. They are honest, hospitable, and kindly disposed towards the whites. They excel most other Indians in simplicity and frankness of character. The Blackfeet, a numerous tribe inhabiting the same region, a treacherous, vindictive, and warlike people, are the implacable enemies of the Flatheads, and harass them continually. This war is of the most uncompromising character; the Blackfeet pursue their enemies with unceasing hostility, driving them from place to place, hunting them down with untiring vigilance, and allowing them no rest. But though forced to fly from their foes, in consequence of their vastly inferior numbers, the Flatheads singly are more than a match for their enemies in boldness and physical strength; and as they never receive any quarter from their cruel oppressors, they fight with the most desperate courage when forced into action. Exposed to the greatest extremes and hardships to which the savage state is incident, and chased continually by their enemies, who use every artifice to decoy and surprise them, they are as wild, as watchful, and almost as fleet as the antelope of the prairies.

They are admirable horsemen. Without any fixed residence, roving throughout the year, engaged often in hunting the buffalo, and more frequently in rapid flight from imminent danger, the Flathead and his horse are inseparable; and such is the skill acquired by constant practice, that one of this tribe will mount an unbroken horse without saddle or bridle, and retain his seat, in spite of all the efforts of the enraged animal to dislodge him. A friend of the writer saw this feat performed by Incilla, the present chief of the tribe, on the plains east of the Rocky Mountains. The chief threw himself upon the back of a wild horse recently taken, holding in one hand a small flag, and in the other a hoop covered with a skin, after the fashion of a tambourine. On being turned loose, the animal dashed off, rearing and pitching, and using the most violent exertions to disengage himself from his fearless rider, who, clinging with his heels, maintained his seat, in spite of the efforts of the horse to throw him. When he wished to check the speed of the animal, he blinded him by throwing the flag across his face; while he guided him, by striking him with the tambourine, on the one side or the other of the head. This exercise he continued, scouring the plain at full speed, and directing the course of the furious steed at will, until the latter was wearied out and subdued.

Westward of the Flatheads, a number of small tribes are found scattered along the shores of the Columbia to the Pacific Ocean, all of whom belong to the Nez Percés nation, by which we mean only that they acknowledge the tie of kindred, and speak a common language, for they do not appear to be united by any other bond, and have no national organisation. They are on friendly terms with the Flatheads, but have not the bold and manly character of that tribe; on the contrary, they are ignorant and timid. They subsist by hunting and fishing, but chiefly by the latter; are miserably poor, inoffensive, and peaceable. They pierce the dividing cartilage of the nose, and thrust a bone several inches in length through the orifice, to remain until the wounded part is completely healed; and they flatten the head by confining it between boards, one of which passes across the forehead, flattening that part, so that the ascent from the nose to the top of the head is almost without a curve. The effect produced is said to be extremely disgusting.

The Indians in the vicinity of the mountains excel in horsemanship, those on the Columbia are expert in the management of their canoes, in which they embark fearlessly on the waves of the Pacific in the roughest weather ; and such is their skill that they keep afloat amid the angry billows when it would seem impossible that such frail vessels could live. The upsetting of a canoe in such circumstances is of little consequence, for these Indians are such admirable swimmers, that they right their canoes when overturned, bail out the water, and resume their seats ; or if necessary abandon them, and swim to the shore.

The women are admitted to a greater degree of equality with the men than among the other American tribes, because in fishing and in managing the canoe they are equally expert, and as they share all the toils and dangers of the other sex, they naturally become the companions and equals, and in virtue of their superior industry, the *better* halves, of their lords and masters. In the savage state, where the employments of the men are confined to war and hunting, a certain degree of contempt attaches to the weaker sex, who are unfit for such rude toils, and a timid or imbecile man is, in derision, compared to a woman. But a different relation exists between the sexes where the employments are such that both engage in them alike, and where both contribute equally to the support of their families.

The Columbia River was discovered by Captain Gray,[3] of Boston, in the ship *Columbia*, from which it received its name. Afterwards, Captains Lewis and Clark,[4] of the army of the United States, with a small escort, performed a journey overland to the mouth of that river, under the auspices of the Government, and for the purpose of exploration. This was one of the most remarkable journeys of which we have any account; the extent of the territory explored, the dangers and privations encountered, the great number of the savage tribes visited, and the success-ful prosecution of the enterprise, display a degree of courage and perseverance never excelled by any scientific travellers. A well-digested account of the expedition was published, written, from the notes of Lewis and Clark, by a gentleman, who in that work gave to his country the first fruits of a genius which in its riper brilliancy has since become the pride and admiration of his countrymen. The discoveries made by these tourists turned the atten-tion of the mercantile world to this wild and unfrequented region, which now became the scene of an animated com-petition. John Jacob Astor, of New York, a German by birth, who came in early life an indigent adventurer to our shores, and had by his unwearied industry and unrivalled talents for business amassed a princely fortune, matured a plan for securing to his adopted country the fur trade of that coast. The Government, to whom he communicated his project, was too weak at that time to give any aid to an uncertain enterprise, which might involve a heavy expenditure, and by possibility endanger its relations with foreign powers; and could only encourage the scheme by its approbation. A fine ship was equipped for the voyage by Mr Astor, and placed under the charge of Captain Thorn, an intelligent officer bred in the American navy, and who had been but a short time previous enrolled in the gallant band that gained so much glory in the Tripolitan war; while a party of hardy men under Mr Theodore Hunt set out from St Louis to cross the continent,[5] and meet the vessel at the mouth of the Columbia. After a prosperous voyage round Cape Horn, the ship reached her destination; but an unfortunate affray

STUM-A-N-U
A Flathead Boy

occurring with the natives, Captain Thorn suffered himself
to be surprised, the whole crew were massacred and the
vessel destroyed. Mr Hunt was more successful. After
a protracted journey, attended by toils and perils the
most incredible and discouraging, this dauntless party
found themselves on the shores of the Columbia River, but
in a condition too exhausted to enable them to carry out
the plan proposed. They had accomplished much in
overcoming the difficulties of the journey, and inspecting
that vast field for commercial enterprise, of which scarcely
anything had been known but its existence. Mr Astor
persevered in his design ; a trading post, called Astoria,
was established on the Columbia, a few miles from its
mouth, and hunters were employed who scattered themselves over the whole region watered by the tributaries
of that river. The British fur traders,[6] who had already
pervaded the whole of the vast territory lying north of
the Great Lakes, as well as the wilderness country lying
within the north-western boundaries of the United States,
penetrated also into these solitudes, and established a
strong post called Fort Vancouver, in honour of the
navigator for whom, without any sufficient evidence, the
discovery of the Columbia was claimed, and another called
Fort Colville. When the war of 1812, between the United
States and Great Britain, was declared, the Americans
were compelled to abandon this country, to which their
Government could not extend its protection ; but when,
by the treaty of peace negotiated at Ghent, it was provided that the belligerent parties should mutually surrender the places taken during the war from each other,
Astoria was formally delivered up by the British Government, which, by this act distinctly recognised the territorial rights of the American people. Subsequently,
however, the question of jurisdiction was opened, and to

prevent collision, it was agreed that for a period of ten years the subjects and citizens of both Governments might occupy the disputed territory for the purposes of hunting and traffic, without prejudice to the claims of either country. Since then, the whole region west of the Rocky Mountains has been traversed by numerous bands of British and American trappers. A few wealthy and enterprising individuals residing chiefly at St Louis, in the state of Missouri, have organised regular companies, for the purpose of carrying on this trade, which has been prosecuted with an admirable degree of efficiency and success. Large parties, composed of hunters well mounted and armed, annually leave St Louis, attended by pack horses, and on some occasions by waggons, carrying merchandise and stores for the expedition. The leaders are men of talent and courage, and the discipline that of a rigid military police. After passing the settlements of the United States, and the hunting grounds of the Indian tribes with whom pacific relations have been established by treaty, they have to traverse immense wilds inhabited by the Blackfeet, and other roving bands, who live in perpetual war, and among whom safety can be secured only by unceasing vigilance. The march is conducted with the greatest precaution, and the camp is always guarded by sentinels. All this is beautifully told in Washington Irving's *Astoria*, a work which is not more commendable for the gracefulness of its style, than for the fidelity with which it describes the adventures of the trappers in the wilderness. The subject is one with which we are familiar, and we therefore refer to Mr Irving's delightful work with confidence; and forbear from repeating what has been narrated with an ease of style which would render dull the recital of any other pen, upon the same topic.

Those who have seen those wild and hardy trappers, and who know anything of the severe privations and fearful dangers encountered by them in the wilderness, would scarcely expect to find science or religion marching in such rude companionship. But danger itself is alluring to the ardent temperament, while true piety and the genuine love of science are unappalled by its terrors. Many gentlemen have been induced by curiosity alone to accompany these parties, and a valuable family of missionaries, under the charge of the Rev. Jason Lee,[7] of the Methodist Episcopal Church, has already settled on the Willamette River, a branch of the Columbia. Although missions have not heretofore been successful among the Indians, we think that, considering the pacific character of the people and the favourable auspices under which this attempt has been commenced, much good from it may be confidently expected.

The portrait which accompanies this article represents an interesting individual.[8] He is one of that distant tribe inhabiting the most western extremity of our continent—a Chinook, belonging to a band of the great family of Nez Percés.[9] The name Stumanu has no particular meaning that we have been able to discover; the only account he could give of it himself, is that he was called by it after his grandfather, who is still living. He was born at a Chinook village on the Columbia River, about seven miles from its mouth; and having lost his father when he was but two years old, was brought up by an uncle, who at an early age initiated him in the business of fishing, and in such other employments as engage the attention of that indolent race. In speaking of the skill of his tribe in the management of their canoes, he stated that he had often been alone on the ocean, when overtaken by storms, and had never felt the slightest alarm, but would right his little vessel, when overturned, and pursue his voyage as if nothing had happened.

Shortly after the establishment of the mission family on the Willamette, this youth, being favourably impressed in regard to the advantages of civilisation, voluntarily determined to place himself at the school, and applied to Doctor M'Loughlin,[10] a benevolent gentleman, at the British fort Vancouver, who had taken a lively interest in the missionary enterprise, for his advice on the subject. He cheerfully gave the applicant a letter of introduction to the Rev. Mr Lee, superintendent of the Willamette station; and thus encouraged, Stumanu, taking his younger brother by the hand, proceeded to the school, to offer himself and his brother as pupils. They were cheerfully admitted, and this youth soon proved himself a valuable acquisition to the school. He quickly showed a great fondness, as well as an aptitude, for learning, was industrious and useful on the farm, and won esteem by the most amiable qualities of temper. He possessed, what was remarkable in an Indian, a decidedly mechanical genius, and excelled in the construction of tools and implements, and in the imitation of any simple articles of furniture that came under his notice, so that the mission family were fully repaid for the expenses of his education and subsistence by his labour. His good sense, sobriety of temperament, and equability of disposition, rendered him altogether a person of uncommon interest.

Stumanu was about twenty years of age when this portrait was taken; he was about five feet in stature, thick set, and strongly made. He was on a visit to the Atlantic cities in company with the Rev. Mr Lee, who was on a tour for the purpose of raising funds to support his valuable establishment. At New York, Philadelphia, and other places, the young Indian addressed large congregations, in his native tongue, on the destitute condition of his people, their readiness to learn from the white people, and the ample field that was spread open to those whose benevolence might induce them to take pity on the poor savages of the farther West. Some of these addresses were of a very impressive character, and Mr Lee, who interpreted them, assured the congregations that what Stumanu said was wholly his own in conception and language.

On the eve of the departure of the Rev. Mr Lee to the scene of his labours on the Willamette, Stumanu, flushed with the prospect of once more mingling with his kindred and friends, and gratified with all he had seen of the white man's capacity and powers, was taken suddenly ill in New York and after a short but severe attack, died on the 29th of May, 1839.

NOTES

1. " The [Chinook are the] best-known tribe of the Chinookan family. They claimed the territory on the north side of Columbia River, Washington, from the mouth of Gray's Bay, a distance of about 15 miles, and north along the sea-coast as far as the north part of Shoalwater Bay, where they were met by the Chehalis, a Salish tribe. The Chinook were first described by Lewis and Clark, who visited them in 1805, though they had been known to traders for at least twelve years previously. Lewis and Clark estimated their number at 400, but referred only to those living on Columbia River."—*Handbook of American Indians*, pt. 1, p. 272.

2. The custom of artificially flattening the heads of children appears to have been practised by nearly all the tribes of south-eastern United States, but not by the Algonquian tribes farther north.

3. Robert Gray, of Boston, born 1755, died 1806. May 11, 1791, he discovered the mouth of the river which he named *Columbia*, after his own vessel.

4. Meriwether Lewis, born near Charlottesville, Virginia, 1774; died in Tennessee, 1809. About 1801 he became private secretary to President Jefferson.

William Clark, born in Virginia, 1770; died at St Louis, Missouri, 1838. Governor of Missouri Territory from 1813 to 1820.

The "Lewis and Clark" Expedition started from the mouth of the Missouri, May 14, 1804; returning the party reached St Louis, September 23, 1806. They crossed from the valley of the Mississippi to the Pacific Ocean; the distance from the mouth of the Missouri to the mouth of the Columbia is more than 3500 miles.

5. John Bradbury, F.L.S., London, *Travels in the Interior of America, in the Years* 1809, 1810, *and* 1811, London, 1819, p. 18:—"On my return to St Louis, I was informed that a party of men had arrived from Canada, with an intention to ascend the Missouri, on their way to the Pacific Ocean, by the same route that Lewis and Clark had followed, by descending the Columbia River. . . . Mr Wilson P. Hunt, the leader of the party, in a very friendly and pressing manner invited me to accompany them up the River Missouri. . . . I gladly accepted the invitation, to which an acquaintance with Messrs Ramsey Crooks and Donald M'Kenzie, also principals of the party, was no small inducement."

6. For a full discussion of this subject, consult Hiram M. Chittenden, *American Fur Trade in the Far West*, 3 vols., New York, 1902.

7. Rev. Jason Lee was born at Stanstead, Canada, in 1803. His parents, of English descent, were born in the United States, but went to Canada. For a number of years Jason worked in the pineries of northern Canada; in 1826 he was "converted" and joined the Wesleyan Church, and in the following year entered the Wesleyan Academy at Wilbraham, Mass., where he remained a short time. Returning to his home in Canada he taught school and afterward became a preacher of the Wesleyan Church. In 1832 or 1833 he offered his services to the Wesleyan Missionary Society of London as a missionary to the Indians, and in 1833, while awaiting a reply to his application, was offered an appointment by the New England Conference of the Methodist Church as missionary to the Flathead Indians. He started overland for Oregon in the spring of 1834, with Nathan J. Wyeth's second expedition, arriving at Fort Vancouver, September 16. As the original site for his mission Lee selected a place at French Prairie on the eastern side of Willamette River, ten miles north of the present Salem, Oregon, and therefore within the territory of the Kalapooian Indians. In its establishment and subsequent support Lee was substantially aided by Dr John M'Loughlin, "the Father of Oregon" and chief factor of the Hudson's Bay Company at Fort Vancouver. Lee married Anna Maria Pittman, a member of a party of missionaries who arrived at Fort Vancouver in May, 1837. On April 4, 1838, Lee left Fort Vancouver on a trip to the Eastern States for the purpose of raising funds for his mission. His wife died in June, before her husband had covered more than half of his long journey across the continent. Accompanying the missionary were two Chinook boys, known as W. M. Brooks and

Thomas Adams, who had been at the mission for some time. Adams was taken ill at Peoria, Illinois, and was compelled to spend the winter there, but joined Lee later. Stumanu, therefore, was W. M. Brooks. Lee's journey was very successful. The Missionary Board was induced to raise $42,000 to provide for sending thirty-six adults (including Lee's new wife) and sixteen children, and a cargo of goods and supplies for the Oregon mission. The missionary was received everywhere with great enthusiasm during the winter of 1838 and the summer of 1839, which he devoted to travelling and delivering addresses in the cities and larger towns of the Atlantic states, the presence and intelligent speeches of the boys adding greatly to the popular interest. Notwithstanding this large endowment, the mission was not successful. The Indians, who belonged to several tribes, did not receive Christianity kindly, their numbers had become wasted by disease, and the men refused to work for the reason that they regarded labour as fit only for women and slaves. In 1843 trouble arose between Lee and the Missionary Board in New York, and he was summarily removed as superintendent of the Oregon Methodist Mission, but was afterward exonerated of the charges of misapplication of the Mission's resources. He died at Lake Memphremagog, Canada, on March 2, 1845. His body was buried at Stanstead. Consult: Holman, Frederick V., *Dr John M'Loughlin, the Father of Oregon*, 1907; Hines, Gustavus, *Oregon, its History, Condition, etc.*, 1851; Lee and Frost, *Ten Years in Oregon*, 1844; Wyeth, Nathan J., *Correspondence and Journals*, 1899; Townsend, John K., *Narrative of a Journey Across the Rocky Mountains*, 1839; Bancroft, H. H., *History of Oregon*, 2 vols., 1886.

8. The artist is unknown. The portrait is not listed in the Rhees *Catalogue*.

9. This, of course, is an error, the Nez Percés being the principal tribe of the Shahaptian family, whose language is totally distinct from that of the Chinook. (See note 1, above.)

10. See Holman, F. V., *Dr John M'Loughlin, the Father of Oregon*, 1907, cited in note 7, above.

LE SOLDAT DU CHENE

(AN OSAGE CHIEF)

THE name of this chief, as pronounced in the tongue of his own people, has not reached us; we know it only in the French translation, which introduces him to us as "*The Soldier of the Oak.*"[1] The name refers, we understand, to a desperate fight, in which, having sheltered himself behind a large oak, he successfully defended himself against several enemies. His portrait was taken in Philadelphia, in 1805 or 1806, while he was on a visit to the President of the United States,[2] under charge of Colonel Chouteau, of St Louis, and was presented to the American Philosophical Society, in whose valuable collection we found it.[3]

He was an Osage chief of high reputation, and is mentioned by Pike in his *Travels*. The Osages inhabit the prairies lying south of the Missouri River, and west of the states of Missouri and Arkansas.[4] The buffalo is found in their country, and the wild horse roams over the plains immediately beyond them. They are horsemen, therefore, and not only manage the steed with dexterity, but bestow great pains upon the appearance and equipment of their horses. Living in a sunny climate, and roving over plains covered with rich verdure and well stocked with game, they present a striking contrast to the unhappy Chippewa, to whom they are superior in stature, in cheer-

LE SOLDAT DU CHIENE
An Osage Chief

fulness, and in social qualities. The privations of the northern Indian subdue his spirit, while the Osage exhibits all the pride and all the social elevation of which the savage is capable. The difference between them results solely out of the disparity in their respective physical comforts; but it is so great as to be obvious to the most casual observer, and goes far towards demonstrating how much of the savage character is the consequence of poverty and the want of the common comforts of life.[5]

NOTES

1. Major S. H. Long, *Account of an Expedition from Pittsburgh to the Rocky Mountains,* compiled by Edwin James, Philadelphia, 1823, Vol. II., p. 245, refers to "Big Soldier" and "The Soldier of the Oak" of the Little Osage as "great war captains."

2. Z. M. Pike, *An Account of Expeditions to the Sources of the Mississippi and through the Western Parts of Louisiana,* Philadelphia, 1810.
Page 111 : "15th *July,* 1806, *Tuesday.*—We sailed from the landing at Belle Fontaine, about 3 o'clock P.M., in two boats. . . . We had also under our charge, chiefs of the Osage and Pawnees, who, with a number of women and children, had been to Washington. These Indians had been redeemed from captivity among the Potowatomies, and were now to be returned to their friends at the Osage towns. The whole number of Indians amounted to fifty-one. . . ." During the journey up the Missouri to the Osage, the Indians went on foot, joining Pike's camp each night. Page 116 : "29th *July, Tuesday.*—All the Indians arrived very early and the Big Soldier, whom I had appointed the officer to regulate the march, was much displeased that Sans Oreille and the others had left him. . . ." In the Appendix to the second part, facing p. 53, Pike mentions "Soldat de Chien, Soldiers' Dog, second chief of the Little Osage."
Morse, *Report to the Secretary of War,* 1882, p. 206, refers to Big Soldier as "a very sensible Osage . . . who has twice been at Washington."
In view of the above facts it would appear that Big Soldier and the subject of this sketch were one and the same person.

3. The following is gleaned from the jumble of names following the various early treaties with the Osage: Treaty of Portage des Sioux, September 12, 1815, signed by "Akidatangga, the big soldier." Treaty at "the United States Factory on the M. De Cigue Augt.," August 31, 1822, signed by "Big Soldier." Treaty of St Louis, June 2, 1825, signed by "Paigaismanie, or Big Soldier." Treaty of Camp Holmes, August 24, 1835, signed by " Ah-te-kah, or the soldier."

4. At the beginning of the nineteenth century the Osage claimed a vast territory in Missouri, Arkansas, Kansas, and Indian Territory, but by treaty of November 10, 1808, they ceded to the United States all that part lying between the Arkansas River in Arkansas and the Missouri River in Missouri lying east of a line extending from Fort Clark on the Missouri River southward to the Arkansas, and also surrendered all claim to lands north of the Missouri. By treaty of September 25, 1818, they relinquished a considerable area in north-western Arkansas and eastern Indian Territory, north of Arkansas River. By treaty of June 2, 1825, they ceded all claim to the remainder of their lands in Missouri and Arkansas, all of that part of the present Oklahoma north of the Canadian River (excepting the area in the eastern part ceded by previous treaty), comprising the greater part of the state, together with a vast area extending almost entirely across central Kansas from east to west. To this enormous area the Osage ceded an adjoining strip in Kansas, more than 250 miles in length, by treaty of September 29, 1865. Again, by Act of Congress of July 15, 1870, the remainder of the lands held by the Osage in Kansas was ceded to the United States, and a reservation set aside for them in north-eastern Indian Territory (Oklahoma), embracing lands that had been purchased from the Cherokee (see also Executive order of March 27, 1871, and Act of Congress of June 5, 1872).

5. Population of the tribe in 1912, 2056. (See also WATCHEMONNE, note 5, p. 171, this volume.)

POWASHEEK

(A FOX CHIEF)

THE word Powasheek,[1] in the Musquakee language, signifies
"*To dash the water off.*" The individual who bears this
name is a celebrated brave of the Musquakee or Fox
nation, and is numbered among their chiefs or leading
men. A few years ago he was better known to the whites
than any other person of his nation, and was probably
at that time the most influential man among them. The
superior talents of Keokuk have, however, thrown into
the shade all the leaders who once stood high in the
combined Saukie and Musquakee nation, and Wapella[2]
the Fox leader, being a chief of great address and a friend
of Keokuk,[3] Powasheek has been little heard of during
late years in public life. He was a daring warrior, and
held a respectable standing in council, as a man of
prudence and capacity. The likeness is a good one, and
gives a correct idea of his character.[4]

Powasheek is one of those men who, though highly
respected, and holding a rank among the first men of
his nation, is not distinguished by brilliant talents.
Nothing very striking in his history has reached us.

NOTES

1. Powasheek, according to Dr Truman Michelson, is correctly *Pāwashĭk·*, "one who shakes his (own) body while lying down."

2. See biography, p. 99, this volume.

3. See biography, p. 115, this volume.

4. Pawasheek was a signer of the following treaties: Fort Armstrong, September 21, 1832, his name appearing as "Pow-sheek, or the roused bear"; Debuque (Dubuque) county, Wisconsin Territory, September 26, 1836, as "Po-we-seek," and September 28, 1836, as "Pow-a-sheek"; Washington, October 21, 1837, as "Po-we-sheek, Shedding Bear, a (principal chief)"; and Sac and Fox agency, Iowa, October 11, 1842, as "Pow a shick." Of the last-mentioned treaty he was the first signer for the Foxes.

The portrait of "Paw-a-shick, *To dash the water off*," bears No. 34 in the Rhees *Catalogue*. It was painted by Cooke in 1837, during which year a large delegation visited Washington and signed the treaty of October 21.

POW-A-SHEEK
A Fox Chief

SHARITARISH

(A PAWNEE CHIEF)

THE Pawnee nation is divided into several parts, the original or main body of which are called Grand Pawnees, while the bands which have separated from them and form independent, though somewhat subordinate communities, are designated as Pawnee Loups, Republican Pawnees, Pawnee Mahas, etc. These divisions of larger into smaller communities, which are continually taking place, present a curious subject in the study of Indian history, which we propose to treat more at large in another place.

Sharitarish[1] was principal chief, or head man, of the Grand Pawnees. He was descended from a line of chiefs, and according to the law of descent, which selects the next of kin, if worthy, succeeded his elder brother, Tarecawawaho. They were sons of Sharitarish, a chief who is mentioned in *Pike's Expedition*[2] under the name of Characterish.

Tarecawawaho was a brave and enterprising leader, as indeed those usually are who obtain power in these warlike tribes ; for the office of chief is no sinecure among a people so continually exposed to various dangers. He had also a large share of that pride, the offspring of ignorance, which is often the principal ingredient in the magnificence of sovereignty, and especially in the savage state. When invited to visit the President of the United States, he refused to do so, upon the ground that it would be too great a condescension. The Pawnees, he asserted, were the greatest people in the world, and himself the most important chief. He was willing to live at peace with the American people, and to conciliate the Government by reciprocating their acts of courtesy. But he argued that the President could not bring as many young men into the field as himself, that he did not own as many horses, nor maintain as many wives; that he was not so distinguished a brave, and could not exhibit as many scalps taken in battle; and that therefore he would not consent to call him his Great Father. He did not object, however, to returning the civilities of the President, by sending a delegation composed of some of his principal men; and among those selected to accompany Major O'Fallon to Washington[3] on this occasion was the subject of this sketch. Sharitarish returned with enlarged views of the numbers and power of the white men, and no doubt with more correct opinions than he had before entertained, of the relative importance of his own nation. As he travelled league after league over the broad expanse of the American Territory, he became convinced of the vast disparity between a horde of wandering savages and a nation of civilised men, and was satisfied that his people could gain nothing by a state of warfare with a power so superior.

Sharitarish was a chief of noble form and fine bearing; he was six feet tall, and well proportioned; and when mounted on the fiery steed of the prairie, was a graceful and very imposing personage. His people looked upon him as a great brave, and the young men especially regarded him as a person who was designed to great distinction.[4] After his return from Washington his popularity increased so greatly as to excite the jealousy of his elder

SHAR-I-TAR-ISH
A Pawnee Chief

brother, the head chief, who, however, did not long survive that event. He died a few weeks after the return of Sharitarish, who succeeded him, but who also died during the succeeding autumn, at the age of a little more than thirty years. He was succeeded by his brother Ishcatape, the wicked chief, a name given him by the Omahas, or Pawnee Mahas, and which also has been applied by some to the subject of this notice.[5]

NOTES

1. His name is correctly given by John B. Dunbar ("The Pawnee Indians," *Magazine of American History*, Vol. VIII., 1882, p. 740) as Sa'-re-cĕr-ish (c = ch). Of the son of the subject of this sketch, he says: "Sa'-re-cĕr-ish (Angry Chief), second chief of the Cau'-i [*i.e.*, Chawi or Grand Pawnee] band, was a man of unusually humane disposition, and had strenuously endeavoured to secure the suppression of the practice [of human sacrifice]. In the spring of 1817 The Ski'-di arranged to sacrifice a Comanche girl. After Sa-re-cĕr-ish had essayed in vain to dissuade them, Pit'-a-le-sha-ru . . . conceived the bold design of rescuing her." Mr Dunbar states (*ibid.*, Vol. IV., April, 1880, p. 261) that this Sa'-rĕ-chĕr-ish died in 1838.

2. Lieut. Z. M. Pike met the elder Sharitarish (whom he calls Characterish) near the Pawnee village on the Republican River in Webster county, Nebraska, on September 25, 1806. The chief was accompanied by his two sons and the chief Iskatappe. Characterish, it appears (Pike, September 27), had been given a commission from the Governor of New Mexico, dated Santa Fe, June 15, 1806, and also a grand medal and two mules (Pike, *Exped.*, Coues ed., Vol. II., pp. 409, 414, 544). Lieut. Wilkinson of Pike's force (pp. 542, 551) refers to "Characterish, or White Wolf," while Pike in his "Statistical Abstract" (p. 591) gives his Pawnee, French, and English names respectively as Characterish, Loup Blanche, and White Wolf.

"Sâ-ni'-tsă-rish" the second was met by Charles Augustus Murray during his visit to the Pawnee country, and is several times mentioned by him in *Travels in North America during the Years* 1834, 1835, *and* 1836, London, 1839. This son served Murray as a guide from the Pawnee village to Fort Leavenworth, and just before starting on their journey, Murray wrote (Vol. I., p. 305): "Old Sâ-ni'-tsă-rish gave a warm embrace at parting, as before, but he was grave and thoughtful, and said there were bad men in the prairie; adding a significant sign that we should look out while we slept." (See PETALESHARRO, Vol. I., note 12, p. 216, this work.)

"Shah-re-tah-riche" the second was the first signer, in behalf of the Grand Pawnees, of the treaty made at the Grand Pawnee village on Platte River, Nebraska, October 9, 1833. The treaty of Fort Childs, Nebraska, August 6, 1848, was signed by Sha-re-ta-riche, but he is the third chief of this name, his father, the son of the subject of this sketch, having died ten years before, as we have seen. See note 5, below.

3. A reference to the arrival of Major O'Fallon and his party of Indians in Washington appears in *Niles' Register*, under date of December 15, 1821. (See Vol. I., note 8, p. 163.) Several interesting accounts of the events that transpired during their stay in Washington have come down to us. W. Faux (*Memorable¡Days in America*, London, 1823, p. 378 *et seq.*), an Englishman visiting America at that time, wrote "Some account of the Indians who visited all the chief cities in the Eastern States, and made a long stay in Washington in the winter of 1821." "These Indians," he says, "were the chiefs and half-chiefs of tribes from the most western part of this continent with which we are acquainted, and came under the guidance of Major O'Fallon from the Council Bluffs. All of them are men of large stature, very muscular, having fine countenances, with the real Roman nose, dignified in their manners, and peaceful and quiet in their habits. There was no instance of drunkenness among them during their stay here. . . . Their portraits, which are gone with them, were taken in oil by Mr King in their native costume, buffalo skins, with the hair inside, turned back at the neck and breast, which looked very handsome, like fur collars. Eight, however, the chiefs and the squaw, Mr King copied and keeps himself. He received 400 dollars from *Uncle Sam* for it. There was a notice in the papers that the Indians would dance and display their feats in front of the President's house on a certain day, which they did to at least 6000 persons. They showed their manner of sitting in council, their dances, their war whoops, with the noises, gesticulations, etc., of the sentinels on the sight of an approaching enemy. They were in a state of perfect nudity, except a piece of red flannel round the waist and passing between the legs. . . . The Otta half-chief (evidently Shaumonekusse or L'Ietan ; see Vol. I., p. 156, this work) and his squaw have taken tea. . . . She was a very good-natured, mild woman, and he showed great readiness in acquiring our language." It may be added that no portrait of the Deligation referred to by Faux is in the King collection in the Redwood Library at Newport, R.I., with the exception of that of " Peskelechaco, or Republican Pawnee. A Pawnee chief, killed by a war party of the Osages, 1826."

James Buchanan (His Majestey's Counsul for the State of New York), in *Sketches of the History, Manners, and Customs of the North American Indians*, London, 1824, pp. 38-46, records the "Speeches of

Several of the Chiefs of the Deligation of Indians, under Major O'Fallen, to the President of the United States, in Council, on the 4th of February, 1822."

4. Major Stephen H. Long met Sharitarish at the Pawnee village in April, 1820 (*An Account of an Expedition from Pittsburgh to the Rocky Mountains, Compiled by Edwin James*, Philadelphia, 1823, Vol. I., p. 354): "Sharetarish said, that, if agreeable to his father (Major O'Fallon), he would return in a reasonable time, and bring some of his young warriors, for the purpose of performing a dance. Towards evening Sharetarish arrived with his dancers, thirty or forty in number, who were all accoutred and painted for the occasion. . . . At the termination of the dance, Sharetarish presented Major O'Fallon with a painted bison robe, representing several of his own combats with the enemy, as well as those of his friends, all of which he explained to us."

5. In the Rhees *Catalogue*, the portrait of "Is-ca-ta-pe, Wicked Chief —Great Pawnee," bears No. 93. It was painted by King, but no date appears. This was probably the portrait of Sharitarish painted during his visit to Washington with Major O'Fallon in 1821. "Esh-ca-tar-pa, the bad chief," was the first name attached to the treaty of Fort Atkinson, Council Bluffs, September 30, 1825.

WAKAUNHAKA

(A WINNEBAGO CHIEF)

THIS individual is of mixed blood; his father is a French-man, and his mother a woman of the Winnebago nation. He is one of the finest-looking men among that people, and has for many years been one of their principal speakers on all public occasions. The qualifications for this office are not very extensive, and in general comprise little else than fluency, a graceful manner, and a familiar acquaint-ance with the current transactions of the day. Wakaun-haka, or the *Snake Skin*, possesses these qualities in a high degree; his stature is about six feet three inches, his person erect and commanding, and his delivery easy. He is between fifty and sixty years of age, and is one of the war chiefs of the Winnebagoes.[1]

In the early years of the Snake Skin, he was a success-ful hunter, a warrior of fair standing, and a person of decided influence among his people. But the sin that most easily besets the Indian has destroyed his usefulness; habits of dissipation, with the premature decrepitude incident to the savage life, have made him an old man at the age at which the statesmen of civilised nations are in the enjoyment of the highest degree of intellectual vigour. His influence has declined, and many of his band have left him and joined the standards of other chiefs.

298

WA-KAUN-HA-KA, *or* "SNAKE SKIN"
A Winnebago Chief

This personage has been the husband of no less than eleven wives, and the father of a numerous progeny. With all the savage love of trinkets and finery, he had his full share of the personal vanity which nourishes that reigning propensity, and of which the following anecdote affords a striking illustration. In one of the drunken broils which had not been unfrequent in the latter part of his life, a fight occurred between himself and another person, in which the nose of the chief was severely bitten. The Reverend Mr Lowry, superintendent of the school, on hearing of the accident, paid the chief a visit of condolence, hoping that an opportunity might offer which might enable him to give salutary advice to the sufferer. He was lying with his head covered, refusing to be seen. His wife, deeply affected by the misfortune, and terrified by the excited state of her husband's mind, sat near him weeping bitterly. When she announced the name of his visitor, the chief still concealing his mutilated features, exclaimed that he was a ruined man, and desired only to die. He continued to bewail his misfortune as one which it would be unworthy in a man and a warrior to survive, and as altogether intolerable. His only consolation was found in the declaration that his young men should kill the author of his disgrace; and accordingly the latter was soon after murdered, though it is not known by whom. Had not this injury been of a kind by which the vanity of Wakaunhaka was affected, and his self-love mortified, it might have been forgotten or passed over ; we do not say *forgiven*, as this word, in our acceptance of it, expresses an idea to which the savage is a stranger. Regarding an unrevenged insult as a trader views an outstanding debt, which he may demand whenever he can find the delinquent party in a condition to pay it, he is satisfied by a suitable compensation, if the injury be of a character to admit of compromise. Had his wife, for instance, eloped with a lover, or his brother been slain, the offender might have purchased peace at the expense of a few horses; but what price could indemnify a great chief for the loss of his nose? Happily, the wound proved but slight, and Wakaunhaka lost neither his nose nor his reputation.

We do not intend, however, by the last remark, to do injustice to this chief, who on another occasion nursed his resentment under the influence of highly creditable feelings. We have had occasion to mention elsewhere [2] a striking incident of border warfare which occurred in 1834, when a war party of Sauks and Foxes surprised a small encampment of the Winnebagoes, and massacred all the persons within it, except one gallant boy, about twelve years of age, who, after discharging a gun and killing a Sauk brave, made his escape by swimming the Mississippi, and brought the news of the slaughter to Fort Crawford, at Prairie du Chien. That boy was the son of Wakaunhaka, and among the slain was one of the wives and several of the children of this chief. The exploit was considered as conferring great honour on the lad, as well as upon his family, and the father evinced the pride which he felt in his son, while he lamented over the slain members of his family with a lively sensibility. An exterminating war was expected to follow this bloody deed; but by the prompt interposition of the agent of the United States, and the military officers, a treaty was held, and a peace brought about, chiefly through the politic and conciliatory conduct of Keokuk, the head man of the offending nation. Forty horses were presented to the Winnebagoes, as a full compensation for the loss of about half that number of their people, who had been massacred in cold blood; the indemnity was accepted, the peace pipe was smoked, and the hands of the murderers, cleansed of the foul stains of midnight assassination, were clasped in the embrace of amity by the relatives of the slain. Wakaunhaka, with a disdain for so unworthy a compromise, which did honour to his feelings as a husband and father, stood aloof, and refused either to participate in the present or to give his hand to the Sauks and Foxes.

The Snake Skin, like many other influential men among the Indians, has always been obstinately opposed to all changes in the condition of his people, and has declined taking any part in the benevolent plans of the American Government, or of individuals, for the civilisation of his race. On one occasion, when the superintendent of the school called his attention to the subject, and urged the advantages which the Winnebagoes might derive from those benevolent measures, his reply was, that the Great Spirit had made the skin of the Indian red, and that soap and water could not make it white. At another time, when urged to use his influence to procure the attendance of the Indian youth at the Government school, he replied that their children were all asleep, and could not be waked up. These answers were figurative, and contain the substance of the objection invariably urged by the savages on this subject : " The Great Spirit has made us what we are—it is not his will that we should be changed ; if it was his will, he would let us know ; if it is not his will, it would be wrong for us to attempt it, nor could we by any art change our nature."

NOTES

1. As evidence of the important position he held in the tribe, we find his name attached to numerous treaties. At Prairie du Chien, he was the fourth representative of his tribe to sign the important treaty of August 19, 1825, his name appearing as Wau-ca-ha-ga. At Green Bay, on August 25, 1828, he was the ninth signer of the treaty, signing as Wau-kaun-haw-kaw. On August 1, 1829, he signed another treaty concluded at Prairie du Chien. At Fort Armstrong, Rock Island, Illinois, he was a signer of the treaty dated September 15, 1832, being the second signer, and his name appearing as Wau-kaun-hah-kaw. And lastly, he signed the treaty at Washington, November 1, 1837.

It was evidently during this visit to Washington that his portrait, bearing No. 127 in the Rhees *Catalogue,* was painted. Although the name of the artist does not appear, it may safely be attributed to King. (See Introduction, Vol. I., p. xlvii. No. 20; p. xlix. No. 61; p. lii., No. 127, this work.)

2. See KEOKUK, p. 136, this volume.

PES-KE-LE-CHA-CO
A Pawnee Chief

PESKELECHACO

(A PAWNEE CHIEF)

WE regret that so few particulars have been preserved of
the life of this individual, who was one of the most prominent men of his nation, and whose character afforded
a favourable specimen of his race. He was a person of
excellent disposition, who, to the qualities proper to the
savage mode of life, added some of the virtues which
belong to a more refined state of society. But such is the
evanescent nature of traditionary history, that while we
find this chief invariably spoken of with high commenda-
tion, we have been scarcely able to trace out any of the
circumstances of his life.

Peskelechaco was a noted war chief of the Pawnees,
who visited Washington City as a delegate from his nation
in 18—.[1] We have had frequent occasions of remarking
the salutary effect produced upon the minds of the more
intelligent of the Indian chiefs and head men, by giving
them the opportunity of witnessing our numbers and
civilisation; our arts, our wealth, and the vast extent of
our country. The evidences of our power which they
witness, together with the conciliatory effect of the kindness shown them, have seldom failed to make a favourable
impression. Such was certainly the case with this chief,
who, after his return from Washington, acquired great
influence with his tribe, in consequence of the admiration

with which they regarded the knowledge he had gained in his travels. He had spent his time profitably in observing closely whatever passed under his notice, and in proportion to his shrewdness and intelligence his opinions became respected. He spoke frequently of the words he had heard from his Great Father, the President of the United States, who had, in pursuance of the benevolent policy which has governed the intercourse of the administration at Washington with the Indians, admonished his savage visitors to abandon their predatory habits and cultivate the arts of peace. Peskelechaco often declared his determination to pursue this salutary advice. He continued to be uniformly friendly to the people of the United States, and faithful to his engagements with them, and was much respected by them. He was a man of undoubted courage, and esteemed a skilful leader.

The only incident in the active life of this chief which has been preserved was its closing scene. About the year 1826, a war party of the Osages marched against his village with the design of stealing horses and killing some of his people. The assailants were discovered, and a severe battle ensued. The chief, at the head of a band of warriors, sallied out to meet the invaders, and the conflict assumed an animated and desperate character. Having slain one of the enemy with his own hand, he rushed forward to *strike the body*, which is considered the highest honour a warrior can gain in battle. To kill an enemy is honourable, but the proudest achievement of the Indian brave is to strike, to lay his hand upon, the slain or mortally wounded body of his foeman, whether slain by himself or another. To strike the dead is therefore an object of the highest ambition ; and when a warrior falls, the nearest warrior of both parties rush forward, the one to gain the triumph, and the other to frustrate the attempt. Peskelechaco was killed in a gallant endeavour to signalise himself in this manner.

NOTE

1. Peskelechaco was probably one of the party of Pawnee that visited Washington in 1821, and his portrait was evidently painted by King at that time. It bears No. 89 in the Rhees *Catalogue*, although neither the date nor the name of the artist appears. The original is now in Redwood Library, Newport, Rhode Island, having been one of the collection bequeathed to that institution by King.

HOOWANNEKA

(A WINNEBAGO CHIEF)

HOOWANNEKA, the *Little Elk*, was a chief of the Winnebago nation, who served with some reputation on the side of the British in the late war between Great Britain and the United States. At the termination of hostilities, when it was found that the British had made peace for themselves, leaving their Indian allies residing within the United States at the mercy of the latter Government, the Winnebagoes reluctantly sought protection under the American flag. Hoowanneka was among the first who became convinced that his nation had been seduced by specious promises into an unnatural war against those whose enmity must be fatal to their existence, and under whose friendship alone they could continue to have a resting place or a name. Uniting with those who held similar opinions, he exerted a salutary influence over his fierce associates, in restraining them from further outrage upon the American frontiers; and he remained afterwards a friend of our people and Government.[1]

The Little Elk was descended from the Caromanie[2] family, the most distinguished band of his nation. He was a tall, fine-looking man, and had some reputation as a speaker, but has left no specimen of his eloquence upon record. In the portrait which accompanies this sketch, he appeared in the costume in which he presented himself

HOO-WAN-NE-KA, *or* " LITTLE ELK "
A Winnebago Chief

before the President of the United States, at Washington, in 1824,[3] when he visited the seat of Government as a delegate from his nation. It must have been a singular scene, which exhibited the savage orator, painted in fantastic style, and clad in these wild and picturesque habiliments, addressing the grave and dignified head of the American people, in one of the saloons of the White House. The President and his Cabinet, with the diplomatists and other visitors who are usually invited when a spectacle of this kind is presented, must have afforded a striking contrast to the war chiefs and orators of a savage horde decked out in all the barbarian magnificence of beads, paint, and feathers, with their war clubs, pipes, and banners.

NOTES

1. He was the eleventh and last of his tribe to sign the treaty at Prairie du Chien, August 19, 1825, his name appearing as "Ho-wa-mick-a, the little elk"; at Green Bay, Michigan Territory, August 25, 1828, his name was the third signed to the treaty as "Hoo-waun-ee-kaw, or little elk"; again at Prairie du Chien, August 1, 1829, he signed as "Hoo-wan-noo-kaw"; lastly, in the treaty signed at Fort Armstrong, September 15, 1832, his name appears as "Hoo-wau-nee-kaw, or little elk (orator), one of the Kay-ra-men-nees."

2. See Vol. I., p. 146, this work.

3. The portrait reproduced in this sketch was probably that bearing No. 58 in the Rhees *Catalogue*, although another, from a drawing by Lewis in 1826, is included in the same list, being numbered 16.

WAKAWN

(A WINNEBAGO CHIEF)

WAKAWN, *The Snake*, was a war chief of the Winnebagoes. He was born on St Mary's River, near Green Bay, in the Michigan Territory, and died in 1838, at the age of nearly sixty years. He was of the middle stature, but athletic in form, and was exceeded by none of his nation in ability to endure fatigue. Although his countenance displayed but an ordinary intellect, the expression was mild, and he had an honest eye, such as is not often seen among his people, who are among the most fierce and treacherous of their race. The Snake was a well-disposed man, who maintained a good character through life.

In 1811, and previously to that time, the Winnebagoes, under the influence of the British agents and traders, were unfriendly to the United States, and were actively engaged in the depredations committed upon the frontier settlements. The broad expanse of wilderness which intervened between them and the settlements in Ohio and Indiana, afforded no protection to the latter, whose log cabins were burned and sacked by savages who travelled hundreds of miles to enjoy the gratification of murdering a family, and plundering the wretched homestead of a hunter whose whole wealth consisted in the spoils of the chase. The prospect of a war between Great Britain and the United States, to which they had long been taught to look for-

WA-KAWN, *or* "THE SNAKE"
A Winnebago Chief

ward, as an event which would give them temporary employment and great ultimate advantage, stimulated this warlike people into a high state of excitement; and when the Shawanee Prophet[1] raised his standard, they were among the first of the deluded band who rallied around it. Wakawn and some of his people formed a part of the motley assemblage collected at the Prophet's town[2] in the autumn of 1811, and against whom was directed the campaign of General Harrison, which eventuated so honourably to the American arms and to the personal fame of that distinguished leader. Wakawn was in the battle of Tippecanoe,[3] where he was slightly wounded, and is said to have borne himself bravely on that occasion. He was occasionally on the war - path during the remainder of the war, at the close of which he buried the hatchet, and has since been uniformly friendly to the American people.

Since the establishment of friendly relations between his nation and the United States, The Snake has been conspicuous for his faithful observance of the existing treaties; and after the several cessions of land made by the Winnebagoes to the American Government, he always led the way in abandoning the ceded territories, while a majority of the tribe were disposed to rescind the contract. In the late removal of his people to the west of the Mississippi,[4] he was the first Winnebago of any note who crossed the river, when a great portion of the nation, including most of the influential men, were inclined to remain upon the lands they had sold to the United States. The readiness with which the Indians sell their titles to large tracts of country, contrasted with their subsequent reluctance to deliver the possession, may be attributed in part to the fickleness of the savage character, in which notions of property, of obligation, or of abstract right are but feebly developed, if indeed they can be said to have palpable existence. But the immediate causes of those breaches of faith may be usually traced to the intrigues of unprincipled traders, who seek pecuniary profit in fomenting dissension. The refusal of an Indian nation to comply with its engagements affords an occasion for a new treaty, attended with all the parade and expenditure of the original convention, with new stipulations, additional presents, and increased disbursements of money for various purposes, all which afford opportunities for peculation to those rapacious men. No subject has been more greatly misunderstood, or has afforded a more prolific theme for vituperation towards the American Government and people, than the oppression supposed to have been exercised in removing Indians from their ceded lands, and which has been inferred from their reluctance to abandon them; when in fact, the only fault on the part of the Government is, that in effecting a laudable object, and with humane intentions towards the Indian, they have unwisely adopted a system which is liable to gross abuses.

In 1834, the Government established at Prairie du Chien a school and farm for the instruction of the Winnebagoes,[5] under the direction of the Rev. David Lowry, who engaged assiduously in the duty of instructing that tribe in the rudiments of an English education, as well as in the labours of agriculture, combining with these such religious information as his opportunities enabled him to inculcate. The Snake was the first of the chief men to appreciate the value of this establishment; he applied himself to the study of husbandry, and placed his family under the tuition of Mr Lowry. His example was the more valuable, as the Indians generally are opposed to all such innovations; and the Winnebagoes were obstinately hostile to the efforts made to induce them to adopt the

habits of civilised life. The decision of Wakawn, and
the zeal with which he advocated the benevolent views of
the Government, brought him into collision with the other
chiefs, who viewed his predilection for the knowledge and
habits of the white men as an alien and degenerate par-
tiality, inconsistent with the duty which he owed to his
own race; and on one occasion he defended his opinions
at the risk of his life.

Notwithstanding the disgrace attached to the practice
of manual labour among the Indian braves, The Snake
often threw aside his blanket, and joined his wife in her
rude but persevering attempts to support the family by
tilling the soil. The fertile prairies of Wisconsin, where
the soil has never been exhausted by culture, yields
abundant returns, and he soon became convinced that
he could more easily obtain a livelihood in this manner
than by the fatiguing and precarious labours of the chase.
But when urged by the superintendent of the school to
give the full weight of his character and influence to the
proposed reformation, by laying aside the character of the
brave and adopting entirely the habits of the civilised
man, he replied that he was too old—that the Indians
who had been reared in the free and roving pursuits of
savage life could not abandon them, but that their children
might; and while he declined doing what would be a
violence to his own nature, he strongly advocated the
employment of means to civilise the youth of his nation.

The difficulty of changing the habits of a people was
exemplified, in an amusing manner, in the family of this
chief. At his own request a log house, such as constitutes
the dwelling of the American farmer in the newly settled
parts of the country, was erected for him, at the expense
of the Government, under the expectation that by giving
his family a permanent residence, one step would be taken

towards their civilisation. The house was arranged in the ordinary way, with a chimney and fireplace; the operations of cooking were commenced in due form, at the fireplace, and the family assembled round the hearth, pleased and amused, no doubt, with this new form of social economy. But it was not long before the newly adopted contrivance was abandoned — the floor was removed, and a fire kindled in the centre of the house— the family gathered in a circle about it—a hole was cut in the roof for the smoke to pass through—and the mansion of The Snake family became once more thoroughly, and completely, an Indian lodge.

Nor could Wakawn himself resolve to abandon the superstitions of his race; while he recommended civilisation to others, he clung to the customs of his forefathers. Believing in the existence and the superiority of the true God, he could not sever the tie that bound him to the ideal deities of his people. He continued to join his tribe in their religious feasts and dances, and usually presided at the exercises. He probably had the faculty of veneration strongly developed, for his grave and solemn demeanour on such occasions is said to have rendered them interesting, and to have given an imposing effect to the ceremonies.

Unfortunately this respectable chief, who possessed so many estimable qualities, and so just a sense of the true interests of his people, was subject to the weakness which has proved most fatal to them. He was addicted to intoxication, and unhappily there is nothing in the religion or the ethics of the savage, nothing in their public opinion or the economy of their domestic life, to impose a restraint upon this vice. When a fondness for ardent spirits is contracted, it is usually indulged, with scarcely any discredit to the individual, and without a limit, except that imposed by the want of means to gratify this insatiable appetite. Wakawn lived in the neighbourhood of Prairie du Chien, where the temptation was continually before him, and where ardent spirit was easily procured; and he was often drunk. This vice was the cause of his death. In November, 1838, after receiving their annuities from the United States, the Winnebagoes indulged themselves in a grand debauch, a kind of national *spree*, in which all engaged, without distinction of age, sex, or condition; and scenes of drunkenness, of violence, and of disgusting indecency were exhibited such as had never before been witnessed among this people. Wakawn indulged freely, and becoming entirely helpless, wandered off, and threw himself on the ground, where he slept without any protection from the weather, during the whole of a very cold night. The next day he was attacked with a pleurisy, which soon terminated his existence.

The Snake was buried according to the Indian customs. A pipe, and several other articles of small value were deposited with his remains in the grave. As those had been intended for the use of the spirit, in the happy hunting grounds of the blessed, his wife was desirous of adding some other articles, and brought them to the place of interment, but they were claimed by a rapacious chief, in remuneration of his services in doing honour to the deceased, and actually carried away. Previous to filling up the grave, the family and relations of Wakawn stepped across it, uttering loud lamentations, and then, after marching from it, in single file, for several hundred yards, returned by a circuitous route to their several lodges. This custom, which the Winnebagoes usually pursue, is practised from a regard for the living, and is supposed to be efficacious in diverting the hand of death from the family of the deceased.

The grave of this chief is often visited by convivial parties of his friends, who gather around it and pour whisky on the ground, for the benefit of the departed spirit, which is supposed to return and mingle in their orgies. It would not be difficult to point out in the bacchanalian lyrics of the most refined nations some ideas more absurd and less poetical than this.

The wife of this chief still survives, and is a pattern to her nation, in point of morality and industry. She had the sagacity to see the advantages which civilisation offered to her sex, and became an early advocate for extending its benefits to her children. She has uniformly resisted the temptation to which most of the Indian women yield, and has never been known to taste whisky. Always industrious, she contributed largely to the support of her family, during her husband's life, by cultivating the soil, and since his decease has maintained them decently by the same means. Shortly after she became a widow, a brother of her late husband offered to marry her, in conformity with a custom of the tribe, but she declined the proposal.[6]

NOTES

1. That is, Tenskwautawa. See Vol. I., p. 75, this work.

2. It was situated on the west side of the Wabash, just below the mouth of Tippecanoe River, in the present Tippecanoe county, Indiana. The site had been successively occupied by different tribes, but the last occupants were the Potawatomi, by whose invitation, in 1808, it became the headquarters of Tecumseh and his brother, the Prophet.

3. The battle of Tippecanoe was fought November 7, 1811. In the appendix to *History of the Discovery of America.* . . By Henry Trumbull, Norwich, 1812, appears one of the earliest accounts of the battle, from which the following notes are extracted : " . . . The conduct of the Wabash Indians, becoming suspicious to our Government, in consequence of their many thievish excursions and hasty preparations for an offensive attack, Gov. Harrison, with 1200 men (350 regulars and the remainder militia), were ordered to proceed from the neighborhood of Vincennes to the line, and demand of the Prophet the object of his real intentions. The troops commenced their march on the 26th September, and nothing important occurred until they arrived on the line, where they remained near a month, and built a strong fort which in honor of the commander-in-chief was called Fort Harrison. The Indians in a friendly manner almost every day visited camp and held councils with the Governor, but would not accede to his terms, which were that their leader (the Prophet) should give up the property stolen from the Americans, and send all their warriors to their different tribes; the Governor therefore determined to attack them. On the 29th October the troops left Fort Harrison and took up their line of march for the Prophet's town, where they arrived on the 6th November. When within about half a mile of the town the troops formed the line of battle, which the Indians perceiving, sent three of their chiefs with a flag of truce, begging that their lives might be spared, pledging themselves that they would not take up the tomahawk against the troops and that if they would encamp near the town, in the morning they would come to such terms as the Governor should propose. This lulled the troops into security, and they encamped about half a mile back of the town. . . However, early the next morning the Indians attacked the Americans, but the latter were victorious, although sustaining a loss of 179 killed and wounded. The troops returned to Vincennes, where they in safety arrived after a most fatiguing campaign of 55 days, and marching the distance of 320 miles."

4. By treaty signed at Fort Armstrong, September 15, 1832, the Winnebago ceded "to the United States, forever, all the lands, to which said nation have title or claim, lying to the south and east of the Wisconsin River, and the Fox River of Green Bay." By article 2 of this treaty the Winnebago were granted a tract of land to the west of the Mississippi, to which they subsequently removed.

5. Article 4, treaty of September 15, 1832, reads: "It is further stipulated and agreed, that the United States shall erect a suitable building, or buildings, with a garden and a field attached, somewhere near Fort Crawford, or Prairie du Chien, and establish and maintain therein for the term of twenty-seven years, a school for the education, including clothing, board and lodging, of such Winnebago children as may be voluntarily sent to it."

6. The portrait, here reproduced, bears No. 57 in the Rhees *Catalogue*; it was painted by Ford from a sketch by Lewis in 1826, and is numbered 69 in the Lewis *Portfolio*. The original sketch was no doubt made at Prairie du Chien.

" Wau-kaw-saw-kaw, or snake," was a signer of the treaty made at Green Bay, August 25, 1828; he also signed the following treaties: Prairie du Chien, August 1, 1829; Fort Armstrong, Rock Island, Illinois, September 15, 1832; and lastly, the treaty at Washington, November 1, 1837.

KATAWABEDA[1]

(A CHIPPEWAY CHIEF)

THERE is, in general, so great a sameness in the Indian character, that the individuals may be said to differ rather in the degree of physical and mental strength, with which they are endowed, than in the qualities of their minds. The pursuits of all being the same, there must naturally be a similitude of intellectual development, and we find accordingly but little variety of character, except that arising from extraordinary instances of bodily vigour, or still more rarely, from superior native talent. Their hunters and warriors are great, greater, and greatest, but still they are but warriors and hunters, practising with more or less success the same arts of sylvan warfare against the brute inhabitants of the lake and forest, or snatching by similar devices the bloody trophies of victory, in perpetual feuds with each other.

It is therefore an agreeable relief to turn from the monotonous recital of the wiles of battle and ambuscade to the contemplation of a pacific character.[2] The chief whose portrait[3] is before us deserves honourable mention as one of the very few of his race who condemned, by precept and example, the vindictive and bloody wars so common and so fatally destructive among the ill-starred aborigines. Although we do not learn that his courage was ever questioned, he never took an active part in war,

KA-TA-WA-BE-DA
A Chippeway Chief

but discouraged it on all occasions, as far as his situation and influence allowed. At the councils, in which, as an able speaker, he was a prominent person, he usually harangued in favour of pacific measures, recommended negotiation and remonstrance rather than revenge and violence, and sought to allay the excitement which ordinarily prevails at the meetings of the antagonist and turbulent denizens of the wild.

Katawabeda was an orator of no small repute.[4] Expert and ready in debate, his speeches were marked by shrewdness, ingenuity, and subtlety of argument, and by a simple brevity and force of expression. Some of these displays of native eloquence were well worthy of preservation, but we are not aware that any of them have been recorded except in the memory of those who sat in the councils of that lonely region of lakes and forests of which this remarkable Indian was a native and a ruler.

He was the principal village chief—the civil head, as distinguished from the war chief, or military leader—of a band of the Chippeway nation, who reside at Sandy Lake or Kometongogomog, among the head springs of the Mississippi, and was a sensible, prudent, politic man, who was revered by his own people, and looked up to as a safe counsellor by the surrounding villages.[5]

NOTES

1. This name, according to the late Dr William Jones, is correctly *Kä'täwābidä*, "old tooth."

2. Katawabeda is thus mentioned by Warren ("History of the Ojibways," *Minn. Hist. Soc. Coll.*, Vol. V., p. 365, 1885): "Shortly after this Dakota war party had returned to their homes [*circa* 1810], emboldened by the cordial and unexpected manner in which they had met their advances for peace, a small war party of Ojibways, under Broken Tooth,

the chief of Sandy Lake, proceeded in their birch canoes down the Mississippi to the mouth of the Minnesota, to pay the Dakotas a visit of peace at their own villages. On the low point over which now towers the American fortress known as Fort Smelling, the Ojibways first discovered their old enemies congregated in a large camp. Broken Tooth, to denote his rank, approached with the American flag hanging over the stern of his canoe. On their being perceived, the wildest excitement ensued in the camp. The men ran out of their lodges with guns in their hands. The Dakotas were preparing to go on a war party against the very people who now made their appearance, and the warriors made demonstrations to fire on them. Their chiefs interfered, but with little effect, and bullets were already flying about the ears of the Ojibways, when Renville, an influential Dakota trader and half-breed, made his timely appearance, and with a loud voice quelled the disturbance and took the peace party under his protection. . . . Broken Tooth and his party made but a short stay in the midst of a people who were so anxious to spill their blood and handle their scalps. Under an escort provided by the kind trader, who guarded them some distance towards their country, they succeeded in reaching their homes in safety and felt thankful for escaping from such a fearful predicament."

Schoolcraft (*Personal Memoirs*, Philadelphia, 1851) wrote at the agency at Sault Ste Marie, July 19, 1828 :

"The Brèche, *alias* Catawabeta (Broken Tooth), entered the office with one or two followers. . . . This venerable chief is the patriarch of the region around Sandy Lake, on the Upper Mississippi. He made his first visit to me a few days after the landing of the troops at this post, in 1822. In turning to some minutes of that date, I find he pronounced himself 'the friend and advocate of peace,' and he referred to the facts to prove that his practice had been in accordance with his professions. He discountenanced the idea of the Indians taking part in our wars. He said he was a small boy at the taking of *old* Mackinac (1763). The French wished him to take the war-club, but he refused. The English afterwards thanked him for this, and requested him to raise the tomahawk in their favor, but he refused. The Americans afterwards thanked him for his refusal, but they did not ask him to go to war. 'They all talked of peace,' he said, 'but still, though they talk of peace, the Sioux continue to make war upon us. Very lately they killed three people.'"

3. The portrait, which bears No. 66 in the Rhees *Catalogue*, was a copy, somewhat changed, of the painting by Lewis, numbered 27 in his *Portfolio*.

4. Evidently the only treaty ever signed by the subject of this sketch was at Prairie du Chien, August 19, 1825, in which document his name appears as "Kaw-ta-waubeta, or broken tooth of Sandy lake."

5. Lieut. Z. M. Pike (*An Account of Expeditions to the Sources of the*

Mississippi, etc., Philadelphia, 1810), who visited Sandy Lake during the winter of 1805-6, computed the census as follows: "Warriors, 45. Women, 79. Children, 224. Lodges, 24. Catawabata, or Broken Teeth, first chief of the band."

On August 8, 1828, Schoolcraft (*Personal Memoirs*, Philadelphia, 1851), then at the agency at Sault Ste Marie, wrote: "Katewabeda, having announced his wish to speak to me on the 6th instant, came into the office for that purpose. He took a view of the standing his family had maintained among the Sandy Lake Indians from an early day, and said that he had in his possession until very lately a French flag, which had been presented to some of his ancestors, but had been taken to exhibit at Montreal by his son-in-law (Mr Ermatinger, an English trader recently retired from business). He had received a *muzinniégun* (a paper; any written or printed document) from Lieut. Pike, on his visit to Sandy Lake, in 1806, but it had been lost in a war excursion on the Mississippi."

FOKE LUSTE HAJO

(A SEMINOLE CHIEF)

THIS distinguished individual was at one time the principal war chief of the Seminoles, but being friendly to the United States, was superseded in that post by Holato Micco, the *Blue King*. His name, Foke Luste Hajo, signifies *Black craggy clay*, but he is usually called *Black Dirt*, an epithet which seems to have no reference to his character, for he is described as a brave and high-minded man of more than ordinary abilities.

He was one of the chiefs who assisted at the council of Payne's Landing, and assented to the celebrated treaty, of which the results have been so disastrous to the country and so ruinous to the Seminoles; and he was one of the seven who were appointed to visit and explore the country offered to his people for their future residence. His associates were Holata Amathla, Jumper, Charley Amathla, Coa Hajo, Arpiucki, and Yaha Hajo. Having examined and approved the country, the delegation proceeded to ratify the treaty of Payne's Landing, at Fort Gibson, on the 28th of March, 1833. This was one of the several fatal mistakes committed in the course of this unfortunate negotiation; for the chiefs were only deputed to examine the country, and should have reported the result of their inquiries to a council of the nation, who alone were competent to ratify the treaty. Colonel Gadsden,[1] the commissioner who negotiated the treaty, in a letter to the Secretary of War, says : "There is a condition prefixed to the agreement, without assenting to which, the Florida Indians *most positively refused* to negotiate for their removal west of the Mississippi. Even with the condition annexed, there was a reluctance—which with some difficulty was overcome—on the part of the Indians, to bind themselves by *any* stipulations before a knowledge of the facts and circumstances would enable them to judge of the advantages or disadvantages of the disposition the Government of the United States wished to make of them. They were finally induced, however, to assent to the agreement."

The same gentleman remarks further : "The payment for property alleged to have been plundered, was the subject most pressed by the Indians, and in yielding to their wishes on this head, a limitation has been fixed in a sum, which I think, however, will probably cover all demands which can be satisfactorily proved. Many of the claims are for negroes, said to have been enticed away from their owners during the protracted Indian disturbances of which Florida has been for years the theatre. The Indians allege that the depredations have been mutual, that they have suffered in the same degree, and that most of the property claimed was taken as reprisal for property of equal value lost by them. They could not, therefore, yield to the justice of restitution solely on their part ; and probably there was no better mode of terminating the difficulty than by that provided for in the treaty now concluded. The final ratification of the treaty will depend upon the opinion of the seven chiefs selected to explore the country west of the Mississippi River. If that corresponds with the description given, or is equal to the expectations formed of it, there will be no difficulty on the part of the Seminoles."

The mistake made by the agents of our Government in accepting the ratification of an important treaty by a few chiefs, instead of requiring the action of the whole Seminole nation properly convened in council, was a fatal one for the country.

We have stated in another place the conduct of this chief, at the council held on the 23rd of April, 1835,[2] where he boldly and eloquently advocated the treaty of Payne's Landing. We find him also assisting at a council on the 19th of August in the same year, and still adhering firmly to the pacific policy which he had from the first embraced.[3]

At the close of the year 1835, a general council of the Seminoles was held, at which they resolved to retain possession of their country at all hazards, and condemned all who opposed their views to death. This was in effect a declaration of war : and all who had taken side with the United States were admonished by it to seek safety in flight. Accordingly, Holata Amathla, Otulkee Amathla, Foke Luste Hajo, Conhatkee Micco, Fushutchee Micco and about four hundred and fifty of their followers fled to Fort Brooke, and encamped under the protection of its guns. Since that time this chief has remained with our troops, using his best efforts to put an end to this unhappy war, which is rapidly wasting away the strength of the Seminoles, while to the American army, it has been a field of gallant and untiring effort, filled with daring and brilliant events, but equally fraught with disaster and fruitless of good results.[4]

NOTES

1. See HALPATTER-MICCO, note 6, p. 14, this volume.

2. The following notes are abstracted from [Woodburn Potter] *The War in Florida*, Baltimore, 1836.

".... 22d of April, 1835, several hundred met in council.

"The business of the convention having been opened, General Thompson expressed his hope that they had assembled to fulfill their promise, and to act like honest men. The treaty of Payne's Landing was read and explained to them, and the following talk of President Jackson was then delivered :—

"'*To the Chiefs and Warriors of the Seminole Indians in Florida.*

"' My Children,—I am sorry to have heard that you have been listening to bad councils. You know me, and you know that I would not deceive nor advise you to do anything that was unjust or injurious. Open your ears and attend to what I shall now say to you. They are the words of a friend, and the words of truth.

"'The white people are settling around you. The game has disappeared from your country. Your people are poor and hungry. All this you have perceived for some time. And nearly three years ago, you made an agreement with your friend Colonel Gadsden, acting on the part of the United States, by which you agreed to cede your lands in Florida, and remove and join your brothers, the Creeks, in the country west of the Mississippi. You annexed a condition to this agreement, that certain chiefs named therein, in whom you placed confidence, should proceed to the western country, and examine whether it was suitable to your wants and habits ; and whether the Creeks residing there were willing to permit you to unite with them as one people ; and if the persons thus sent were satisfied on these heads, then the agreement made with Colonel Gadsden was to be in full force.

"'In conformity with these provisions, the chiefs named by you proceeded to that country, and having examined it, and having become satisfied respecting its character and the favourable disposition of the Creeks, they entered into an agreement with commissioners on the part of the United States, by which they signified their satisfaction on these subjects, and finally ratified the agreement made with Colonel Gadsden.

"' I now learn that you refuse to carry into effect the solemn promises thus made by you, and that you have stated to the officers of the United States, sent among you, that you will not remove to the western country.

"' My Children,—I have never deceived, nor will I ever deceive, any of the red people. I tell you that you must go, and that you will go. Even if you had a right to stay, how could you live where you now are ? You have sold all your country. You have not a piece as large as a blanket to sit down upon.   What is to support yourselves, your women and children? . . .

"'But lest some of your rash young men should forcibly oppose your arrangements for removal, I have ordered a large military force to be sent among you.   I have directed the commanding officer, and likewise the agent, your friend General Thompson, that every reasonable indulgence be held out to you.   But I have also directed that one-third of your people, as provided for in the treaty, be removed during the present season.   If you listen to the voice of friendship and truth, you will go quietly and voluntarily.   But should you listen to the bad birds that are always flying about you and refuse to remove, I have directed the commanding officers to remove you by force.   This will be done. I pray the Great Spirit, therefore, to incline you to do what is right.

"'Your friend,

"'A. JACKSON.

"'WASHINGTON, *February* 16, 1835.'

"The reading of this talk having been enforced with such observations as were deemed necessary by General Thompson, he requested them to retire and consult among themselves, and then to give him their final decision upon the subject.

"In a short time the chiefs signified their desire to be heard, when Jumper arose and expressed sentiments opposed to the treaty and to a removal from their present homes; yet, sentiments solicitous of our friendship, and advice to a hostile resistance should we employ force to oblige them to go.

"He was followed in turn by Miconopy, Charley Amathla, Arpincki, Coa Hajo, Holata Mico, Moke Is Sha Larni, Tutenuggee, and others, who advocated his views with more or less power; and as the day was wasting and the Indians were not disposed to listen to the agent's entreaties for a voluntary removal, General Clinch arose and briefly, yet friendly, declared to the chiefs, that the time of expostulation had passed; that already too much had been said, and nothing had been done. . . ."

"The firmest friend to emigration was Fucta Lusta Hajo (Black Dirt).   In consequence of sickness he did not arrive in time for the council of the first day. . . ."

"On the morrow, the 23d [April, 1835], the chiefs and warriors again convened in council, and sent word to the agent that they were ready to talk with him.   On his arrival at the council General Thompson discovered that Miconopy was absent, and, on inquiry, he was informed that the chief was sick—that he had a pain in the stomach; but the agent viewed this as a shuffling trick, and that his object was to shun responsibility.   Jumper was again speaker, and when asked the result of their deliberations, similar replies to the preceding day were made. After several of the leading chiefs had spoken, the veteran Fucta Lusta

FOKE-LUSTE-HAJO
A Seminole Chief

Hajo (or Black Dirt) then arose, and in the firmest and most decisive manner denounced all who opposed the execution of the treaty, and that if they were his brethren and wished him to value them, they must act consistently with the wishes of their Great Father. . . ."

A document was then produced by General Thompson. It acknowledged the validity of the treaties of Payne's Landing, signed May 9, 1832, and of Fort Gibson, signed March 28, 1833. This document was then (April 23, 1835) signed by Fucta Lusta Hajo, eight chiefs, and eight sub-chiefs. However, Miconopy, Jumper, Holata Mico, Coa Hajo, and Arpincki refused to sign. "The agent promptly declared that he no longer considered Miconopy as chief; that his name should be struck from the council of the nation; that he should treat all who acted like him in the same manner. . . . In consequence of this the *names* of the above *five opposing chiefs were struck from the council of the nation.*

" Now the injurious tendency of this act must be obvious to all who will for a moment reflect upon the already disastrous state of things. . . .

" On this subject the Secretary of War remarks : ' I understand that the President deemed this course an incorrect one ; and it seems to me obviously liable to strong objections. We do not assume the right of determining who shall be the chiefs in the various Indian tribes ; this is a matter of internal policy which must necessarily be left to themselves. . . .' "

3. Foke Luste Hajo signed many treaties, beginning with that of Moultrie Creek, September 18, 1823, in which his name appears, " Fake lustee Hajo " ; at the treaty of Payne's Landing, on the Ocklawaha River, May 9, 1832, he was the third to sign for his tribe, as " Fuch-ta-lus-ta Hadjo " ; on the document (it should not be designated as a " treaty ") signed at Fort Gibson, March 28, 1833, the subject of this sketch did not sign for himself, as the name " Ne-ha-tho-clo, representing Fuch-a-lusti-hadgo" appears. The treaty of January 4, 1845, signed at the Creek agency, bears the name " Black Dirt," this time the English translation of his Seminole name.

4. The portrait of Foke Luste Hajo was painted in Washington by King in 1826. It bears No. 68 in the Rhees *Catalogue*, where it is recorded as " Folke-tuste-najo, *Craggy Black Clay*, Seminole War Chief."

JOHN RIDGE

(A CHEROKEE INTERPRETER)

THE subject of this sketch was a son of Major Ridge,[1] a distinguished Cherokee chief, whose biography is given in Vol. I. That individual was a remarkable instance of one born and brought up in savage life, accustomed to war and hunting, and to the habits and modes of thought of the Indian warrior, yet abandoning those habits, and by deliberate choice adopting the customs of civilised men, and persevering in them unchangeably through life. There have, doubtless, been other instances, but we know of none in which the change was so thorough and the result so successful. Commencing life as a mere savage, with no knowledge but that of the hunter, he adopted with energy the forms of civilisation, became a successful farmer, and a public spirited citizen, and reared his family in the observance of the social duties and virtues of civilised life. His wife zealously seconded his views, and though bred in a wigwam, learned after her marriage the domestic arts appertaining to good housewifery, and became as skilful in housekeeping and agriculture as she was industrious and persevering.

John Ridge was second of the five children of this sensible and worthy couple. The pains and expense bestowed upon his education show how thoroughly his parents were imbued with the principles of civilisation, and how high an estimate they placed upon the possession of knowledge. He was first put to school to the Rev. Mr and Mrs Gambold, Moravian missionaries at Spring Place,[2] who taught him the alphabet, spelling, reading, English grammar, and some arithmetic. He was first sent to Brainerd,[3] a missionary station established by the American Board of Commissioners for Foreign Missions; then to a school at Knoxville, Tennessee; and afterwards to the Foreign Mission school at Cornwall in Connecticut,[4] where he spent four years under the able instruction of the Rev. Herman Daggett. These opportunities seem to have been well improved, and Ridge acquired the essential parts of a good education; his attainments in literature were respectable, and, what was of more importance, his morals were correct and firmly established, his habits good, and his disposition mild and amiable.

While a student in Connecticut, he fell in love with a beautiful and excellent young lady, Miss Northrop, who reciprocated his affection, and after an engagement of two years they were married. It must have required great strength of affection in this young lady to enable her to overcome the aversion which is usually entertained against alliances with a race so different from ourselves in many important particulars, as well as to nerve her for a life in which she could foresee little else than trouble. A contest had already commenced between the United States and the Cherokees,[5] which promised to be fruitful in discord, and which could only end in the discomfiture of the latter—and then a new home, new neighbours, fresh troubles, and unknown difficulties awaited them in the wilderness. All this, however, she was willing to brave. She loved the young Indian, who, abandoning the bow and the tomahawk, had successfully cultivated the arts of peace, and the literature of the white man, and had exhibited a mildness and benevolence of character peculiarly interesting in the descendant of a wild and ferocious race.   She possessed too, a missionary spirit, a deeply seated and fervent piety, which impressed her with the belief that it was her duty to embrace the opportunity offered her, of becoming a messenger of peace to the savage; and she followed her Indian husband to the Western forests, full of enthusiastic hope, pious aspirations, and plans for the civilisation and conversion of the heathen.

We are happy to say that the noble courage of this truly excellent lady was not exhibited in vain, nor were her hopes of usefulness disappointed.   It is true that the plan of a separate government formed by some of the leading men of the Cherokees failed, and with it were crushed some benevolent schemes and some infant institutions which promised well; for they carried with them the elements of premature decay in the erroneous political views with which they were connected.   But the pious labours of the devoted woman bud and blossom like the violet, untouched by the storm that rages in the political atmosphere.   Her assiduity was unabated through all the vicissitudes which attended the Cherokees, and there is reason to believe that her example and her counsels were eminently useful to her adopted countrymen.   And the full extent of her influence is yet to be developed and expanded by the character of her children, who are numerous, and are receiving the best education the United States can afford.

John Ridge was a conspicuous man among the Cherokees.   He returned from college and commenced his active career as a public man at the period when his people were attempting to erect themselves into an independent nation

—when the invention of the alphabet by George Guess[6] gave them a written language—and when the establishment of schools, missions, and a newspaper afforded them the facilities for instruction. Ridge was fitted for the crisis in which he was an actor. He had youth, education, talents, piety, enthusiasm, and was a son of the race out of which it was proposed to rear a new nation. He was the son of a distinguished and popular chief, and had all the advantage of family influence. His fault, and that of those with whom he acted, was in cherishing a zeal without knowledge—a zeal which, confiding in pure intentions, and in the goodness of the end in view, overlooked the impracticability of the scheme by which it was attempted to accomplish the object. Ridge was an active man in all these scenes. He accompanied several of the delegations to Washington, and though not a chief, was usually an interpreter, a secretary,[7] or an agent, and exerted great influence in the negotiations. He was a writer for the Cherokee newspaper,[8] and a civil functionary under the Cherokee government during its brief existence.

We know little of the life of John Ridge after the removal of his people to their lands west of the Mississippi. He continued to be a conspicuous man until about two years ago, when in consequence of a violent quarrel growing out of political differences, he was cruelly and basely murdered by a party of the opposing faction of his own countrymen.[9] We forbear a detail of the circumstances of this outrage, and any comment, because we are aware that, distant as we are from the scene, and limited as our knowledge of the parties and the facts must necessarily be, we could scarcely touch on such an event without the risk of injustice to some of the actors or sufferers.

NOTES

1. See Vol. I., p. 368, this work.

2. "In 1799, hearing that the Cherokee desired teachers—or perhaps by direct invitation of the chiefs—two missionaries visited the tribe to investigate the matter.   Another visit was made in the next summer, and a council was held at Tellico agency, where, after a debate in which the Indians showed considerable difference of opinion, it was decided to open a mission.   Permission having been obtained from the government, the work was begun in April, 1801, by Rev. Abraham Steiner and Rev. Gottlieb Byhan at the residence of David Vann, a prominent mixed-blood chief, who lodged them in his own house and gave them every assistance in building the mission, which they afterward called Spring place, where now is the village of the same name in Murray county, north-western Georgia.   They were also materially aided by the agent, Colonel Return J. Meigs.   It was soon seen that the Cherokee wanted civilisers for their children, and not new theologies, and when they found that a school could not at once be opened, the great council at Ustanali sent orders to the missionaries to organise a school within six months or leave the nation.   Through Vann's help the matter was arranged and a school was opened, several sons of prominent chiefs being among the pupils.   Another Moravian mission was established by Reverend J. Gambold at Oothcaloga, in the same county, in 1821.   Both were in flourishing condition when broken up, with other Cherokee missions, by the state of Georgia in 1834. The work was afterward renewed beyond the Mississippi."—Mooney, "Myths of the Cherokee," *Nineteenth Annual Report of the Bureau of American Ethnology*, pt. 1, p. 84, Washington, 1900.

3. "In 1817 the American Board of Commissioners for Foreign Missions established its first station among the Cherokee at Brainerd, in Tennessee, on the west side of Chickamauga creek, two miles from the Georgia line.   The mission took its name from a distinguished pioneer worker among the northern tribes.   The government aided in the erection of the buildings, which included a schoolhouse, gristmill, and workshops, in which, besides the ordinary branches, the boys were taught simple mechanic arts while the girls learned the use of the needle and the spinning wheel.   There was also a large work farm. The mission prospered and others were established at Willstown, Hightower, and elsewhere by the same board, in which two hundred pupils were receiving instruction in 1820.   Among the earliest and most noted workers at the Brainerd mission were Reverend D. S. Butrick and Reverend S. A. Worcester, the latter especially having done much for the mental elevation of the Cherokee, and more than once having suffered imprisonment for his zeal in defending their cause. The missions flourished until broken up by the state of Georgia at the beginning of the Removal troubles, and they were afterwards renewed in the western country. Mission ridge preserves the memory of the Brainerd establishment."—Mooney, *op. cit.*, pp. 104-105.

4. The school at Cornwall, Connecticut, was established in May, 1817, by the American Board of Commissioners for Foreign Missions. In 1820 it was attended by thirty-five pupils, and received an allowance of $1433.00 from the U.S. Government.

5. This probably refers to "White Path's" rebellion in 1828. Consult Mooney, "Myths of the Cherokee," *Nineteenth Report of the Bureau of American Ethnology,* Washington, 1900, p. 113.

6. Sequoyah, or George Guess. See biography, Vol. I., pp. 130-46, this work.

7. The portrait of John Ridge was painted by King in 1825; it bears No. 69 in the Rhees *Catalogue.* At that time Ridge was "Secretary to the Creek delegation to Washington."

8. "In 1827 the Cherokee council having formerly resolved to establish a national paper in the Cherokee language and characters, types for that purpose were cast in Boston, under the supervision of the noted missionary, Worcester, of the American Board of Commissioners for Foreign Missions, who, in December of that year, contributed to the *Missionary Herald* five verses of Genesis in the new syllabary, this seeming to be its first appearance in print. Early in the year the press and types arrived at New Echota, and the first number of the new paper, *Tsa'lagi Tsu'lehisanuñ'hǐ, the Cherokee Phœnix,* printed in both languages, appeared on February 21, 1828. The first printers were two white men, Isaac N. Harris and John F. Wheeler, with John Caudy, a half-blood apprentice. Elias Boudinot (Gălagi-na, 'The Buck'), an educated Cherokee, was the editor, and Reverend S. A. Worcester was the guiding spirit who brought order out of chaos and set the work in motion. The office was a log house. The hand press and types, after having been shipped by water from Boston, were transported two hundred miles by wagon from Augusta to their destination. The printing paper had been overlooked and had to be brought by the same tedious process from Knoxville. Cases and other equipments had to be dressed and fashioned by the printers, neither of whom understood a word of Cherokee, but simply set up the characters, as handed to them in manuscript by Worcester and the editor. After a precarious existence of about six years, the *Phœnix* was suspended, owing to the hostile action of the Georgia authorities, who went so far as to throw Worcester and Wheeler into prison. Its successor, after the removal of the Cherokee to the West, was the *Cherokee Advocate,* of which the first number appeared at Tahlequah in 1844, with William

P. Ross as editor." Until the dissolution of the Cherokee Nation it was " still continued under the auspices of the Nation, printed in both languages and distributed free at the expense of the Nation to those unable to read English—an example without parallel in any other Government."—Mooney, *op. cit.*, p. 111.

9. He was murdered at his home at Park Hill, Indian Territory, June 22, 1839. (See Vol. I., p. 401, note 45, this work.)

JOHN RIDGE
A Cherokee Interpreter

THE CHIPPEWAY WIDOW

THE CHIPPEWAY WIDOW

THIS picture,[1] which we copy from Colonel McKenney's *Tour through the North - Western Lakes*, is not the portrait of any individual, but is intended to represent a singular custom which prevails among the Chippeway Indians, and we insert it to give variety to our pages.

A Chippeway widow, on the death of her husband, selects from his scanty wardrobe, a complete suit of his best clothes, which she makes up into a bundle. This is placed near her while at work, and is carried wherever she goes. She calls it her husband, treats it with the respect which would be due to a living lord and master, and would be considered as disgracing herself and treating his memory with disrespect, if she was to part with it even for a moment.

The custom is a beautiful and affecting one, which, had it prevailed in the days of the Greeks or Romans, would have been immortalised by the poet and historian, and been often quoted and referred to as a graceful instance of the classic taste of the ancients. It is the more remarkable as occurring in the most inhospitable region of our country, where the inclemency of the climate and the sterile nature of the soil impose upon the inhabitants the necessity of constant exertion to procure a scanty subsistence. This state of penury falls especially hard upon the women, who are doomed to continual labour.

From a class so wretchedly poor and so severely tasked, we should scarcely expect the exhibition of so refined a sentiment as is indicated by the custom we have described ; nor is it less remarkable that the wretched inhabitants of a frozen region should encumber their toils by an addition which must often be burthensome and inconvenient. But what will not woman do—what does she not do, in every clime—in compliance with the laws of fashion, or in obedience to the dictates of the heart ?

The Chippeway widow carries her "husband" during the season of mourning, which is one year, and during that time cannot marry without gross impropriety. If she does not marry at the close of the year, she usually continues to carry the badge of her widowhood until she is relieved of it by the nearest relatives of her deceased husband, who may at any time, when they conceive she has mourned long enough, call upon her, and take away the bundle, after which she is at liberty to contract a second marriage.

NOTE

1. The original picture is a crude lithograph showing a " Chippeway Widow" sitting on a bench under a shelter. The illustration faces p. 292 of McKenney's *Sketches of a Tour to the Lakes*, Baltimore, 1827. The sketch was made by Lewis, in whose *Portfolio* it likewise appears under the name Ta-ma-kake-toke.

A " Chippeway woman in mourning" was drawn by the Swiss artist Kurz, at Fort Union, mouth of the Yellowstone, September 28, 1851. See *American Anthropologist*, Vol. X., 1908, p. 14.

MICANOPY

(A SEMINOLE CHIEF)

THE early Spanish writers describe Florida as an earthly paradise, blessed with a delightful climate, and abounding in the richest fruits and flowers of the tropics. According to their accounts the population must have been very numerous; but unfortunately, there is little trace to be found of the many tribes named by them; and the probability is that no dependence can be placed upon any information derived from that source. The celebrated expedition of De Soto is now believed to be fabulous.[1]

The Palanches,[2] Eamuses,[3] and Kaloosas,[4] the ancient possessors of Florida—if such nations ever existed—are all extinct. The present race of Indians inhabiting Florida settled there about a century ago, and are called Seminoles, or "Runaways,"[5] being fugitives from various tribes residing in the region bordering on the Mississippi, but chiefly from the Lower Creek nation. They were the restless, dissolute, and abandoned individuals who fled from punishment, or who were unwilling to submit even to the loose restraints of the savage community. So long as Florida belonged to a foreign power, the fugitives from the Indian tribes residing within the American colonies or states found the boundary line a convenient protection, and thither fled the lawless and the disaffected. They found here some small remnants of the Yemasses,[6] once a powerful and warlike people, whose name occurs frequently in the early history of South Carolina and Georgia. Exhausted by fierce and long continued wars with the Creek Indians, as well as the English colonists, they sought refuge in the hammocks of Florida, where the Seminoles assailed and nearly exterminated them about the year 1721. The small number who survived became slaves to the conquerors, and were finally incorporated with them. The Yemasses were of a darker complexion than any other Indians, and the Ochlewahaw tribe of the Seminoles, who are descended from them, betray their origin by the dark colour of their skins. The American traveller, Bartram,[7] relates a tradition of the Creeks, that a beautiful race of Indians, whose women they called " Daughters of the Sun," resided among the lakes and swamps of the great Oahefanoke wilderness, where they lived in uninterrupted felicity, upon islands of eternal verdure, inaccessible to the approach of human footsteps. He supposes, with much plausibility, that some little colony of the fugitive Yemasses, having taken shelter at that retired spot, were seen by a party of Creek hunters, and that the fable grew out of this circumstance.

The wilds of Florida have, for a long series of years afforded a harbour to the runaway slaves from the Southern States, who were eagerly received by the Seminoles, as well on account of the dislike they bore to the people of the United States, as from the value they placed on the services of the negroes, who performed their agricultural labours, and in consequence of their knowledge of the arts were useful in various ways. They were kindly treated, and not severely worked; were soon admitted to a footing of equality, and finally amalgamated with the Indians.

Such were the Seminoles, who, so long as Florida was a colony of Spain, found protection there, while they carried on a constant and lawless predatory war upon the frontier settlements of the United States, not only by the commission of murders, but more frequently by enticing away the slaves and stealing the cattle of the inhabitants.

The hostile feeling engendered by this conduct was greatly aggravated by the course pursued by the British authorities during the war which commenced in 1812. In August, 1814, a British fleet anchored in Pensacola Bay, and a body of troops, under the command of Colonel Nichols, took possession of the Spanish forts Barrancas and St Michael, and hoisted the British flag.[9]   On the 31st of the same month, he published the infamous proclamation which rendered his name notorious in our history, in which he called upon the people of Louisiana and Kentucky to throw off the slavish yoke of the United States and join his standard, encouraged the Indians to butcher the unarmed inhabitants of the frontier, and the slaves to rise upon their masters.   Arms and ammunition were furnished abundantly to the Indians, and a reward of ten dollars each was offered for the scalps of the Americans, without distinction of age or sex.   A person called Woodbine,[10] who was announced as a Colonel in the British service, was also engaged in the same nefarious warfare ; and two spies, named Ambrister and Arbuthnot,[11] who were taken in company with the Indians, were executed by order of General Jackson.

When Florida was afterwards ceded to the United States,[12] and the American people began to settle within its limits, it will readily be conceived that no very friendly dispositions existed between them and the Seminoles. Nor were our settlers free from blame in regard to the hostilities which ensued.   A frontier is always infested by lawless men, and however respectable the majority may be, a few such individuals may embroil the whole community by acts which may be condemned but which cannot be prevented.   The rights of the Florida Indians were in many instances violently outraged by unprincipled speculators and loose marauders, who perpetrated the most scandalous frauds and cruelties upon that unhappy people.

In all such cases there is one inevitable result— whoever may be in fault, or whatever may be the character of the quarrel, the whites and the Indians respectively espouse opposite sides, and prepare for the last resort. The leaders on both sides may be disposed to conciliate, but there are always individuals in either party who at such a juncture seize the occasion to plunder and to shed blood, and thus bring on a war.   There is, then, but one alternative on the part of our Government, which is, to separate the belligerents by the removal of one party, and the Indians, being the weakest, must emigrate.

After years of disturbance, and the commission of numberless acts of violence by individuals on both sides, it became necessary that some measure should be adopted to prevent a general war; and on the 9th of May, 1832, Colonel Gadsden,[18] a commissioner on the part of the United States, met the Seminoles in council at a place called Payne's Landing, and effected a treaty, by which the Seminoles ceded all their country to the United States, in exchange for lands to be assigned them west of the Mississippi; provided that, on examination by a committee of their chiefs, they should approve the lands offered them. The examination was made, and the chiefs being satisfied with the country, made a treaty at Fort Gibson on the

28th of March, 1833, ratifying the former cession of their lands; and on the 23rd of April, 1835,[14] sixteen of their chiefs and sub-chiefs entered into a new agreement ratifying the former treaties. When, however, the Government, after years of negotiation, at length determined to enforce the removal of the Florida Indians, the larger portion refused to go, disavowed the cession made by their chiefs, and the late disastrous war was the consequence.

Micanopy is, by inheritance, the principal chief or head man of all the bands of Seminoles, and is by some writers styled king, and by others governor of the Seminoles. We prefer the title of chief, as we do not find in the office of head man any difference between this and any other Indian nation, nor do we discover in any of them the slightest resemblance to the state or authority of a king. Those governments, so far as they can be termed such, are military and republican, and the leader mingles with his people on terms of the most perfect equality, except when acting officially.

King Payne,[15] the grandfather of Micanopy, is said to have established and united the Seminoles as a people. He married a Yemassee woman, his slave, who was the mother of the late chief Payne, whose origin from the Yemassee stock was distinctly marked in the darkness of his complexion. Micanopy also is very black. The elder King Payne lived to the age of nearly one hundred years. The word "Micco," which we find compounded into many of the Creek and Seminole names, means *chief*, and *Micconopy* is *head chief*. He is also called "the Governor," and the "Pond Governor."

Micanopy was among those who from the beginning opposed the views of our Government in relation to the removal of his people.[16] He does not appear to have been a man of much activity or enterprise, but in regard to this matter he remained firm, in consequence perhaps of the influence of Asseola [17] and others, who constantly urged him to adhere to his purpose.

At a council with the Seminole chiefs, held by General Wiley Thompson on the 22nd of April, 1835, Micanopy boldly opposed the agreements of the agent, and objected to the removal of his people. The next day when the council reassembled he was absent, and General Thompson was informed that the chief was sick, but this was considered as a subterfuge, and as an indication that he was not disposed to listen to any further discussion of a question which he had settled in his own mind. A veteran chief, Foke Luste Hajo, who had always advocated the removal, and remained firm in his attachment to the United States, denounced all who opposed the execution of the treaty. During this speech he was frequently interrupted by those who held different views — a circumstance which shows that great excitement must have existed among them—for the Indians are remarkable for their decorum in council, and for the patience with which they listen to the speakers, to interrupt whom is considered a flagrant breach of good manners. The writer of *The War in Florida, by a late Staff Officer*, [18] from whose pages we compile these facts, adds :—

" In consequence of the bold and manly declaration of the chief Foke Luste Hajo, eight of the principal chiefs of the nation and eight sub-chiefs advanced and signed the article (affirming the treaty of Payne's Landing). Five of the principal chiefs remained opposed, viz., Micanopy, Jumper, Holato Micco, Coa Hajo, and Arpiucki. The former chief, as before mentioned, was absent, and as the agent knew that Micanopy controlled the movements of many of them, he demanded of Jumper, 'whether Micanopy intended to abide by the treaty or not?' And

MICANOPY
A Seminole Chief

when Jumper finally confessed that he was authorised to
say that Micanopy did not, the agent promptly declared
that he no longer considered Micanopy as chief; that his
name should be struck from the council of the nation;
that he should treat all who acted like him in the like
manner; and that he would neither acknowledge nor do
business with him, nor with any other as a chief, who did
not honestly comply with the terms of his engagements;
that the door was, however, still open to them, if they
wished to act honestly. In consequence of this, the names
of the above five opposing chiefs were struck from the
council of the nation."

We are happy to be able to record the fact that this
high-handed and unjustifiable measure of the agent was
promptly rebuked by the President, General Jackson, in a
letter written by Governor Cass, Secretary of War, who
treats it as follows [19] :—

"It is not necessary for me to enter much into detail
on the subject presented by you. I understand from
Mr Harris, that he communicated to you the President's
views on the subject of the chiefs whom you declined to
recognise in all questions connected with the removal of
the Seminoles. I understand that the President deemed
this course an incorrect one; and it seems to me obviously
liable to strong objections. We do not assume the right
of determining who shall be the chiefs in the various
Indian tribes; this is a matter of internal policy which
must necessarily be left to themselves. And if, when we
have a grave matter for adjustment with one of the tribes,
we undertake to say *it shall* be determined by a particular
class of individuals, we certainly should render ourselves
obnoxious to censure. It appears to me the proper course
upon important questions, to treat directly with the tribe
itself; and if they depute their chiefs, or any other indi-

vidual to act for them, we must either recognise such
authority or abandon the object in view."

Micanopy does not seem to have distinguished himself
as a warrior in the late contest.   He is said to be an unwieldy man in his person, and inactive in his habits.   He
commanded, however, in the disastrous defeat and massacre
of the gallant party under the command of Major Dade.[20]

After a series of outrages on the part of the Seminoles,
and various attempts at conciliation by our Government
and the friendly chiefs, an open and general war broke
out in November, 1835.

On 24th of December, 1835, Major Dade's command
marched from Fort Brooke for Fort King.   It consisted
of Captain Gardiner's company C. 2nd Artillery, and
Captain Frazer's company B. 3rd Infantry, of fifty men
each, with eight officers, having with them ten days'
provisions, and a light six-pounder.   A noble display of
disinterested gallantry attended the setting out of this
party.   Major Dade was not originally detailed for duty
with this detachment, to make up which, his own
company had been transferred to those of Gardiner and
Frazer.   The service was considered dangerous in the
highest degree, as it was probable the Indians would
attempt to cut off the detachment.   The wife of Captain
Gardiner was exceedingly ill at Fort Brooke, and it was
feared that if he then left her she would die; but he
could not be prevailed upon to relinquish the command,
and after making every preparation, mounted his horse,
and placed himself at the head of the party.   At this
moment Major Dade voluntarily proposed to take the
place of his friend Captain Gardiner, and Major Belton,
the commanding officer, accepted the offer.   Dade
mounted his horse and took the command, Gardiner
retired to the sick chamber of his wife, and the gallant

little party moved off. Before they had proceeded far, Captain Gardiner ascertained that a transport schooner was on the eve of departure for Key West, where Mrs Gardiner's father and children then were, and she consented to go there and leave him at liberty to join his company. She was accordingly placed on board the transport, and he resumed his post in the ill-fated expedition, while Dade, unwilling now to give up the command, remained with it.

A series of untoward circumstances attended the march. The oxen that drew the field-piece broke down early in the first day, and the command was obliged to halt until horses could be procured from Fort Brooke. The next day, on reaching the Hillsborough River, they found the bridge destroyed, and were obliged to halt until the ensuing morning, when they crossed, but with such difficulty and delay that they made but six miles that day. On the 27th they crossed the Big and Little Ouithlacoochee Rivers, and encamped three miles north of the latter. Aware that the enemy were watching his movements, Major Dade had, during all this time, adopted every precaution that military skill suggested, carefully avoiding surprise while marching, and throwing up a small breastwork every night. On the 28th they marched early, and had only proceeded about four miles, when the advanced guard passed through a plat of high grass, and had reached a thick cluster of palmettoes, where a heavy and destructive fire was opened upon them, by an enemy concealed at a distance of fifty or sixty yards. The column was thrown into confusion by this sudden attack, but they were quickly rallied, and as the enemy were observed to rise in front, a charge was made, by which the Indians were dislodged, but not until knives, bayonets, and clubbed muskets were used. Major Dade fell dead on the first fire, and Captain Gardiner, having driven back the Indians, but finding they were gathering for another onset, attempted to throw up a breastwork of logs. This was not effected before the attack was renewed. The Indians being reinforced, and having stationed about a hundred mounted warriors on the opposite side to cut off retreat, advanced to the second attack, yelling in so terrific a manner as to drown the reports of the firearms. The field-piece was now used with effect for a short time, but the enemy surrounding the little breastwork, shot down every man who attempted to work the gun, and soon rendered it useless. Gallantly did these heroic men defend themselves and maintain the honour of their flag; but, overpowered by numbers, and fighting under every disadvantage, they fell one by one, without the prospect of any change of fortune. At length the ammunition gave out, the Indians broke into the enclosure, and every man was either killed or so badly wounded as to be incapable of resistance. The work of havoc done, the dead were plundered, and the Indians retreated; then came a party of negroes, who despatched and mutilated all who showed signs of life. Three persons only escaped to tell the story of this dreadful massacre.

Mr Cohen,[21] in his *Notices of Florida*, gives the following description of Micanopy: "The Governor is of low, stout, and gross stature, and what is called loggy in his movements—his face is bloated and carbuncled, eyes heavy and dull, and with a mind like his person. Colonel Gadsden told me, at Payne's Landing, after having *double* rations he complained of *starving*. He reminds me of the heroes of the Trojan War, who could eat up a whole lamb, or half a calf. He owns a hundred negroes, and a large stock of cattle and horses. The 'top Governor' has two wives, one a very pretty squaw, and the other a half-breed negress. She is the ugliest of all ugly women, and recalls the image of Bombie, of the Frizzled Head, in Paulding's *Koningsmarke*."

NOTES

1. Rather than being fabulous, it was, in reality, one of the most important as well as the most wonderful expeditions in North America of which we have record.

2. The Palanches, or Apalachee, were one of the principal native tribes of Florida, formerly holding the region north of the bay now called by the name, from about the neighbourhood of Pensacola eastward to Ocilla. The chief towns were about the present Tallahassee and St Mark's. They were of Muskhogean stock and linguistically more nearly related to the Choctaw than the Creeks. See *Handbook of American Indians*, pt. 1, p. 67.

3. The Eamuses, or Yamasee, were a Muskhogean tribe, formerly living in South Carolina, although their earlier home was evidently the coastal area of Georgia, extending into northern Florida.

4. The Kaloosas, or Calusa, were formerly an important and powerful tribe of south-western Florida, extending from Lake Okeechobee to the coast and the outlying keys. As only one or two words of their language have come down to us, it is not possible to say to what linguistic stock they may have belonged.

5. See OPOTHLE-YOHOLO, note 14, p. 34, this volume.

6. See note 3, above. War was waged by the Government of Carolina against the Yamasee in 1715; after their final defeat they were driven from the colony and many fled to Florida.

7. William Bartram, *Travels Through North and South Carolina, Georgia, East and West Florida*, etc., London, 1792.—" The river St Mary has its source from a vast lake or marsh, called Ouaquaphenogaw, which lies between Flint and Oakmulge Rivers, and occupies a space of near three hundred miles in circuit. This vast accumulation of waters, in the wet season, appears as a lake, and contains some large islands or knolls of rich high land; one of which the present generation of Creeks represent to be a most blissful spot of the earth : they say it is inhabited by a peculiar race of Indians, whose women are incomparably beautiful; they also tell you that this terrestrial paradise has been seen by some of their enterprising hunters when in pursuit of game, who being lost in inextricable swamps and bogs, and on the point of perishing, were unexpectedly relieved by a company of beautiful women, whom they call daughters of the sun, who kindly gave them such provisions as they had with them, which were chiefly fruit, oranges, dates, etc., and some corn cakes, and then enjoined them to fly for safety to their own country ; for that their husbands were fierce men, and cruel to strangers: they further say that these hunters had a view of their settlements, situated on the elevated banks of an island, or promontory, in a beautiful lake ; but that in their endeavour to approach it, they were involved in perpetual labyrinths, and, like enchanted land, still as they imagined they had just gained it, it seemed to fly before them, alternately appearing and disappearing.   They resolved, at length, to leave the delusive pursuit, and return, which, after a number of inexpressible difficulties, they effected " (p. 24).

8. The Seminole and the negroes have always been regarded by each other in a degree of equality.   At the present time a band of Seminole Negroes resides on the Mexican side of the Rio Grande, not far from Eagle Pass, Texas.

9. "Colonel Nichols, an Irishman by birth, and now a British officer, arrived at Pensacola with a small squadron of his majesty's ships, immediately manned Forts Barancas and St Michael, and hoisted the British flag upon their ramparts.   Making the house of Governor Manrequez his head-quarters, Nichols sought to draw around his standard the malcontents and traitors of the country, by issuing a proclamation, stating that he had come with a force sufficient to relieve them from the chains which the Federal Government was endeavouring to rivet upon them.   This presumptious appeal was even extended to the patriotic people of Kentucky and Louisiana.   At the same time, in conjunction with Captain Woodbine, he employed himself in collecting and clothing in British uniform, the Red Sticks and Seminoles, whom he publicly drilled in the streets of Pensacola.   To these, and all the Red Sticks, he promised a bounty of ten dollars for every scalp, whether of men, women or children."— Pickett, *History of Alabama*, Vol. II., p. 359, Charleston, 1851.

10. See note 9, above.

11. See HALPATTER-MICCO, note 2, p. 13, this volume.

12. See HALPATTER-MICCO, note 2, p. 13, this volume.

13. See HALPATTER-MICCO, note 6, p. 14, this volume.

14. See FOKE LUSTE HAJO, note 2, p. 323, this volume.

15. See HALPATTER-MICCO, note 3, p. 13, this volume.

16. See FOKE LUSTE HAJO, note 2, p. 323, this volume.

17. See biography of Osceola, p. 360, this volume.

18. [Woodburn Potter], *The War in Florida*, Baltimore, 1836, p. 83 *et seq.*

19. *Cf.* note 2, p. 323, under Foke Luste Hajo, this volume.

20. See Halpatter-Micco, note 12, p. 15, this volume.

21. M. M. Cohen, *Notices of Florida and the Campaigns*, Charleston, 1836, p. 238. Micanopy's name is attached to the following treaties: Moultrie Creek, Florida, September 18, 1823, signed Miconope; Payne's Landing, May 9, 1832, signed Mico-Noha; Creek Agency, January 4, 1845, signed Miccanope, the first of his tribe to sign.

The portrait of Micanopy is evidently No. 63 of the Rhees *Catalogue*: " Mi-co-a-na-pas, Second Chief of the Seminoles; owns seventy slaves. [Painted by] King." Catlin made a full-length portrait of " Mick-e-no-pah" while at Fort Moultrie, Charleston Harbour; it is reproduced as plate 305, facing p. 243, Vol. II., of his *Letters and Notes of the Manners, Customs and Conditions of the North American Indians*, London, 1841.

SELOCTA

(A CREEK CHIEF)

ONE of the most unhappy circumstances attending the late war between the United States and Great Britain, was its effect upon the Indian tribes residing within our limits. That all of these tribes have grievances to complain of, there can be no question; it would be impossible for two distinct races, differing so widely in character and in power, to inhabit the same country without frequent collisions, in which the weaker would generally be the injured and oppressed party. We have said elsewhere, and we take pride in repeating, that the American nation and Government have acted towards that unfortunate race with great magnanimity. The intentions of our people, and the official action of our Government towards them, has been decidedly benevolent; but irritating causes have continually occurred to thwart the generous intentions entertained towards them; dishonest agents have diverted the liberality of the Government from its intended direction; and the selfishness or violence of unprincipled individuals have kindled hatred, jealousy, and bloodshed. Naturally prone to war, and habitually vindictive, the passions of the Indians are easily aroused, and those who have tampered with them, for sinister purposes, have ever been but too successful in the accomplishment of their detestable ends.

SE-LOC-TA

A Creek Chief

When the war of 1812 was about to break out, the British Government availed itself of the precarious relations existing between the American Government and the Indian tribes within its boundaries; and the agents of that power traversed the whole frontier upon the fatal errand of discord. The famous Tecumthe was the missionary sent to excite the Southern tribes, by inflammatory harangues and lavish promises of assistance. Bribes were scattered among their influential men, and their prophets were seduced to utter predictions such as were but too well calculated to mislead an ignorant and inflammatory people. Inferior as the Indians were in numbers, and in all the elements of physical power—surrounded by the white population—and dependent as they were upon us for their very existence—we can hardly conceive a more cruel project than that which would lead them into a hopeless and ruinous contest with the only power which could at pleasure protect or destroy them.

The Creek Indians, the most powerful of the Southern tribes, were, on this occasion, divided into two parties, one of which adhered to the United States, and proposed to take no part in the expected war, while the other madly engaged in the conspiracy against their own best interests. The latter were called *Redsticks*,[1] because, in preparing for hostilities, each individual armed himself with a war-club which was painted red.

The first demonstration of this spirit betrayed itself in a series of murders and other outrages, which were committed upon the white settlements, attended by the most atrocious circumstances of savage cruelty. The massacre at Fort Mims[2] was the earliest act of open war. This was a frontier post in the Mississippi territory, containing about one hundred and fifty men, under the command of

Major Beasley, besides a number of women and children who had fled to it for protection. Weatherford,[3] a distinguished chief of the hostile Creeks, having procured a supply of ammunition from the Spaniards[4] at Pensacola, and assembled a force of six or seven hundred warriors, surprised this place on the 30th of August, 1813, and slaughtered nearly three hundred persons, including women and children, in cold blood, and with every aggravation of deliberate cruelty. None were spared; the mother and child fell under the same blow; seventeen individuals only escaped.

The news of this unprovoked outrage carried terror and indignation throughout the south-western frontier, and in all the neighbouring states the people flew to arms. In Tennessee large bodies of gallant men volunteered their services, and Andrew Jackson, a citizen already distinguished for his abilities and patriotism in civil life, was placed at their head. It is not our purpose to follow this distinguished leader through the perils, difficulties, and embarrassments of this war, to its brilliant victories and successful result.

Among the Creek warriors who adhered to the United States in this war, and rendered efficient services in the field, were Chinnaby,[5] a principal chief of that people, and his son Selocta, the subject of this notice. The former occupied a fort on the Coosa River—a rude primitive fortress of logs, surrounded by a stockade such as are commonly resorted to in our border wars. Upon General Jackson's first advance into the savage territory, he was met by Selocta, who sought his camp to fight under his banner, and to solicit aid for his father, whose decided measures had already excited the vengeance of the war faction, by whose forces his fort was surrounded and threatened. From this time until the close of the Indian

war, Selocta continued with our army, an intelligent and
sagacious guide during its marches, and a brave warrior
and leader in battle.

It was during this war that the striking scene [6] occurred
between General Jackson and Weatherford, the leader in
the atrocious butchery at Fort Mims. After a series of
active hostilities, and several general engagements in which
the Indians had been beaten, and their forces cut up and
dispersed, a number of the chiefs of the hostile party
sought the presence of General Jackson, and offered sub-
mission upon his own terms. The victor treated them
with clemency, admonished them to a pacific course of
conduct for the future, but demanded as a preliminary to
any amicable intercourse, that Weatherford should be
delivered up to him. A few days afterwards an Indian
presented himself at the camp, and desired to be conducted
to the General, to whom he announced himself as Weatherford. The American commander expressed his astonishment that one whose hands were stained with an inhuman
murder of captives, should dare to appear in his presence,
knowing as he must, that his arrest had been ordered
for the purpose of bringing him to punishment. The
undaunted chieftain replied: "I am in your power, do
with me as you please. I am a warrior. I have done
the white people all the harm I could; I have fought
them, and fought them bravely; if I had any warriors left,
I would still fight, and contend to the last. But I have
none; my people are all gone; and now I can only mourn
over the misfortunes of my nation." Struck with a
magnanimity so nearly akin to his own high spirit, the
General explained to his visitor the terms upon which his
people might have peace, adding that he should take no
advantage of his voluntary surrender, that he was now at
liberty to remain and be protected, or retire, and reunite

himself with the war party; but that if taken, his life should pay the forfeit of his crimes.

The undismayed savage, maintaining the self-possession which distinguishes his race, replied : " I may well be addressed in such language now.   There was a time when I could have answered you ; I then had a choice, but now I have none—even hope has ended.   Once I could lead my warriors to battle ; but I cannot call the dead to life. My warriors can no longer hear my voice ; their bones are at Talladega,[7] Talluschatchee,[8] Emuckfaw,[9] and Tohopeka.[10] I have not surrendered myself without reflection.   While there was a chance of success, I never left my post, nor asked for peace.   But my people are gone, and I now ask for peace for my nation and for myself.   I look back with sorrow upon the miseries and misfortunes brought upon my country, and wish to avert still greater calamities. Our best warriors are slain, our cattle and grain are destroyed, and our women and children are destitute of provisions.   If I had been left to contend with the Georgia army, I would have raised my corn on one bank of the river and fought them on the other, but your people have destroyed my nation.   You are a brave man ; I rely on your generosity.   You will exact no terms from a conquered people but such as they should accept ; whatever they may be, it would be madness in us to oppose them.   If any oppose them you will find me stern in enforcing obedience.   Those who would still hold out, can be influenced only by a spirit of revenge, and to this they must not, and shall not, sacrifice the last remnant of their nation.   You have told us where we must go, and be safe. This is a good talk, and they ought to listen to it.   They shall listen to it."

At the conclusion of the war, a council was held by General Jackson, at which the chiefs and warriors of both

factions of the Creeks attended, and the subject of the
removal of that people to the lands assigned them west of
the Mississippi was discussed.[11] A majority were opposed
to the scheme, and several of the chiefs denounced it in
bold and eloquent language. The speech of the Big
Warrior on that occasion, has been quoted as a fine
specimen of savage elocution. Major Eaton,[12] in his *Life
of General Jackson*, from which we have gathered the
preceding facts, after describing the speeches of some of
the chiefs, adds, "but the inflexibility of the person with
whom they were treating, evinced to them, that however
just and well-founded might be their objections, the policy
under which he acted was too clearly defined for any
abandonment of it to be at all calculated upon. Selocta,
one of their chiefs, who had united with our troops at the
commencement of the war, who had marched and fought
with them in all their battles, and had attached to himself
strongly the confidence of the commanding general, now
addressed him. He told him of the regard he had ever
felt for his white brothers, and with what zeal he had
exerted himself to preserve peace, and keep in friendship
with them; when his efforts had failed, he had taken up
arms against his own country, and fought against his own
people; that he was not opposed to yielding the lands
lying on the Alabama, which would answer the purpose
of cutting off any intercourse with the Spaniards, but the
country west of the Coosa he wished to preserve to the
nation. To effect this he appealed to the feelings of
Jackson; told him of the dangers they had passed
together, and of his faithfulness to him in the trying
scenes through which they had gone."

"There were, indeed, none whose voice ought sooner
to have been heard than Selocta's. None had rendered
greater services, and none had been more faithful. He

had claims growing out of his fidelity that few others had."

The sequel of this interview has become matter of history, and is too well known to need repetition. The Creeks assented to the terms proposed by the American Government, and, abandoning the graves of their fathers, sought a new home.[13]

NOTES

1. "Among the Creeks and their cousins, the Seminole, all warlike functions, including the declaration of war, the organising of war parties, and the burning of captives, were in charge of officers of certain clans, which clans were designated for this reason, 'bearers of the red' in contradistinction to the 'white' or peace clans, in the towns of which peace treaties were negotiated and where it was forbidden to shed human blood.   The symbol of the declaration of war was the erection of a tall pole, painted red, in the public square, as a rallying point for the warriors, whence the popular term 'Red Sticks' applied by writers both to these towns and to the hostile war element, which at various periods made headquarters in them particularly during the Creek and Seminole war.   The most noted towns controlled by the war clans were Atasi of the Upper Creeks, Kawita of the Lower Creeks, and Mikasuki of the Seminole." — Mooney in *Handbook of American Indians*, pt. 2, p. 365.

2. See Vol. I., note 32, p. 400 ; also Tustennuggee Emathla, note 1, p. 176, this volume.   Referring to the fight at Fort Mims : "The courage of Major Beasley amounted to desperation.   Although often warned, he turned a deaf ear to all idea of danger.   At the outset of the enemy, in the blaze of three hundred rifles, he wished to close the front gate, which opened into the outward work not yet completed.   Here he fell—too soon to perceive his inability to repel a superior force fighting on equal terms ; too late to enable the gallant officer who succeeded him, to gain possession of the bastions and blockhouse, which were now occupied by the enemy."—J. F. H. Claiborne, *Mississippi as a Province, Territory and State*, Jackson, Miss., 1880, Vol. I., p. 336.

3. In connection with the massacre at Fort Mims, Pickett (*History of Alabama*, Charleston, 1851, Vol. II., p. 267 *et seq.*) wrote : "Associated with M'Queen and Francis was William Weatherford, the son of Charles Weatherford, a Georgian, who had lived almost a lifetime in the Creek nation.   His mother, Sehoy, was the half-sister of General M'Gillivray and a native of Hickory Ground.   William was uneducated, but was a man of great native intellect, fine form, and commanding person. His bearing was gentlemanly and dignified, and was coupled with an intelligent expression, which led strangers to suppose that they were in the presence of no ordinary man. His eyes were large, dark, brilliant and flashing. He was one of 'nature's noblemen,' a man of strict honor and unsurpassed courage." Page 251: "After the war was over, Weatherford became a permanent citizen of the lower part of the county of Monroe, where, upon a good farm, well supplied with negroes, he lived, maintained an excellent character, and was much respected by the American citizens for his bravery, honor and strong native sense. He died in 1826, from the effects of fatigue, produced by a desperate bear hunt."

4. From existing documents it is known that about July 27, 1813, the Spanish Governor at Pensacola gave the Creek chief M'Queen and the assembled warriors "about 1000 lb. Gunpowder & proportion of Balls, &c."

5. Eaton (*Life of Andrew Jackson*, p. 50) refers to ". . . old Chinnaby, a leading chief of the Creek nation, and sternly opposed to the war party." Page 40: "On the night of the 8th [January, 1813] a letter was received from him [Colonel Coffee], dated two days before, advising that two Indians, belonging to the peace party, had just arrived at the Tennessee River, from Chinnaby's fort, on the Coosa, with information that the war party had dispatched 800 or a 1000 warriors to attack the frontiers of Georgia. . . ." Page 43: "Shelocta, the son of Chinnaby, a principal chief among the friendly Creeks, arrived at his [Jackson's] camp, to solicit his speedy movement for the relief of his father's fort which was then threatened by a considerable body of the war party, who had advanced to the neighbourhood of the Ten Islands, on the Coosa."

6. Consult Pickett, *History of Alabama*, Vol. II., p. 350, Charleston, 1851.

7. Eaton (*Life of Jackson*, p. 57) wrote: ". . . On the evening of the 7th [November, 1813] a runner arrived from Talladega, a fort of the friendly Indians, distant about thirty miles below, with information that the enemy had that morning encamped before it in great numbers, and would certainly destroy it, unless immediate assistance could be afforded. Jackson confiding in the statement determined to lose no time in extending the relief which was solicited. . . . He now gave orders for taking up the line of march, with twelve hundred infantry, and eight hundred cavalry and mounted gun men; leaving behind the sick, the wounded, and all his baggage, with a force which was deemed sufficient for their protection until the reinforcements from Turkey Town should arrive." The following day the American forces attacked the Indians who were besieging the fort, and won a decisive victory. The Indian loss being stated at 600; the American, 15 killed and 80 wounded.

8. Eaton, *Life of Jackson*, p. 53: "Learning now [October 30, 1813] that a considerable body of the enemy had posted themselves at Tallushatchee, on the south side of the Coosa, about thirteen miles distant, General Coffee was detached with nine hundred men (the mounted troops having been previously organised into a brigade, and placed under his command) to attack and disperse them. With this force he was enabled, through the direction of an Indian pilot, to ford the Coosa, at the Fish-dams, about four miles above the Islands; and having encamped beyond it, very early the next morning proceded to the execution of his orders." As a result of this engagement 186 Indians were killed. "Of the Americans, five were killed, and forty-one wounded. Two men were killed with arrows, which, on this occasion, formed a principal part of the arms of the Indians; each one having a bow and quiver, which he used after the first fire of his gun, until an opportunity occurred for reloading." (See also Pickett, *History of Alabama*, Vol. II., p. 293 *et seq.*) Pickett (p. 298) gives November 3, 1813, as the date of the battle of "Tallasehatche."

9. The battle of Emuckfaw was fought January 22, 1814, at the mouth of Emuckfaw creek, on the Tallapoosa River, in Tallapoosa county, Alabama. (Consult Pickett, *History of Alabama*, Vol. II., p. 332, Charleston, 1851; Eaton, *Life of Andrew Jackson*, p. 134, Philadelphia, 1824.)

10. That is, the battle of the "Horseshoe," March 27, 1814, Tohopeka being the Creek name. (See MENAWA, note 4, p. 192, this volume.)

11. "Articles of agreement and capitulation, made and concluded this ninth day of August, one thousand eight hundred and fourteen, between Major General Andrew Jackson, on behalf of the President of the United States of America, and the chiefs, deputies and warriors of the Creek nation." By Article 1 of this treaty the Creek nation ceded to the United States territory equal in value to the expense of the war. The treaty was signed at Fort Jackson, at the junction of Coosa and Tallapoosa Rivers, Alabama. This post occupied the site of the old Fort Toulouse.

12. John Henry Eaton, *The Life of Andrew Jackson*, Philadelphia, 1824.

13. The portrait of Selocta, No. 70 of the Rhees *Catalogue*, was painted by King in 1825. Selocta was one of the party of Creeks who visited Washington during the winter of 1825-26, and was a signer of the treaty of Washington, January 24, 1826. He likewise signed the supplementary article to the same treaty, March 31, 1826; consequently he must have remained in Washington for some time.

KAI-POL-E-QUA, *or* " WHITE-NOSED FOX "
A Sauk Brave

KAIPOLEQUA [1]

(OR, WHITE-NOSED FOX)

THIS distinguished warrior is the chief of a division of the Sauk nation, which forms part of a singular institution, which, so far as we know, is peculiar to that people.

The warriors of the Sauk nation are divided into two bands, or parties,[2] one of which is called Kishkoquis, or the *Long Hairs*, and the other Oshcush, or *The Brave*; the former being considered as something more than merely brave. In 1819 each party numbered about four hundred warriors; in 1826 they numbered about five hundred each, but have not increased since that time. The Kishkoquis, or Long Hairs, are commanded by the hereditary war chief Keokuk, whose standard is red; the head man of the Oshcushies is Kaipolequa, the subject of this sketch, whose standard is blue. The Long Hairs take precedence in point of rank. The formation of these parties is a matter of national concern, and is effected by a simple arrangement. The first male child who is born to a Kishkoqui is marked with white paint, the distinguishing colour of the Kishkoquis, and belongs to that party; the next male of the same family is marked with black paint, and is attached to the Oshcushies, and so on alternately—the first son belonging to the same band with his father, and the others being assigned in turn, first to one band and then to the other. Thus all the warriors are attached to one or the other band, and the division is as nearly equal as it could be by any arrangement commencing with infancy.

Whenever the whole nation, or any large party of warriors, turn out to engage in a grand hunt, or a warlike expedition, or for the purpose of performing sham battles or ball-plays, the individuals belonging to the two bands are distinguished by their appropriate colours. If the purpose of the assemblage is for sham-fighting, or other diversion, the Kishkoquis daub their bodies all over with white clay, and the Oshcushies blacken themselves with charcoal; the bands are ranged under their respective leaders, and play against each other, rallying under the red and blue banners. In war and hunting, when all must be ranged on one side, the white and black paints are mingled with other colours, so that the distinction is kept up, and after the close of the expedition the scalps, plunder, game, and other trophies of each band collectively are compared, and the deeds of each repeated.

The object of these societies will be readily seen. They form a part of the simple machinery of a military government, and are founded in consummate wisdom, with the view of exciting emulation, and of placing every warrior in the nation under the constant observation of all the others. From early youth each individual is taught to feel, that whether engaged in war, in hunting, or in athletic sports, the honour of his band, as well as his own, is concerned in his success or failure, and thus a sense of responsibility is awakened and kept alive which has all the moral force of a constant and rigid discipline.

Kaipolequa attained the high rank of leader of his band through his military abilities; and he is considered as one of the most distinguished braves of the nation.[3]

NOTES

1. According to the late Dr William Jones, the name is derived from *Kepanigw*, " closed eye."

2. See KEOKUK, note 15, p. 147, this volume.

3. The portrait of " Kai-pol-e-quah, White-nosed Fox," bears No. 44 in the Rhees *Catalogue*, and although both the date and the name of the author are lacking, it may be attributed to King and the date 1824 assigned to it. On August 4, 1824, Kaipolequa was in Washington, where he signed the treaty concluded that day. His name appears in *Nile's Register*, July 31, 1824, among the list of Indians then in Washington transacting business with the Government. Other members of this delegation were Taiomah (p. 107, this volume); Keesheswa (p. 154, this volume); Peahmuska (Vol. I., p. 231).

OSCEOLA (ASSEOLA)

(A SEMINOLE LEADER)

WE have already, in our notices of Micanopy and other
Seminoles, touched in a cursory manner upon the history
of that people, and the causes of the war between them
and the United States. We have shown that the Seminoles were chiefly renegades from the Creek and other
nations within the United States, who, taking refuge in
the wilds of Florida, while that province was a dependency
of Spain, united in bands, and carried on a predatory
war against the frontiers of the United States. During
the war between this country and Great Britain, they
joined our enemies, and afterwards, in 1816, made war
upon us. They not only, therefore, had no title to the
lands of Florida, but their claims upon the generosity
of our Government were equally slender. In 1821
General Jackson, then Governor of Florida, urged upon
the Government at Washington the propriety of sending
back to the Creek country all the refugees from that
nation, as he foresaw the most disastrous consequences
from their continuance in the territory. Colonel White,[1]
a representative in Congress from that territory, in a letter
to the Secretary of War, written in 1822, pressed the
same considerations upon the Administration, and urged
the removal of those intruders as the only efficient means
of giving quiet to the country. Had those suggestions

been adopted, the restless spirits who have since given animation to these ferocious bands would have been removed, and we should have been spared the pain and expense of a protracted war. A contrary policy was unfortunately pursued; humanity dictated a temporising course, which has proved eminently disastrous; the Seminoles were recognised as a separate people, and treaties were held with their chief men for the purchase of the wilds through which they roamed, and the removal of their people. By the treaty of Camp Moultrie, held on the 18th September, 1823, they were permitted to remain in the territory for twenty years,[2] and were thus established in the country, and their claims acknowledged to lands to which they had not the shadow of a title.

The forbearance of the American Government towards the Seminoles was in accordance with the humane policy which has marked all its measures in regard to the aborigines. In no instance have the Indians been treated with cruelty or injustice by the deliberate action of the national executive or legislature, whose whole course towards them has been beneficent and forbearing. When it has been found necessary to remove them from their hunting-grounds, the most ample remuneration has always been provided, and other lands assigned them, better suited to their condition. Their lands have never been taken from them, except by purchase; and so careful has the Government been to avoid even the appearance of injustice, that where several tribes have claimed the same lands, they have paid the full equivalent to each; and in cases where the tribes have refused to comply with the treaties made by their chiefs, the same lands have been purchased over and over from the same people, and as repeatedly paid for.

But while the Government and people of the United

States have been actuated by the most benevolent intentions, their views have been signally frustrated by the inefficiency of the system by which their intercourse with Indians has been attempted to be regulated, by the weakness or misconduct of their own agents, and by a variety of causes inseparable from transactions conducted in a wilderness far distant from the seat of Government. The wrongs perpetrated against the Indians have been numerous and flagrant. The wide scheme of peculation and pillage practised by bands of expert knaves who invest the frontiers, has been shaped into a system which has now become so complicated and enormous as almost to defy the hand of reform. The Indian Department is one of the most expensive branches of our Government,[3] consuming annually vast sums, liberally appropriated for the good of the red men, but of which a small portion ever reaches its destination; and they are constantly subject to abuse and insult of the most ignominious character. The desperate and dissolute men who fly to the frontier as a place of refuge, or seek it as a theatre for intrigue or violence, find easy victims in the ignorant savage, who claims no protection from the law, and whose demand for protection or revenge cannot reach the ear of a distant Government.

In no part of our country were the Indians worse used than in Florida, where the most scandalous outrages were perpetrated upon their persons and property, provoked often by their own ferocity and bad faith, but, nevertheless, wholly inexcusable.[4] Under the pretence of reclaiming property alleged to have been stolen by the Indians, their country was entered by lawless persons, whose sole object was plunder, their houses pillaged, their cattle driven away, and themselves cruelly maltreated. Frauds in pecuniary transactions, of gross criminality and enormous amount, were practised both upon the Government and the Indians. Complaints of these abuses, and evidence of their existence have reached the ears of the Executive, and of Congress, but no sustained effort has ever been made to investigate or correct them; no patriot has been found who would devote himself to a cause so worthy of the highest efforts of the Christian and the statesman; and thus has the political paradox been presented, of a people practically oppressed by a magnanimous nation, entertaining towards them the kindest sympathies, and annually expending millions for their defence, support, and welfare.

The celebrated individual of whom we are about to give a brief account, is known to the public under the various appellations of Powell, Osceola, Oceola, Asseola, Osiniola, and Assini Yahola; but his true name is that which we have placed at the head of this article. Powell is the surname of a white man who married the mother of Asseola, after the death of his father, and whose name was very naturally given to the youth who had thus become one of his family. Osceola signifies the *Rising Sun*, and has been erroneously adopted by many, as well on account of its similarity of sound to the true name, as from its supposed adaptation to the character and position of this daring leader. The true name is derived from *Asse*, "the black drink," and *Ola*, "a waterfall." We have, in another place,[5] mentioned a peculiar custom of the Creeks, who, previous to entering into council, assemble in groups and drink freely of the decoction of a certain herb of their country, which operates as an emetic, and whose effect, they imagine, is to purify and invigorate both the mind and body, so as to prepare them for the business of thought and debate. This beverage, which is taken warm, and in large quantities, is called the

"Black drink," from its colour, and among the several names applied to it, to express its quality or effects, are those of *asse, assiniola,* and *assini yahola.* The name Asseola, when freely translated, signifies the plentiful drinker of the black drink, or, one who imbibes this fluid in torrents; and it may or may not be descriptive of a peculiarity of this individual, as Indian names are given in childhood, as with us, for the mere purpose of convenience, while they are afterwards often superseded by others, descriptive of a prominent feature in the character of the person, or of some of his exploits. We have not been able to ascertain whether Asseola bore this name in infancy, or acquired it by his devotion to the nauseating draught, by which the Creek statesman makes a clean breast, preparatory to the solemn duties of the council.

The paternal grandfather of Asseola was a Scotsman, who married a Creek woman; his father, therefore, was a half-breed, but his mother was a Creek of the pure blood. He was born on the Tallapoosa River, in the Creek nation, somewhere between the years 1800 and 1806, and must have been between thirty and thirty-five years of age at the time of his death. His European descent is said to have been distinctly indicated in his complexion and eyes, which were lighter than those of his people, as well as in the features and expression of his countenance. The following spirited description of him is from a work entitled *Notices of Florida and the Campaigns,* by M. M. Cohen.[6]

"When conversing on topics agreeable to him, his countenance manifests more the disposition of the white than of the red man. There is great vivacity in the play of his features, and when excited, his face is lighted up as by a thousand fires of passion, animation, and energy. His nose is Grecian at the base, and would be perfectly

Phidean, but that it becomes slightly arched. There are indomitable firmness and withering scorn in the expression of his mouth—though the lips are tremulous from intense emotions, which seem ever boiling up within him. About his brow, care, and thought, and toil have traced their channels, anticipating on a youthful face the work of time.

"To those who have known Oceola long, his fame does not appear like a sunburst, but as the ripening fruit of early promised blossoms. For years past he has enjoyed the reputation of being the best ball-player and hunter, and the most expert at running, wrestling, and all active exercises. At such times his figure, whence all the superfluous flesh is worn down, exhibits the most beautiful development of muscle and power. He is said to be inexhaustible from the ball-play, an exercise so violent, that the struggle for mastery has been known to cause the death of one of the combatants. When this occurs in a fair contest, the survivor is not punished for murder, as in all other cases of taking life. On one occasion Oceola acted as guide to a party of horsemen, and finding, at starting, that they proceeded slowly, inquired the cause. On being told that it was on his account, with one of those smiles he alone can give, he bade them proceed more rapidly. They put spurs to their steeds, and he, afoot, kept up with them during the entire route, nor did he exhibit the slightest symptoms of fatigue at the close of day, but arrived at the point proposed as early as the mounted body."

Another writer,[7] the author of the *War in Florida, by a late Staff Officer*, speaks of this individual in the following terms :—

"It will be seen that the standing of Asseola, prior to the war, was much inferior to that of a number of the other chiefs, and although his influence was seemingly great, it was still less than that of Micanopy, Jumper, Holata Micco, Coa Hajo, Arpiucki, Abraham, and several others; but he was with the mass of the warriors who were the anti-removal party, and themselves possessing as much influence as their chiefs; so that the marvellous reports of him, and the influence which it is supposed he exerts over the Indians, are very exaggerated, and have their origin only in the bold, desperate, and reckless murders which have been perpetrated by the band of Micosukees, of which he is sub-chief. Holata Micco is the chief leader of that band, and decidedly superior to Asseola in every point of view. The latter is a *Redstick*, not a Micosukee, by descent, and prior to the breaking out of hostilities, was leader of but seven warriors. His talents are not above mediocrity, and he was never known, by those who were most intimate with him, to possess any of the nobler qualities which adorn the Indian character; all his dealings have been characterised by a low, sordid, and contracted spirit, which often produced difficulties with those with whom he had intercourse. Perverse and obstinate in his disposition, he would frequently oppose measures which it was the interest of his people that he should advocate. The principal chiefs were favourable to the project of emigration, but the mass of warriors were opposed to it; and as Holata Micco and his band, with Asseola, were the first to be removed by the provisions of the treaty, and these warriors having been averse to the treaty from the first, they sowed discord among the others by threatening to murder all who should advocate the measure; and it was doubtless through fear that Asseola joined the hostile party, after the pledge he had made to leave the country. This description of Asseola may, perhaps, serve to disabuse the public mind as to the 'noble character,' 'lofty bearing,' 'high soul,' 'amazing powers,' and 'magnanimity' of the 'Micosukee chief.'"

It will be seen that there is some discrepancy in the views of the character of Asseola given by these writers, both of whom were witnesses of his conduct; we apprehend that both are correct in the main, differing chiefly in the colouring given to their pictures. Referring occasionally to these and some other authorities, we shall, in the remainder of this sketch, depend principally upon a manuscript statement in our possession, prepared with much care by an intelligent officer of the United States army, serving in the Indian Department throughout the whole of the Florida war.

The death of his father probably threw Asseola at a very early age upon his own guidance, and some of the strong points of his character, especially its vices, may be referred to this cause, the fruitful source of evil in the formation of ardent minds. While yet a boy of not more than from twelve to fifteen years of age, he joined the "Redsticks," or hostile Creeks, and fought against the Tennessee troops, commanded by Generals Jackson and Floyd. When peace was established, he was one of the many unruly spirits who emigrated to Florida, where the Redsticks [8] became known as a party hostile to the United States. In 1817, when the repeated depredations of the Florida Indians caused the invasion of that country by General Jackson, he was in arms, and being driven across the Suwanee, retreated with a small party of his companions down into the peninsula, and settled upon Peas' Creek. Here he remained unknown to fame, and probably engaged in no other pursuit than that of hunting, and occasionally participating in those athletic games in which he was so expert, until a few years ago, when he removed to the Big Swamp, in the neighbourhood of Fort King, and united himself with the Micosukees, with whom he has since lived.

It was at that time, probably about 1832, that Asseola, who was then somewhat more than twenty-five years of age, became known to the American officers. He had neither rank nor property, nor any followers, except two Indians, who had accompanied him from his late residence ; but his deportment and appearance were such as to point him out as a person likely to become important. He was of light frame, a little above the common stature, and finely formed, his complexion light, and the expression of his countenance cheerful and agreeable. His habits were active and enterprising, evincing an entire freedom from that indolence of mind which degrades the great mass of this race into merely sensual beings, who are only roused into action to indulge the appetites of hunger or revenge, and sink into apathy when those passions have been satiated. The mind of Asseola was active rather than strong, and his conduct that of a cunning and ambitious man, who was determined to rise by his own exertions.

The frontier was at that time in a state of great excite-ment, and our intercourse with the Seminoles becoming daily more complicated and uncertain. There was no war existing, nor expected, but there was neither peace nor safety. The Indians had been advised of the determina-tion of the Government to remove them from Florida, and were holding a temporising course with our agents, while divided among themselves as to the policy to be pursued. The most intelligent of their chiefs, and a minority of the braves, respectable in number and character, were decidedly in favour of emigration, not merely as an unavoidable alter-native, but as a measure positively advantageous in itself. Experience had demonstrated the impossibility of living in contact with the whites. The superiority of the civilised over the savage man, however reluctantly admitted, was practically felt and acknowledged. The pressure of the white population was recognised as a continual and accumulating force, operating to the destruction of the Indian race, almost imperceptibly, yet with the swiftness and certainty of the laws of Nature. They saw that the decree had gone out which compelled the weak to give place, and allowed the strong to possess. Those who had marked the signs of the times, and had reflected calmly upon the traditions of their ancestors, discerned but too clearly the gigantic growth of the white man's power, and saw its shadow extending over the land of the Indian, with a progress as irresistible as that of the shades of night. Wherever that shadow fell, the Indian felt its chilling influence, which thickened around him until he sunk under its blighting effect. They saw all this, and determined to seek safety in flight. Nor was this all : they were offered not merely safety from present danger, but decided advantages—a better climate, a more abundant country, a wider range of hunting ground, and a permanent separation from the white man—peace, and the protection of a powerful nation, instead of inevitable and hopeless war. In addition to these advantages, they were to be paid for the improvements they abandoned, to be supported for one year after their arrival in the new country, to receive an annuity of three thousand dollars for fifteen years, and their cattle and other property were to be sold for their benefit by the United States.

The mass of the Seminoles,[9] however, were opposed to emigration. To many, the prospect of war was, in itself, a sufficient inducement to remain. The savage is habitually improvident, and seldom looks beyond the present. War gives him employment, excitement, and, above all, plunder

—that fatal lure is not without its attraction, even among the armies and the councils of the most refined nations, but to the savage mind, it is the first, the best, and the most irresistible of arguments.   The love of war, the ardent lust for carnage, was not the least of the incitements operating on a people swift to shed blood.   The passion of revenge, too, had its influence; not only the national and general hatred against the whites, but the personal resentment rankling in the bosoms of individuals for actual wrongs for which they were eager to seek redress.   Then there was ambition, the small ambition of the sub-chiefs, the captains of ten, and captains of twenty, who desired to increase their own importance, and to swell the number of their followers.   Besides all which, the country they occupied suited them; its peninsular conformation, its wild and tangled forests interspersed with swamps and hammocks impenetrable to the foot of the white man, and which seemed to bid eternal defiance to the approach of civilisation, rendered this region the fit and favourite abode of savage men.

There was also an objection to the removal, which was felt by all the Seminoles, and gave so much plausibility to the arguments of those opposed to emigration, that it is surprising the Government should not have promptly removed it.   By the treaty of Payne's Landing,[10] it was provided that the Seminoles should remove west of the Mississippi, and there become a constituent portion of the Creek nation.   They were to settle near the Creeks, and be placed under the charge of the same agent.   To this arrangement they expressed a decided repugnance.   A large number of those who had separated from the Creeks had private reasons for not desiring a reunion; some were debtors, and some held property of which the ownership might be brought in question.   They were refugees, who had outstanding accounts and quarrels with those from whom they had fled. They asked, therefore, to have a separate territory, and especially, an agent of their own. Holata Amathla, in one of the councils, said [11] : "If our Father, the President, will give us our own agent, our own blacksmith, and our ploughs, we will go to this new country, but if he does not, we shall be unwilling to remove; we should be among strangers, they may be friendly or they may be hostile to us, and we want our own agent whom we know, who will be our friend, take care of us, do us justice, and see justice done us by others." "We have been unfortunate in the agents sent us by our Father. General Thompson, our present agent, is the friend of the Seminoles. We thought at first that he would be like the others, but now we know better. He has but one talk, and what he tells us is the truth; we want him to go with us. He told us he could not go, but he at last agreed to do so, if our Great Father would permit him; we know our Father loves his red children, and will not let them suffer for want of a good agent." General Clinch, the gallant and able commander of the troops then in Florida, in presenting this subject to the Government, said: "It is a law of Nature for the weak to be suspicious of the strong. They say the Creeks are much more numerous and powerful than they are; that there is a question of property, involving the right to a great many negroes, to be settled between them and the Creeks, and they are afraid that justice will not be done them, unless they have a separate agent to watch over and protect their interests. The manly and straightforward course pursued towards them by General Thompson appears to have gained their confidence, and they have again petitioned the President to make him their agent, and have requested me to forward their petition, with such remarks as my long acquaintance with their views and interests would authorise me to make. The experiment they are about to make is one of deep interest to them.   They are leaving the birthplace of their wives and children, and many of them the graves of those they hold most dear ; and is it not natural they should feel, and feel deeply, on such a trying occasion, and wish to have someone that they had previously known, whom they could lean upon and look up to for protection."   To this rational appeal the Government replied by a cold negative ; the preparations for the removal were going forward, the friendly chiefs were using their influence to urge on that desirable measure, while the disaffected stood aloof, or gave manifestations of their dissatisfaction in sudden and secret acts of violence, in pillaging by night, or murdering the solitary traveller in the wilderness.

Such was the state of things when Asseola began to take an active part as a Tustennugge, or sub-chief, of the Micosukees, of which tribe Holato Micco, or the *Blue King,* was chief.   The term sub-chief, which we use, is not descriptive of any actual office or formal appointment, but merely designates those individuals who, by their talents or popular qualities, obtain followers, and become leaders or persons of influence.   Those who are expert in war or hunting are followed by the young braves, who desire to learn under them, at first, perhaps, only by their own relatives who depend on them ; but as their reputation increases, the train swells in number : and there are, therefore, leaders of every grade, from those who head a few men, up to him who controls his hundred warriors, vies with the chief in influence and authority, and at last supplants him, or supersedes him in every particular except in name.   Thus we have seen Powell,[12] a young man with two followers, beginning to mingle in public affairs. He had carefully noted the path to popular favour, and

OSCEOLA (ASSEOLA)
A Seminole Leader

pursued it with sagacity and boldness. His first step was to gain the confidence of the American officers, and by making himself useful, to gain employment which would render him important in the eyes of his own people. He visited the Fort[13] frequently, and his services were always at the command of the officers, to suppress the depredations of those lawless Indians who would clandestinely cross the frontier to plunder, and arrest the offenders, as well as to apprehend deserters from the army. On these occasions, he would call on the neighbouring chiefs for men, and having formed a party, placed himself at their head, and recommended himself, as well to his employers as to his own people, by his diligence and efficiency. He soon pushed himself into notice, and was continually engaged in some active service; he became a favourite with the military officers, and in consequence of the estimation in which he was held by them, rose rapidly in the eyes of his adopted tribe. He now gained adherents; for the Indians are a fickle people, and there are always many among them who are ready to surround the banner of a rising leader; until at length, without apparently holding any positive rank, he became a leading man among the Micosukees. He continued for some time to cultivate with assiduity the goodwill of the whites, was quiet and unassuming in his deportment, submissive even to humility towards the officers, and pacific in his sentiments, while he insinuated himself into the affections of his own people by his courtesy and his martial qualities.

But there was another source of popularity which he failed not to improve to the utmost, as it was that on which he chiefly depended for promotion. The chiefs and more intelligent of the braves were, as we have said, in favour of emigration, while the majority of the people, comprising all the ignorant and lawless portions, were opposed to the removal. The conjuncture was one which offered a tempting opportunity to an aspiring demagogue. Asseola took the side of the majority, and while, at first, he did not venture openly to oppose the chiefs, he artfully fomented the discontents of the people, and encouraged them in their obstinate refusal to leave the country. He was always opposed to the treaty of Payne's Landing; but at first, his tone with regard to it was quiet and unobtrusive, and it might have been inferred, that while his feelings revolted against the proposed arrangement, he was ready to sacrifice his own wishes to preserve peace and secure the welfare of his countrymen. With consummate art he continued to pay court to the chiefs and the American officers and agents, and to affect a sympathy for the people, until he found himself sufficiently strong in the affections of the latter to throw aside the mask. He grew into favour with the factious multitude, who needed only an unscrupulous leader who would play out the game of revolt, regardless of consequences; and when he felt that he was the leader and dictator of a party, he began to avow the principles he had long secretly cherished. His conduct now became as conspicuous for boldness and insolence as it had been for the opposite qualities; he was loud, querulous, and bitter in his opposition; his language was coarse and inflammatory; and his whole course was that of one who had resolved to bring on a crisis which should draw a broad line of separation between the respective parties, oblige the neutral to take sides, and force on an issue of the contest. In his interviews with General Thompson, the agent for the removal of the Seminoles,[14] he now openly avowed his opposition, declared that he never would be carried from the country alive, that rather than submit to such injustice, the Indians would fight, that he could kill two or three white men

himself before he could be slain ; and finally, he denounced
in the most vehement manner the friendly chiefs, declaring
they should not go peaceably to another country, that the
first who took a step towards emigration should be put to
death, and that if required he would himself become the
executioner.

There can be little doubt as to the decision which
history will record as to the conduct of Asseola.   The line
of distinction is clear and definite between the patriot who
calmly and firmly places himself in the breach between his
country and her oppressors, exposing himself to procure
safety, or even a temporary advantage for her, and the
demagogue, who, seizing for his own aggrandisement an
occasion of popular excitement, fans into a blaze the
embers of discord, and affecting to administer that public
will which he has secretly created, becomes the agitator
and the soul of a bad cause.   The one controls and gives
a proper direction to the judgment of his people, while the
other stimulates their worst passions, and leads them
blindfold to their own destruction.   The former course
gives employment to talents and virtues of the highest
grade, the latter may be successfully pursued by an instinct
of no greater capacity than that of the fox or the wolf.
There could scarcely be a difference of opinion as to the
true interest of the Seminoles.   Setting aside the question
of the right of occupation, as between civilised and savage
man, as having no direct bearing here, we must view the
Seminoles as themselves intruders into a land previously
occupied by the Europeans, from whom the American
Government derived title by purchase.   They seized on
this wilderness while it was protected, as they supposed,
by a foreign flag,[15] as a stronghold from which they could
with impunity annoy the American citizen.   The United
States, having the right as well as the power to remove

them, resistance could only lead to a war, wholly unjustifiable because hopeless. Under the circumstances it is scarcely probable that this aspiring leader was impelled by any higher motive than that of taking the side opposed to the chiefs, whom he desired to supplant, and favoured by the multitude, through whom he hoped to rule—a course of which history affords but too many examples, and which the experience of every day shows to be the natural path of reckless ambition.

Throwing aside entirely the mask he had worn, Asseola became more and more insolent, until at last he ceased to observe the common forms of courtesy. He either absented himself from the councils which were now frequently held, or disturbed the deliberations by inflammatory speeches. He boldly threatened the chiefs with the vengeance of the people, and in his interviews with General Thompson,[16] the agent, was so rude and so undisguised in his threats of personal violence to that officer, that the latter was obliged on one occasion to order him to leave his presence, and his friends earnestly advised the arrest of the refractory partisan, as a measure due to his own safety. It is only to be regretted that this salutary step was not sooner adopted, and more effectually carried into execution. Asseola was not a chief, but a self-constituted leader, misdirecting the ignorant to their ruin, disturbing the peace, and defeating the benign intentions of the Government. He was accordingly arrested [17] by the orders of Colonel Fanning, at the request of the agent, and placed in close confinement. As he was dragged to the guard-house, he was heard by one who understood the Creek tongue, to exclaim, "The sun," pointing to its position, "is so high; I shall remember the hour! the agent has his day, I will have mine!"

The conduct of Powell while in confinement threw a

new light upon his character, evincing the coolness and deliberation of his designs, and showing how completely he was master of the arts of dissimulation. At first sullen, and apparently alarmed, he seemed to abandon all hope. A new light seemed gradually to gleam upon him; and then, as if convinced of his error, he requested to see the friendly chiefs, who were accordingly permitted to visit him. To them he figured a humility and contrition which completely deceived them. He spoke of his past conduct in terms of regret and pointed self-condemnation; depicted in glowing language the hopes he had entertained of uniting the several factions of the nation, so that by organising a firm opposition they might be permitted to occupy a little longer their present homes; and admitted the fallacy of these expectations. He spoke of himself as a martyr, whose vain efforts to unite the people for their common good had brought upon him the vengeance of their oppressors, and bitterly deplored the weakness and ingratitude of those who he said had deserted him in his hour of trouble; but avowed a sincere determination to yield to what now appeared an unavoidable destiny, and remove peaceably to a new country. The chiefs, whom he had violently denounced and opposed, were so completely deceived by his ostensible conversion, that a full reconciliation took place; and Asseola professing a conviction that his former course, though intended for the best, had been fatally erroneous, promised to become as active in promoting the cause of emigration as he had been zealous in retarding it. Satisfied of the sincerity of the change which they supposed had taken place, the chiefs interceded for him, pledged themselves for his faith, and Powell was set at liberty.[18] This act of mistaken humanity was the cause of much evil; for had Asseola been kept a prisoner, the removal might have gone on, and the cruel war which succeeded would never have taken place.

For awhile Asseola seemed to act in full accordance with his promises.[19] He not only signed the articles agreeing to emigrate himself, but brought over sixty or seventy Micosukees to do the same, assumed a conspicuous stand in the ranks of the party friendly to removal, was consulted on all measures leading to that object, and was always treated with the consideration due to an influential chief. Such was his position for some time; but, as the season for emigration approached, his visits to the agent became less frequent, and various plausible reasons were assigned for his absence, until the friendly chiefs began to suspect, and then to declare openly, that Powell "had one talk for the white man and another for the red," that many of the Indians were bent on war, and that the removal must be effected by force.

In the autumn of 1835,[20] the negotiations with the Seminoles were brought to a crisis. The friendly party, prepared to remove, and the hostile to resist, and the excitement on the border was increased. The following incident, recited in the *War in Florida, by a Staff Officer* will serve to illustrate the temper of the times [21] :—

" The Long Swamp and Big Swamp Indians, principally the Micosukee tribe, were, from the causes heretofore stated, again reduced to the greatest distress for the want of provisions, and their depredations upon the neighbouring settlements became daily more extensive. On one of these occasions three of the Long Swamp Indians were surprised, and two of them secured by the owner of the land, who tied them by the hands and feet with a rope, and carried them to his barn, where they were confined without sustenance for three days, unable to extricate themselves, and obliged to remain in one position. Not returning to their homes, their friends became alarmed for their safety, and the chief of the town where they resided went forward and demanded them. Being refused, he returned to his town, and, taking several of his people with him, again demanded the release of the prisoners, and was again refused, with a threat by the white fellows, that if the chief dared to effect their release, complaint should be entered against him. Upon this the whole party rushed to the barn whence they heard the moaning of their friends, and where they beheld a most pitiable sight. The rope with which these poor fellows were tied had worn through into the flesh—they had temporarily lost the use of their limbs, being unable to stand or walk —they had bled profusely, and had received no food during their confinement—so it may be readily imagined that they presented a horrible picture of suffering. The owner of the barn in which they were confined then fired upon the Indians, and slightly wounded one of the party, when their exasperation attained to such a height that, in retaliation for this brutal outrage, they set fire to the barn, and would not permit the owner to remove anything therefrom, nor did they leave the spot until the whole was consumed.

"These outrages continued to increase with each succeeding week, and the Indians discovering the hopelessness of their situation, at once concluded to oppose the efforts of the Government and call for a general assemblage of the nation. This course was rendered the more imperative at this particular period, in consequence of a demand having been made upon the Seminoles for a surrender of their cattle, ponies, hogs, etc., which were to be collected at some convenient depot, appraised and sold by the agent, and the Indians reimbursed therefor, on their arrival in their new country. Six of the principal chiefs, viz. : Charley Amathla, Holata Amathla, Foke Luste Hajo, Otulkee Amathla, Conhatkee Micco, and Fushutchee Micco, having returned their cattle, ponies, and hogs, the agent publicly announced that a sale would take place on the first of the ensuing month, December, 1835; but, in consequence of the interference of the anti-removal party, the delivery of the others was prevented, and the sale necessarily postponed to an indefinite period. In the meantime the great meeting of the nation at the Big Swamp resolved on retaining possession of their country, and condemned all who should oppose their views to instant death. This, therefore, was the signal for an immediate abandonment of the friendly towns, and no time was lost by those who had gone too far to retract, in seeking the protection of the forts. Accordingly, Holata Amathla, Otulkee Amathla, Foke Luste Hajo, Conhatkee Micco, and Fushutchee Micco, with about four hundred and fifty of their people, fled to Fort Brooke on the 9th of November, and encamped on the opposite side of the river."

The war was commenced by a tragedy of deep and affecting interest. Charley Amathla, a noble, intelligent, and honest chief, was preparing to retreat to Fort Brooke, on the 26th of November, when his house was surrounded by four hundred warriors, led by Holata Micco, Abraham, and Asseola, who demanded of him a promise that he and his people would oppose the removal. He replied, that having pledged his word to their Great Father, he would adhere to it even at the risk of his life. He said he had lived to see his people degraded, and on the verge of ruin, and their only hope of being saved from utter destruction depended on their removing to the West; he had made arrangements for his people to go, and had now no excuse for not complying with his engagements. He was told that he must join the opposition or suffer death, and that two hours would be allowed him to consult his people, and make his choice. He replied, that his mind was unalterable, and that his people could not make him break his word; but if he must die, he desired time to make some arrangements, which were required for the welfare of his people. At this moment, Asseola raised his rifle, pointed it at the bosom of the unresisting chief, and would have fired, had not Abraham arrested his arm, and called off the party to a council. They shortly after retired, having probably decided to defer, if not to retract, their murderous purpose; and the chief proceeded to the agency to complete his preparations. He appeared cheerful, but said to some of his friends, that perhaps they might never see him again, as persons had been appointed to kill him. He left the agency accompanied by his two daughters, and preceded by a negro on horseback, and had travelled homewards a few miles, when Asseola, with twelve other Indians, rose from an ambush, gave the war whoop, and fired upon him. The noble chief, comprehending instantly his situation, rose in his stirrups, sent back a whoop of defiance, charged into the midst of his assassins, and fell like a hero, perforated by eleven bullets. Thus died the chief of the Witamky band, a gallant, high-minded leader, and a man of sterling integrity, by the hands of Asseola, whom he had delivered from prison but a few months before, and for whose good conduct he stood pledged. The ingratitude and bad faith of Asseola greatly aggravate the heinousness of his participation in this cold-blooded murder, and stamp his character with a viciousness wholly incompatible with a great mind.

This atrocious deed was succeeded by open hostilities, and on the 28th of December following, occurred the melancholy massacre of the detachment under Major

Dade which we have described in another place. On
the same day, and while that melancholy scene of butchery
was going forward in the hammock, General Thompson,
the agent, was surprised and basely murdered. He had
dined at the Agency Office, about one hundred yards from
Fort King, and shortly after was walking unguardedly
near the woods, beyond the Office, when a band of fifty or
sixty Micosukees, led by Asseola, rushed upon him, and
having slain him, Lieutenant Smith and several others
hastily retired. The body of General Thompson was
perforated with fourteen bullets and a knife wound; all
the killed were shockingly mangled, and the whole affair
evinced the worst feelings on the part of the perpetrators.
The functions of the agent were not military, but civil,
and his relation to the Indians such as should have
rendered his person sacred. He had been their friend
and advocate; and, by their own evidence, had been kind
and just in his dealings with them. Asseola especially,
who had been employed by him, and whose intercourse
with him had been intimate, was acquainted with the
uprightness of his conduct, and was bound above all
others to respect his character and hold his person sacred
from violence. But if such sentiments had ever made any
impression on his vicious nature, that impression was
eradicated by a single offence towards himself, which
rankled in his bosom, and instigated a brutal revenge.

The writer last quoted thus continues the narrative of
these events.[22] "Marauding parties now commenced their
operations almost simultaneously, in various sections of
the country, pillaging and destroying everything of value.
Those who had inflicted injuries on the Indians were
forthwith repaid, and many barely escaped with their
lives. Conflagration succeeded conflagration, until the
whole country from Fort Brooke to Fort King was laid

waste; while those who lived in the interior were compelled to abandon their crops, their stock, their implements
of husbandry, and indeed every article of value, and seek
protection within the forts, or concentrate themselves in
the neighbouring towns, around which pickets were erected
for their better security." The war soon assumed the
most appalling character; whole families were butchered,
and wherever the war whoop was heard, the most shocking cruelties were perpetrated.

We cannot pretend to follow the narrative of this war
throughout its details; the events are too numerous for
the space to which we are confined, and are too similar
to each other to be either interesting or instructive. We
have already, in this and other articles, given sufficient
specimens of the horrors of Indian warfare. It is enough
to say, that the war in Florida was one of unmitigated
ferocity. The Seminoles were not numerous, but they
were scattered over a wilderness almost impenetrable, and
surrounded by an atmosphere fatal to the white man. In
their fastnesses they were secure from pursuit, while our
troops could scarcely move without imminent danger
from ambuscades, from climate, from the impracticable
nature of the country, and from the difficulty of transport-
ing supplies. The Seminoles kept up the war with
unceasing activity and indomitable courage, acting continually on the offensive, and with the determination of
men who were resolved to succeed or perish. Their
system of tactics was the only one which the savage can
practise with effect, and that which is most harassing to a
regular army opposed to them. Divided into small parties,
widely scattered, and constantly scouring the country—
striking by stealth, and chiefly at night—surprising small
parties, and cutting off supplies—harassing the settlements
—and giving no quarter to prisoners, they made the most

of their own small force, and wearied the strength of their opponents. Our gallant army was continually on service, performing labours and exploits which, on a more conspicuous theatre, would have won for them unfading laurels. Many noble fellows perished miserably in this wretched service, and all who were engaged in it fought and suffered with a heroism which should entitle them to the lasting gratitude of their country.

Asseola engaged ardently in the war, of which he was one of the principal instigators, and was an influential and daring leader. How far his mind directed and controlled the movements of the Seminoles is not fully known, but that he is entitled to a full share of whatever credit may be due to the leaders, there can be little doubt. He was present at most of the more important engagements, acting a conspicuous part, and was concerned in many of the outrages that were perpetrated by marauding parties. All who came in contact with this remarkable man, concede to him the possession of intellectual qualities superior to those of the people by whom he was surrounded; while the public voice, too prone to exaggeration, has gifted him with moral attributes of the highest order. We have some difficulty in reconciling the dignified and noble traits of character attributed to him with the duplicity which unquestionably ran through the whole of his short but brilliant career. His martial qualities, his daring, his talent, and his commanding influence over the minds of his people, were as conspicuous as his double-dealing towards both parties in producing hostilities, and his cruelty during their continuance.

After prosecuting the war with vigour and various fortune until the summer of 1837, the Seminoles intimated a willingness to submit, and some negotiations took place, the result of which was, that a number of the chiefs declared their determination to emigrate, and requested a cessation of hostilities until they could collect and bring in their people. This was cheerfully granted; and Micanopy, with some others, were delivered up as hostages for the faithful performance of the stipulations. The prospect of peace proved delusive. The hostages remained but a few days, when they were forcibly rescued, and the war renewed with all its former virulence. In the autumn of the same year, a similar stratagem was attempted. General Hernandez, a citizen of Florida, serving at the head of a gallant band of volunteers, having captured an active partisan called Philip, the occasion was seized by the Seminoles to open another negotiation, which resulted in the captivity of Micanopy, Asseola, and several other leaders.

General Jesup, the commanding general of the Florida army, in a letter dated Picolata, November 17, 1837, says :—

" Powell, Coacochee, the two Hickses, and several other sub-chiefs, organised the abduction of Micanopy and other hostages in June last. Coacochee, John Cavallo (the latter one of the hostages), with several others, carried the hostages off, and with them their people. I then resolved to take all who were concerned in the measure, whenever the opportunity might be found. The capture of Philip by General Hernandez opened the way to effect my object sooner than I hoped. Coacochee carried off Micanopy by force, and if he had been a white man I would have executed him the moment he came into my hands. His father Philip, however, asked permission to send him out with messages to the chiefs and warriors. He returned with one of my hostages, John Cavallo, and with most of the sub-chiefs and warriors who were concerned in the abduction. I determined at once that they should be seized and held as hostages for the conduct of the chiefs and warriors out."

The persons who thus accompanied John Cavallo to the neighbourhood of Fort Peyton, with a purpose avowedly friendly, could not be prevailed upon to enter the fort, but halting at some distance, sent a message to General Hernandez desiring him to meet them at their camp, without an escort, with the assurance that he would be perfectly safe with them without troops. Knowing the perfidious character of these people, and of John Cavallo especially, General Jesup was satisfied that some treachery was intended, probably to seize a sufficient number of his officers to exchange for Philip and the Euchee chiefs, and directed General Hernandez to go to the meeting with a strong escort. He was also furnished with the heads of a conversation to be held with them, the result of which was to be communicated to the commanding general before the termination of the interview. The suspicions entertained were justified by the event. The answers of the Indians to all the questions put to them were evasive and unsatisfactory; they stood warily on the defensive, evincing no frankness nor confidence, and obviously on the watch to gain advantages; and it became sufficiently apparent that they had sought this interview for some sinister purpose. It became the duty of General Jesup to protect his own force, and disarm that of a perfidious enemy. He accordingly gave orders to have the place of meeting surrounded by a squadron of dragoons, under Major Ashby,[23] who executed the measure with such skill and celerity, that although the Indians stood on the alert, with rifles loaded and primed, ready for action, they were all taken before a gun could be fired.

The political excitement existing in the country during the whole of the Florida war has caused many of its events

to be misrepresented, and in some instances has produced
great injustice towards the gallant officers engaged in that
arduous service. With regard to the transaction just
related, we should suppose there could be but one opinion;
yet the capture of Asseola and his associates has been
denounced as a flagrant breach of confidence, and a gross
violation of the laws of war. A very slight examination of
the facts will show the fallacy of such denunciations.

The Indians were in arms to resist an attempt on the
part of the Government to remove them from a country in
which it was alleged they were intruders; and if it was
lawful to remove them, there could be no moral wrong
in taking them wherever they could be found. The
military officer could not judge of the justice of the
removal. He was to effect the object by lawful means;
and the purpose was as well effected by taking them when
they came to parley as it would be by seizing them when
in arms, or shooting them down in battle. To insist on the
observance of all the etiquette of military law in conducting such an operation, would be as absurd as to hold a
police officer to a nice observance of the rules of politeness
in his dealings with a fugitive from justice.

It is also to be recollected that the Indians do not
acknowledge any international law, or military usage, as
existing during a state of war. They do not recognise the
sanctity of a flag of truce—they steal upon the defenceless
in the hour of sleep—waylay the unarmed—murder without respect to age or sex—and consider every stratagem
fair by which an advantage is gained. With what propriety then can the protection of the laws of war be claimed
for them? Those laws can only operate between parties
who reciprocally acknowledge their obligation; and to claim
the advantage of them for those who habitually set them
at defiance, would be unreasonable.

But allowing that the Seminoles were entitled to the full benefit of the laws of war as observed by civilised nations, there was no infraction of them on this occasion. The persons in question had violated those laws by rescuing hostages, and suffering themselves to be rescued when held as hostages. The parties to the laws of war have no common tribunal to which to appeal; if an infraction is alleged, there is but one mode of retribution : the offending party is placed out of the pale of the protection of these laws by the other party, who, from the necessity of the case, becomes judge and executioner. And after all, there was no trust violated by General Jesup. These Indians were not under the protection of a flag of truce; they were not in the fort, nor under its guns. They halted at a distance from the fort, and standing warily upon the defensive, requested that an officer be *sent to them*, and that he be sent without an escort. The only trust placed in the American commander was in apprising him of the spot at which they awaited his decision. He took them partly by stratagem and partly by force; and the use of the one was as justifiable as that of the other. The purpose was humane. By securing the most active of the agitators, the duration of the war was abridged and its horrors decreased. The act was not only justifiable, but meritorious; the national honour was not stained, nor did General Jesup tarnish the laurels he had gallantly won on nobler fields.

The prisoners were immediately transferred to Charleston, South Carolina, where they were confined upon Sullivan's Island, until arrangements were made for their removal to their new homes. While a prisoner there, Asseola was an object of much curiosity. His fame was widely extended; he was not only considered as the hero of the war, but had been extravagantly praised in the newspapers for brilliant and noble qualities which probably existed only in the imaginations of the writers. He was visited by many persons, and among others by several artists,[24] who took likenesses of him, one of the finest of which is that taken for the War Department.

Asseola had two wives, both of whom were young and pretty, and one of them was particularly attractive in her personal appearance. They lived together in perfect harmony, having one table in common, to use our own phraseology, or, to speak more in accordance with the fact, sitting around the same kettle, but occupying separate lodges. They accompanied him in his confinement, and during his illness watched and nursed him with great solicitude and tenderness. He was attacked, in the spring of 1838, with an inflammation of the throat, which hurried him rapidly to the grave. He died with the dignity of a brave warrior, and his remains were respectfully interred by those against whom he had fought with a courage and skill worthy of a nobler field and a better fate.[25]

NOTES

1. Colonel Joseph M. White was born in Franklin county, Kentucky, May 10, 1781; he received a liberal education; studied law and commenced the practice of his profession at Pensacola, Florida. He was elected delegate from Florida to the 19th Congress as a Democrat; re-elected to the 20th, 21st, 22nd, 23rd, and 24th Congresses; defeated for the 25th Congress. He died at St Louis, Mo., October 19, 1839.

2. This is an error. The only reference to "twenty years" is contained in Article 4 of the treaty: "An agent, sub-agent, and interpreter, shall be appointed, to reside within the Indian boundary aforesaid, to watch over the interests of said tribes; and the United States further stipulate, as an evidence of their humane policy towards said tribes, who have appealed to their liberality, to allow for the establishment of a school at the agency, one thousand dollars per year for twenty successive years; and one thousand dollars per year, for the

same period, for the support of a gun and blacksmith, with the expenses incidental to his shop."

3. This statement is not exaggerated. It is estimated that between 1789 and 1907, Government expenditures on account of the Indian service aggregated $472,823,935, and since the latter year the appropriations by Congress for the conduct of Indian affairs approximate $80,000,000.

4. See [Woodburn Potter], *The War in Florida*, Baltimore, 1836, p. 15 *et seq.*

5. See OPOTHLE-YOHOLO, note 11, p. 33, this volume.

6. M. M. Cohen, *Notices of Florida and the Campaign*, p. 235, Charleston, 1836.

7. [Woodburn Potter], *The War in Florida*, p. 10 *et seq.*, Baltimore, 1836

8. See SELOCTA, note 1, p. 354, this volume.

9. See FOKE LUSTE HAJO, note 2, p. 323, this volume.

10. The now famous treaty of " Payne's Landing, on the Ocklawaha River in the territory of Florida," was signed May 9, 1832. " Article 1. The Seminole Indians relinquished to the United States, all claim to the lands they at present occupy in the Territory of Florida, and agree to emigrate to the country assigned to the Creeks, west of the Mississippi River; it being understood that an additional extent of territory, proportioned to their numbers, will be added to the Creek country, and that the Seminoles will be received as a constituent part of the Creek nation, and be readmitted to all the privileges as members of the same."

11. [Woodburn Potter], *op. cit.*, p. 89 *et seq.*

12. That is, Osceola.

13. This refers to Fort King.

14. The subject is discussed at length by Woodburn Potter, *op. cit.*

15. This refers to the possession of Florida by Spain. *Cf.* HALPATTER-MICCO, note 2, p. 13, this volume.

16. See note 14, above.

17. This happened early in June, 1835.

18. That is, Osceola, who was again taken, with others of his tribe, on October 21, 1837.

19. Woodburn Potter, *op. cit.*, p. 86 : " The General refused to set him [Osceola] at liberty unless he would give him security for his future good behaviour, accordingly Asseola sent for some of the friendly chiefs

and solicited their intercession on his behalf; under the most solemn pledge that he would throw no further obstacles in the way of the agent, and in consideration of his fulfilling the promise, that he would come forward and meet those friendly chiefs in a council within five days from that time, and subscribe to the acknowledgment of the treaty, he was released. On the fifth day after he appeared with seventy-nine men, women and children and redeemed his promise."

20. The council mentioned in the preceding note convened August 19, 1835, and it is evident that Osceola's treachery was soon suspected by the chiefs of the peace party.

21. Woodburn Potter, *op. cit.*, p. 93.

22. *Ibid.*, p. 98.

23. James A. Ashby, born in New York; he was captain in the Second Dragoons, June 8, 1836; brevet captain, July 19, 1836, for gallant and good conduct in the affair at Walika, Florida; resigned December 15, 1841; died July 30, 1846.

24. No reference is made in the Rhees *Catalogue* to the portrait of Osceola, nor is there a copy in the Peabody Museum. Catlin visited Charleston, S.C., during the time Osceola and many other Seminole were prisoners of war at Fort Moultrie. A portrait of Osceola, painted by Catlin five days before the death of this celebrated chief, is reproduced as figure 298, facing p. 219 of Vol. II. of the artist's *Letters and Notes on the Manners, Customs and Conditions of the North American Indians*, London, 1841.

25. Osceola died at Fort Moultrie, South Carolina, in January, 1838. Regarding his last moments Catlin (*op. cit.*, p. 221) has left the following account, communicated to him by Dr Weedon, post surgeon: "About half an hour before he died, he seemed to be sensible that he was dying; and although he could not speak, he signified by signs that he wished me to send for the chiefs and for the officers of the post, whom I called in. He made signs to his wives (of whom he had two, and also two fine little children by his side) to go and bring his full dress, which he wore in time of war; which having been brought in, he rose up in his bed, which was on the floor, and put on his shirt, his leggings, and moccasins, girded on his war-belt, his bullet-pouch, and powderhorn, and laid his knife by the side of him on the floor. He then called for his red paint, and his looking-glass, which was held before him, when he deliberately painted one half of his face, his neck and his throat, his wrists, the backs of his hands, and the handle of his knife, red with vermilion, a custom practised when the irrevocable oath of war and destruction is taken. His knife he then placed in its sheath, under his belt, and he carefully arranged his turban on his head, and his three ostrich plumes that he was in the habit of wearing in it.

Being thus prepared in full dress, he laid down a few minutes to recover strength sufficient, when he rose up as before, and with most benignant and pleasing smiles, extended his hand to me and to all of the officers and chiefs that were around him, and shook hands with us all in dead silence, and also with his wives and his little children. He made a signal for them to lower him down upon his bed, which was done, and he then slowly drew from his war-belt his scalping-knife, which he firmly grasped in his right hand, laying it across the other, on his breast, and in a moment smiled away his last breath, without a struggle or a groan."

YAHA-HAJO
A Seminole War Chief

YAHA HAJO

(A SEMINOLE WAR CHIEF)

On the 29th of March, 1836, as the main body of the American troops in Florida was about to encamp on the banks of the Ocklewahah, two fires were discovered, newly lighted, on the opposite side of one of those lakes which abound in this country. Supposing them to be signal fires lighted by the Indians to communicate intelligence from one party to another, Colonel Butler's command was detached in search of the enemy. The troops had proceeded three or four miles, when four Indians were discovered and pursued by the advance guard. General Joseph Shelton, of South Carolina, a gallant gentleman who accompanied the army as one of a band of volunteers from that patriotic state, dashed forward and charged upon one of the Indians, who, finding he could not elude the attack, halted and faced his opponent. When but a few steps apart, both parties levelled their guns at each other; the general fired first, wounded his adversary in the neck, and, dropping the gun, drew a pistol. Advancing on the Indian, he placed the pistol at his breast, and drew the trigger, but the weapon missed fire. The Indian brought his rifle to his shoulder and shot the general in the hip; at the same moment the brave savage received a fatal wound from another hand, fell on his knees, attempted to load his rifle in that position, and died, resisting to the last gasp, with the obstinacy which always marks the death of the Indian warrior.

Near the scene of this rencounter were several lodges, forming a temporary hamlet, whose inmates had been hastily scattered by the approach of the troops. Here, among the few articles abandoned by the inhabitants in their flight, were found forty or fifty human scalps, the sad memorials of the vindictiveness of savage warfare. They were attached to small pine sticks, in the form of flags, so as to be used at the dances and feasts of the warriors, when these trophies are exultingly displayed. The locks of hair attached to some of them were long and fine, and were evidently those of women, perhaps of young and beautiful women, who had fallen under the edge of the tomahawk; some were the scalps of children and grey-haired men; and all were preserved with equal care, as if the warrior regarded with the same pride the slaughter of the helpless and the defeat of an able adversary.

The warrior who was slain in the manner just described was Yaha Hajo, or the *Mad Wolf*, a Creek chief, who visited Washington City in 1826 as one of the delegates from that nation, but afterwards emigrated to Florida, where he held the same rank. His name is not expressive of his character, which was comparatively mild and benevolent. He was especially noted as a successful hunter, and was considered one of the best in Florida. For this exercise he seemed admirably fitted by his finely-moulded form, which evinced both strength and agility, and exhibited a fine specimen of savage beauty. He was erect and slender. His chest was broad and high, his limbs round and elegantly turned, and his muscles greatly developed by constant exercise. The hands of the Indians

never being employed in labour, are usually small, bearing
that evidence of gentility which Sir Walter Scott lays
down as an indubitable sign of aristocratic birth. Those
of Yaha Hajo were remarkably small and delicately
formed; while his feet had the hollow sole and high
instep common to his race, and might have served as
models for the sculptor, except that they were too small
for just proportion. His nose was Roman, and all his
features fine and prominent.

The Mad Wolf was second principal war chief of
the Seminoles, and was one of the deputation of seven
chiefs appointed to examine the country west of the
Mississippi, assigned to the Florida Indians by the treaty
of Payne's Landing, and who reported favourably; and
also one of the sixteen who signed the treaty at Fort
Gibson, ratifying that of Payne's Landing.[2] But although
thus far committed on the subject, and favourably disposed
towards emigration, he united with the majority of the
people in their opposition to it, and became an active
leader in the war. The truth is, that the measures adopted
to bring about this result were neither conciliatory nor
efficient; the wishes and interests of the Indians, in several
particulars, were not consulted as they should have been,
nor were the means for effecting the removal forcibly
either adequate or promptly applied.

We find in Mr Cohen's book[3] a report of a phrenological
examination of the head of this chief, which we shall
copy, because it will be interesting to those who have
confidence in phrenology, not because we have any faith
in it ourselves.

"Exceedingly circumspect in all his actions, he must
have been remarkable for persevering in every undertaking
on which he had determined, how cruel soever the means.
His cunning and courage ably fitted him for the station he

PHRENOLOGICAL EXAMINATION OF THE SKULL OF YAHA HAJO.

Affective Faculties.	Very Large.	Large.	Moderate.	Small.
Propensities.	Destructiveness. Combativeness. Acquisitiveness. Secretiveness.	Adhesiveness.	Philoprogenitiveness. Amativeness. Inhabitiveness. Constructiveness.	Desire to live. Alimentiveness.
Sentiments.	Cautiousness. Firmness.	Approbativeness. Self-esteem. Imitation. Ideality. Hope.	Mirthfulness. Conscientiousness. Marvellousness. Reverence. Benevolence.	
Intellectual Faculties.				Colour. Order. Calculation.
Perceptive Faculties.	Eventuality. Locality.	Individuality.	Size. Configuration.	Tune. Time.
Reflective Faculties.			Comparison. Causality.	

is supposed to have held among his countrymen ; acquisitiveness, although very large, would not, from his relative size, have formed a prominent feature in his character. His eloquence must have been of the persuasive kind, and his images not wanting in boldness—his attachments must have been firm. The recollection of events and places is strongly marked on his skull, but the reflective organs are small. Grave in his demeanour, moderate mirthfulness, large love of approbation."

NOTES

1. It was during this visit to Washington that his portrait was painted by King; it bears No. 67 in the Rhees *Catalogue*. Yaha Hajo's name is attached to the following treaties: Payne's Landing, Florida, May 9, 1832, signed "Ya-ha Hadjo"; Fort Gibson, March 28, 1833, signed "Ya-ha-hadge"; Creek Agency, January 4, 1845, signed "Yo-ho-lo Harjo."

2. See FOKE LUSTE HAJO, note 2, p. 323 ; also OSCEOLA, note 10, p. 390, both in this volume.

3. M. M. Cohen, *Notices of Florida and the Campaigns*, p. 170, Charleston, 1836.

TOOAN TUH[1]

(OR, SPRING FROG)

THIS individual is a Cherokee of highly respectable character. He was born near the mouth of Chuckamogga Creek,[2] in the vicinity of Lookout Mountain, about the year 1754, within the limits of the State of Tennessee. The place of his birth is no longer known as a wilderness tenanted by savage men, but is now a civilised country, inhabited by another race. The villages of his people and the sepulchres of his fathers have disappeared, the forests have been levelled, and the plough has effaced the scattered vestiges of their dwellings and places of assemblage.

In early youth, and throughout his life, until old age had impaired the elasticity and vigour of his muscles, *Spring Frog* was remarkable for his activity in the chase, his skill in trapping and killing game, and his success in the athletic sports of his people. With little of the ferocity of the Indian, yet excelling in all the arts of sylvan life, brave, but not addicted to war, he was a fine specimen of the savage man. He loved to roam the forest in pursuit of game; could sit patiently for hours by the sequestered stream, devising stratagems to entrap its tenants, or wander for whole days among the haunts of the deer, with no companions but his gun and dog. His mind, trained to these pursuits, was acute, and richly stored with

observation on all subjects connected with his occupation.
He watched the seasons, noted the changes of the weather,
marked the hues of the water, and the appearances of the
vegetation. Wherever he went his keen eye rested, with
a quiet but observant glance, on all the indications of the
surrounding objects which might serve to forward the
present purpose, or furnish information for future operations. He knew the habits of animals and their signals;
the voices of birds were familiar to his ear; and he could
sit for hours in the lone wilderness an interested listener to
sounds, in which one unused to the forest could detect
nothing but the rustling of leaves, the rush of the winds,
or the creaking of boughs. His practised eye detected the
footmarks of animals upon the ground, and his quick ear
distinguished, even in the night, the difference between the
tramp of the deer and the stealthy tread of the wolf.

This is the poetry of savage life. If there be any real
enjoyment apart from civilisation, it is in this close communion with Nature. The exposure, the perils, the
extremes of hunger and satiety, which fill up the whole
life of those who depend on the precarious supplies of the
chase for subsistence, throw a forbidding gloom around this
mode of existence; but there are rich and noble enjoy-
ments combined with the toils of the hunter, in the freedom
from all restraint, and in the opportunities it affords for
contemplating the beauties and the mysteries of Nature.
Few, especially among savages, have the heart and the
intellect to appreciate such luxuries. The general tendency
of the savage life is monotonous and debasing. But there
are some gifted minds—some of Izaak Walton's " fishermen
and honest men "—to be found in every region, whether
civilised or savage, over whom such pursuits exercise an
elevating and soothing influence. To this class belonged
the subject of this notice; uniting with the keen and hardy

character of the sportsman, the humane and meditative cast of the philosopher. He was an artless and harmless, but a shrewd and thoughtful man.

Spring Frog was passionately fond of all the manly sports of his people, but was particularly remarkable for his love of ball-playing, in which he greatly excelled. This game requires the greatest muscular strength, swiftness of foot, and clearness of vision. The ball, similar in materials and construction to that used by our own schoolboys, is played with two sticks, one in each hand. These sticks are bent at the end, with strings drawn across the bow, so as to form an implement resembling a battledore. The ground on which the game is to be played is a plain, marked off by measuring a space of about three hundred feet in length, and placing two poles erect at each extremity, and one in the centre. The ball-players are divided, as nearly as possible, into two parties of equal skill, each of which has its leader, and its side of the play-ground. The ball is thrown into the air, at the centre pole, and each party exert themselves to drive it through the poles on their own side. The party first carrying the ball twelve times through their poles, win the game. To effect this, it is considered fair to employ strength, activity, and stratagem in every form, provided that the ball is always propelled by the use of the stick. The parties may strike, trip, or grapple each other, knock away each other's sticks, or take any advantage which strength or cunning may give them.

These games are intensely exciting. The number engaged is often great, comprising the principal men, the most distinguished warriors, and the most promising young men of the band; for this is the great theatre on which the ambitious and aspiring exhibit those personal qualities that are held in the highest repute by the savage

TOOAN-TUH, *or* "SPRING FROG"
A Cherokee Chief

warrior. The whole population of the village pours out to witness the inspiring spectacle, and like the spectators of a horse-race in Virginia, all take sides, and feel as if the honour of the country was staked upon the contest. The excitement is often increased by gambling to immense amounts—immense for these poor savages, who have little to lose, and who freely stake all upon the game. The women and children share in the interest, watch the progress with intense anxiety, and announce the result by loud shouts. The contest is active and even fierce. The parties exercise great command over their tempers, and usually conduct their sports with good humour and great hilarity; but the excitement is always high, and sometimes the deeper passions are awakened. The struggle then becomes fearful. A number of muscular men, innured to toil and danger, savage, irascible and revengeful, by nature and habit, are seen, with their limbs and bodies naked, and oiled to enable them the more readily to elude the grasp of an adversary—now rushing after the ball with uplifted sticks, now gathered round it, striking at it with rapid blows, darting upon each other, pulling, wrestling, and presenting a medley in which it seems hardly possible that heads or limbs must not be broken. Blows are received as if upon bodies of iron. Men are prostrated and trodden under foot. But none are killed; the wounded soon forget their bruises, and the beaten bear their discomfiture without murmur.[3]

Though Spring Frog was an ardent and successful ball-player, and the most patient of anglers, he devoted much of his time to the more profitable, though less genteel employment, of raising cattle, trading in horses, and cultivating beans, corn, and pumpkins. His agriculture was not upon an extensive scale; but it was enough to furnish the means of a comfortable subsistence and a generous hospitality; his friends were always welcome to his cheerful fireside, and the stranger, to use the figure of one of the noblest spirits of our land, "never found the string of his latch drawn in."

Gifted with a discriminating mind, he was a strong man in the council. Amiable, kind, placid in his disposition—loving peace and pursuing it, he always advocated conciliatory measures, and was useful on many occasions in softening and restraining the fiercer passions of his warlike countrymen. But although his inclinations were pacific, he lacked neither energy nor courage when the interest or honour of his nation required the exercise of those qualities. In 1818, the Osages murdered several Cherokees in cold blood. Upon the reception of the news of this injury, the Cherokees flew to arms, and instantly adopted measures to revenge the outrage.[4] Spring Frog, although he was then in his sixty-fourth year, was among the first to take up the war club in this quarrel; and uniting himself with a party of his tribe, marched in pursuit of the murderers. So rapid and secret was the movement, that the track of the offenders was found and pursued, and they, ignorant that any pursuit was on foot, were scarcely arrived at their village when the avengers of blood were at their heels. The village was surprised and burned; eighty of the Osages were killed and captured, all their provisions were destroyed, and the band, for the present, broken up. Thus Spring Frog and his party appeased, as they supposed, the *manes* of their slaughtered friends; and thus dearly did the Osages atone for an outrage committed in mere wantonness by one of their marauding parties.

He served also under General Jackson in the campaign against the Creeks, and fought gallantly in the battle of Emuckfaw[5] and in that of the "Horse-shoe."[6] His coolness in battle, and his habits of discipline and obedience, on all occasions were conspicuous.

He was among the earliest of the emigrants to the country assigned the Cherokees, west of Arkansas,[7] and we hope that he lived to be satisfied of the advantages of that movement. The change has thus far proved eminently successful. Many of the Cherokees have large farms, under a good state of cultivation, and large droves of cattle and horses. Their dwellings and other improvements are comfortable and well constructed. They have mills, schools, mechanics, and many other of the evidences and arts of civilised life. An intelligent traveller, who lately visited their country, says : "We passed many fine farms on our way, and as evening fell came to the missionary station of Dwight, with which we found ourselves much pleased. This institution has for its object the advancement, scientifically and morally, of the Cherokees. It was founded some twenty years ago, and has continued faithful to the Indians through all that long period. It was first commenced in the year 1821, in what is now called Pope County, on the waters of Illinois bayou, where suitable buildings were erected, farms opened, and schools established, in which were gathered the children of the then wild Cherokees, to the yearly number of one hundred. The Cherokees were a portion who had removed from their old country at an early period, and were denominated *Western* Cherokees, but are now distinguished as the *old settlers.*"

Those missionaries have resided there for many years undisturbed, in the peaceful discharge of their duties, and on the kindest terms with the Cherokees. They have witnessed the commencement and whole progress of this interesting colony, and have been identified with its entire history. They have done great good to the Cherokees, and are entitled to their gratitude.

NOTES

1. The correct form of the name of this Cherokee is *Dústŭ*, which signifies a species of frog which makes its appearance very early in spring; the name is intended for an onomatope. See Mooney, "Myths of the Cherokee," *Nineteenth Report of the Bureau of American Ethnology*, pt. 1, p. 517, Washington, 1900.

2. Chickamauga is the popular adaptation of *Tsĭkămă'gĭ*, a name occurring in at least two places in the old Cherokee country, which has lost its meaning, and appears to be of non-Cherokee origin. It is applied to a small creek at the head of Chattahoochee River, in White county, Georgia, and also to the district about the southern Chickamauga creek coming into Tennessee River a few miles above Chattanooga, in Hamilton county, Tennessee. In 1777 the more hostile portion of the Cherokee withdrew from the rest of the tribe and established here a large settlement, from which they removed about five years later to settle lower down the Tennessee in what were known as the Chickamauga towns, or Five Lower Towns. See Mooney, *op. cit.*, p. 537.

3. This was the favourite game over the greater part of the eastern section of North America. Consult *Handbook of American Indians*, pt. 1, p. 127, and authors therein cited, and particularly Mooney, "Cherokee Ball Play," in *American Anthropologist*, Washington, 1890.

4. The two tribes had been enemies for many years, and "the distressing war, which has raged for some time between these Cherokees and the Osages, has created insurmountable obstacles to the progress and success of the infant Establishments among them."—Morse, *A Report to the Secretary of War*, p. 216, New Haven, 1822.

5. January 22, 1814. (See SELOCTA, note 9, p. 356, this volume.)

6. March 27, 1814. (See SELOCTA, note 10, p. 356, this volume; also MENAWA, note 4, p. 192, this volume.)

7. Previous to 1820, many members of the Cherokee tribe had left their ancient villages and moved westward, across the Mississippi, into the present state of Arkansas. Finally, by treaty of New Echota, December 29, 1835, they ceded to the United States all their lands east of the Mississippi. Under the name Spring Frog, "Tooan Tuh" signed the treaty "At the Chickasaw council house," September 14, 1816, and "At the Cherokee Agency," July 8, 1817. In the Rhees *Catalogue* (No. 26) the name of the subject of the portrait is given as "Yoosto, Spring Frog," which more closely approximates the correct form.

TSHIZUNHAUKAU

(A WINNEBAGO WARRIOR)

TSHIZUNHAUKAU, or *He who runs with the deer*, is a Winnebago warrior of remarkable genius and singular character.
He unites the characters of the conjurer and medicine-man[1]
with that of the brave, without losing any of his reputation
for manliness and courage.

It is a peculiarity of savage life that but one highroad
to distinction exists. War is the only occupation which
is considered as capable of giving exercise to the highest
powers of manhood. Hunting is the business of their life,
and expertness in this employment and in the various arts
belonging to it is highly estimated ; but to be a successful
hunter confers respectability rather than distinction. The
spoils of the chase afford sustenance, and to the able or
fortunate hunter give that competency which stands in the
place of wealth ; but the standing gained by this employment, in its best aspect, is only equal to that of a successful man of business in civilised communities. Oratory
ranks a little higher, and carries with it a certain
degree of popular influence which is eagerly sought
after by the aspiring savage. Strength, swiftness, expertness in horsemanship, and other qualities which enable
their possessor to triumph in athletic sports, and give
grace and manliness to his movements, are highly prized.
But all these are but the accomplishments considered

desirable to give finish to the character of the warrior; for without military distinction all else is as the sounding brass and tinkling cymbal.

A few men among the Indians have gained high repute, and maintained a commanding influence through life, without the aid of a military reputation. One of these was Red Jacket,[2] who never attained any standing as a warrior, nor set up any pretensions to martial skill or fame; and some other instances have been recorded in this work. But these were men of consummate ability, whose talents were useful to their people, and whose genius elevated them above the operation of general rules; and, in the case of Red Jacket, there was a nationality, a zeal and tenacity, with which he adhered to the side of his own people, right or wrong, in all their controversies with the whites, and clung to the customs and prejudices of his ancestors, that endeared him to the Senecas. But these are rare examples, in which the strong law of human nature prevails over the peculiarities of national character.

It follows that those who are incapacitated by indolence, bodily debility, and mental weakness, from earning laurels on the field of battle, sink into insignificance and even contempt, unless they can strike out some other mode of securing respectability. The same causes which render them unfit for warriors operate equally against their success in either of the occupations we have alluded to. But no debility, either physical or mental, prevents a man from becoming a doctor; as in this occult science, skilful practice and skilful imposture approach as nearly as the sublime and the ridiculous. We think that the majority of the Indian prophets, conjurers, and medicine-men have their origin in this principle. Though indolent, or pusillanimous, or unfortunate in labouring under some physical deficiency, they have been compensated by a sufficient portion of that cunning which Nature bestows upon inferior creatures, to enable them to impose on the credulity of the people. A few of these persons have undoubtedly been fanatics who were self-deluded; but we suppose the greater part of them to be crafty impostors, whose highest motive is to gain a livelihood without incurring the danger and fatigue of war or hunting, and to rise above the contempt of a wholly idle and useless life.

The standing of this class may be readily imagined. A savage people, without arts or literature, who scarcely ever reason, and act almost entirely from impulse, are easily imposed upon. Superstition is one of the thriftiest plants in the wilderness of an uncultivated intellect; it flourishes under the rude culture of the most bungling impostor. The number of such persons is small, for the reasons indicated above; inactive employments are unsuited to the habits and genius of the savage; few will condescend to follow such pursuits, and still more few will undertake the mental exertion of thought and deception required for the office. The conjurers, therefore, rank high, because they are a small class, practising an occult art among a superstitious people.

The failures of this class, on the other hand, are numerous, because the capital of intellect embarked in it is small, and the indolence and improvidence of the race is such that few persevere in any occupation requiring continued attention. The medicine-men and prophets, therefore, often fall into disrepute, either from a repeated want of success in their incantations and predictions, or from the laziness and dissoluteness of life consequent upon a brief harvest of successful practice; and the same man who was revered on account of his supposed intercourse with the world of spirits, is heartily despised when discovered to be a cheat. The brother [3] of Tecumthe, whose reputation was very high, and whose influence, extending through several tribes besides his own, lasted for several years, dwindled into a very insignificant person, and in his old age there were "none so poor to do him reverence."   There are some who, from honesty of purpose or great native sagacity, become skilful in public business, or useful counsellors in sickness and domestic calamity, and retain the confidence of the people ; but we think that usually this class of persons, like the quacks and humbugs of civilised society, enjoy a short-lived celebrity ; the delusion itself survives in ever-blooming vigour ; the gullibility of mind which sustains it remains fresh and prolific as the bountiful earth, while the impostors flourish and fade, like the annual plants, in rapid succession.

We need not enlarge upon the practice of the Indian conjurer, for although the details of the modes of operation may exhibit considerable variety, none of them exhibit much ingenuity, and the leading features are few and exceedingly superficial. The Indians are not an imaginative people ; they have no poetry, no sprightliness of fancy, scarcely any perceptible creative faculty. They have no mythology, no belief nor theory in regard to another world which is general or which lasts from one generation to another. The whole subject is to them a blank. The conception or idea inseparable from the existence of spirit, and which the human mind in a sane state nourishes under every modification of life, of a hereafter, and a superhuman power, is prevalent among them ; but the conception is so vague and feeble as to be fruitless of any practical result. No system of worship obtains amongst them, no fabric of superstition has been reared. When their minds awaken for a moment from the lethargy that

TSHI-ZUN-HAU-KAU
A Winnebago Warrior

benumbs them, and soar into the regions of speculation, the flight is too feeble, and the newly acquired vision too dim, to yield materials for any connected chain of reasoning, and the only product of such efforts consists of the most puerile and shapeless vagaries. A few traditions are handed down from times past, but so mutilated as to be scarcely traced from one generation to another. The legends, dreams, and visions in current circulation are mostly of modern date, but are fabricated from the fragments and reminiscences of other times.

Their knowledge of the medicinal qualities of herbs is not extensive. The medicine-men have a few simple remedies of this character, which are efficacious in ordinary cases of disease and injury, and in the use of these the women are equally expert. In more difficult cases they resort to incantations and prayers addressed to good or evil spirits. To produce dreams they resort to fasting and bodily penance, carried often to the utmost power of endurance, and by these means a disturbed state of the mind is induced which gives rise to visions of more or less coherence. Great confidence is placed in these dreams; and this circumstance affords a sufficient temptation to cunning men to feign them, while it points out to sagacious chiefs an efficient mode through which a secret though powerful influence may be exerted over the people.

Tshizunhaukau was not a regular medicine-man, but he practised the art when it suited his convenience, and had the reputation of possessing the gift. He was a sagacious man, who knew and thought more than those around him. He noticed the seasons and changes of the atmosphere, and had a strong memory for dates and events. The portrait represents him holding in his hand a rod, which was an invention of his own, and was covered with marks and figures representing the divisions of time, and certain changes of the seasons, to which were added signs indicating the results of certain calculations he had made respecting the weather.   It was a curious and original invention, the fruit of an inquisitive and active mind, and the indication of a spirit that rose above the sluggish incuriousness of his race.   He had noticed the phenomena which took place around him with deep attention, and had recorded upon the tablet of a retentive memory all that seemed worthy of remark.   He had endeavoured, to the extent of his limited knowledge and means of information, to trace effects to their causes, and to find out the reasons of uncommon events.   The results of these inquiries were carved upon his wand, which became thus an almanac, and doubtless as complete a one, in reference to his wants, as our common almanacs are to the enlightened astronomer.   He maintained a high character as a warrior, and was one of the deputation who accompanied Nawkaw,[4] the principal chief of the Winnebagoes, to Washington, in 1828.[5]

NOTES

1. See Keesheswa, note 1, p. 156, this volume.

2. See biography of Red Jacket, Vol. I., p. 5, this work.

3. That is, Tenskwautawaw, or the Shawnee Prophet. See the biography, Vol. I., p. 75, this work.

4. See biography, Vol. I., p. 146, this work.

5. The portrait of "Tshi-zhun-kaw-kaw, he who runs with the deer —of the Day-kau-ray family," bears No. 126 in the Rhees *Catalogue*, but no reference is made to the name of the artist nor to the date of the painting. It may, however, possibly be identical with the Too-sha-na-gan-ka of Lewis, No. 13.

WAKECHAI

(A SAUK CHIEF)

WAKECHAI, or the *Crouching Eagle*,[1] was one of the village chiefs, or civil magistrates, of the Sauk nation, and resided at the principal town of that people, near the confluence of Rock River with the Mississippi, in one of the most beautiful regions of Illinois. This neighbourhood has been abandoned by its Indian inhabitants, who have recently removed to the Iowa Territory, on the opposite shore of the Mississippi; but it will always be considered as classic ground by those who shall be engaged in researches into the history of the aborigines, as well on account of the unrivalled beauty of the scenery, as from the many interesting recollections connected with the soil.

The subject of this notice was a person of low stature, with a stooping and ungraceful form, a shuffling gait, a stern savage expression of countenance, and a deportment altogether displeasing and undignified. Though named after the noble bird regarded by the Indians as the most warlike of the feathered tribes, and whose plumage is appropriated to the decoration of the warrior's brow, this chief never acquired any reputation as a brave, nor do we know that he ever performed any warlike feat worthy to be mentioned. That he has been upon the war-path is most probable, for among a people so entirely military, some service is expected of every individual.

But it is certain that the Crouching Eagle, or as we should interpret the name, *The Eagle stooping upon his prey*, gained no laurels in the fields and never rose to be a leader in any expedition. Neither did he excel in manly sports, or in the ceremonious dances so highly esteemed in savage life.

It may be very naturally inquired by what means a person destitute of the qualities which are held in the highest repute among his people, became a chief and a person of influence among them. Without the physical powers which are so greatly valued in savage life, with no reputation for valour, nor any trophy snatched from the enemy by force or cunning, it would not seem that there was any community of feeling between him and his associates through which he could conciliate their kindness or command respect.

The answer to the inquiries which we have suggested shows the vast superiority of mind over any and all endowments that are merely physical. Even in the savage state, under all the disadvantages which surround it, prevent its culture, and cramp its exercise, the intellect silently asserts its supremacy, and the warrior, while he affects to despise it, unconsciously yields to its sway. The Eagle was a man of vigorous and clear mind, whose judicious counsels were of more advantage to his tribe than any services he could have rendered in the field, even supposing his prowess to have been equal to his sagacity. If Nature denied him the swift foot and the strong arm of the warrior, it endowed him with a prompt and bold heart, and a cool judgment to direct the energies of others. He was not an orator, to win the admiration of multitudes, nor had he those popular and insinuating talents and manners which often raise individuals of little solid worth to high station and extensive influence. He was a calm and sage man. His nation had confidence in his wisdom; he was considered a prudent and safe counsellor. He gave his attention to public business, became skilled in the affairs of his people, and acquired a character for fidelity which raised him to places of trust. Perhaps the braves and war chiefs, the hot-blooded, turbulent, and ambitious aspirants for place and honour, submitted the more readily to the counsels of one who was not a rival, and cheerfully yielded him precedence in a sphere in which they were not competitors.

It is recorded of Tecumthe and of Red Jacket,[2] that each of them in his first engagement with the enemy showed discreditable symptoms of fear; the former became afterwards the most distinguished Indian leader of his time, and both of them enjoyed deservedly the most unlimited influence over their respective nations. These facts are interesting from the evidence they afford of the supremacy of the intellectual over the physical man, in savage as well as in civilised life.

The man of peace, however valuable his services, seldom occupies a brilliant page in history; and Wakechai, though a diligent and useful public man, has left but little trace of his career. The only striking incident which has been preserved in relation to him is connected with his last moments. He had been lying ill some days and was labouring under the delirium of a fever, when he dreamed, or imagined, that a supernatural revelation directed him to throw himself into the water at the spot where Rock River unites with the Mississippi, where his good *Manito*,[3] or guardian spirit, would meet him, and instantly restore him to health. The savage who knows no God, and

"Whose soul proud science never taught to stray
Far as the solar walk, or milky way,"

is easily deluded by the most absurd superstitions. Every

human spirit looks up to something greater than itself; and when the helplessness induced by disease or misfortune brings a humbling sense of self-abasement, the savage, as well as the saint and the sage, grasps at that which to each, though in a far different sense, is a religion—the belief in a superior intelligence.   The blind credulity of the Indian in this respect is a singular feature in his character, and exhibits a remarkable contrast between the religion of the savage and that of the Christian.   In his intercourse with men, whether friends or enemies, the savage is suspicious, cautious, and slow in giving his confidence; while in regard to the invisible world, he yields credence to the visions of his own imagination and the idlest fables of the ignorant or designing, not only without evidence, but against the plain experience of his own senses.   In the instance before us, a man of more than ordinary common sense, a sagacious counsellor, accustomed to the examination of facts and to reasoning upon questions of difficulty, suffered himself to be deceived into the belief that he could plunge with impunity into the water, while enfeebled by disease, and that in the bosom of that element he should meet and converse with a supernatural being, such as he had not only never seen, but of which he could have heard no distinct, rational, or credible account.   We cannot avoid the persuasion that such a fact, while it evinces the imbecility of the human intellect in reference to the contemplation of the hidden things of another life, does also strongly indicate an innate belief working in the natural mind, and a want which nothing but revelation can rightly direct or fully satisfy.

Wakechai believed and obeyed the vision, nor did any venture to interpose an objection to the performance of that which seemed a religious duty.   He arose, and with much difficulty proceeded to the margin of the river. He paused for a moment at that romantic spot, which presents one of the loveliest landscapes ever offered to the human eye. Perhaps he paused to contemplate the great river, which, rising in far-distant lakes on the one hand, and rolling away to the ocean on the other, and washing far distant and to him unknown lands in its course, may have figured to him his own existence, the beginning and the end of which were equally beyond his comprehension. The fatal plunge was made with undaunted courage, and doubtless with unaltered faith, and the deluded man awoke to the consciousness that he was deceived. The clear stream received and enclosed him in its cold embrace, but no mysterious form met his eye, nor did any friendly voice impart the desired secret. The limbs that should have been renovated scarcely retained sufficient strength to enable the deluded sufferer to rise again into his native element; he regained the shore with difficulty, where he sunk exhausted, and being carried back to his lodge, died in the evening of the same day.

Wakechai was a popular and respected chief, and was a great favourite of the whites, who found him uniformly friendly, honest, and disposed to maintain peace between his own nation and the American people. He was a person of steady mind, and may be regarded as one of the few statesmen of this little republic who watched and reflected over its interests and directed its affairs, while others fought its battles. His death was greatly regretted by his own people, and by the American residents of Rock Island.

He was one of the delegation who accompanied General Clark to Washington in 1824, when his portrait was taken.[4]

NOTES

1. The name, according to the late Dr William Jones, is derived from *Wâ-kushe-shiᵃ*, "Little Fox," of the Fox clan.

2. See biography of RED JACKET, Vol. I., p. 5, this work.

3. See the article "Manito" in *Handbook of American Indians*, pt. 1, p. 800, and the authors thereunder cited.

4. The portrait of "Wai-kee-chai, Crouching Eagle," bears No. 65 in the Rhees list, and although the name of the artist and the date of the painting are lacking from the *Catalogue*, the latter is supplied by McKenney's text. It is also known that the portrait was the work of King, as it is listed among the collection of paintings bequeathed by him to the Redwood Library, Newport, Rhode Island. (See Introduction, p. xlv., this work.)

In 1824, a large deputation from the Sauk and Foxes visited Washington for the purpose of concluding a treaty with the Government. The treaty was signed August 4, 1824, and "Wash-kee-chai, or Crouching Eagle," appears as the third signer, being followed by Kee-o-kuck.

WAKECHAI, *or* "CROUCHING EAGLE"
A Sauk Chief

KANAPIMA

(AN OTTAWA CHIEF)

THIS is an admirable likeness, by Otis, of the ruling chief of the Ottawas, a tribe which was formerly numerous and powerful, but is now dwindled to a comparatively small number. They once occupied as hunting grounds the finest lands of Ohio,[1] and are mentioned by the early writers as among the most warlike of the nations with whom the Europeans held intercourse, in the first settlement of the country. With the common fate of their race, they were driven from their former haunts to the sterile and inclement shores of Lake Superior, where a portion of them now derive a precarious subsistence by fishing and hunting, while the remainder have emigrated to the far West.

One of the most celebrated of all the northern Indians was Pontiac,[2] the head chief of this tribe, whose daring exploits and able opposition against the early British settlements on the lakes are too well known to require repetition in this place. He lived on the south bank of the river St Clair, above Detroit. His son Tisson, with a part of the tribe, lived on the lands at the junction of the Maumee with Lake Erie,[3] since, and perhaps before, the revolutionary war. Tisson led his people in an expedition against the post of Vincennes, about the time of the first settlement of Kentucky. The Indians were defeated;

and the chief, with a number of his warriors, were taken prisoners, and sentenced or threatened to be shot, according to the usages of retaliation too often practised at that period.   Tisson was rescued by a stratagem put in operation by a Frenchman named Navarre, and after being concealed by the latter for some time, was enabled to make his escape.   For this service, the Ottawas granted to the Navarre family eight hundred acres of choice land at the mouth of the Maumee River, on which they now live.   We are indebted for these and some other particulars to the politeness of a friend, who received them from Pierre Navarre, grandson of the man who rescued Tisson.

Waskonoket, *A cloud far off*, the only surviving son of Tisson, was dwelling on the reserve land of his tribe, on Maumee Bay, at the mouth of the river of that name, a few years ago.   His mother was a French half-breed, and he exhibited in his countenance and complexion strong indications of the European blood which ran in his veins. He was five feet nine inches in height, erect, and well made for action or fatigue, with a round body and full chest.   His forehead was large and inclining backward, his nose straight, but rather broad, his eyes a dark grey, and his lips prominent.   He was affable, courteous, and hospitable in his intercourse with the whites, but dignified, firm, and somewhat reserved in his manners towards his own people, by whom he was much beloved, and over whom he maintained a strict rule.   When the Government purchased the lands of this band of the Ottawas,[4] with a view to their removal to the West, he received twenty-five hundred dollars for his proportion, after which he became profuse in his expenditure.   He had two wives, who lived together in perfect harmony.   Our intelligent correspondent adds: "He, and this branch of the tribe, have moved over the Mississippi, to the lands appropriated for them by the Government. When about leaving his inheritance, he appeared sometimes thoughtful, but neither expressed hope, nor joy, nor regret. Near the time of his departure, I observed him standing in the principal street of the town we had laid out on a part of their council-ground and burial-place, with his arms folded on his breast, looking on the land, the river, and the bay with that deep composure of features which the Indian so commonly preserves, but which is so difficult to describe, for the closest observer could not discover in his countenance the indication of a single passion that moved in his breast."

The larger portion of the Ottawas dwell in the province of Upper Canada. At the commencement of the war between the United States and Great Britain, the Canadian Ottawas joined the British, and were received into service, and they required the bands residing within the American boundaries to repair to the same standard. The latter gave an evasive answer; and shortly after sent a message to General Hull,[5] offering to fight under his command if he would engage to protect them from the Canadian tribes. The general, in pursuance of the humane policy adopted by the American Government, informed them that he did not require their assistance, and advised them to remain peaceably at home, without embroiling themselves in a war in which they had no interest. But neutrality is by no means a condition suited to the Indian taste; and the Canadian tribes, on the defeat of General Hull, compelled their American friends to join them. They were, however, not very active; they had no chief of any energy to lead them, and little relish for the British service. Tisson died by poison, administered by some of his tribe, in the gratification of revenge or jealousy, and was buried on the east bank of the Maumee, in sight of the present town of Manhattan, in Ohio.

The subject of this sketch, Kanapima, or *One who is talked of*, is the chief of another branch of the Ottawas, who are settled at L'Arbre Croche,[6] in Michigan, about forty miles south of Michilimackinac. He is otherwise called Augustin Hamelin, jr. He was born at the place of his present residence, on the 12th of July, 1813. In 1829 he was sent to Cincinnati, in company with a younger brother, named Maccoda Binnasee, *The Blackbird*, to be educated at the Catholic Seminary at that place. They remained here three years, not making any remarkable progress that we can learn, but still receiving instruction with a degree of profit which encouraged the benevolent persons who had undertaken their education to persevere in their generous design. Kanapima was said to be the more sprightly of the two, but his brother was probably the better scholar. They both exhibited much restlessness under the confinement of the school, and a decided fondness for the athletic exercises. They loved the open air; when the sun shone they could scarcely be restrained from wandering off to the romantic hills which surround this beautiful city; and when it rained, however hard, they delighted to throw off their upper garments and expose themselves to the falling showers.

It has been a favourite project with the Roman Catholic missionaries to rear up a native priesthood among the American Indians, and they have taken great pains to induce some of their converts to be educated for the holy office. It seems strange that so rational a project, and one which would appear to promise the most beneficent results, should have entirely failed, especially when undertaken by a Church of such ample means and persevering spirit—yet it is a fact, that not a single individual

KA - NA - PI - MA
An Ottawa Chief

of this race in North America, among the many who have
been educated, and the still larger number who have been
converted to Christianity, has ever become a minister of
the gospel.

Kanapima and his brother were of the number upon
whom this experiment was tried, and they were accordingly sent to Rome in 1832, to prosecute their studies in
the Propaganda Fide. After remaining there about two
years, Maccoda Binnasee died, and Kanapima immediately
afterwards returned to this country, became the chief of
his tribe, and resumed the costume and habits of his people.
His manners have much of the ease and polish of civil life;
but his feelings, his affections, and his opinions have
resumed their native channels. In the latter part of 1835,
he conducted a party of his tribe to Washington City, and
was one of those who were specially appointed by the
Ottawas to make a treaty.[7]

The affecting circumstance of the death of the young
Ottawa student at Rome has been commemorated in the
following beautiful lines by the Rev. Edward Purcell, of
Cincinnati :—

ON THE DEATH OF MACCODA BINNASEE, AT ROME.

THE morning breaks, see how the glorious sun,
Slow wheeling from the sea, new lustre sheds
O'er the soft climes of Italy. The flower
That kept its perfume through the dewy night,
Now breathes it forth again. Hill, vale, and grove,
Clad in rich verdure, bloom, and from the rock
The joyful waters leap. Oh! meet it is,
That thou, Imperial Rome, should lift thy head,
Decked with the triple crown, when cloudless skies
And lands, rejoicing in the summer sun,
Rich blessings yield.

But there is grief to-day :
A voice is heard within thy marble walls,
A voice lamenting for the youthful dead ;
For o'er the relics of her forest boy
The " Mother of dead Empires " weeps.   And lo !
Clad in white robes, the long procession moves ;
Youths throng around the bier, and high in front,
Star of our hopes ! the glorious cross is reared,
Triumphant sign !   The low sweet voice of prayer,
Flowing spontaneous from the spirit's depths,
Pours its rich tones, and now the requiem swells,
Now dies upon the ear.

But there is one
Who stands beside the grave, and though no tear
Dims his dark eye, yet does his spirit weep.
With beating heart he gazes on the spot
Where his young comrade shall forever rest ;
For they together left their forest home,
Led on by him, who to their fathers preached
Glad tidings of great joy, the holy man,
Who sleeps beneath the soil his labours blessed.
How must the spirit mourn, the bosom heave,
Of that lone Indian boy !   No tongue can speak
The accents of his tribe, and as he bends,
In melancholy mood, above the dead,
Imagination clothes his tearful thoughts
In rude but plaintive cadences :

" Soft be my brother's sleep !
At Nature's call the cypress here shall wave,
The wailing winds lament—above the grave
    The dewy night shall weep.

" And he thou leavest forlorn,
Oh ! he shall come to shade thy bed with moss,
To plant, what thou didst love, the mystic cross,
    To hope, to pray, to mourn.

" No marble here shall rise ;
But o'er thy grave I'll teach the forest tree
To lift its glorious head, and point to thee,
    Rejoicing in the skies :

" And when it feels the breeze,
I'll think thy spirit wakes the gentle sound ;
Such was our father's thought, when all around
  Shook the old forest leaves.

" Dost thou forget the hour
When first we heard the Christian's hope revealed,
When fearless warriors felt their bosoms yield
  Beneath Almighty power ?

" Then truths came o'er us fast,
Whilst on the mound the Missionary stood,
And through the list'ning silence of the wood
  His words, like spirits, passed.

" And oh ! hadst thou been spared,
We too had gone to bless the fatherland,
To spread rich stores around, and, hand in hand,
  Each holy labour shared.

" But here thy relics lie,
Where Nature's flowers shall bloom o'er Nature's child,
Where ruins stretch, and classic art has piled
  Her monuments on high.

" Sleep on, sleep peaceful here ;
The traveller from thy native land will claim this spot,
And give to thee, what kingly tombs have not,
  The tribute of a tear ! "

NOTES

1. Only a fragment of the tribe ever lived within the limits of the present State of Ohio (see note 3 below). The Ottawa (name derived from *ădāwe*, " to trade," an Algonquian term) were first met by Champlain in 1615, near the mouth of French River, on Georgian Bay. He described them as being armed only with bows, arrows, and clubs ; their bodies were tattooed and their faces painted ; their noses were pierced and their ears decorated with trinkets. The Ottawa were frequently mentioned in the Jesuit Relations, as well as by the early historians of Canada. Consult *Handbook of American Indians*, part 2, pp. 167-172, and the works therein cited.

2. Pontiac, the greatest of the Ottawa chiefs, was born about 1720, probably near the Maumee River, within the present State of Ohio, and died in 1769, being murdered by a Kaskaskia Indian near Cahokia, Illinois. He is supposed to have been present at Braddock's defeat, leading his Ottawa and Chippewa warriors. Later, in 1763, he attempted the capture of Detroit, but without success. Consult Francis Parkman, *Conspiracy of Pontiac*, Boston, 1851; *Handbook of American Indians*, part 2, p. 280, and works cited therein.

3. Certain bands, known as the Ottawa of Roche de Bœuf on the Maumee River, and the Ottawa of Blanchard's Fork of Great Auglaize River, both within the limits of the present State of Ohio, removed west of the Mississippi about 1832 and their descendants are now living in Oklahoma.

4. The treaty was concluded at Maumee, in the State of Ohio, February 18, 1833. The first signer of the treaty, after the commissioner, was Wau-see-on-o-quet, evidently identical with Waskonoket.

5. William Hull, 1753-1825. Served in the Revolution, and was in many engagements during the war, receiving a vote of thanks by Congress for his services in the expedition against Morrisiana. After the war he was appointed a major-general in the Massachusetts militia, and in 1805 was named Governor of the Territory of Michigan by President Jefferson. In 1812 he was appointed to the command of the North-Western army, and in August of that year surrendered with an army of 2000 men to General Brock, the British commander at Detroit. For this he was tried by court-martial, found guilty, and condemned to be shot, but the sentence was remitted by President Madison.

6. L'Arbre Croche, or Waganakisi, was near the lower end of Lake Michigan. The Ottawa reached the point sometime earlier in the 18th century, and thence appear to have spread in all directions. Many settled along the eastern shore of Lake Michigan, others passed around the southern end of the lake and reached the northern part of the present State of Illinois and south-eastern Wisconsin; still others reached the northern part of the present State of Ohio (see note 1, above).

7. This refers to the important treaty of Washington, signed March 28, 1836, by virtue of which the Ottawa ceded a vast territory to the United States. The subject of this sketch was a signer of this treaty, his name appearing as Augustin Hamelin, jr., as mentioned in a previous paragraph of the text.

RED BIRD

(A WINNEBAGO WARRIOR)

WE present to the patrons of this work a spirited likeness of the celebrated chief, *Red Bird*, with another, at his side, of his accomplice, We-Kau, in a work of murder, at Prairie du Chien, in which a party of Indians, in 1827, headed by Red Bird, killed and scalped two men, taking at the same time a scalp from a child.

This bloody tragedy came suddenly and most unexpectedly upon the inhabitants of that village, and created a deep excitement all along the frontier. Tidings of it were brought to Governor Cass and Colonel McKenney, who were, as United States Commissioners, then about negotiating a treaty at *Le Butte de Morts*, on Fox River, with several of the surrounding tribes of Indians, when an expedition was set on foot—Governor Cass moving at once to the seat of the outbreak, and thence, after putting the place in the best possible state of defence, to St Louis, to confer with General Atkinson,[1] then in command at Jefferson Barracks,[2] where arrangements were promptly made for ascending the Mississippi, with troops in command of General Atkinson, in person; whilst Major Whistler, then stationed at Green Bay, with a part of his command, including about a hundred Menominie Indians, ascended the Fox River to the portage, where, by an order from General Atkinson, he encamped, awaiting the general's arrival.

News of these movements reached the Red Bird and his party, who were then at the Four Lakes, when, to save their people from the calamity of war, it was agreed the Red Bird and We-Kau should voluntarily surrender.

Colonel McKenney, who accompanied Major Whistler's command, addressed a letter from the portage to the Secretary of War, which gives a graphic account of this memorable event, describing so minutely the Red Bird's person, and the imposing ceremonies attending the surrender, that we transfer it, as giving a better account of the Red Bird, and also of We-Kau, than any other sketch which at this day it would be in our power to procure.

We copy the following from Colonel McKenney's *Memoirs, Personal and Official*[3] :—

"The military had been previously drawn out in line. The Menominie and Wabanackie Indians were in groups upon their haunches, on our left flank. On the right was the band of music, a little in advance of the line. In front of the centre, at about ten paces distant, were the murderers. On their right and left were those who had accompanied them, forming a semicircle, the magnificent Red Bird and the miserable-looking We-Kau a little in advance of the centre. All eyes were fixed upon the Red Bird; and well they might be—for of all the Indians I ever saw, he is, without exception, the most perfect in form, in face, and gesture. In height, he is about six feet; straight, but without restraint. His proportions are those of the most exact symmetry, and these embrace the entire man, from his head to his feet. His very fingers are models of beauty. I have never beheld a face that was so full of all the ennobling and at the same time the most winning expression. It were impossible to combine with such a face the thought that he who wore it could be a murderer! It appears to be a compound of grace and dignity; of firmness and decision, all tempered with mildness and mercy. During my attempted analysis of this face, I could not but ask myself, Can this man be a murderer? Is he the same who shot, scalped, and cut the throat of Gagnier? His head, too—sure no head was ever so well formed. There was no ornamenting of the hair, after the Indian fashion; no clubbing it up in blocks and rollers of lead, or bands of silver; no loose or straggling parts—but it was cut after the best fashion of the most civilised.

"His face was painted, one side red, the other intermixed with green and white. Around his neck he wore a collar of blue wampum, beautifully mixed with white, which was sewn on to a piece of cloth, the width of the wampum being about two inches—whilst the claws of the panther, or wild-cat, distant from each other about a quarter of an inch, with their points inward, formed the rim of the collar. Around his neck were hanging strands of wampum of various lengths, the circles enlarging as they descended. He was clothed in a *yankton dress*—new and beautiful. The material is of dressed elk, or deer-skin, almost a pure white. It consists of a jacket, the sleeves being cut to fit his finely formed arm, and so as to leave outside of the seam that ran from the shoulder, back of the arm, and along over the elbow, about six inches of the material, one-half of which was cut into fringe; the same kind of fringe ornamenting the collar of the jacket, its sides, bosom, and termination, which was not circular, but cut in point; and which also ran down the seams of his leggings, these being made of the same material. Blue beads were employed to vary and enrich the fringe of the leggings. On his feet he wore moccasins.

"A piece of scarlet cloth of about a quarter of a yard

deep, and double that width, a slit being cut in its middle, so as to admit the passing through of his head, rested, one-half on his breast (and beneath the necklace of wampum and cloths), and the other on his back. On one shoulder, and near his breast, was a beautifully orna-mented feather, nearly white ; and about opposite, on the other shoulder, was another feather, nearly black, near which were two pieces of thinly shaven wood in the form of compasses, a little open, each about six inches long, richly wrapped round with porcupine's quills, dyed yellow, red, and blue. On the tip of one shoulder was a tuft of horse-hair, dyed red, and a little curled, mixed up with ornaments. Across his breast, in a diagonal position, and bound tight to it, was his war-pipe, at least three feet long, brightly ornamented with dyed horse-hair, the feathers and bills of birds. In one of his hands he held the white flag, and in the other the calumet or pipe of peace.

"There he stood. Not a muscle moved, nor was the expression of his face changed a particle. He appeared to be conscious that, according to Indian law, and measur-ing the deed he had committed by the injustice, and wrongs, and cruelties of the white man, he had done no wrong. The light which had shone in upon his bosom from the law which demanded an eye for an eye and a tooth for a tooth, so harmonised with his conscience as to secure its repose. As to death, he had been taught to despise it, confiding in that heaven, that spirit land, where the game is always plenty—the forests always green—the waters always transparent, tranquil, and pure —and where no evil thing is permitted to enter. He was there, prepared to receive the blow that should consign his body to the ground, and send his spirit to that blissful region, to mingle with his fathers who had gone before him.

"He and We-Kau were told to sit down. His motions, as he seated himself, were no less graceful and captivating than when he stood or walked. At this moment the band struck up Pleyel's Hymn. Everything was still. It was indeed a moment of intense interest to all. The Red Bird turned his eyes towards the band; the tones operated upon his feelings in such a way as to produce in his countenance a corresponding pensiveness. The music having ceased, he took up his pouch (which I forgot to say was a handsomely ornamented otter-skin, that hung on his left side), and taking from it some *kinnakinic*[4] and tobacco, cut the latter in the palm of his hand, after the Indian fashion, then rubbing the two together, filled the bowl of his calumet, struck fire into a bit of spunk with his flint and steel, and lighted it, and smoked. All the motions employed in this ceremony were no less harmonious and appropriate than had characterised his other movements. He sat after the Turkish fashion, with his legs crossed.

"If you think there was anything of affectation in all this, you are mistaken. There was just the manner and appearance and look you would expect to see in a nobly built man of the highest order of intelligence, and who had been taught all the graces of motion, and then escorted by his armies to the throne where the diadem was to be placed upon his head.

"There is but one opinion of the man, and that I have attempted to convey to you. I could not refrain from speculating on his dress. His white jacket, having upon it but a single piece of red, appeared to indicate the purity of his past life, which had been stained by only a single crime; for all agree that the Red Bird had never before soiled his fingers with the blood of the white man, or committed a bad action. His war-pipe, bound close to his heart, seemed to indicate his love of war, in common with his race, which was no longer to be gratified. The red cloth, however, may have been indicative of his name.

"All sat, except the speakers. The substance of what they said was—We were required to bring in the murderers. They had no power over any, except two— the third had gone away—and these had voluntarily agreed to come in, and give themselves up. As their friends, they had come with them. They hoped their white brothers would agree to accept the horses—of which there were, perhaps, twenty—the meaning of which was, to take them in commutation for the lives of their two friends. They asked kind treatment for their friends, and earnestly besought that they might not be put in irons— and concluded by asking for a little tobacco, and something to eat.

"They were answered, and told, in substance, that they had done well thus to come in. By having done so, they had turned away our guns, and saved their people. They were admonished against placing themselves in a like situation in the future, and advised, when they were aggrieved, not to resort to violence, but to go to their agent, who would inform their Great Father of their complaints, and he would redress their grievances; that their friends should be treated kindly, and tried by the same laws by which their Great Father's white children were tried; that for the present, Red Bird and We-Kau should not be put in irons; that they should all have something to eat, and tobacco to smoke. We advised them to warn their people against killing ours; and endeavoured also to impress them with a proper notion of their own weakness, and the extent of our power, etc.

"Having heard this, the Red Bird stood up—the commanding officer, Major Whistler, a few paces in front

of the centre of the line, facing him. After a moment's
pause, and a quick survey of the troops, and with a
composed observation of his people, he spoke, looking at
Major Whistler, saying, '*I am ready.*' Then advancing
a step or two, he paused, saying, 'I do not wish to be put
in irons. Let me be free. I have given away my life—it
is gone—(stooping and taking some dust between his
finger and thumb, and blowing it away)—like that'—
eyeing the dust as it fell, and vanished from his sight,
then adding—'I would not take it back. It is gone.'
Having thus spoken, he threw his hands behind him, to
indicate that he was leaving all things behind him, and
marched briskly up to Major Whistler, breast to breast.
A platoon was wheeled backwards from the centre of the
line, when Major Whistler stepping aside, the Red Bird
and We-Kau marched through the line, in charge of a
file of men, to a tent that had been provided for them in
the rear, where a guard was set over them. The comrades
of the two captives then left the ground by the way they
had come, taking with them our advice, and a supply of
meat and flour, and tobacco.

"We-Kau, the miserable-looking being, the accomplice
of the Red Bird, was in all things the opposite of that
unfortunate brave. Never before were there two human
beings so exactly, in all things, so unlike one another.
The one seemed a prince, and as if born to command, and
worthy to be obeyed; the other as if he had been born to
be hanged. Meagre—cold—dirty in his person and dress,
crooked in form—like the starved wolf, gaunt, hungry,
and blood-thirsty—his entire appearance indicating the
presence of a spirit wary, cruel, and treacherous. The
heart, at sight of this, was almost steeled against
sympathy, and barred against the admission of pity.
This is the man who could scalp a child, not eleven

months old, and in taking off its fine locks as a trophy, and to exhibit as a scalp, cut the back of its neck to the bone, and leaving it to languish and die on the floor, near the body of its murdered father? But his hands, and crooked and miserable-looking fingers, had been accustomed to such bloody work.

"The Red Bird did not appear to be over thirty years old, and yet he is said to be past forty. We-Kau looks to be forty-five, and is no doubt as old as that. I shall see on my arrival at Prairie du Chien, the scene of these butcheries; and, as I may write you upon all matters connected with my tour, I will introduce you to that. The child, I forgot to say, by the latest accounts, yet lives, and promises to survive. The widow of Gagnier is also there, and I shall get the whole story from her mouth, and shall then, doubtless, get it truly. You shall have it all, and a thousand things besides, that, when I left home, I never expected to realise; but having once entered upon the scenes I have passed, no matter with how much of personal risk they were to be encountered, there was no going back. I see no danger, I confess, especially now— but, anyhow, my way is onward, and I shall go."

The foregoing narrative might suffice, and answer all the purposes for which this sketch of the Red Bird is intended, but we prefer following Colonel McKenney a little further, at least to the scene of the murders at Prairie du Chien, where, as he supposed he should, he found the widow of Gagnier, of whom he received all the circumstances connected with the killing of her husband.

The object of the military movement having been accomplished, in the surrender of the murderers, Colonel McKenney parted from Major Whistler and his command, and crossing the portage which separates the Fox from the Ouisconsin[5] River, pursued his voyage in his bark canoe down the latter, when, arriving at *Le Petit Roche*, he fell in with General Atkinson's command, on its way up to unite with that of Major Whistler's, when, if the Indians had not come in, a junction would have been formed the next day and an attack made upon them, near the Four Lakes, whither they were congregated.

A fleet in the interior and upon these far-distant waters being a new feature, and this being, doubtless, the first that had ever been seen, on the Ouisconsin, we have no fear of fatiguing the reader by introducing here Colonel McKenney's description of its appearance.

"At *Le Petit Roche*, forty-five miles from the portage, at eight o'clock in the evening, fell in with General Atkinson and his command. His barges were ranged alongside the bank of the river, and moored there. These long keel-boats, some as much as thirty tons burden, with the sails of several of them hanging quietly in the calm of the evening against the masts; the numerous fires that lined the shores, around which a large portion of the general's command of seven hundred men were gathered, gave to the place the appearance of a seaport. The general hum of voices, the stroke of the axe, with the confused noises, made of it, in so out-of-the-way a place, where never before had such circumstances combined, a sort of spirit-scene; especially as the moon's light invested the whole, being made pale by the many lights, and yet paler with an occasional half-obscuration caused by the rolling up of denser portions of the smoke from these numerous fires. Everything in Nature by which we were surrounded was still, save only the sounds that proceeded from this spot, and the plash of the paddles of our canoes. Presently a sentinel challenged, and demanded the countersign. I told him who I was, and that I was bearer of tidings from Major Whistler's command (which

I had left that morning at the portage), to General Atkinson. The sergeant of the guard was called, who making this message known to General Atkinson, we were invited to come alongside his barge, and (he being confined to his berth by a slight attack of fever) down into the cabin to see him.

"We were received with the courtesy that always distinguished this gallant officer, when I went rapidly over the events that had transpired, and informed him of the surrender of the murderers; commended the Red Bird to all the kind usage which his unfortunate condition would permit, and especially urged that he might not be put in irons. I did this, because I very well knew that he would suffer a thousand deaths rather than attempt to regain his liberty. There was no mistake in this matter. The man had literally already parted from life, and had his eyes fixed more upon the spirit land than upon coming in contact again with the bitter realities of the world around him. All this passed, and pledging each other in a glass of wine, and our best wishes for the general's health, we continued our voyage till ten at night, when we landed on a sand-bar for repose.

"Arriving at the Prairie," our author continues, "I rode to the scene of the recent murders, attended by my companions, including Ben, who manifested great anxiety to see the place where the Indians had actually carried out, upon others, those plans of destruction which he had so often anticipated would be made personal to himself. The scene of these butcheries is distant from the village, in an easterly direction, about three miles. I received the whole story from the widow of one of the murdered men, Gagnier by name, who was at the time proprietor of the log-house in which he was killed. Gagnier was a half-breed, his mother having been Indian and his father

French. The door of this one-storey log tenement fronts east, and a window opposite, of course, west. A large tree grows near its south-western corner. Gagnier was sitting on a chest, on the left of the door. At the window, his wife was washing clothes. On her left was the bed, in which a child, eleven months old, was sleeping. On her right, and a little back of her, sat a discharged soldier, named Liepcap; and this was the situation of the family when Wan-nig-sootsh-kau—the Red Bird—We-Kau, or the Sun, and a third Indian, entered. Visits of Indians being common, no particular attention was paid to them. They were, however, received with the usual civility, and asked if they would have something to eat. They said yes, and would like some fish and milk.

"Gagnier had, meantime, seen something peculiar in the looks and movements of these Indians, as is supposed, which led him to reach up and take from brackets just over his head his rifle, which, as Mrs Gagnier turned to get the fish and milk, she saw lying across Gagnier's lap. At the moment she heard the *click* caused by the cocking of the Red Bird's rifle, which was instantly followed by its discharge. She looked, and saw her husband was shot. At the same moment, the third Indian shot old Liepcap, when Mrs Gagnier seeing We-Kau, who had lingered about the door, about to rush in, she met him, made fight, and wrested from him his rifle. He ran out, she pursuing him, employing all her energies to cock the rifle and shoot him, but by some mysterious cause, was rendered powerless—'feeling,' as she expressed it, 'like one in a dream, trying to call, or to run, but without the ability to do either.' To save himself, We-Kau kept running round the big tree at the corner of the house, well knowing if he should put off in a line, she would have better aim, and be more likely to kill him. After a few turns round the tree, and finding she had no power over the rifle, she turned short about, and made for the village, bearing the rifle with her to give the alarm ; which, being given, she returned, followed by a posse of armed men, and found her infant, which she had left, covered up in the bed on the floor, scalped, and its neck cut just below the occiput, to the bone.   This was the work of We-Kau, who, being intent on having a scalp—the other two having secured theirs—there being no other subject, took one from the head of the child.   The knife, from the examination made of the head, was applied in front of the crown, and brought round by the right ear, and far down behind, and up again on the other side, the object seeming to be, to get as much hair as he could.   In the turn of the knife, at the back of the head, the deep cut was given which found its way to the bone.

"The child, when I saw it, was comfortable, and I believe it recovered—but the sight of a rifle, even at that tender age when one might suppose it could not distinguish between a rifle and anything else, would terrify it almost into fits.   Young as it was, it must from its place in the bed have seen a rifle in connection with what it was made itself, so immediately after, to suffer.   I made the mother presents for herself and child.

"Notwithstanding we bore to the Prairie the tidings of the surrender, there still remained in the minds of the inhabitants some lingering apprehensions that more of the same kind of bloody work might await them.   They thought the war-cloud had not yet spent itself.   But nothing surprised them so much as that the hitherto peace-loving 'Red Bird' should have been guilty of such conduct.   He was not only well known, but was also the pride of the Prairie.   Such was the confidence reposed in him that he was always sought after as a protector, and

RED BIRD
A Winnebago Warrior

his presence was looked upon as a pledge of security against any outbreak that might be attempted. Indeed, when husbands, and brothers, and sons had occasion to leave their homes, the families considered themselves quite secure if the Red Bird could be procured to see to their safety. What had happened to induce him to act the part he had acted, was a mystery to all. As to We-Kau, he was known and abhorred as one of the most bloody-minded of his race. Of the third, whose name I could not learn, they knew but little.

"All this mystery, however, was at last solved. There had been great indignities offered to the band near the St Peter's,[6] to which Red Bird had become allied, and personal violence committed upon some of their lead-ing men, and by those whose station ought to have taught them better, and whose authority and power should have been differently exercised. The leading chiefs counselled upon those acts of violence, and resolved on enforcing the Indian's law—*retaliation*. Red Bird was called upon to go out and take 'meat,' as they phrase it. Not wishing to appear a coward, he undertook the enterprise, secretly rejoicing that the business had been referred to him; for he resolved to make a circuit, and return, saying he could find no meat. He did so, and was upbraided, and taunted, and called '*coward*,' and told he knew very well, if he had the spirit to avenge the wrongs of his people, he could, by going to the Prairie, get as much meat as he could bring home. This fired him, and he resolved to redeem his character as a *brave!* when, beckoning to We-Kau and another Indian, he told them to follow him. They proceeded to the Prairie. Gagnier's was not the first house they entered, with the view of carrying out their purpose. If I mistake not, their first visit was to the house of Mr Lockwood, who was then absent. His interesting wife was at home, and her life was undoubtedly saved by the presence of an old Frenchman on a visit to her, who not only understood the Winnebago language, but knew the parties; and he, also, was known to them. They had respect for him—he had been their friend. So, after lingering about the house for a season, they quit the premises, and crossed the Prairie to Gagnier's, and there executed their bloody purpose, as I have narrated.

"Addressing a few lines to General Atkinson, still urging a lenient treatment for the Red Bird, I prepared for the descent of the Mississippi."

General Atkinson having taken charge of the prisoners, put them, as was doubtless his duty, in irons, and proceeding with them to Prairie du Chien, handed them over to the civil authority, where they were placed in close confinement, and in chains. The proud spirit of Red Bird could not brook this. His thoughts, doubtless, were busy with the past. He was conscious of being a man of peace; of having at no time, and under no previous circumstances, given way to any unbridled passions. He reflected, doubtless, also, upon the provocation that had forced his people to strike; and upon the incentive that had overcome all his better purposes, and forced him to give the blow. And then the heroism of his self-surrender and the humanity that led to it—for it was to save his people from having a track made through their country, not with axes, but guns—as well as to atone for his deed of blood, that determined him, voluntarily, to give himself up. In that noble act he thought also, no doubt, of his assurance that, as he had blown the dust from his fingers, so had he parted from his life. And yet to find himself suspected—and to have that prison, and those irons telling him, whenever he saw the one, or heard the clanking of the other, that he was looked upon by the whites as meanly cherishing the purpose, cowardly to escape, if he could, came like a mildew upon his heart, perishing it. Death was what he expected, and was prepared at any moment to meet, but such suspicions of his cowardice, and those "chains and slavery," were more than he could bear. Like Osceola, the victim of a similar treatment, the Red Bird died in prison,[7] of crushed hopes, and a broken heart!

NOTES

1. Henry Atkinson, born in North Carolina about 1780; died June 14, 1842. He reached the grade of Brigadier-General in 1820, and commanded the Western army at the battle of Bad Axe, when Black Hawk was defeated, August 2, 1832.

2. Established in 1821 on the west bank of the Mississippi, a few miles below St Louis.

3. Published in 1846. See Introduction, Vol. I., p. xxii., this work.

4. *Kinnikinnick*, the more common form of the word, meaning literally "what is mixed," is applied to various mixtures of tobacco, sumac leaves, the bark of willow, etc., used for smoking in pipes.

5. That is, Wisconsin River. The portage was in the present Columbia county, Wisconsin.

6. Minnesota River, formerly called St Peter's, enters the Mississippi about five miles below the Falls of St Anthony, the site of the present city of Minneapolis. Fort Snelling is situated on the bluff at the mouth of the Minnesota.

7. Red Bird, or *Zitkaduta*, died in prison at Prairie du Chien, February 16, 1828. A deputation of his tribe visited Washington during the winter of 1827-28 for the purpose of appealing to President Adams for the release of Red Bird and his companions in misery (Wekau and Chickhousic). The pardon was granted, November 3, 1828, but Red Bird died before the word reached the prisoners. (See Nawkaw, Vol. I., p. 146, especially notes 4 and 6, p. 153, this work).

INDEX

A

Acee-Yoholo, in Seminole battles, 203

Acts of the Apostles in Mohawk tongue, 216

Adams, Captain, at battle of Callabee, 56 (*note* 3)

Adams, President John Quincy, 33 (*note* 7)

Ahyouwaighs. See Brant, John

Alabama, 17; Clement Comer Clay, Governor of, 30, 34 (*note* 16)

Algonquian tribe, 146 (*note* 3); linguistic stock, 146 (*note* 4)

Alligator clan, 13 (*note* 1)

Alphabet, Cherokee, 329, 331 (*note* 6)

Amathla, Charley, a prominent chief, 10, 14 (*note* 10); waylaid and killed for selling his cattle, 10, 14 (*note* 10), 381; signs treaty of Payne's Landing, 14 (*note* 10); noble conduct of, 380-381

Ambrister, British spy, executed, 337

American Government, prospects of war with Great Britain, 62; purchases of land by, 62

American Revolution, policy pursued by British officers a cause of, 217-218

Ames' (E.) portrait of Joseph Brant, 255 (*note* 33)

Amisquam, or "Wooden Ladle," a Winnebago brave, 274; parents of, 274; his successful military enterprises, 275; portrait of, in Rhees *Catalogue*, 275 (*note* 2)

Appanoose, Sauk chief, 105; delegate to Washington, 105; his speech at Governor Everett's Reception, 105; meaning of name, 105, 106 (*note* 1); portrait of, by Cooke, in Rhees *Catalogue*, 106 (*note* 2); signs treaty at Washington (1837), 106 (*note* 2)

Arbor. See Lee Compere

Arbuthnot, executed, 13 (*note* 2), 14 (*note* 6)

Arizona, Southern, and New Mexico. See "Gadsden Purchase"

Arkansas, Creek nation living in harmony at, 30, 34 (*note* 21)

Arpiucki (Sam Jones), 9

Arsee, the "black drink," 25, 33 (*note* 11), 363; *ássi-lupútski*, Creek name for, 33 (*note* 11)

Ashby, Major J. A., 386, 391 (*note* 23)

Asseola, or Osceola, Seminole leader, 9, 14 (*note* 8), 340, 360; opposes treaty of Payne's Landing, 9; implicated in murder of General Thompson and Lieutenant Smith, 10; rules Micanopy's councils, 10; death of, 10, 15 (*note* 13), 389, 391-392 (*note* 25); grave of, 15 (*note* 13); derivation of name, 33 (*note* 11), 363-364; mother of, marries a white man, 363; various appellations of, 363; birthplace and parentage of, 364; description of, by Cohen. 364-365; by Woodburn Potter, 365-367; joins "Red Sticks" and fights against Tennessee troops, 367; settles at Peas' Creek, 367; unites with Micosukees, 368; openly avows opposition to emigration, 374-376; arrested by General Thompson, 376, 390 (*note* 17); set at liberty on promise of future good behaviour, 377-378, 390 (*note* 19); arrested with Micanopy, 385; transferred to Charleston, 385

Astor, John Jacob, plan of, to secure fur trade, 280, 281

Astoria, Washington Irving's (quoted), 282

Astoria, trading post on Columbia River, 281

Atkinson, General, 75, 93 (*note* 16); 425, 433, 434, 438, 439 (*note* 1)

B

"Bad Axe," 79

Balloon ascent at New York, witnessed by captive members of Black Hawk's band, 81-82

441